AF660623

MAHATMA GANDHI SPEAKS

Selected Speeches and Writings

Anil Dutta Mishra
Dr. P.V. Sarma

Centre for Gandhian Philosophy and Human Development
Gayatri Vidya Parishad Degree and P.G. College, Autonomous
Vishakapatnam
in collaboration with
CONCEPT PUBLISHING COMPANY PVT. LTD.
NEW DELHI-110059

© Authors

All rights reserved. No part of this work may be reproduced, stored, adapted, or transmitted in any form or by any means, electronic, mechanical, photocopying, micro-filming recording or otherwise, or translated in any language, without the prior written permission of the copyright owner and the publisher. The book is sold subject to the condition that it shall not, by way of trade or otherwise, be lent, resold, hired out, or otherwise circulated without the prior publisher's written consent in any form of binding or cover other than that in which it is published.

The views and opinions expressed in this book are author(s) own and the facts reported by them/her have been verified to the extent possible, and the publishers are not in any way liable for the same.

ISBN-13 : 978-93-5125-046-3

First Published 2014

Published and Printed by

Concept
Since 1974

Concept Publishing Company Pvt. Ltd.
A/15-16, Commercial Block, Mohan Garden
New Delhi-110059 (India)
T: 25351460, 25351794, *F*: 091-11-25357109
E: publishing@conceptpub.com, W: www.conceptpub.com
Editorial Office: H-13, Bali Nagar, New Delhi-110 015, India.

Cataloging in Publication Data—*Courtesy:* D.K. Agencies (P) Ltd. <docinfo@dkagencies.com>

Gandhi, *Mahatma*, 1869-1948.
[Works. Selections]
Mahatma Gandhi speaks : selected speeches and writings / Anil Dutta Mishra, P.V. Sarma.
p. cm.
Includes bibliographical references (p.) and index.
ISBN 9789351250463

1. Gandhi, Mahatma, 1869-1948— Philosophy. 2. Nationalism—India—History. 3. India—Politics and government—1765-1947. 4. India—Religion. I. Mishra, Anil Dutta, 1965- II. Sarma, P. V. (Pulugurtha Vyaghreswara), 1944- III. Gayatri Vidya Parishad Degree and P.G. College. Centre for Gandhian Philosophy and Human Development. IV. Title.

DDC 954.035 23

Preface

This work is an outcome of collaborative efforts of two dedicated friends' work miticulously without any financial support who are trained in Social Sciences. Dr. Mishra is trained in political science and specialized in Gandhi and Peace Research having wide experience of teaching, research, administration and field experience. He has a first hand experience of so called Gandhians and Gandhian Institutions. Whereas, Dr. Sarma is trained in Economics and having taught more than three decades in university having wide experience of teaching, research and administration and founder of Gayatri Vidya Parishad Trust which runs number of colleges and imparting education to the youths on principle of Gandhian Concept of Trusteeship. Both are unique in the sense that Dr. Mishra born, brought up and worked in North India and Dr. Sarma born, brought up and worked in South India but they have same vision of how to promote Gandhian values in the contemporary world where immorality is taught in the name of morality. The purpose of this book is to understand the evolution of Gandhi through his speeches and writings without any distortion.

There are three types of man in this world. One who reads history. One who takes part in the making of history. And one who creates history. In fact Mohandas Karamchand Gandhi was a creative man, creating history for himself and rest of the world to follow. He was the most simple but complex thinker; a unique personality and master strategist. He was greatly admired all over the world even by critiques and opponents but also misunderstood by followers, admirers and critiques. There is lot of misconceptions about Gandhi. Neither his political mentor [*Guru*] Gopal Krishna Gokhle, nor his political heir, Pandit Jawaharlal Nehru could fully understand him. Finally, Nathuram Godse killed Gandhi. Everyday so called Gandhians, Gandhian Institutions and followers of Gandhi are killing Gandhi because they killed their self respect, self esteem and integrity. Now the time has come to follow the basic tenets of Gandhism which is core of all religious thoughts and essential for human centric approach. One can learn much from the successful experiment of Gandhian values from Gayatri Vidya Parishad with whom we are associated and proud of it.

In recent years there is a revival of Gandhi everywhere in form of Arab spring or various movements in India. Gandhi represents the continuum of Indian culture and aspirations of downtrodden and underprivileged, voiceless and powerless people.His concerns were contemporary but timeless. Gandhi reached at the top step by step where no one has reached before. Gandhi an iconic personality, who inspired millions of people during his lifetime, is still inspiring people around the globe. His thoughts are everlasting, time tested and written for common man in a simple language. He emerged as a giant among men and brought awareness of political, social and human freedom to many millions of people, and also gave them a practical method for achieving redress against wrongs, by practice of non-violent assertion of rights. Through practice of non-violence Gandhi became a powerful symbol of protest for people in most adverse circumstances.

Gandhi inspired masses and masses inspired Gandhi. Gandhi derived power from masses. Gandhi was a mass mobilizer who redefined India's struggle for *swaraj* in a way as to solicit support for the cause. Fear is a greatest sin. Gandhi removed fear from the masses and masses rose in revolt against humiliation and injustice done by Britishers. Gandhi converted Indian National Congress into mass party. He brought in people from all walks of life. He spoke the language of the masses. He dressed himself like them. In a sense he lived, spoke, dressed like an ordinary man and by doing so he won the heart of the most ordinary man. In fact it was a masterstroke by a master strategist who transformed himself and the Indian masses and emerged as the undisputed leader of the Indian National Congress.

Being a leader, Gandhi used to deliver speeches and write the letters every day. These speeches and letters are treasure of information and function like a lighthouse in the journey of thought in the ocean of knowledge. These speeches and letters are reproduced here without any distortion and alteration so that the readers drew their own conclusions. We have arranged the Seventy-Seven Selected Speeches and Writings chronologically and put headings to enable the reader to understand Gandhi's thinking over the years. We are sure that the book *Mahatma Gandhi Speaks: Selected Speeches and Writings* will open new vistas of research and proper understanding of Gandhi.

Last but not the least, we are grateful to all those who helped us in completing this work.

Anil Dutta Mishra
P.V. Sarma

Contents

Glossary

Adharma	Opposite of *dharma* or duty
Adhikar	Authority
Acharya	Teacher, preceptor
Ahimsa	Non-violence
Anasakti	Non-attachment
Aparigraha	Non-possession
Artha	Pursuit of wealth and power
Ashram	Stages of life—*Brahamacharya*, *Grihastha*, *Banaprastha* and *Sanyasi*
Atman	Soul
Bania	Person of commercial caste
Behn	Sister
Bhakti	Devotion
Bhai	Brother
Bhangi	Sweeper
Brahmacharya	Celibacy
Brahman	The ultimate reality
Brahmin	The highest caste in Hindu society
Charkha	Spinning wheel
Daridranarayan	God embodied as the poor
Darshan	The sight of a holy person
Dewan	Prime Minister
Dharma	Duty; one of the four *purusharthas*—*Dharma*, *Artha*, *Kama* and *Moksha*
Dharna	A form of sit-down strike
Dhoti	Loin cloth worn by men
Duragraha	Stubborn persistence
Ek-praja	One nation
Gram	Village
Gram Pradhan	Head man of the Village
Guru	Holy man, teacher
Hartal	Strike
Itihas	History

Kaliyuga	The dark age
Karma	The ethical law of causation
Khadi	Hand-spun cloth
Khilafat	Movement in support of Khalifah
Kisan	Farmer
Maharaj	King; suffixed to person's name as a mark of respects
Mandir	Temple
Mantra	A sacred formula
Moksha	Salvation, release from the cycle of rebirth; one of the four *purusharthas—Dharma, Artha, Kama* and *Moksha*
Purdha	The custom of veiling women
Poorna Swaraj	Complete Independence
Praja	People, nation
Raj	Kingdom, rule, regime
Ramrajya	The rule of Ram, the rule of God
Rishi	Seer
Sanatani	Follower of Vedic *dharma* (religion)
Sanyasi	One who has renounced from ordinary life for religious meditation
Sena	Army
Sarvodaya	Welfare of all
Satyagraha	Truth force; Insistence on Truth
Swadeshi	Insistence on local products
Swaraj	Self Rule, Home Rule, Self-government
Varna	Caste
Varnashrama	Four-fold division in Hindu society
Vaishnava	Follower of Lord Vishnu
Yajna	Sacrificial offering to Fire God
Yogi	One who practices *yoga*

A Chronology of Gandhi's Life

1869 Born at Porbandar, now in Gujarat, India, on 2nd October.

1876 Betrothed to Kasturbai.

1883 Married to Kasturbai

1887 Passed Matriculation Examination; Entered the Sanwaldas College at Bhavnagar.

1888 Proceeded to England on 4th September, to study Law.

1889 First Public Speech in England to a gathering of vegetarians.

1891 Became Barrister on 10th June; Sailed back to India: Reached Bombay on 7th July, where he received news of his mother's death.

1892 Started legal practice at Rajkot and Bombay.

1893 First time left for South Africa in April to appear in a Civil Suit.

1894 Civil suit decided by compromise.

1895 Enrolled as an Advocate of Natal Supreme Court; organised Natal Indian Congress.

1896 Returned from South Africa to India where he remained for six months and met Indian leaders, Tilak, Gokhale and others; went to South Africa again on 28th November.

1897 Anti-Gandhi demonstrations in Durban, which marked the beginning of a great change in his life.

1899 Helped the British in Boer War.

1901 Returned to India; Organised public service in plague affected areas of Rajkot, Participated in Calcutta Congress.

1902 Went to Burma; Started travelling in India in third class Railway Compartment, Opened an office in Bombay in July; Again proceeded after 3 months to South Africa.

1903 Established 'Transvaal British India Association; Started editing *Indian Opinions*.

1904 Studied *Gita* and Ruskin's *Unto This Last* which led to a revolutionary change in his life; Established 'Phoenix Ashram'.

1906 Zulu Revolt, Rendered service to the injured in the revolt; Took a vow to observe *Brahmacharya*; The word *Satyagraha* was coined for the first time; Proceeded to England as a member of the Indian deputation.

1907 Started *Satyagraha* against 'Black Act.'

1908 Interim agreement with British; attacked by a Pathan; Restarting of *Satyagrah*, resulting in his arrest.

1909 Wrote his first letter to Tolstoy; Proceeded to England as a member of the second Indian deputation. While returning from England he wrote *'Hind Swaraj'* or *'Indian Home Rule'*.

1910 Established Tolstoy Farm in Johannesburg.

1912 Gokhale arrived in South Africa; The book entitled *Niti Dharma* was published: wrote another book of general information on nature-cure for health.

1913 Restarting of *Satyagrah*: Arrested and released; observed fast for seven days and thereafter took one meal a day for four and a half months.

1914 Fast for 14 days; Success of *Satyagraha*, resulting in on agreement; Proceeded to England on 18th July; First World War broke out on 4th August; Meeting with Sarojini Naidu; Service in World War.

1915 Awarded Kaiser-e-Hind medal on return to India; widely travelled in India; Meeting with Kaka Kalelkar and Acharya Kripalani; Death of Gokhale on 19th February; on 25th May Sabarmati Ashram was established.

1916 Historical speech on the occasion of the establishment of Kashi Vishwavidyalaya; First meeting with Jawaharlal Nehru in Lucknow Congress.

1917 First meeting with Dr. Rajendra Prasad; Started Champaran Satyagraha on 10th April; Abolition of Indentured Labour Act on 31st May; First meeting with Mahadev Desai.

1918 Mill Worker's strike in Ahmedabad, followed by three days fast; Khera Satyagraha; Revival of spinning wheel.

1919 Rowlatt Act; observed 6th April as prayer-cum-fast day; Jallianwala Bagh massacre on 13th April; Started editing of *Young India* and *Navajivan* ; Khilafat Movement; Amritsar Congress

1920 Death of Lokmanya Tilak on 1st August; Tilak Swaraj Fund was established on 2nd October; Congress Constitution prepared by Gandhi was approved; Started Non-cooperation Movement; Establishment of Gujarat Vidyapeeth.

1921 Establishment of other national educational institutions; Boycott of the visit of Prince of Wales, followed by riots; Five day fast; Ahmedabad Congress.

1922 Revolt of Chauri Chaura on 5th February; *Satyagrah* suspended, five days fast; Arrested on 10th March; Six years of imprisonment.

1924 Operated for appendicitis; Released from Jail on 5th February; Twenty-one days fast from 24th September; Presided over Belgaum Congress.

1925 Death of Deshbandhu Chitranjandas on 16th June; One week fast; Kanpur Congress; Establishment of Charkha Sangh.

1927 Extensively toured throughout India for the revival of *Khadi*; Death of Hakim Ajmal Khan on 19th September.

1928 Simon Commission; Bardoli Satyagraha; Death of Manganlal Gandhi in Patna on 22nd April; Death of Lala Lajpat Rai on 17th November; Nehru Report, Compromise resolution in Calcutta Congress.

1929 Resolution for complete Independence passed in Lahore Congress.

1930 Pledge for complete Independence on 26th January; Dandi March on 12th March to break the Salt Law; Arrested on 5th May.

1931 Death of Mohammed Ali in England on 4th January; Gandhiji released from Jail on 25th January; Death of Pandit Motilal Nehru on 6th February; Gandhi -Irwin Pact on 4th March; Bhagat Singh hanged on 23rd March; Karachi Congress; Martyrdom of Ganesh Shankar Vidyarthi on 25th March; Participated in the Second Round Table Conference as the sole representative of India, but returned disappointed in December.

1932 Congress declared unlawful organisation; Restarted *Satyagrah*; Arrested on January 4th, Publication of *Young India* and *Navajivan* stopped; From September 20 fast unto death against communal Award; Yarvada Pact on September 24; fast ended on 26th September.

1933 Twenty-one days fast from 8th May; Started *Harijan* weekly; Released from jail and again arrested; one year imprisonment; Fast unto death from 16th August, which ended after one week; Released from jail on 23rd August; Death of Annie Besant on 30th September; Death of Vitthalbhai Patel on 22nd September; Left Sabarmati Ashram to live at Wardha; Undertook tour from November 7th for 'Harijan' uplift.

1934 Bihar earthquake; *Satyagraha* suspended on 7th May; Seven days fast; Gram Udyog Sangh established on 26th October; Bombay Congress.

1935 Golden Jubilee of Indian National Congress.

1936 Sewagram Ashram established.

1937 Accepted Congress membership in July; Started 'Nai Talim' programme.

1939 Death of Maulana Shaukat Ali on 4th January; Fast unto death in Rajkot, which ended after 4 days on the intervention of the Viceroy; Tripura Congress; Subhash Chandra Bose resigned from the presidentship of Indian National Congress; Second World War broke out on September 3rd; Congress Government in all provinces resigned on 8th November.

1940 Individual *Satyagraha* started from 11th October, Vinoba offered arrest as first *Satyagrahi*; Publication of *Harijan* Weekly suspended.

1941 Death of Rabindranath Tagore on 7th August; Gave up leadership of Indian National Congress; Established 'Go-Seva-Sangh' on September 30.

1942 Again accepted the leadership of Indian National Congress; Death of Shri Jamnalal Bajaj on 11th February; Cripps Mission; established Hindustani Prachar Sabha,; 'Quit India' resolution on 8th August; Collective arrest of Indian leaders all over India on 9th August; Death of Mahadev Desai on 15th August.

1943 Twenty-one days fast in Agha Khan Palace.

1944 Death of Kasturba Gandhi on February 22; Released from Jail on 6th May; Gandhi-Jinnah talks.

1945 Indian leaders released from jail; 1st Simla Conference. 1946 Cabinet Mission; 'Direct Action' Programme of Muslim League from August 16; Communal riots; *Padyatra* in Noakhali; Death of Madan Mohan Malaviya on 12th November.

1947 India declared independent on 15th August; Seventy-three hours fast for peace in Calcutta.

1948 Fast unto death undertaken to establish peace in Delhi, which continued for five days; Martyrdom on January 30, with Last words; '*Hey Ram*, '*Hey Ram*' !

1. Protest

A mass meeting of British Indians was held to protest against the draft Asiatic Law Amendment Ordinance. Abdul Gani, Chairman, British Indian Association, presided. Several speakers opposed the Ordinance and called for non compliance in case it became law. The following is a report of Gandhiji's speech:

JOHANNESBURG,
September 11, 1906

Mr. M. K. Gandhi, (Johannesburg), Hony. Secretary of the British Indian Association, then addressed the meeting. He pointed out that by some critics it might be thought that there was a defect in the chain of reasoning as outlined by their resolutions, because they asked for redress of their grievances, and then went on immediately to threaten to go to gaol if their prayer was not granted. He contended, however, that there was no real flaw in the chain, because they were not holding out a threat. It was merely a question of one ounce of practice which was worth whole tons of speeches and writings. He had thought the matter over seriously and earnestly before he had given his opinion upon the step they should take, and he felt that it was their bounden duty to adopt the course laid down if their prayer was not granted. He contended that every adjective used that day was justified for the occasion, and said that if he could find a stronger adjective he would use it. He had studied the whole of the anti-Asiatic legislation throughout South Africa; but he never, in the whole course of his experience, came across anything like this present Ordinance. Even the legislation of the O.R.C., drastic as it was, was far superior to that now introduced here, which was so bad that no self-respecting Indian could live under it. He admitted that the responsibility for the serious step he had taken was upon his shoulders, and he took the responsibility in its entirety. He felt he had done the right thing in advising them to take this step as loyal British subjects. In all their action in this respect they were full of loyalty. No shadow of disloyalty could rest upon them. Some people might say that they were foolish, and he would say that their action was foolish if he had not full confidence in his fellow-countrymen. But he knew them; he knew that he could trust them, and he knew also that, when occasion required an heroic step to be taken,—he knew that every man among them would take it. (Loud Cheers.)

INDIAN OPINION, 22-9-1906

At the meeting, Haji Habib proposed that they should take a solemn oath to oppose the Ordinance. Explaining the implications of the suggestion, Gandhiji made a speech, which he recapitulates in *Satyagraha* in South Africa:

I wish to explain to this meeting that there is a vast difference between this resolution and every other resolution we have passed up-to-date and that there is a wide divergence also in the manner of making it. It is a very grave resolution we are making, as our existence in South Africa depends upon our fully observing it. The manner of making the resolution suggested by our friend is as much of a novelty as of a solemnity. I did not come to the meeting with a view to getting the resolution passed in that manner, which redounds to the credit of Sheth Haji Habib as well as it [*sic*] lays a burden of responsibility upon him. I tender my congratulations to him. I deeply appreciate his suggestion, but if you adopt it you too will share his responsibility.

You must understand what is this responsibility, and as an adviser and servant of the community, it is my duty fully to explain it to you.

We all believe in one and the same God, the differences of nomenclature in Hinduism and Islam notwithstanding. To pledge ourselves or to take an oath in the name of that God or with Him as witness is not something to be trifled with. If having taken such an oath we violate our pledge we are guilty before God and man. Personally I hold that a man, who deliberately and intelligently takes a pledge and then breaks it, forfeits his manhood. And just as a copper coin treated with mercury not only becomes valueless when found out but also makes its owner liable to punishment, in the same way a man who lightly pledges his word and then breaks it becomes a man of straw and fits himself for punishment here as well as hereafter. Sheth Haji Habib is proposing to administer an oath of such a serious character. There is no one in this meeting who can be classed as an infant or as wanting in understanding. You are all well advanced in age and have seen the world; many of you are delegates and have discharged responsibilities in a greater or lesser measure. No one present, therefore, can ever hope to excuse himself by saying that he did not know what he was about when he took the oath.

I know that pledges and vows are, and should be, taken on rare occasions. A man who takes a vow every now and then is sure to stumble. But if I can imagine a crisis in the history of the Indian community of South Africa when it would be in the fitness of things to take pledges, that crisis is surely now. There is wisdom in taking serious steps with great caution and hesitation. But caution and hesitation have their limits, which we have now passed. The Government has taken leave of all sense of decency. We would only be betraying our unworthiness and cowardice, if we cannot stake our all in the face of the conflagration which envelopes us and sit watching it with folded hands. There is no doubt, therefore, that the present is a proper occasion for taking pledges. But every one of us must think out for himself if he has the will and the ability to pledge himself. Resolutions of this nature cannot be passed by a majority vote. Only those who take a pledge can be bound by it. This pledge must not be taken with a view to produce an effect on outsiders. No one should trouble to consider what impression it might have upon the local Government, the Imperial Government, or the Government of India. Every one must only search his own heart, and if the inner voice assures him that he has the requisite strength to carry him through, then only should he pledge himself and then only would his pledge bear fruit.

A few words now as to the consequences. Hoping for the best, we may say that, if a majority of the Indians pledge themselves to resistance and if all who take the pledge prove true to themselves, the Ordinance may not even be passed and, if passed, may be soon repealed. It may be that we may not be called upon to suffer at all. But if on the one hand one who takes a pledge must be a robust optimist, on the other hand he must be prepared for the worst. It is, therefore, that I would give you an idea of the worst that might happen to us in the present struggle. Imagine that all of us present here numbering 3,000 at the most pledge ourselves. Imagine again that the remaining 10,000 Indians take no such pledge. We will only provoke ridicule in the beginning. Again, it is quite possible that in spite of the present warning some or many of those who pledge themselves might weaken at the very first trial. We might have to go to gaol, where we might be insulted. We might have to go hungry and suffer extreme heat or cold. Hard labour might be imposed upon us. We might be flogged by rude warders. We might be fined heavily and our property might be attached and held up to auction if there are only a few resisters left. Opulent today, we might be reduced to abject poverty tomorrow. We might be deported. Suffering from starvation and similar hardships in gaol, some of us might fall ill and even die. In short, therefore, it is not at all impossible that we might have to endure every hardship that we can imagine, and wisdom lies in pledging ourselves on the understanding that we shall have to suffer all that and worse. If someone asks me when and how the struggle may end, I may say that, if the entire community manfully stands the test, the end will be near. If many of us fall back under storm and stress, the struggle will be prolonged. But I can boldly declare, and with certainty, that so long as there is even a handful of men true to their pledge, there can only be one end to the struggle, and that is victory.

A word about my personal responsibility. If I am warning you of the risks attendant upon the pledge, I am at the same time inviting you to pledge yourselves, and I am fully conscious of my responsibility in the matter. It is possible that a majority of those present here might take the pledge in a fit of enthusiasm or indignation but might weaken under the ordeal, and only a handful might be left to face the final test. Even then there is only one course open to the like of me, to die but not to submit to the law. It is quite unlikely but even if every one else flinched leaving me alone to face the music, I am confident that I would never violate my pledge. Please do not misunderstand me. I am not saying this out of vanity, but I wish to put you, especially the leaders upon the platform, on your guard. I wish respectfully to suggest it to you that, if you have not the will or the ability to stand firm even when you are perfectly isolated, you must not only not take the pledge yourselves, but you must declare your opposition before the resolution is put to the meeting and before its members begin to take pledges and you must not make yourselves parties to the resolution. Although we are going to take the pledge in a body, no one should imagine that default on the part of one or many can absolve the rest from their obligation. Everyone should fully realize his responsibility, then only pledge himself independently of others and understand that he himself must be true to his pledge even unto death, no matter what others do.

[*M. K. Gandhi: Satyagraha in South Africa*, Chapter XII; S. Ganesan, Madras; 1928]

RESOLUTIONS PASSED AT THE MEETING[1]

Resolution I

This mass meeting of British Indians here assembled, respectfully urges the Honourable the President and Members of the Legislative Council of the Transvaal not to pass the Draft Asiatic Ordinance to amend Law No. 3 of 1885, now before that Honourable House, in view of the facts that :

(1) It is, so far as the Indian community of the Transvaal is concerned, a highly contentious measure.
(2) It subjects the British Indian community of the Transvaal to degradation and insult totally undeserved by its past history.
(3) The present machinery is sufficient for checking the alleged influx of Asiatics.
(4) The statements as to the alleged influx are denied by the British Indian community.
(5) If the Honourable House is not satisfied with the denial, this meeting invites [an] open, judicial, and British enquiry into the question of the alleged influx.

Resolution II

This mass meeting of British Indians here assembled respectfully protests against the Draft Ariatic Low. Amendment Ordinance now being considered by the Legislative Council of the Transvaal, and humbly requests the local Government and the Imperial Authorities to withdraw the Draft Ordinance, for the reasons that :

(1) It is manifestly in conflict with the past declarations of His Majesty's representatives.
(2) It recognises no distinction between British and alien Asiatics.
(3) It reduces British Indians to a status lower than that of the aboriginal races of South Africa and the Coloured people.

1. In accordance with Resolution V, copies of Resolutions II, III and IV were sent to the Secretary of State for India through the Governor of the Transvaal, who was also requested to telegraph their substance to the Viceroy of India. Vide "The Mass Meeting", 11-9-1906 and Cd. 3308 issued in February 1907.

(4) It renders the position of British Indians in the Transvaal much worse than under Law 3 of 1885, and, therefore, than under the Boer regime.
(5) It sets up a system of passes and espionage unknown in any other British territory.
(6) It brands the communities to which it is applied as criminals or suspects.
(7) The alleged influx of unauthorised British Indians into the Transvaal is denied.
(8) If such denial is not accepted, a judicial, open and British enquiry should be instituted before such drastic and uncalled for legislation is enforced.
(9) The measure is otherwise un-British and unduly restricts the liberty of inoffensive British subjects and constitutes a compulsory invitation to British Indians in the Transvaal to leave the country.
(10) This meeting further and especially requests the Right Honourable the Secretary of State for the Colonies and the Right Honourable the Secretary of State for India to suspend the Royal sanction and to receive a deputation on behalf of the British Indian community of the Transvaal in connection with this Draft Ordinance.

Resolution III

This meeting hereby appoints a delegation with power from the Committee of the British Indian Association to add to its membership or to change its personnel, to proceed to England and to lay before the Imperial Authorities the complaint of the British Indian community of the Transvaal regarding the Draft Asiatic Law Amendment Ordinance.

Resolution IV

In the event of the Legislative Council, the local Government, and the Imperial Authorities rejecting the humble prayer of the British Indian community of the Transvaal in connection with the Draft Asiatic Law Amendment Ordinance, this mass meeting of British Indians here assembled solemnly and regretfully resolves that, rather than submit to the galling, tyrannous, and unBritish requirements laid down in the above Draft Ordinance, every British Indian in the Transvaal shall submit himself to imprisonment and shall continue so to do until it shall please His Most Gracious Majesty the King-Emperor to grant relief.

Resolution V

This meeting desires the Chairman to forward copy of the first resolution to the Honourable the President and Members of the Legislative Council, and copies of all the resolutions to the Honourable the Colonial Secretary, to His Excellency the Acting Lieutenant Governor, and to His Excellency the High Commissioner, and to request His Excellency the High Commissioner to cable the text of resolutions Nos. 2, 3 and 4 to the Imperial Authorities.

[*Indian Opinion*, 15-9-1906]

2. The Settlement Explained[1]

SPEECH AT THE MEETING OF BRITISH INDIAN ASSOCIATION

[JOHANNESBURG,
January 31, 1908]

It is God in whom I placed my trust while launching on this struggle and advising the people to do likewise; it is He who has given us this unexpected victory, and it is to Him therefore that we must give our thanks. It is because I have always believed that God helps the cause of truth that I started this movement in His name. The success we have achieved is there for all of us to see. What has made the Government remit the sentences and open the prison gates and let the people out? Surely our truthfulness and strength. I used to say that, if we scrupulously followed the path of truth, the white Colonists themselves would veer to our side, and that is exactly what has happened. We are also thankful to the whites for the pains they took to further our just cause. They did so because they were inspired by God within to have sympathy for His oppressed devotees, and to fight on their behalf.

I need not refer to the remark General Smuts made in the course of a speech[2] that it was impossible to send everyone to gaol. All these things indicate that, if the [Indian] community remains united, it will always win through. We will now register voluntarily for purposes of identification and the scrutiny [of our rights of domicile] and the Government has accepted this [offer]. That means that the obnoxious law will die altogether. The stigma that attached to us under the law will now disappear. Under the proposed arrangement, the Government will accept signatures by educated persons and by owners of property, but unlettered

1. On the evening of the day of his release, Gandhiji explained the terms of "the compromise" to fellow-Indians at a public meeting held under the auspices of the British Indian Association. The text of this speech was published only in the Gujarati section under the title "The Settlement Explained".
2. His Mayville speech; vide 1st footnote of "Inter to the Transvaal Leader", 6-1-1908.

people have to give ten finger-prints on the application forms. Though I am against this myself and will strive with the Government to the best of my ability to have the requirement waived, I see nothing wrong in having to give finger-impressions if the Government does not come round. For after all we shall be giving them of our own free choice. They must not be given if they are made compulsory. And the Government has allowed us a period of three months for the matter to be settled. I will, therefore, strive to obtain the best [terms] that I can for the Indian community.

Under the law, the Government wanted the compulsory registration of children, and this [provision] too, has now been dropped. The question of amending the law suitably will be taken up when Parliament meets in Pretoria. For the present, however, the sentences of imprisonment against us have been set aside, and it is now up to us to prove that we are honourable men. It will be no use having anything in writing from the Government, since the final authority is that of Parliament. We have thus to depend only on what Parliament does. Just as Lord Roberts and others used to make promises to us on behalf of the Imperial Parliament, so has the Colonial Secretary set us free in anticipation of Parliament's approval. When Parliament meets, we shall be delivered from this law[1]. That is, the Act will be repealed and the Immigration Bill will be suitably amended. The object of the Government will thus be secured, and we shall get the freedom that we have been demanding.

The reason why we have won is that people went to gaol,—150 from Johannesburg, 25 from Pretoria and many persons from other towns as well. Women did their true duty. The pickets in particular displayed unsurpassed skill which even the Government could not help admiring; the selfsame Government [which had resisted our demands earlier] came round clearly because it perceived the strength of the community. A campaign that is carried on in the name of God cannot but end in success. I am hopeful that I shall succeed in the matter of fingerprints also.

We have, however, no reason to feel triumphant over the measure of success that we have achieved, neither have the whites any cause to complain against the Government. Even God is won over by humility. It is, therefore, humility which will ensure our success in a just struggle. We must not play foul with the Government; rather, by adopting the highest standard of conduct for ourselves, we must convince the Government and the white Colonists that we do respect laws which uphold our dignity. If, through an oversight on the part of the Government, the door is left open and there is scope for some kind of fraud, our duty will be to shut that

1. Asiatic Registration Act.

door. The Government will see for itself that we do not practise deception. When we have thus created a [favourable] impression on the minds of the Colonists by acquitting ourselves as befits us, the redress of our grievances is bound to follow.

Equally, the Government will be unable to go back on its commitment to us, for we have the great weapon of passive resistance.

That was the weapon with which we brought the Government to its senses. Whatever the Government does now, it will do with the consent of our people. As long as we are ready to go to gaol and fight on, we shall wield sufficient power over the Government to make it do the right thing.

Whatever, we plan to do now must be kept wholly confidential. Should anyone among us be found carrying information to the Government or some other party, he will have proved himself a veritable traitor. Nothing can be gained by playing the spy to the Government; on the contrary, it will be of advantage to remain with the community. Even those who have taken out registers[1] under the new law may gain their freedom if they take out registers under the proposed arrangement. We must also prove ourselves to be as good as our word, and thus furnish an earnest of our sincerity. As soon as Parliament meets, the [Asiatic Registration Act] will be repealed and the immigration law amended. That is to say, domicile certificates will be issued as they are in Durban.

We have to thank those who gave us real help. We should pass a resolution expressing our gratitude to Mr. Polak[2], Mr. Ritch[3], and he took to life in Phoenix "like a duck takes to water" and "we began to live like blood brothers", says Gandhiji who was also best man at his wedding. Became Editor, *Indian Opinion* in 1906 during Gandhiji's absence in England and a full-fledged attorney in 1908 after having served an

---

1. In the Gujarati Gandhiji uses "register" for "registration certificate".
2. Harry Solomon Leon Polak ; assistant editor of *The Transvaal Critic* who joined *Indian Opinion* ("Our Trial", 31-12-1904) after Gandhiji had struck up a "casual" acquaintance with him in the Johannesburg vegetarian restaurant; "had a wonderful faculty of translating into practice anything that appealed to his intellect".
3. L. W. Ritch; Theosophist and manager of a Johannesburg commercial firm before he joined Gandhiji as an articled clerk; passed his Bar examination in London (*vide* "Letter to A.H. West", 2-11-1906 and "The Deputation's Voyage—V", 1-12-1906); Secretary, South Africa British Indian Committee ("Letter to Lord Reay", 24-11-1906) of which he eventually became the "moving spirit". Vide *Autobiography*, Part IV, Ch. IV and XIII and *Satyagraha in South Africa*, Ch. XIV and XXIII. For his pamphlet on British Indians in South Africa, vide Vol. VII, Appendix.

apprenticeship with Gandhiji; was arrested after the "Great March" into the Transvaal in 1913; visited India and England to help African Indian cause vide *Autobiography*, Part IV, Ch. XVIII, XXI and XXII and Satyagraha in South Africa, Ch. XXIII and XLV.

Mr. Cartwright[1], the editor of The [Transvaal] *Leader*, as also to the others who joined the struggle.

[From Gujarati]

[*Indian Opinion*, 8-2-1908]

1. Albert Cartwright; Editor of the *Transvaal Leader*, was "as broad-minded as he was able" and "always supported the Indian cause in his columns"; the "Angel of Peace" who mediated betroun Transvaal Indians and Smuts in the controversy regarding the Asiatic Registration Act. Gandhiji described him as "duply shoked" at stute' failure to keep his promise. Vide *Satyagraha in South Africa*, Ch. XXI and XXV.

3. Role of Asiatic and the Coloured Races in British Empire

SPEECH AT Y.M.C.A.

[JOHANNESBURG,
May 18, 1908]

The following address was given by Mr. M. K. Gandhi, Bar-at-Law, before the Y.M.C.A., Johannesburg, in moving the negative in a debate on the question, "Are Asiatics and the Coloured races a menace to the Empire?"

It seems to me somewhat remarkable that a question of this description should arise at all, or that there should be any debate whatsoever as to whether Coloured races are a menace to the Empire. I think that a question of that description could arise only in the Colonies or, better still, only in some of the Colonies. In a well-ordered society industrious and intelligent men can never be a menace. If they have any defects, the very order of the society corrects them. At the same time, we, as practical men and women living in this very practical age, have to face facts as they are and, seeing that questions of this description arise in the Colonies, it is undoubtedly well that we should discuss them and debate upon them; and, to my mind, it is a very happy augury for the future that your humble servant can be called upon to give his views on the question before an audience like this, and I think it is also a happy augury that this hall is so well filled, showing the keen interest taken in the subject.

By the term "Coloured people" generally, I think we understand only offspring of mixed marriages, but in connection with the question before us this evening, the term "Coloured people" has been taken more comprehensively, and has been made to include the Coloured people proper—the Africans and the Asiatics. My own observations and experience, as you know, are confined very largely to British Indians, my own fellow-countrymen, but in studying the Indian question, I have endeavoured to study the question as it affects the Africans and the Chinese. It seems to me that both the Africans and the Asiatics have advanced the Empire as a whole; we can hardly think of South Africa without the African races. And who can think of the British Empire without India? South Africa would probably be a howling wilderness without the Africans. I do not think that the white man would have come to South Africa at all if there had been no Native races.

This brings me to the White Man's Burden as Kipling has called it. His writings, to my mind, have been very much misunderstood. We know now also that he himself has very considerably, with extended experience, revised his views, and he no longer thinks that the Coloured people are a menace to the Empire, or that the white man may not coexist with the Coloured man. Be that as it may, he has certainly shown in some of his writings that it was really a responsibility thrown on the white people, more particularly on the British people, to act as trustees for the Coloured races. But have the white people acted as trustees? Would you consider that your own wards were a menace to yourselves? The majority of people in South Africa, the majority of people in most of the Colonies, have become impatient of colour, and it behoves every right-minded man and woman to think twice before he or she jumps to the conclusion that the Coloured people are a menace and that, therefore, they ought to be got rid of with the greatest possible despatch.

We hear nowadays a great deal of the segregation policy, as if it were possible to put people in water-tight compartments. Captain Cooke has written to the papers[1] and has taken the trouble of discussing the same question with me, and has propounded a policy of segregation. I had no hesitation in telling him that, in my own opinion, based now on 14 years' observation and study, such a scheme, if it was meant to people some portions of East Africa with Coloured people only or, better still, with Asiatics only, was not possible of fulfilment. How are you going to restrict Asiatics to some parts of the earth only? Will they be content to have those portions of the earth which may be apportioned to them and which are unfit for white occupation? I have certainly never been able to find any justification for the colourbarrier. In the words of Mr. Chamberlain, it is possible to make distinctions on the ground of want of education, on the ground of criminality, or some such ground. Then there will be no cry of segregation. But from the present civilisation, or, rather, from western civilization, there flow two propositions which have almost become maxims to live by—I call them fallacious maxims.

They are "might is right" and "survival of the fittest". Those who

1. Vide "Johannesburg Letter", 16-5-1908.

have propounded these two maxims have given a meaning to them. I am not going into the meaning that might be attached in our minds to them, but they have said undoubtedly, by [saying] "might is right", that physical might is right, that physical strength is right and supreme. Some of them have also combined intellectual strength with physical strength, but I would replace both these with heart-strength, and I say that nobody with merely physical might and intellectual might can ever enjoy that strength that can proceed from the heart. It never can be that mere intellectual or mere physical strength can ever supersede the heart-strength or, as Ruskin would say, social affections.

A quickening and quickened soul responds only to the springs of the heart.

That[1] is the difference between western and eastern civilization?

I know that I am treading on very dangerous and delicate ground. We had the distinction given to us by so great an authority as Lord Selborne only a short time ago, and I have very humbly and very respectfully to differ from His Excellency's views.[2] It appears that western civilization is destructive, eastern civilization is constructive. Western civilization is centrifugal, eastern civilization is centripetal. Western civilization, therefore, is naturally disruptive, whereas eastern civilization combines. I believe also that western civilization is without a goal, eastern civilization has always had the goal before it. I do not mix up or confuse western civilization with Christian progress. I decline to believe that it is a symbol of Christian progress that we have covered a large part of the globe with the telegraph system, that we have got telephones and ocean greyhounds, and that we have trains running at a velocity of 50 or even 60 miles per hour. I refuse to believe that all this activity connotes Christian progress, but it does connote western civilization. I think western civilization also represents tremendous activity, eastern civilization represents contemplativeness, but it also sometimes represents lethargy. The people in India, the people in China—I leave Japan for the time being—having been sunk in their contemplative mood, have forgotten the essence of the thing, they have forgotten that, in transferring their activity from one sphere of life to another sphere of life, they had not to be idle, they had not to be lazy. The result is that immediately they find an obstacle in their way, they simply sit down. It is necessary that that civilization should come in contact with

1. Misprint for "What"?
2. *Vide* "Lord Selborne's View", 4-4-1908.

that of the West, it is necessary that that civilization should be quickened with the western spirit.

Immediately that fact is accomplished, I have no doubt also that the eastern civilization will become predominant, because it has a goal. I think you will see easily that a civilization or a condition in which all the forces fly away from the centre must necessarily be without a goal, whereas those which converge to a point have always a goal. It is then necessary for these two civilizations to meet and we shall have a different force altogether, by no means a menacing force, by no means a force that disunites, but a force that unites. The two forces are undoubtedly opposing forces, but perhaps in the economy of nature both are necessary. Only we, as intelligent human beings with heart and soul, have to see what those forces are, and have to use them, not blindly but intelligently, not anyhow and haphazard, but with a goal in view. Immediately that is done, there is no difficulty whatsoever in [the] two civilizations meeting and meeting for a good purpose.

I have said that the African races have undoubtedly served the Empire, and I believe so have the Asiatic races or, rather, British Indians. Have not the British Indians fought on many a battle field? A people, moreover, who have religion as the basis of life, cannot be a menace. And how can the African races be a menace? They are still in the history of the world's learners. Able-bodied and intelligent men as they are, they cannot but be an asset to the Empire. I believe with Mr. Creswell that they ought not to be protected. We do not want protection for them in any shape or form, but I do believe this—that they are entitled to justice, a fair field and no favour. Immediately you give that to them, you will find no difficulty. Whilst, therefore, Asiatics and other Coloured people cannot be a menace, Asiatics at least have been made a menace in some Colonies. We have been told that Natal and Mauritius are awful examples to every white man throughout the world. I do not know that they are such awful countries, but I, at the same time, believe that, if what happened in Natal had not happened, it would have been different—whether better or worse, we are not for the present discussing; but, if these countries have been ruined, they have been ruined purposely by white men, or, rather, by a few of them who were in a hurry to get rich. If they had only bided their time and opportunity, no such thing need, would, have happened. They did not hesitate to import indentured labour, which might be called semi slave labour, from India. Posterity has to pay for it. If, therefore, Natal or Mauritius has suffered, it has suffered not from Asiatics as such, but from a system of labour of which Asiatics happened to form part. Had there been white indentured labour instead, the result would have been the same. It is not the free Indian population that can ever do any harm whatsoever to the Colonies.

But I do also admit that there are some reasonable complaints with reference to British Indians. I venture, however, to submit that these complaints have no real basis. It is complained that they live in dirty hovels. Yes, some of them do. They are said to live very cheaply.

But if you were to examine these complaints, I think, you would come to the conclusion that they could be dealt with very easily and very effectively by municipal regulations. There are many complaints against the people living in the East End of London by the people living in the West End, but no one has suggested that, therefore, the people in the East End should be swept away. Sweep away the rack-rent and the conditions prevailing in the East End, and its inhabitants will be just as good as those in the West End. Similarly also, sweep away the conditions under which British Indians are called upon to live, sweep away the condition that they cannot own a patch of land which they can call their own, that they cannot live, and move, and have their being on God's earth in South Africa with any degree of freedom, self-respect and manliness, and they will realize that in Rome they must live as the Romans do, and will respond to every real and reasonable call that can be made upon them by the white man; but I ask you to be patient with them just as you would be patient with any fellow-man. Treat him as a real, live human being, and you will have no such thing as the Indian question in the country. Please do not forget I do not advocate that there should be absolutely free immigration. On the contrary, I have always said, and British Indians admit, that there may be regulation of immigration, but never based on colour. Anyone who is accepted as an immigrant ought to be entitled to all the rights that a man who lives in the country should possess. Whether he should have political rights or not is another question. I am not here today to discuss the political question at all.

But there should be no two opinions as to whether he may live freely without being restricted, move freely without being restricted, own land, or trade honestly.[1] British Indians and Englishmen have come together by Divine Providence. I may add, and I believe it is true, that, when the British occupied India, it was not owing to humanitarian grounds, but that the act was selfish and often tinged with dishonesty.

But Nature's ways are inscrutable. She often unmakes what man

1. Vide "Letter to the Press", 30-11-1906.

makes and produces good out of evil. Such is, in my opinion, the case with the British connection with India. I believe that the two races, the British and the Indian, have been brought together, not only for their own mutual advantage, but to leave an impress on the history of the world. Believing that, I also believe that it is well for me to be a loyal subject of the Empire, but not I hope a member of a subject race. I trust it is the mission of the English race, even where there are subject races, to raise them to equality with themselves, to give them free institutions and make them absolutely free men. If that be the mission of the Empire, the mission of the British race, then is it not as well that the millions of human beings should be trained for self-government? If we look into the future, is it not a heritage we have to leave to posterity, that all the different races commingle and produce a civilization that perhaps the world has not yet seen? There are difficulties and misunderstandings, but I do believe, in the words of the sacred hymn, "We shall know each other better when the mists have rolled away."

[*Indian Opinion*, 6-6-1908 and 13-6-1908]

4. Breach of Compromise

SPEECH AT MASS MEETING[1]

[JOHANNESBURG
June 24, 1908]

The receipt of so many telegrams shows the unanimity with which the object of this meeting has been received, but though I have read these telegrams to you, it is due to this meeting, due to the executive of the British Indian Association, and due to the Transvaal public to state also that there is, at this meeting, electric; in the air, and these telegrams by no means demonstrate the whole truth. The whole truth is that there is, even in this meeting, a number of Indians who are seething with discontent over what the leaders have done, and over what especially I myself have done, in connection with the compromise. There is a number of Indians in this meeting who believe, as the Chairman has stated in his speech, that the whole Indian community has been sold for selfish purposes. The Chairman has repudiated the charge, and so do I, but I do not blame my countrymen who bring that charge against me especially.[2]

Some of my countrymen tell me and, perhaps, with some justification that I did not take them into confidence, when I approached General Smuts on the strength of the letter that was placed before me in the gaol-yard, and it is better that I myself should voice their complaint I believe that, in seeing General Smuts as I saw him, I acted correctly and

1. The meeting, which was held under the auspices of the British Indian Association at 3.45 p.m. to discuss the situation arising out of the "breach", by the Transvaal Government of "the spirit of the compromise" of January 30, 1908, was attended by delegates from all over the Transvaal. For resolutions passed at the meeting, *vide* Appendix V.
2. The Chairman had said: "They who assaulted the Chairman and the Secretary distrusted the Government. In their opinion, we had misled them, and, when the proper time came, we had sold the community to the Government. Whilst I emphatically repudiate any such suggestion, it is impossible for me to deny that the Government have, by their recent conduct, lent colour to the suspicion and distrust."

in accordance with my conscience, but time has shown that they were right, time has shown also that I need not have gone to General Smuts as I did. What I did was simply and solely to accept voluntary registration that was placed before him for over a year by the whole Indian community. I felt that I was yielding nothing, not a single new principle, not a single concession, in accepting this voluntary compromise. I believed that I had full instructions from my countrymen to do so, but I believed too much. I did not know what was to come after. I did not know that there was to be repudiation of the emphatic promise that was made in connection with the repeal of the Act. I know now that the compromise is not to be respected by the Government.

General Smuts says that he never made any promise of repeal but there are documents, which the world will see, which will show, at least that there was a talk and a conversation with reference to the repeal of the Act. There are witnesses also in connection with it but as the Chairman has rightly said, that is left for the lawyers to decide.[1] The Indian community only knows that the repeal of the Act was the object, and that was the object which was to be gained by undergoing voluntary registration, but today the Indian community finds that voluntary registration has not sufficed [for] the purpose. It finds also that it has become necessary to hold this Mass Meeting again, and it has become necessary again, perchance, if it is the will of God, to undergo the same measure of suffering, only far more bitterly.

If, therefore, you find there is electricity in the air, I do plead guilty. I am responsible for it responsible because I had too great faith in the statesmanship of General Smuts, in his honesty, and in his integrity. If any countrymen today believe that I have sold them, they have good reason to believe so, although [there is] no justification for it, in my own estimation. They can only judge me by the results obtained. They cannot judge, the world is not today so constituted that it will judge men by the motives they ascribe to themselves, but by the result of their actions; and they judge me by the result of my action, the result of having foisted the

---

1. The Chairman again: "We went to prison to buy liberty of conscience and freedom from molestation and restraint, and we did not come out of the prison gates in order to submit to a law, or a revised edition of it, which was calculated to take away those priceless possessions. We want to no bandying of legal phrases and subtleties of lawyers. We, as common sense men, want our honour to be respected, and it is for that this great meeting has come to plead."

compromise on the whole of the Indian community, and I include also the Chinese community, because although there were two other gentlemen who signed the letter that was addressed to General Smuts they did so fully believing in my own good faithfully believing that what I was doing was what they were all working for, namely, the repeal of the Act not only in word but in deed, not indeed, to secure a revised edition of the Act, but to obliterate the Act and all its consequences, if the Indian community and the Chinese community voluntarily proved that they were capable of being trusted without any legal restraint. If they proved that the large majority of the Asiatics had entered the Transvaal with perfect right, and if they proved that the documents that they held were correct documents and were properly obtained by them, and were not fraudulent documents, then they undoubtedly believed that the Act would be repealed, that their position was to be much better than it would have been under the Asiatic Act. They believed also that they had fought for 16 months, not merely to secure a nominal repeal of the Act, but to secure recognition for themselves as human beings, to secure a voice in the management of their own affairs, to secure a voice in the legislation that may be passed so far as they are concerned; not a voting paper by any means a voting paper for the Indians or the Asiatics may not be worth the paper on which the signature might be put but they wanted a real voting paper, they wanted to be consulted before any legislation was passed.

And what did they find? They found that there was a Gold Law, they found that there was a Municipal kill, both these Bills still further curtailing the rights of those having a right to remain in this country.

Have they not every reason to believe that Gandhi has misled them?

Have they not every reason to believe that they have no longer any business to suffer because Gandhi advises them to suffer?

I see before me a warrior, a military man, who was my fellow-prisoner. He tells me "How shall I trust you? You have misled your countrymen, you have given 18 finger-impressions. I have not. I hold my medals, and that is my registration."

Another of his fellow-religionists, or A fellow-Pathan, has assaulted me. He deserves every thanks for having assaulted me, because he believed that I was selling the community. He had no grudge against me, he was my client. He had a perfect right to do what he did, as I find now from the consequences that have been entailed on the whole of the Asiatic communities.

Gentlemen, those who are here and whose influence reaches far beyond the four corners of this building, go away from this meeting knowing full well what the consequence of General Smuts' act will be General Smuts' act undertaken in the name of the white communities.

I may understand, I may distinguish, but, just as my fellow-countrymen could not distinguish and they only had the remedy of assaulting me, another had the remedy of telling me that I had sold my countrymen; similarly it is not possible for them to distinguish between one white man's word and another white man's word, especially when that word happens to be the word of almost the highest man in the State.

I state most emphatically and definitely that General Smuts did promise that he was going, to repeal the Act, in the presence of the Registrar of Asiatics, if the Asiatic communities abided fully, frankly, and freely by the terms of the compromise, if the Asiatic communities enabled General Smuts to identify every Asiatic in the country, and if the Asiatic communities enabled General Smuts to see to it that there was no Asiatic who could surreptitiously enter into the country and not be found out by his Police. These terms the Asiatic communities have fulfilled, and yet we find today, we meet this afternoon to find out, that this Act is not to be repealed as it should be repealed, and that the promise of repeal is hedged in on all sides by such restrictions as could never be accepted by any self-respecting man.

The passive resistance movement has been undertaken only to gain rights for the whole of the Asiatics who have a right to remain in this country and not for a chosen few, and if—there is one man, whom I can recall, who is in Ladysmith, who came to the country in 1885 and paid £25 to the Boer Government for remaining in this country, carried on a trade, and possesses European credentials—if he cannot enter this country, I, for one, do not wish to remain in this country, if my countrymen before that time do not remove this head which seems to have done grievous wrong to them.

[*Indian Opinion*, 4-7-1908]

5. Speech at *Madras* Law Dinner

April 24, 1915

Under the auspices of the Madras Bar Association, the Annual Madras Law Dinner, the third of its kind, came off on Saturday evening last in the open air under bright moonlight on the extensive grounds adjoining the Moore Pavilion, People's Park, Madras. The Hon'ble Mr. F.H.M. Corbet, Advocate-General, was in the chair.... Mr. Gandhi, who is now in Madras, and who, as a Barrister, had been invited to the Dinner, was honoured with a seat on the left of the Hon'ble the Advocate-General. . . . The Chairman asked Mr. Gandhi to propose the toast of "The British Empire". . . .In proposing the toast of "The British Empire", Mr. Gandhi said:

MR. CHAIRMAN, MR. LORD CHIEF JUSTICE,
MY LORDS AND GENTLEMEN,

When the learned Advocate-General came to me and asked me to propose this toast, I must confess that I was taken aback a little. I don't think he noticed it himself, but I make that confession to you. I felt that I was invited to be present here as at one time I belonged to the profession to which you or most of you belong and as I happen to be in Madras, but that I would be allowed to remain a silent spectator of what was going on here. But when he mentioned the thing I did not hesitate to say, "Yes, I shall be pleased to speak to this toast." During my three months' touring in India as also in South Africa, I have been often questioned how I, a determined opponent of modern civilization and an avowed patriot, could reconcile myself to loyalty to the British Empire of which India was such a large part, how it was possible for me to find it consistent that India and England could work together for mutual benefit. It gives me the greatest pleasure this evening at this very great and important gathering to redeclare my loyalty to this British Empire and my loyalty is based upon very selfish grounds. As a passive resister I discovered that I could not have that free scope which I had under the British Empire. I know that a passive resister has to make good his claim to passive resistance, no matter under what circumstances he finds himself, and I discovered that the British Empire had certain ideals with which I have fallen in love,

("Hear, hear.") and one of those ideals is that every subject of the British Empire has the freest scope possible for his energies and efforts and whatever he thinks is due to his conscience. I think that this is true of the British Empire as it is not true of any other Governments that we see. ("Hear, hear.") I feel as you have perhaps known that I am no lover of any Government and I have more than once said that Government is best which governs least, and I have found that it is possible for me to be governed least under the British Empire. Hence my loyalty to the British Empire. (Loud applause.) And may I before I sit down and ask you to drink to the prosperity of the British Empire remind you of one singular incident that happened during this campaign in far-off South Africa. General Beyers, the trusted Commander of one of the Forces of the British Empire, rose against that Empire in open rebellion. It was only possible for him under that Empire and that Empire alone not to have himself shot on sight.

General Smuts wrote to him in a memorable letter that he himself was at one time a rebel. He wrote to General Beyers that it was only under the British Empire that it was possible for him to save his life. Hence my loyalty to the British Empire. (Loud applause.)

The toast was very enthusiastically honoured.

[*The Hindu*, 26-4-1915]

6. Spiritualizing Politics

SPEECH AT Y. M. C. A., MADRAS[1]

[April 27, 1915]

MR. CHAIRMAN AND DEAR FRIENDS,

Madras has well nigh exhausted the English vocabulary in using adjectives of virtue with reference to my wife and myself and, if I may be called upon to give an opinion as to where I have been smothered with kindness, love and attention, I would have to say: it is Madras.

(*Applause.*) But, as I have said so often, I believe it of Madras. So it is no wonder to me that you are lavishing all these kindnesses with unparalleled generosity, and now the worthy President of the Servants of India Society—under which Society I am going through a period of probation—has, if I may say so, capped it all. Am I worthy of these things? My answer from the innermost recesses of my heart is an emphatic "No". But I have come to India to become worthy of every adjective that you may use, and all my life will certainly be dedicated to prove worthy of them, if I am to be a worthy servant.

1. The first four pages of the letter are not available.
2. The month and year have been inferred from Gandhiji's itinerary.
3. In reply to the Madras students' address, V. S. Srinivasa Sastri presiding.

And so it is that you have sung that beautiful national song[2], on hearing which all of us sprang to our feet. The poet[3] has lavished all the adjectives that he possibly could to describe Mother India. He describes Mother India as sweet-smelling, sweet-speaking, fragrant, all-powerful, all-good, truthful, a land flowing with milk and honey, and having ripe

---

1. In reply to the Madras Students' address, V.S. Srinivasa Sastri presiding.
2. The proceedings had begun with the "Vande Mataram" song, all standing.
3. Bankim Chandra Chatterji.

fields, fruits and grains, and inhabited by a race of men of whom we have only a picture in the great Golden Age. He pictures to us a land which shall embrace in its possession the whole of the world, the whole of humanity by the might or right not of physical power but of soul-power. Can we sing that hymn? I ask myself, "Can I, by any right, spring to my feet when I listen to that song?" The poet no doubt gave us a picture for our realisation the words of which simply remain prophetic, and it is for you, the hope of India, to realise every word that the poet has said in describing this Motherland of ours. To-day I feel that these adjectives are very largely misplaced in his description of the Motherland, and it is for you and for me to make good the claim that the poet has advanced on behalf of his Motherland.

THE REAL EDUCATION

You—the students of Madras as well as students all over India— are you receiving an education which will make you worthy to realise that ideal and which will draw the best out of you, or is it an education which has become a factory for making Government employees or clerks in commercial offices? Is the goal of the education that you are receiving that of mere employment whether in the Government departments or other departments? If that be the goal of your education, if that is the goal that you have set before yourselves, I feel and I fear that the vision which the poet pictured for himself is far from being realised. As you have heard me say perhaps, or as you have read, I am and I have been a determined opponent of modern civilization. I want you to turn your eyes today upon what is going on in Europe and if you have come to the conclusion that Europe is today groaning under the heels of the modern civilization, then you and your elders will have to think twice before you can emulate that civilization in our Motherland. But I have been told: "How can we help it, seeing that our rulers bring that culture to our Motherland?"

Do not make any mistake about it at all. I do not for one moment believe that it is for any rulers to bring that culture to you unless you are prepared to accept it, and if it be that the rulers bring that culture before us, I think that we have forces within ourselves to enable us to reject . that culture without having to reject the rulers themselves.

(*Applause.*) I have said on many a platform that the British race is with us. I decline to go into the reasons why that race is with us, but I do believe that it is possible for India if she would but live up to the tradition of the sages of whom you have heard from our worthy President, to transmit a message through this great race, a message not of physical might, but a message of love. And then, it will be your privilege to conquer the conquerors not by shedding blood but by sheer force of spiritual predominance. When I consider what is going on today in India, I think it is necessary for us to say what our opinion is in connection with the political assassinations and political dacoities.

I feel that these are purely a foreign importation which cannot take root in this land. But you the student world have to beware, lest mentally or morally you give one thought of approval to this kind of terrorism. I, as a passive resister, will give you another thing very substantial for it. Terrorise yourself; search within; by all means resist tyranny wherever you find it; by all means resist encroachment upon your liberty, but not by shedding the blood of the tyrant. That is not what is taught by our religion. Our religion is based upon *ahimsa*, which in its active form is nothing but love, love not only to your neighbours, not only to your friends but love even to those who may be your enemies.

One word more in connection with the same thing. I think that if we were to practise truth, to practise *ahimsa*, we must immediately see that we also practise fearlessness. If our rulers are doing what in our opinion is wrong, and if we feel it our duty to let them hear our advice even though it may be considered sedition, I urge you to speak sedition but at your peril. You must be prepared to suffer the consequences. And when you are ready to suffer the consequences and not hit below the belt, then I think you will have made good your right to have your advice heard even by the Government.

RIGHTS AND DUTIES

I ally myself with the British Government, because I believe that it is possible for me to claim equal partnership with every subject of the British Empire. I today claim that equal partnership. I do not belong to a subject race. I do not call myself a member of a subject race. But there is this thing: it is not for the British governors to give you; it is for you to take the thing. I want and I can take the thing.

That I want only by discharging my obligations, Max Muller[1] has told us—we need not go to Max Muller to interpret our own religion but he says, our religion consists of the four letters "D-u-t-y" and not the

1. (1823-1900), German Orientalist.

five-letters "R-i-g-h-t". And if you believe that all that we want can grow from better discharge of our duty, then think always of your duty and fighting along those lines, you will have no fear of any man, you will fear only God. That is the message that my master—if I may say so, your master, too—Mr. Gokhale has given to us. What is that message then? It is in the constitution of the Servants of India Society and that is the message by which I wish to be guided in my life. The message is to spiritualize the political life and the political institutions of the country. We must immediately set about realising its practice. The students cannot be away from politics. Politics is as essential to them as religion. Politics cannot be divorced from religion. Politics divorced from religion becomes debasing. Modern culture and modern civilization are such politics.[1] My views may not be acceptable to you, I know. All the same I can only give you what is stirring me to my very depths. On the authority of my experiences in South Africa, I claim that your countrymen who had not that modern culture but who had that strength of the *rishis*[2] of old, who have inherited the *tapascharya*[3] performed by the *rishis*, without having known a single word of English literature and without knowing anything whatsoever of the present modern culture, they are able to rise to their full height.

And what has been possible for the uneducated and illiterate countrymen of ours in South Africa is ten times possible for you and for me today in this sacred land of ours. May that be your privilege and may that be my privilege ! (*Applause.*)

[*Speeches and Writings of Mahatma Gandhi*]

---

1. These two sentences are from *The Hindu*, 28-4-1915.
2. Sages.
3. Penance.

7. Speech at Benares Hindu University

[February 6, 1916]

The following is the full text of the speech delivered on February 4th[1] on the occasion of the opening of the Benares Hindu University. Gandhiji, who edited the report for G. A. Natesan, wrote:

I have merely removed some of the verbiage which in cold print would make the speech bad reading:

Friends, I wish to tender my humble apology for the long delay that took place before I was able to reach this place. And you will readily accept the apology when I tell you that I am not responsible for the delay nor is any human agency responsible for it. (*Laughter*.)

The fact is that I am like an animal on show and lay keepers in their over-kindness always manage to neglect a necessary chapter in this life and that is pure accident. In this case, they did not provide for the series of accidents that happened to us—to me, my keepers ! and my carriers. Hence this delay.

Friends, under the influence of the matchless eloquence of the lady (Mrs. Besant) who has just sat down, pray, do not believe that our University has become a finished product and that all the young men who are to come to the University that has yet to rise and come into existence, have also come and returned from it finished citizens of a great empire. Do not go away with any such impression and if you, the student world to which my remarks are supposed to be addressed this evening, consider for one moment that the spiritual life, for which this country is noted and for which this country has no rival, can be transmitted through the lip, pray, believe me you are wrong. You will never be able merely through the lip to give the message that India, I hope, will one day deliver to the world. I myself have been "fed up" with speeches and lectures. I except the lectures that have been delivered here during the last two days from this category, because they were necessary. But I do venture to suggest to you that we have now reached almost the end of our resources in speech-

1. Misprint for 6th.

making, and it is not enough that our ears are feasted, that our eyes are feasted, but it is necessary that our hearts have got to be touched and that our hands and feet have got to be moved. We have been told during the last two days how necessary it is, if we are to retain our hold upon the simplicity of Indian character, that our hands and feet should move in unison with our hearts. But this is only by way of preface, I wanted to say it is a matter of deep humiliation and shame for us that I am compelled this evening under the shadow of this great college, in this sacred city, to address my countrymen in a language that is foreign to me. I know that if I was appointed an examiner to examine all those who have been attending during these two days this series of lectures most of those who might be examined upon these lectures would fail.

And why? Because they have not been touched. I was present at the sessions of the great Congress in the month of December. There was a much vaster audience, and will you believe me when I tell you that the only speeches that touched that huge audience in Bombay were the speeches that were delivered in Hindustani? In Bombay, mind you, not in Benares where everybody speaks Hindi. But between the vernaculars of the Bombay Presidency on the one hand; and Hindi on the other, no such great dividing line exists as there does between English and the sister-languages of India; and the Congress audience was better able to follow the speakers in Hindi. I am hoping that this University will see to it that the youths who come to it will receive their instruction through the medium of their vernaculars. Our language is the reflection of ourselves, and if you tell me that our languages are too poor to express the best thought, then I say that the sooner we are wiped out of existence, the better for us. Is there a man who dreams that English can ever become the national language of India? (Cries of "Never"). Why this handicap on the nation? Just consider for one moment what an unequal race our lads have to run with every English lad. I had the privilege of a close conversation with some Poona professors. They assured me that every Indian youth, because he reached his knowledge through the English language, lost at least six precious years of life. Multiply that by the number of students turned out by our schools and colleges and find out for yourselves how many thousand years have been lost to the nation. The charge against us is, that we have no initiative. How can we have any if we are to devote the precious years of our life to the mastery of a foreign tongue? We fail in this attempt also. Was it possible for any speaker yesterday and today to impress his audience as was possible for Mr. Higginbotham? It was not the fault of the previous speakers that they could not engage the audience. They had more than substance enough for us in their addresses. But their addresses could not go home to us. I have heard it said that after all it is English-educated India which is leading and which is doing all the things for the nation.

It would be monstrous if it were otherwise. The only education we receive is English education. Surely we must show something for it.

But suppose that we had been receiving during the past fifty years education through our vernaculars, what should we have had today?

We should have today a free India, we should have our educated men, not as if they were foreigners in their own land but speaking to the heart of the nation; they would be working amongst the poorest of the poor, and whatever they would have gained during the past 50 years would be a heritage for the nation.

(*Applause.*) Today even our wives are not the sharers in our best thought. Look at Professor Bose[1] and Professor Ray[2] and their brilliant researches. Is it not a shame that their researches are not the common property of the masses?

Let us now turn to another subject.

The Congress has passed a resolution about self-government and I have no doubt that the All-India Congress Committee and the Moslem League will do their duty and come forward with some tangible suggestions. But I, for one, must frankly confess that I am not so much interested in what they will be able to produce as I am interested in anything that the student world is going to produce or the masses are going to produce. No paper contribution will ever give us self-government. No amount of speeches will ever make us fit for self-government. It is only our conduct that will fit us for it.

(*Applause.*) And how are we trying to govern ourselves? I want to think audibly this evening. I do not want to make a speech and if you find me this evening speaking without reserve, pray, consider that you are only sharing the thoughts of a man who allows himself to think audibly, and if you think that I seem to transgress the limits that courtesy imposes upon me, pardon me for the liberty I may be taking.

I visited the Viswanath Temple last evening and as I was walking through those lanes, these were the thoughts that touched me. If a stranger dropped from above on to this great temple and he had to consider what we as Hindus were, would he not be justified in

1. Sir J. C. Bose, F.R.S., botanist.
2. Sir P. C. Ray, chemist.

condemning us? Is not this great temple a reflection of our own character? I speak feelingly as a Hindu. Is it right that the lanes of our sacred temple should be as dirty as they are? The houses round about are built anyhow. The lanes are tortuous and narrow. If even our temples are not models of roominess and cleanliness, what can our self-government be? Shall our temples be abodes of holiness, cleanliness and peace as soon as the English have retired from India, either of their own pleasure or by compulsion, bag and baggage?

I entirely agree with the President of the Congress that before we think of self-government, we shall have to do the necessary plodding.

In every city there are two divisions, the cantonment and the city proper. The city mostly is a stinking den. But we are a people unused to city life. But if we want city life, we cannot reproduce the easy-going hamlet life. It is not comforting to think that people walk about the streets of Indian Bombay under the perpetual fear of dwellers in the storeyed buildings spitting upon them. I do a great deal of railway travelling. I observe the difficulty of third-class passengers. But the Railway Administration is by no means to blame for all their hard lot. We do not know the elementary laws of cleanliness. We spit anywhere on the carriage floor, irrespective of the thought that it is often used as sleeping space. We do not trouble ourselves as to how we use it; the result is indescribable filth in the compartment. The so-called better class passengers over-awe their less fortunate brethren. Among them I have seen the student world also.

Sometimes they behave no better. They can speak English and they have worn Norfolk Jackets and therefore claim the right to force their way in and command seating accommodation. I have turned the searchlight all over and as you have given me the privilege of speaking to you, I am laying my heart bare. Surely we must set these things right in our progress towards self-government. I now introduce you to another scene. His Highness the Maharajah, who presided yesterday over our deliberations, spoke about the poverty of India.

Other speakers laid great stress upon it. But what did we witness in the great pandal in which the foundation ceremony was performed by the Viceroy? Certainly a most gorgeous show, an exhibition of jewellery which made a splendid feast for the eyes of the greatest jeweller who chose to come from Paris. I compare with the richly bedecked noblemen the millions of the poor. And I feel like saying to these noblemen: "There is no salvation for India unless you strip yourselves of this jewellery and hold it in trust for your countrymen in India."

("Hear, hear" and *Applause.*) I am sure it is not the desire of the King-Emperor or Lord Hardinge that in order to show the truest loyalty to our King-Emperor, it is necessary for us to ransack our jewellery boxes and to appear bedecked from top to toe. I would undertake at the peril of my life to bring to you a message from King George himself that he expects nothing of the kind. Sir, whenever I hear of a great palace rising in any great city of India, be it in British India or be it in India which is ruled by our great chiefs, I become jealous at once and I say: "Oh, it is the money that has come from the agriculturists." Over 75 per cent of the population are agriculturists and Mr. Higginbotham told us last night in his own felicitous language that they are the men who grow two blades of grass in the place of one. But there cannot be much spirit of self-government about us if we take away or allow others to take away from them almost the whole of the results of their labour. Our salvation can only come through the farmer. Neither the lawyers, nor the doctors, nor the rich landlords are going to secure it.

Now, last but not the least, it is my bounden duty to refer to what agitated our minds during these two or three days. All of us have had many anxious moments while the Viceroy was going through the streets of Benares. There were detectives stationed in many places. We were horrified. We asked ourselves: "Why this distrust? Is it not better that even Lord Hardinge should die than live a living death?" But a representative of a mighty Sovereign may not. He might find it necessary even to live a living death. But why was it necessary to impose these detectives on us? We may foam, we may fret, we may resent but let us not forget that India of today in her impatience has produced an army of anarchists. I myself am an anarchist, but of another type. But there is a class of anarchists amongst us, and if I was able to reach this class, I would say to them that their anarchism has no room in India if India is to conquer the conqueror. It is a sign of fear. If we trust and fear God, we shall have to fear no one, not Maharajahs, not Viceroys, not the detectives, not even King George. I honour the anarchist for his love of the country. I honour him for his bravery in being willing to die for his country; but I ask him: Is killing honourable? Is the dagger of an assassin a fit precursor of an honourable death? I deny it. There is no warrant for such methods in any scriptures. If I found it necessary for the salvation of India that the English should retire, that they should be driven out, I would not hesitate to declare that they would have to go, and I hope I would be prepared to die in defence of that belief. That would, in my opinion, be an honourable death. The bomb-thrower creates secret plots, is afraid to come into the open, and when caught pays the penalty of misdirected zeal. I have been told: "Had we not done this, had some people not thrown bombs, we should never have gained what we have got with reference to the partition movement[1]." (Mrs. Besant: "Please stop it"). This was what I said[2] in Bengal when Mr. Lyons presided at the meeting. I think what I am saying is necessary. If I am told to stop, I shall obey. (Turning to the Chairman) I await your orders. If you consider that by my speaking as I am, I am not serving the country and the Empire, I shall certainly stop. (Cries of "Go on"). (The Chairman: "Please explain your object"). I am explaining my object. I am simply (Another interruption.) My friends, please do not resent this interruption. If Mrs. Besant this evening suggests that I should stop, she does so because she loves India so well, and she considers that I am erring in thinking audibly before you young men. But even so, I simply say this that I want to purge India of the atmosphere of suspicion on either side; if we are to reach our goal, we should have an empire which is to be based upon mutual love and mutual trust. Is it not better that we talk under the shadow of this college than that we should be talking irresponsibly in our homes? I consider that it is much better that we talk these things openly. I have done so with excellent results before now. I know that there is nothing that the students are not discussing. There is nothing that the students do not know. I am therefore turning the searchlight towards ourselves. I hold the name of my country so dear to me that I exchange these thoughts with you and submit to you that there is no reason for anarchism in India. Let us frankly and openly say whatever we want to say to our rulers and face the consequences if what we have to say does not please them. But let us not abuse. I was talking the other day to a member of the much-abused Civil Service. I have not very much in common with the members of that Service, but I could not help admiring the manner in which he was speaking to me. He said: "Mr. Gandhi, do you for one moment suppose that all we, Civil Servants, are a bad lot, that we want to oppress the people whom we have come to govern?" "No", I said. "Then, if you get an opportunity, put in a word for the much-abused Civil Service.", And I am here to put in that word. Yes, many members of the Indian Civil Service are most decidedly overbearing, they are tyrannical, at times thoughtless. Many other

1. The partition of Bengal, which took place in 1905, was annulled in December, 1911.
2. Vide "Speech at Students' Hall, Calcutta", 31-3-1915.

adjectives may be used. I grant all these things and I grant also that after having lived in India for a certain number of years, some of them become somewhat degraded. But what does that signify? They were gentlemen before they came here, and if they have lost some of the moral fibre, it is a reflection upon ourselves. (Cries of "No".) Just think out for yourselves, if a man who was good yesterday has become bad after having come in contact with me, is he responsible that he has deteriorated or am I? The atmosphere of sycophancy and falsity that surrounds them on their coming to India demoralises them as it would many of us. It is well to take the blame sometimes. If we are to receive self-government, we shall have to take it. We shall never be granted self-government. Look at the history of the British Empire and the British nation; freedom loving as it is, it will not be a party to give freedom to a people who will not take it themselves. Learn your lesson if you wish to from the Boer War. Those who were enemies of that Empire only a few years ago have now become friends.

[At this point there was an interruption and there was a movement on the platform to leave; the speech therefore ended here abruptly.]

[*Speeches and Writings of Mahatma Gandhi (4th Edit.),* pp. 317-26]

8. On Swadeshi

AT MISSIONARY CONFERENCE, MADRAS[1]

[February 14, 1916]

It was not without much diffidence that I undertook to speak to you at all. And I was hard put to it in the selection of my subject. I have chosen a very delicate and difficult subject. It is delicate because of the peculiar views I hold upon *swadeshi*, and it is difficult because I have not that command of language which is necessary for giving adequate expression to my thoughts. I know that I may rely upon your indulgence for the many shortcomings you will no doubt find in my address, the more so when I tell you that there is nothing in what I am about to say, that I am not either already practising or am not preparing to practise to the best of my ability. It encourages me to observe that last month you devoted a week to prayer in the place of an address. I have earnestly prayed that what I am about to say may bear fruit and I know that you will bless my words with a similar prayer.

After much thinking, I have arrived at a definition of *swadeshi* that perhaps best illustrates my meaning. *Swadeshi* is that spirit in us which restricts us to the use and service of our immediate surroundings to the exclusion of the more remote. Thus, as for religion, in order to satisfy the requirements of the definition, I must restrict myself to my ancestral religion. That is the use of my immediate religious surroundings. If I find it defective, I should serve it by purging it of its defects. In the domain of politics, I should make use of the indigenous institutions and serve them by curing them of their proved defects. In that of economics, I should use only things that are produced by my immediate neighbours and serve those industries by making them efficient and complete where they might be found wanting. It is suggested that such *swadeshi*, if reduced to practice, will lead to the millennium. And as we do not abandon our pursuit after the millennium because we do not expect quite to reach it

1. Text of the paper read by Gandhiji. It was reprinted in *Young India*, 21-6-1919.

within our time, so may we not abandon *swadeshi* even though it may not be fully attained for generations to come.

Let us briefly examine three branches of *swadeshi* as sketched above. Hinduism has become a conservative religion and therefore a mighty force because of the *swadeshi* spirit underlying it. It is the most tolerant because it is non-proselytising, and it is as capable of expansion today as it has been found to be in the past. It has succeeded not in driving, as I think it has been erroneously held, but in absorbing Buddhism. By reason of the *swadeshi* spirit, a Hindu refuses to change his religion not necessarily because he considers it to be the best, but because he knows that he can complement it by introducing reforms. And what I have said about Hinduism is, I suppose, true of the other great faiths of the world, only it is held that it is specially so in the case of Hinduism. But here comes the point I am labouring to reach. If there is any substance in what I have said, will not the great missionary bodies of India, to whom she owes a deep debt of gratitude for what they have done and are doing, do still better and serve the spirit of Christianity better, by dropping the goal of proselytising but continuing their philanthropic work? I hope you will not consider this to be an impertinence on my part. I make the suggestion in all sincerity and with due humility. Moreover, I have some claim upon your attention. I have endeavoured to study the *Bible*. I consider it as part of my scriptures. The spirit of the *Sermon on the Mount* competes almost on equal terms with the *Bhagavad Gita* for the domination of my heart. I yield to no Christian in the strength of devotion with which I sing, "Lead, kindly Light" and several other inspired hymns of a similar nature. I have come under the influence of noted Christian missionaries belonging to different denominations. And I enjoy to this day the privilege of friendship with some of them. You will perhaps, therefore, allow that I have offered the above suggestion not as a biased Hindu but as a humble and impartial student of religion with great leanings towards Christianity. May it not be that the "Go Ye unto All the World" message has been somewhat narrowly interpreted and the spirit of it missed? It will not be denied, I speak from experience, that many of the conversions are only so called. In some cases, the appeal has gone not to the heart but to the stomach. And in every case, a conversion leaves a sore behind it which, I venture to think, is avoidable. Quoting again from experience, a new birth, a change of heart, is perfectly possible in every one of the great faiths. I know I am now treading upon thin ice. But I do not apologise, in closing this part of my subject, for saying that the frightful outrage that is just going on in Europe, perhaps, shows that the message of Jesus of Nazareth, the Son of Peace, has been little understood in Europe, and that light upon it may have to be thrown from the East.

I have sought your help in religious matters, which it is yours to give in a special sense. But I make bold to seek it even in political matters. I do not believe that religion has nothing to do with politics.

The latter divorced from religion is like a corpse only fit to be buried. As a matter of fact, in your own silent manner, you influence politics not a little. And I feel that if the attempt to separate politics from religion had not been made, as it is even now made, they would not have degenerated, as they often appear to do. No one considers that the political life of the country is in a happy state. Following out the *swadeshi* spirit, I observe the indigenous institutions and the village panchayats hold me. India is really a republican country, and it is because it is that that it has survived every shock hitherto delivered.

Princes and potentates, whether they were Indian born or foreigners, have hardly touched the vast masses except for collecting revenue.

The latter in their turn seem to have rendered unto Caesar what was Caesar's and for the rest have done much as they have liked. The vast organisation of caste answered not only the religious wants of the community, but it answered too its political needs. The villagers managed their internal affairs through the caste system, and through it they dealt with any oppression from the ruling power or powers. It is not possible to deny of a nation that was capable of producing the caste system its wonderful power of organisation. One had but to attend the great *Kumbha Mela* at Hardwar last year to know how skilful that organisation must have been, which without any seeming effort, was able effectively to cater for more than a million pilgrims.

Yet is it the fashion to say that we lack organising ability. This is true, I fear, to a certain extent, of those who have been nurtured in the new traditions. We have laboured under a terrible handicap owing to an almost fatal departure from the *swadeshi* spirit. We the educated classes have received our education through a foreign tongue. We have, therefore, not reacted upon the masses. We want to represent the masses, but we fail. They recognise us not much more than they recognise the English officers. Their hearts are an open book to neither. Their aspirations are not ours. Hence, there is a break. And you witness not in reality failure to organise, but want of correspondence between the representatives and the represented. If during the last fifty years we had been educated through the vernaculars, our elders and our servants and our neighbours would have partaken of our knowledge; the discoveries of a Bose or a Ray would have been household treasure as are the *Ramayan* and the *Mahabharat*. As it is, so far as the masses are concerned, those great discoveries might as well have been made by foreigners. Had instruction in all the branches of learning been given through the vernaculars, I make bold to say that they would have been enriched wonderfully. The question of village sanitation, etc., would have been solved long ago. The village panchayats would be now a living force in a special way, and India would almost be enjoying self-government suited to its requirements and would have been spared the humiliating spectacle of organised assassination on its sacred soil. It is not too late to mend. And you can help if you will, as no other body or bodies can.

And now for the last division of *swadeshi*. Much of the deep poverty of the masses is due to the ruinous departure from *swadeshi* in the economic and industrial life. If not an article of commerce had been brought from outside India, she would be today a land flowing with milk and honey. But that was not to be. We were greedy and so was England. The connection between England and India was based clearly upon an error. But she (England) does not remain in India in error. It is her declared policy that India is to be held in trust for her people. If this be true, Lancashire must stand aside. And if the *swadeshi* doctrine is a sound doctrine, Lancashire can stand aside without hurt, though it may sustain a shock for the time being. I think of *swadeshi* not as a boycott movement undertaken by way of revenge. I conceive it as a religious principle to be followed by all. I am no economist, but I have read some treatises which show that England could easily become a self-sustained country, growing all the produce she needs. This may be an utterly ridiculous proposition, and perhaps the best proof that it cannot be true is that England is one of the largest importers in the world. But India cannot live for Lancashire or any other country before she is able to live for herself. And she can live for herself only if she produces and is helped to produce everything for her requirements within her own borders. She need not be, she ought not to be, drawn into the vortex of mad and ruinous competition which breeds fratricide, jealousy and many other evils.

But who is to stop her great millionaires from entering into the world competition? Certainly, not legislation. Force of public opinion, proper education, however, can do a great deal in the desired direction. The handloom industry is in a dying condition. I took special care during my wanderings last year to see as many weavers as possible, and my heart ached to find how they had lost, how families had retired from this once flourishing and honourable occupation. If we follow the *swadeshi* doctrine, it would be your duty and mine to find out neighbours who can supply our wants and to teach them to supply them where they do not know how to, assuming that there are neighbours who are in want of healthy occupation. Then every village of India will almost be a self-supporting and self-contained unit exchanging only such necessary commodities with other villages where they are not locally producible. This may all sound nonsensical. Well, India is a country of nonsense. It is nonsensical to parch one's throat with thirst when a kindly Mahomedan is ready to offer pure water to drink. And yet thousands of Hindus would rather die of thirst than drink water from a Mahomedan household. These nonsensical men can also, once they are convinced that their religion demands that they should wear garments manufactured in India only and eat food only grown in India, decline to wear any other clothing or eat any other food. Lord Curzon set the fashion for tea-drinking.

And that pernicious drug now bids fair to overwhelm the nation. It has already undermined the digestive apparatus of hundreds of thousands of men and women and constitutes an additional tax upon their slender purses. Lord Hardinge can set the fashion for *swadeshi* and almost the whole of India will foreswear foreign goods. There is a verse in the *Bhagavad Gita*, which, freely rendered, means masses follow the classes. It is easy to undo the evil if the thinking portion of the community were to take the *swadeshi* vow even though it may for a time cause considerable inconvenience. I hate interference in any department of life. At best, it is the lesser evil. But I would tolerate, welcome, indeed plead for, stiff protective duty upon foreign goods. Natal, a British colony, protected its sugar by taxing the sugar that came from another British colony, Mauritius. England has sinned against India by forcing free trade upon her. It may have been food for her, but it has been poison for this country.

It has often been urged that India cannot adopt *swadeshi* in the economic life at any rate. Those who advance this objection do not look upon *swadeshi* as a rule of life. With them, it is a mere patriotic effort not to be made if it involved any self-denial. *Swadeshi*, as defined here, is a religious discipline to be undergone in utter disregard of the physical discomfort it may cause to individuals.

Under its spell, the deprivation of pin or a needle, because these are not manufactured in India need cause no terror. A *swadeshi* will learn to do without hundreds of things which today he considers necessary. Moreover, those who dismiss *swadeshi* from their minds by arguing the impossible forget that *swadeshi*, after all, is a goal to be reached by steady effort. And we would be making for the goal even if we confined *swadeshi* to a given set of articles, allowing ourselves as a temporary measure to use such things as might not be procurable in the country.

There now remains for me to consider one more objection that has been raised against *swadeshi*. The objectors consider it to be a most selfish doctrine without any warrant in the civilized code of morality. With them, to practise *swadeshi* is to revert to barbarism. I cannot enter into a detailed analysis of the proposition. But I would urge that *swadeshi* is the only doctrine consistent with the law of humility and love. It is arrogance to think of launching out to serve the whole of India when I am hardly able to serve even my own family. It were better to concentrate my effort upon the family and consider that through them I was serving the whole nation and, if you will, the whole of humanity. This is humility and it is love. The motive will determine the quality of the act. I may serve my family regardless of the sufferings I may cause to others, as, for instance, I may accept an employment which enables me to extort money from people. I enrich myself thereby and then satisfy many unlawful demands of the family. Here I am neither serving the family nor the State. Or I may recognise that God has given me hands and feet only to work with for my sustenance and for that of those who may be dependent upon me.

I would then at once simplify my life and that of those whom I can directly reach. In this instance, I would have served the family without causing injury to anyone else. Supposing that everyone followed this mode of life, we would have at once an ideal State. All will not reach that state at the same time. But those of us who, realising its truth, enforce it in practice will clearly anticipate and accelerate the coming of that happy day. Under this plan of life, in seeming to serve India to the exclusion of every other country, I do not harm any other country. My patriotism is both exclusive and inclusive. It is exclusive in the sense that in all humility I confine my attention to the land of my birth, but it is inclusive in the sense that my service is not of a competitive or antagonistic nature. *Sic utere tuo ut alienum non laedas*[1] is not merely a legal maxim, but it is a grand doctrine of life.

It is the key to a proper practice of *ahimsa* or love. It is for you, the custodians of a great faith, to set the fashion and show by your preaching,

---

1. This Latin legal maxim means: "Use your property in such a way as not to damage that of others." *Vide* also *An Autobiography*, Part I, Ch. XXV.

sanctified by practice, that patriotism based on hatred "killeth" and that patriotism based on love "giveth life".

[*The Hindu,* 28-2-1916]

9. Ashram Vows

SPEECH AT Y. M. C. A., MADRAS[1]

[February 16, 1916]

MR. CHAIRMAN AND DEAR FRIENDS,

I have so often said that I am not myself fond of hearing my own voice and I assure you that this morning also I retained the same position. It was only, if you will believe me, my great regard for the students, whom I love, whom I respect and whom I consider are the hope of future India that moved me to accept this invitation to speak to you this morning. I did not know what subject to choose. A friend has handed me a slip here asking me whether I would enlighten the students on the Benares incident. ("Hear, hear"). I fear I shall have to disappoint that friend and those of you who associate yourselves with that view. I don't think that you need lay any stress upon that incident. These are the passing waves which will always come and go.

I should, therefore, this morning fear rather if I can possibly do so and pour my soul out to you with reference to something which I treasure so much above everything else.[2]

To many of the students who came here last year to converse with me, I said[3] I was about to establish an institution—an *ashram*—somewhere in India, and it is about that place that I am going to talk to you this morning. I feel and I have felt during the whole of my public life that what we need, what any nation needs, but we perhaps of all the nations of the world need just now, is nothing else and nothing less than character-building. And this is the view propounded by that great patriot, Mr. Gokhale (cheers). As you know, in many of his speeches, he used to say that we would get nothing, we would deserve nothing unless we had character to back what we wished for.

1. With Rev. George Pittendrigh of the Madras Christian College in the chair.
2. This paragraph is from *The Hindu*, 16-2-1916.
3. *Vide* "Speech at Gokhale Club, Madras", 20-4-1915.

This was published with the following note by the Editor, *Indian Review*:

> We have received several enquiries from our readers regarding Mr. Gandhi's new organisation, the Satyagrahashram. We are glad to be able to give the following account of the Ashram from a special report of the speech that Mr. Gandhi delivered sometime ago in Madras. The report has since had the benefit of Mr. Gandhi's revision and may, therefore, be taken as an authoritative exposition of the aims and objects of Mr. Gandhi's Satyagrahashram.

Hence his founding of that great body, the Servants of India Society. And as you know, in the prospectus that has been issued in connection with the Society, Mr. Gokhale has deliberately stated that it was necessary to spiritualise the political life of the country. You know also that he used to say so often that our average was less than the average of so many European nations. I do not know whether that statement by him, whom, with pride, I consider to be my political *guru*, has really foundation in fact, but I do believe that there is much to be said to justify it in so far as educated India is concerned ; not because we, the educated portion of the community, have blundered, but because we have been creatures of circumstances. Be that as it may, this is the maxim of life which I have accepted, namely, that no work done by any man, no matter how great he is, will really prosper unless he[1] has a religious backing. But what is religion? the question will be immediately asked. I, for one, would answer, not the religion which you will get after reading all the scriptures of the world; it is not really a grasp by the brain, but it is a heart-grasp. It is a thing which is not alien to us, but it is a thing which has to be evolved out of us. It is always within us, with some consciously so; with others, quite unconsciously. But it is there; and whether we wake up this religious instinct in us through outside assistance or by inward growth, no matter how it is done, it has got to be done if we want to do anything in the right manner and anything that is going to persist.

Our scriptures have laid down certain rules as maxims of life and as axioms which we have to take for granted as self-demonstrated truths. The *shastras* tell us that without living according to those maxims, we are incapable even of having a reasonable perception of religion.

1. "it" in *New India*.

Believing in these implicitly for all these long years and having actually endeavoured to reduce to practice these injunctions of the *shastras*, I have deemed it necessary to seek the association of those who think with me in founding this institution. And I shall venture this morning to place before you the rules that have been drawn up and that have to be observed by everyone who seeks to be a member of that Ashram.

Five of these are known as *Yamas*, and the first and the foremost is, the VOW OF TRUTH. Not truth simply as we ordinarily understand it, that as far as possible we ought not to resort to a lie, that is to say, not truth which merely answers the saying, "Honesty is the best policy"—implying that if it is not the best policy, we may depart from it. But here Truth, as it is conceived, means that we have to rule our life by this law of Truth at any cost. And in order to satisfy the definition, I have drawn upon the celebrated illustration of the life of Prahlad[1]. For the sake of Truth, he dared to oppose his own father, and he defended himself, not by retaliation by paying his father back in his own coin, but in defence of Truth, as he knew it, he was prepared to die without caring to return the blows that he had received from his father or from those who were charged with his father's instructions. Not only that: he would not in any way even parry the blows. On the contrary, with a smile on his lips, he underwent the innumerable tortures to which he was subjected, with the result that at last, Truth rose triumphant, not that Prahlad suffered the tortures because he knew that some day or other in his very life-time he would be able to demonstrate the infallibility of the law of Truth. That fact was there; but if he had died in the midst of torture, he would still have adhered to Truth. That is the Truth that I would like us to follow. There was an incident I noticed yesterday. It was a trifling incident, but I think these trifling incidents are like straws which show which way the wind is blowing.

The incident was this: I was talking to a friend who wanted to talk to me aside, and we were engaged in a private conversation. A third friend dropped in and he politely asked whether he was intruding.

The friend to whom I was talking said: "Oh, no, there is nothing private here." I felt taken aback a little, because, as I was taken aside, I knew that so far as this friend was concerned, the conversation was private. But he immediately, out of politeness, I would call it

1. Prahlad was a devotee of God persecuted by his unbelieving father, the demon-king, Hiranyakashipu. Gandhiji often spoke of him as an ideal *satyagrahi*.

over-politeness, said there was no private conversation and that he (the third friend) could join. I suggest to you that this is a departure from my definition of Truth. I think that the friend should have, in the gentlest manner possible, but still openly and frankly, said: "Yes, just now, as you properly say, you would be intruding" without giving the slightest offence to the person if he was himself a gentleman—and we are bound to consider everybody to be a gentleman unless he proves to be otherwise. But I may be told that the incident, after all, proves the gentility of the nation. I think that it is over-proving the case. If we continue to say these things out of politeness, we really become a nation of hypocrites. I recall a conversation I had with an English friend. He was comparatively a stranger. He is a Principal of a College and has been in India for several years. He was comparing notes with me, and he asked me whether I would admit that we, unlike most Englishmen, would not dare to say "No" when it was "No" that we meant. And I must admit that I immediately said "Yes". I agree with that statement. We do hesitate to say "No", frankly and boldly, when we want to pay due regard to the sentiments of the person whom we are addressing. In this Ashram, we make it a rule that we must say "No" when we mean "No", regardless of consequences.

This, then, is the first rule. Then we come to the DOCTRINE OF *AHIMSA*

Literally speaking, *ahimsa* means non-killing. But to me it has a world of meaning and takes me into realms much higher, infinitely higher, than the realm to which I would go, if I merely understood by *ahimsa* non-killing. *Ahimsa* really means that you may not offend anybody, you may not harbour an uncharitable thought even in connection with one who may consider himself to be your enemy.

Pray notice the guarded nature of this thought; I do not say "whom you consider to be your enemy", but "who may consider himself to be your enemy". For one who follows the doctrine of *ahimsa*, there is no room for an enemy; he denies the existence of an enemy. But there are people who consider themselves to be his enemies, and he cannot help that circumstance. So, it is held that we may not harbour an evil thought even in connection with such persons. If we return blow for blow, we depart from the doctrine of *ahimsa*. But I go further. If we resent a friend's action or the so-called enemy's action, we still fall short of this doctrine. But when I say we should not resent, I do not say that we should acquiesce; but by resenting I mean wishing that some harm should be done to the enemy, or that he should be put out of the way, not even by any action of ours, but by the action of somebody else, or, say, by Divine agency. If we harbour even this thought, we depart from this doctrine of *ahimsa*. Those who join the Ashram have to literally accept that meaning. That does not mean that we practise that doctrine in its entirety. Far from it. It is an ideal which we have to reach, and it is an ideal to be reached even at this very moment, if we are capable of doing so. But it is not a proposition in geometry to be learnt by heart: it is not even like solving difficult problems in higher mathematics; it is infinitely more difficult than solving those problems. Many of you have burnt the midnight oil in solving those problems. If you want to follow out this doctrine, you will have to do much more than burn the midnight oil.

You will have to pass many a sleepless night, and go through many a mental torture and agony before you can reach, before you can even be within measurable distance of this goal. It is the goal, and nothing less than that, you and I have to reach if we want to understand what a religious life means. I will not say much more on this doctrine than this: that a man who believes in the efficacy of this doctrine finds in the ultimate stage, when he is about to reach the goal, the whole world at his feet, not that he wants the whole world at his feet, but it must be so. If you express your love—*ahimsa*—in such a manner that it impresses itself indelibly upon your so-called enemy, he must return that love. Another thought which comes out of this is that, under this rule, there is no room for organised assassinations, and there is no room for murders even openly committed, and there is no room for any violence even for the sake of your country, and even for guarding the honour of precious ones that may be under your charge. After all, that would be a poor defence of honour. This doctrine of *ahimsa* tells us that we may guard the honour of those who are under our charge by delivering ourselves into the hands of the man who would commit the sacrilege. And that requires far greater physical and mental courage than the delivering of blows. You may have some degree of physical power—I do not say courage—and you may use that power.

But after that is expended, what happens? The other man is filled with wrath and indignation, and you have made him more angry by matching your violence against his; and when he has done you to death, the rest of his violence is delivered against your charge. But if you do not retaliate, but stand your ground, between your charge and the opponent, simply receiving the blows without retaliating, what happens? I give you my promise that the whole of the violence will be expended on you, and your charge will be left unscathed. Under this plan of life, there is no conception of patriotism which justifies such wars as you witness today in Europe. Then there is the VOW OF CELIBACY

Those who want to perform national service, or those who want to have a glimpse of the real religious life, must lead a celibate life, no matter if married or unmarried. Marriage but brings a woman closer together [*sic*] with the man, and they become friends in a special sense, never to be parted either in this life or in the lives that are to come. But I do not think that, in our conception of marriage, our lusts should necessarily enter. Be that as it may, this is what is placed before those who come to the Ashram. I do not deal with that at any length.

Then we have the VOW OF CONTROL OF THE PALATE.

A man who wants to control his animal passions easily does so if he control his palate. I fear this is one of the most difficult vows to follow. I am just now coming after having inspected the Victoria Hostel. I saw there, not to my dismay, though it should be to my dismay, but I am used to it now, that there are so many kitchens, not kitchens that are established in order to serve caste restrictions, but kitchens that have become necessary in order that people can have the condiments, and the exact weight of the condiments, to which they are used in the respective places from which they come. And, therefore, we find that for the Brahmins themselves there are different compartments and different kitchens catering for the delicate tastes of all these different groups, I suggest to you that this is simply slavery to the palate, rather than mastery over it. I may say this: Unless we take our minds off from this habit, and unless we shut our eyes to the tea shops and coffee shops and all these kitchens, and unless we are satisfied with foods that are necessary for the proper maintenance of our physical health, and unless we are prepared to rid ourselves of stimulating, heating and exciting condiments that we mix with our food, we will certainly not be able to control the overabundant, unnecessary, exciting stimulation that we may have. If we do not do that, the result naturally is, that we abuse ourselves and we abuse even the sacred trust given to us, and we become less than animals and brutes. Eating, drinking and indulging passions we share in common with the animals, but have you ever seen a horse or a cow indulging in the abuse of the palate as we do? Do you suppose that it is a sign of civilization, a sign of real life that we should multiply our eatables so far that we do not even know where we are; and seek; dish after dish until at last we have become absolutely mad and run after the newspaper sheets which give us advertisements about these dishes?

Then we have the VOW OF NON-THIEVING.

I suggest that we are thieves in a way. If I take anything that I do not need for my own immediate use, and keep it, I thieve it from somebody else. I venture to suggest that it is the fundamental law of Nature, without exception, that Nature produces enough for our wants from day to day, and if only everybody took enough for himself and nothing more, there would be no pauperism in this world, there would be no man dying of starvation in this world. But so long as we have got this inequality, so long we are thieving. I am no socialist and I do not want to dispossess those who have got possessions; but I do say that, personally, those of us who want to see light out of darkness have to follow the rule. I do not want to dispossess anybody. I should then be departing from the rule of *ahimsa*. If somebody else possesses more than I do, let him. But so far as my own life has to be regulated, I do say that I dare not possess anything which I do not want. In India we have got three millions of people having to be satisfied with one meal a day, and that meal consisting of a chapati containing no fat in it, and a pinch of salt. You and I have no right to anything that we really have until these three million are clothed and fed better. You and I, who ought to know better, must adjust our wants, and even undergo voluntary starvation in order that they may be nursed, fed and clothed. Then there is the vow of non-possession which follows as a matter of course. Then I go to the VOW OF *SWADESHI*.

The vow of *swadeshi* is a necessary vow. But you are conversant with the *swadeshi* life and the *swadeshi* spirit. I suggest to you we are departing from one of the sacred laws of our being when we leave our neighbour and go out somewhere else in order to satisfy our wants. If a man comes from Bombay here and offers you wares, you are not justified in supporting the Bombay merchant or trader so long as you have got a merchant at your very door, born and bred in Madras. That is my view of *swadeshi*. In your village, so long as you have got your village-barber, you are bound to support him to the exclusion of the finished barber who may come to you from Madras. If you find it necessary that your village-barber should reach the attainment of the barber from Madras, you may train him to that. Send him to Madras by all means, if you wish, in order that he may learn his calling. Until you do that, you are not justified in going to another barber. That is *swadeshi*. So, when we find that there are many things that we cannot get in India, we must try to do without them. We may have to do without many things which we may consider necessary, but believe me, when you have that frame of mind, you will find a great burden taken off your shoulders, even as the Pilgrim did in that inimitable book, Pilgrim's Progress: There came a time when the mighty burden that the Pilgrim was carrying on his shoulders unconsciously dropped from him, and he felt a freer man than he was when he started on the journey. So will you feel freer men than you are now, immediately you adopt this *swadeshi* life. We have also the VOW OF FEARLESSNESS.

I found, throughout my wanderings in India, that India, educated India, is seized with a paralysing fear. We may not open our lips in public; we may not declare our confirmed opinion in public; we may hold those opinions; we may talk about them secretly; and we may do anything we like within the four walls of our house,—but those are not for public consumption. If we had taken a vow of silence, I would have nothing to say. When we open our lips in public, we say things which we do not really believe in. I do not know whether this is not the experience of almost every public man who speaks in India. I then suggest to you that there is only one Being, if Being is the proper term to be used, Whom we have to fear, and that is God. When we fear God, we shall fear no man, no matter how high-placed he may be. And if you want to follow the vow of truth in any shape or form, fearlessness is the necessary consequence. And so you find, in the *Bhagavad Gita*, fearlessness is declared as the first essential quality of a Brahmin. We fear consequences and, therefore, we are afraid to tell the truth. A man who fears God will certainly not fear any earthly consequence. Before we can aspire to the position of understanding what religion is, and before we can aspire to the position of guiding the destinies of India, do you not see that we should adopt this habit of fearlessness? Or shall we over-awe our countrymen even as we are over-awed? We thus see how important this "fearlessness vow" is. And we have also the VOW REGARDING THE UNTOUCHABLES.

There is an ineffaceable blot that Hinduism today carries with it.

I have declined to believe that it has been handed to us from immemorial times. I think that this miserable, wretched, enslaving spirit of "untouchableness" must have come to us when we were in the cycle of our lives, at our lowest ebb, and that evil has still stuck to us and it still remains with us. It is, to my mind, a curse that has come to us, and as long as that curse remains with us, so long I think we are bound to consider that every affliction that we labour under in this sacred land is a fit and proper punishment for this great and indelible crime that we are committing. That any person should be considered untouchable because of his calling passes one's comprehension; and you, the student world, who receive all this modern education, if you become a party to this crime, it were better that you received no education whatsoever. Of course, we are labouring under a very heavy handicap.

Although you may realise that there cannot be a single human being on this earth who should be considered to be untouchable, you cannot react upon your families, you cannot react upon your surroundings, because all your thought is conceived in a foreign tongue, and all your energy is devoted to that. And so we have also introduced a rule in this Ashram that we shall receive our EDUCATION THROUGH THE VERNACULARS.

In Europe, every cultured man learns, not only his language, but also other languages, certainly three or four. And even as they do in Europe, in order to solve the problem of language in India, we, in this Ashram, make it a point to learn as many Indian vernaculars as we possibly can. And I assure you that the trouble of learning these languages is nothing compared to the trouble that we have to take in mastering the English language. We never master the English language; with some exceptions, it has not been possible for us to do so; we can never express ourselves as clearly as we can in our own mother tongue. How dare we rub out of our memory all the years of our infancy? But that is precisely what we do when we commence our higher life, as we call it, through the medium of a foreign tongue. This creates a breach in our life for bridging which we shall have to pay dearly and heavily. And you will see now the connection between these two things—education and untouchableness—this persistence of the spirit of untouchableness even at this time of the day in spite of the spread of knowledge and education. Education has enabled us to see the horrible crime. But we are seized with fear also and, therefore, we cannot take this doctrine to our homes. And we have got a superstitious veneration for our family traditions and for the members of our family. You say, "My parents will die if I tell them that I, at least, can no longer partake of this crime." I say that Prahlad never considered that his father would die if he pronounced the sacred syllables of the name of Vishnu[1]. On the contrary, he made the whole of that household ring, from one corner to another, by repeating that name even in the sacred presence of his father. And so you and I may do this thing in the sacred presence of our parents. If, after receiving this rude shock, some of them expire, I think that would be no calamity. It may be that some rude shocks of the kind might have to be delivered. So long as we persist in these things which have been handed down to us for generations, these

1. One of the Hindu trinity, regarded as Preserver of the Universe.

incidents may happen. But there is a higher law of Nature, and in due obedience to that higher law, my parents and myself should make that sacrifice, and then we follow HAND-WEAVING.

You may ask: "Why should we use our hands?" and say "the manual work has got to be done by those who are illiterate. I can only occupy myself with reading literature and political essays." I think that we have to realise the dignity of labour. If a barber or shoe-maker attends a college, he ought not to abandon the profession of barber or shoe-maker. I consider that a barber's profession is just as good as the profession of medicine.

Last of all, when you have conformed to these rules, I think then, and not till then, you may come to POLITICS and dabble in them to your heart's content, and certainly you will then never go wrong. Politics, divorced of religion, have absolutely no meaning. If the student-world crowd the political platforms of this country, to my mind it is not necessarily a healthy sign of national growth; but that does not mean that you, in your student-life, ought not to study politics. Politics are a part of our being; we ought to understand our national institutions, and we ought to understand our national growth and all those things. We may do it from our infancy. So, in our Ashram, every child is taught to understand the political institutions of our country, and to know how the country is vibrating with new emotions, with new aspirations, with a new life. But we want also the steady light, the infallible light, of religious faith, not a faith which merely appeals to the intelligence, but a faith which is indelibly inscribed on the heart. First, we want to realise that religious consciousness, and immediately we have done that, I think the whole department of life is open to us, and it should then be a sacred privilege of students and everybody to partake of that whole life, so that, when they grow to manhood, and when they leave their colleges, they may do so as men properly equipped to battle with life. Today what happens is this: much of the political life is confined to student life; immediately the students leave their colleges and cease to be students, they sink into oblivion, they seek miserable employments, carrying miserable emoluments, rising no higher in their aspirations, knowing nothing of God, knowing nothing of fresh air or bright light, and nothing of that real vigorous independence that comes out of obedience to these laws that I have ventured to place before you.

CONCLUSION

I am not here asking you to crowd into the Ashram, there is no room there. But I say that every one of you may enact that Ashram life individually and collectively. I shall be satisfied with anything that you may choose from the rules I have ventured to place before you and act up to it. But if you think that these are the outpourings of a mad man, you will not hesitate to tell me that it is so, and I shall take that judgment from you undismayed. (Loud cheers.)[1]

[*The Indian Review*, February, 1916]

1. This paragraph is from *New India*, 16-2-1916.

10. The Immediate Need for India

SPEECH AT GURUKUL ANNIVERSARY

[March 20, 1916]

The following is the text of Mr. Gandhi's speech at the anniversary of the Gurukul, as written out by himself:

I propose to reproduce only as much of it as in my opinion is worth placing on record with additions where they may be found necessary. The speech, it may be observed, was delivered in Hindi.

After thanking Mahatmaji, Munshi Ram for his great kindness to my boys to whom he gave shelter on two occasions and acted as father to them and after stating that the time for action had arrived rather than for speeches, I proceeded:

I owe a debt of gratitude to the Arya Samaj. I have often derived inspiration from its activity. I have noticed among the members of the Samaj much self-sacrifice. During my travels in India, I came across many Arya Samajists who were doing excellent work for the country.

I am, therefore, grateful to Mahatmaji, that I am enabled to be in your midst. At the same time, it is but fair to state that I am frankly a Sanatanist. For me Hinduism is all-sufficing. Every variety of belief finds protection under its ample fold. And though the Arya Samajists and the Sikhs and the Brahmo Samajists may choose to be classed differently from the Hindus, I have no doubt that at no distant future they will be all merged in Hinduism and find in it their fullness.

Hinduism, like every other human institution, has its drawbacks and its defects. Here is ample scope for any worker to strive for reform, but there is little cause for secession.

SPIRIT OF FEARLESSNESS

Throughout my travels, I have been asked about the immediate need for India. And, perhaps, I would not do better than repeat this afternoon the answer I have given elsewhere. In general terms, a proper religious spirit is the greatest and most immediate need. But I know that this is too general an answer to satisfy anybody. And it is an answer true for all time. What, therefore, I desire to say is, that owing to the religious spirit being dormant in us, we are living in a state of perpetual fear. We fear the temporal as well as the spiritual authority.

We dare not speak out our minds before our priests and our *pandits*. We stand in awe of the temporal power. I am sure that in so doing we do a disservice to them and us. Neither the spiritual teachers nor our political governors could possibly desire that we should hide the truth from them. Lord Wellington, speaking to a Bombay audience, has been saying recently that he had observed that we hesitated to say 'No' when we really meant it and advised his audience to cultivate a fearless spirit. Of course, fearlessness should never mean want of due respect or regard for the feelings of others. In my humble opinion, fearlessness is the first thing indispensable before we could achieve anything permanent and real. This quality is unattainable without religious consciousness. Let us fear God and we shall cease to fear man. If we grasp the fact that there is a divinity within us which witnesses everything we think or do and which protects us and guides us along the true path, it is clear that we shall cease to have any other fear on the face I if the earth, save the fear of God. Loyalty to the Governor of governors supersedes all other loyalty and gives an intelligent basis to the latter.

MEANING OF SWADESHI

And when we have sufficiently cultivated this spirit of fearlessness, we shall see that there is no salvation for us without true *swadeshi*, not the *swadeshi* which can be conveniently put off.

Swadeshi for me has a deeper meaning. I would like us to apply it in our religious, political and economic life. It is not, therefore, merely confined to wearing on occasion *swadeshi* cloth. That we have to do for all time, not out of a spirit of jealousy or revenge, but because it is a duty we owe to our dear country. We commit a breach of the *swadeshi* spirit certainly if we wear foreign-made cloth, but we do so also if we adopt the foreign cut. Surely, the style of our dress has some correspondence with our environment. In elegance and tastefulness, it is immeasurably superior to the trousers and the jacket.

An Indian, wearing a shirt flowing over his pyjamas with a waist-coat on it without a necktie and its flaps hanging loose behind, is not a very graceful spectacle. *Swadeshi* in religion teaches one to measure the glorious past and re-enact it in the present generation. The pandemonium that is going on in Europe shows that modern civilization represents forces of evil and darkness, whereas the ancient, i.e., Indian, civilization represents in its essence the divine force.

Modern civilization is chiefly materialistic, as ours is chiefly spiritual. Modern civilization occupies self in the investigation of the laws of matter, and employs human ingenuity in inventing of discovering means of production and weapons of destruction; ours is chiefly occupied in exploring spiritual laws. Our *shastras* lay down unequivocally that a proper observance of truth, chastity, scrupulous regard for all life, abstention from coveting others' possessions and refusal to hoard anything but what is necessary for our daily wants is indispensable for a right life; that without it a knowledge of the divine element is an impossibility. Our civilization tells us with daring certainty that a proper and perfect cultivation of the quality of *ahimsa* which, in its active form means purest love and pity, brings the whole world to our feet. The author of this discovery gives a wealth of illustration which carries conviction with it.

THE DOCTRINE OF AHIMSA

Examine its result in the political life. There is no gift so valued by our *shastras* as the gift of life. Consider what our relations would be with our rulers if we gave absolute security of life to them. If they could but feel that, no matter what we might feel about their acts, we would hold their bodies as sacred as our own, there would immediately spring up an atmosphere of mutual trust, and there would be such frankness on either side as to pave the way for an honourable and just solution of many problems that worry us today. It should be remembered that in practising *ahimsa*, there need not be any reciprocation, though, as a matter of fact, in its final stages, it commands reciprocation. Many of us believe, and I am one of them, that through our civilization we have a message to deliver to the world.

I render my loyalty to the British Government quite selfishly. I would like to use the British race for transmitting this mighty message of *ahimsa* to the whole world. But that can only be done when we have conquered our so-called conquerors; and you, my Arya Samaj friends, are perhaps specially elected for this mission. You claim to examine our scriptures critically; you take nothing for granted and you claim not to fear to reduce your belief to practice. I do not think that there is any room for trifling with or limiting the doctrine of *ahimsa*. You dare, then, to reduce it to practice regardless of immediate consequences which would certainly test the strength of your convictions. You would not only produce salvation for India, but you would render the noblest service that a man can render to humanity—a service moreover, which you would rightly assert the great Swami[1] was born for. This *swadeshi* is to be considered as a very active force to be ceaselessly employed with an ever-increasing vigilance, searching self-examination. It is not meant for the lazy, but it is essentially meant for them who would gladly lay down their lives for the sake of truth. It is possible to dilate upon several other phases of *swadeshi*, but I think I have said enough to enable you to understand what I mean. I only hope that you, who represent a school of reformers in India, will not reject what 1 have said without thorough examination. And, if my word has commended itself to you, your past record entitles me to expect you to enforce in your own lives the things of eternity about which I have ventured to speak to you this afternoon, and cover the whole of India with your activity.

WORK OF THE ARYA SAMAJ

In concluding my report of the above speech, I would like to state what I did not in speaking to that great audience and it is this. I have now twice visited the Gurukul. In spite of some vital difference with my brethren of the Arya Samaj, I have a sneaking regard for them, and it, and perhaps the best result of the activity of the Arya Samaj is to be seen in the establishment and the conduct of the Gurukul. Though it depends for its vitality entirely upon the inspiring presence of Mahatmaji Munshi Ram, it is truly a national and self-governing and self-governed institution. It is totally independent of Government aid or patronage. Its war chest is filled not out of monies received from the privileged few, but from the poor many who make it a point of honour from year to year to make a pilgrimage to Kangri and willingly give their mite for maintaining this National College.

Here at every anniversary a huge crowd gathers and the manner in which it is handled, housed and fed evinces no mean power of organisation. But the most wonderful thing about it all is that the crowd consisting of about the thousand men, women and children is managed without the assistance of a single policeman and without any fuss or

1. Dayanand Saraswati

semblance of force, the only force that subsists between the crowd and the managers of the institution is that of love and mutual esteem. Fourteen years are nothing in the life of a big institution like this. What the collegiates who have been just turned out during the last two or three years will be able to show, remains to be seen. The public will not and cannot judge men or institutions except through the results that they show. It makes no allowance for failures, it is a most exacting judge. The final appeal of the Gurukul as of all popular institutions must be to this judge. Great responsibility therefore rests upon the shoulders of the students who have been discharged from the college and who have entered upon the thorny path of life. Let them beware. Meanwhile those who are well-wishers of this great experiment may derive satisfaction from the fact that we have it as an indisputable rule of life, that as the tree is, so will the fruit be. The tree looks lovely enough. He who waters it is a noble soul. Why worry about what the fruit is likely to be?

INDUSTRIAL TRAINING

As a lover of the Gurukul, I may be permitted to offer one or two suggestions to the Committee and the parents. The Gurukul boys need a thorough industrial training if they are to become self-reliant and self-supporting. It seems to me that in our country in which 85 per cent of the population is agricultural and perhaps 10 per cent occupied in supplying the wants of the peasantry, it must be part of the training of every youth that he has a fair practical knowledge of agriculture and hand-weaving. He will lose nothing if he knows a proper use of tools, can saw a piece of board straight and build a wall that will not come down through a faulty handling of the plumber's line. A boy who is thus equipped will never feel helpless in battling with the world and never be in want of employment. A knowledge of the laws of hygiene and sanitation as well as the art of rearing children should also form a necessary part of [the training of] the Gurukul lads. The sanitary arrangements at the fair left much to be desired.

The plague of flies told its own tale. These irrepressible sanitary inspectors incessantly warned us that in point of sanitation all was not well with us. They plainly suggested that the remains of our food and excreta needed to be properly buried. It seemed to me to be such a pity that a golden opportunity was being missed of giving to the annual visitors practical lessons on sanitation. But the work must begin with the boys. Then the management would have at the annual gathering three hundred practical sanitary teachers. Last but not least, let the parents and the Committee not spoil their lads by making them ape European dress or modern luxuries. These will hinder them in their afterlife and are antagonistic to *brahmacharya*. They have enough to fight against in the evil inclinations common to us all. Let us not make their fight more difficult by adding to their temptations.

[*Speeches and Writings of Mahatma Gandhi (4th Ed.)*, pp. 329-35]

11. Morality *vs.* Economics

SPEECH AT MUIR COLLEGE ECONOMIC SOCIETY, ALLAHABAD[1]

[December 22, 1916]

Mr. M.K. Gandhi delivered an instructive lecture on 'Does economic progress clash with real progress?' at a meeting of the Muir Central College Economic Society held on Friday evening in the physical science theatre. The Hon. Pandit Madan Mohan Malaviya presided. There was a good gathering of ladies and gentlemen, European and Indian, besides a large number of students. Among those present were

Dr. E.G. Hill, the Hon. Dr. Sundar Lal, the Hon. Mr. A.W. Pim, the Hon. Mr. H.C. Ferard, the Hon. Dr. Tej Bahadur Sapru, the Hon. Mr. E.H. Ashworth, Mr. H.S.L. Polak, Prof. Gidwani, Prof. Stanley Jevons, Prof. Higginbottom, the Hon. Mr. C.Y. Chintamani, Mr. B.H. Bourdillon, Mr. Mackenzie, Prof. Moody, Prof. Dunn, Prof. Redford, Pandit Baldeo Ram Dave, Mr. Lalit Mohan Banerji, Pandit Rama Kant Malaviya, Pandit Radha Kant Malaviya, Rai Braj Narain Gurtu, Mr. Kichlu,

---

1. Amaranatha Jha's Diary has the following entries:

   December 22, 1916
   From 3 to 5 stayed at Malaviyaji's house, talking to Mr. Gandhi and Mr. Polak. Then to the college physics theatre where Mr. Gandhi read his paper before the Economic Society. I took his paper from him which was written on sheets on which was printed his South African address, "Tolstoy Farm, Johannesburg". He asked me to request Mr. Chintamani [Editor, *The Leader*] to send to him the proofs for correction.

   December 23, 1916
   From 11 to 14 stayed at Malaviyaji's house, talking to Mr. Gandhi and Mr. Polak, Ramdas Gandhi, Mr. Medh (who has been several times to jail for passive resistance). Mr. Chintamani sent the proofs of Mr. Gandhi's lecture for correction.
   I asked for and obtained from Mr. Gandhi the original manuscript. He said, "This lecture is worthier of the waste-paper basket than your desk."
   —*Amaranatha Jha: A Memorial Volume*, Ed. K.K. Mehrotra,

Mr. Shamnath Mushran, Mr. Iswar Saran, Babu Shiva Prasad Gupta, Prof. Sri Prakash, Prof. Ojha, Prof. Karwell, Prof. Thompson, Dr. M. C. Tandon, Mr. Purushottam Das Tandon, Mr. Jagjivan Nath Takru.

Dr. Hill proposed the Hon. Pandit Malaviya to the chair and welcomed Mr. Gandhi in their midst.

The Hon. Pandit Malaviya in introducing Mr. Gandhi said that his was a name honoured throughout India and wherever Indians lived. His name was also appreciated by a large number of Europeans who understood his character.

It was always an instruction to him to read of the work he had done and of the life he had led.

Mr. Gandhi then delivered the following lecture:

When I accepted Mr. Kapildeva Malaviya's invitation to speak to you upon the subject of this evening, I was painfully conscious of my limitations. You are an economic society. You have chosen distinguished specialists for the subjects included in your syllabus for this year and the next. I seem to be the only speaker ill-fitted for the task set before him. Frankly and truly, I know very little of economics, as you naturally understand them. Only the other day, sitting at an evening meal, a civilian friend deluged me with a series of questions on my crankisms. As he proceeded in his cross-examination, I being a willing victim, he found no difficulty in discovering my gross ignorance of the matters. I appeared to him to be handling with a cocksureness worthy only of a man who knows not that he knows not.

To his horror and even indignation, I suppose, he found that I had not even read books on economics by such well-known authorities as Mill, Marshall, Adam Smith and a host of such other authors. In despair, he ended by advising me to read these works before experimenting in matters economic at the expense of the public. He little knew that I was a sinner past redemption. My experiments continue at the expense of trusting friends. For, there come to us moments in life when about some things we need no proof from without. A little voice within us tells us, "You are on the right track, move neither to your left nor right, but keep to the straight and narrow way." With such help we march forward slowly indeed, but surely and steadily. That is my position. It may be satisfactory enough for me, but it can in no way answer the requirements of a society such as yours. Still it was no use my struggling against Mr. Kapildeva Malaviya. I knew that he was intent upon having me to engage your attention for one of your evenings. Perhaps you will treat my intrusion as a welcome diversion from the trodden path. An occasional fast after a series of sumptuous feasts is often a necessity. And as with the body, so, I imagine, is the case with the reason. And if your reason this evening is found fasting instead of feasting, I am sure it will enjoy with the greater avidity the feast that Rao Bahadur Pandit Chandrika Prasad has in store for you for the 12th of January.

Before I take you to the field of my experiences and experiments, it is perhaps best to have a mutual understanding about the title of this evening's address: Does economic progress clash with real progress? By economic progress, I take it, we mean material advancement without limit and by real progress we mean moral progress, which again is the same thing as progress of the permanent element in us. The subject may therefore be stated thus: "Does not moral progress increase in the same proportion as material progress?"

I know that this is a wider proposition than the one before us. But I venture to think that we always mean the larger one even when we lay down the smaller. For we know enough of science to realise that there is no such thing as perfect rest or repose in this visible universe of ours. If, therefore, material progress does not clash with moral progress, it must necessarily advance the latter. Nor can we be satisfied with the clumsy way in which sometimes those who cannot defend the larger proposition put their case. They seem to be obsessed with the concrete case of thirty millions of India stated by the late Sir William Wilson Hunter to be living on one meal a day. They say that before we can think or talk of their moral welfare, we must satisfy their daily wants. With these, they say, material progress spells moral progress.

And then is taken a sudden jump: what is true of thirty millions is true of the universe. They forget that hard cases make bad law. I need hardly say to you how ludicrously absurd this deduction would be.

No one has ever suggested that grinding pauperism can lead to anything else than moral degradation. Every human being has a right to live and, therefore, to find the wherewithal to feed himself and where necessary to clothe and house himself. But, for this very simple performance, we need no assistance from economists or their laws.

"Take no thought for the morrow"[1] is an injunction which finds an echo in almost all the religious scriptures of the world. In well-ordered society, the securing of one's livelihood should be and is found to be the easiest thing in the world. Indeed, the test of orderliness in a country is

1. St. Matthew, VI, 34.

not the number of millionaires it owns, but the absence of starvation among its masses. The only statement that has to be examined is whether it can be laid down as a law of universal application that material advancement means moral progress.

Now let us take a few illustrations. Rome suffered a moral fall when it attained high material affluence. So did Egypt and so perhaps most countries of which we have any historic record. The descendants, kinsmen of the royal and divine Krishna, too, fell when they were rolling in riches. We do not deny to the Rockefellers and the Carnegies possession of an ordinary measure of morality but we gladly judge them indulgently. I mean that we do not even expect them to satisfy the highest standard of morality. With them material gain has not necessarily meant moral gain. In South Africa, where I had the privilege of associating with thousands of our countrymen on most intimate terms, I observed almost invariably that the greater the possession of riches, the greater was their moral turpitude. Our rich men, to say the least, did not advance the moral struggle of passive resistance as did the poor. The rich men's sense of self-respect was not so much injured as that of the poorest. If I were not afraid of treading on dangerous ground, I would even come nearer home and show you that possession of riches has been a hindrance to real growth. I venture to think that the scriptures of the world are far safer and sounder treatises on laws of economics than many of the modern text-books. The question we are asking ourselves this evening is not a new one. It was addressed to Jesus two thousand years ago. St. Mark[1] has vividly described the scene. Jesus is in his solemn mood; he is earnest. He talks of eternity. He knows the world about him. He is himself the greatest economist of his time. He succeeded in economising time and space—he transcended them. It is to him at his best that one comes running, kneels down, and asks: "Good Master, what shall I do that I may inherit eternal life?" And Jesus said unto him: "Why callest thou me good? There is none good but one, that is God. Thou knowest the commandments. Do not commit adultery, Do not kill, Do not steal, Do not bear false witness, Defraud not, Honour thy father and mother." And he answered and said unto him: "Master, all these have I observed from my youth." Then Jesus beholding him, loved him and said unto him: "One thing thou lackest. Go thy way, sell whatever thou hast and give to the poor, and thou shalt have treasure in heaven—come take up the cross and follow me." And he was sad at that saying and went away grieved—

1. Ch. X, verses 17-31.

for he had great possessions. And Jesus looked round about and said unto his disciples: "How hardly shall they that have riches enter into the kingdom of God." And the disciples were astonished at his words. But Jesus answereth again and saith unto them: "Children, how hard it is for them that trust in riches to enter into the kindgom of God. It is easier for a camel to go through the eye of a needle than for a rich man to enter into the kingdom of God !" Here you have an eternal rule of life stated in the noblest words the English language is capable of producing. But the disciples nodded unbelief as we do even to this day. To him they said as we say today: "But look how the law fails in practice. If we sell all and have nothing, we shall have nothing to eat. We must have money or we cannot even be reasonably moral." So they state their case thus. "And they were astonished out of measure saying among themselves: "Who then can be saved?"' And Jesus looking upon them saith: "With men it is impossible but not with God, for with God all things are possible." Then Peter began to say unto him: "Lo, we have left all, and have followed thee." And Jesus answered and said: "Verily I say unto you there is no man that has left house or brethren or sisters; or father or mother, or wife or children or lands for my sake and the Gospels, but he shall receive one hundred fold, now in this time houses and brethren and sisters and mothers and children and lands with persecutions and in the world to come eternal life. But many that are first shall be last and the last first." You have here the result or reward, if you prefer the term, of following the law. I have not taken the trouble of copying similar passages from the other non Hindu scriptures and I will not insult you by quoting in support of the law stated by Jesus passages from the writings and sayings of our own sages, passages even stronger if possible than the Biblical extracts I have drawn your attention to. Perhaps the strongest of all the testimonies in favour of the affirmative answer to the question before us are the lives of the greatest teachers of the world. Jesus, Mahommed, Buddha, Nanak, Kabir, Chaitanya, Shankara, Dayananda, Ramakrishna were men who exercised an immense influence over and moulded the character of thousands of men. The world is the richer for their having lived in it. And they were all men who deliberately embraced poverty as their lot.

I should not have laboured my point as I have done, if I did not believe that, in so far as we have made the modern materialistic craze our goal, in so far are we going downhill in the path of progress. I hold that economic progress in the sense I have put it is antagonistic to real progress. Hence, the ancient ideal has been the limitation of activities promoting wealth. This does not put an end to all material ambition. We should still have, as we have always had, in our midst people who make the pursuit of wealth their aim in life. But we have always recognised that it is a fall from the ideal. It is a beautiful thing to know that the wealthiest among us have often felt that to have remained voluntarily poor would have been a higher state for them.

That you cannot serve God and Mammon is an economic truth of the highest value. We have to make our choice. Western nations today are groaning under the heel of the monster-god of materialism. Their moral growth has become stunted. They measure their progress in £ sd American wealth has become the standard. She [*sic*] is the envy of the other nations. I have heard many of our countrymen say that we will gain American wealth but avoid its methods. I venture to suggest that such an attempt if it were made is foredoomed to failure.

We cannot be 'wise, temperate and furious'[1] in a moment. I would have our leaders to teach us to be morally supreme in the world. This land of ours was once, we are told, the abode of the gods. It is not possible to conceive gods inhabiting a land which is made hideous by the smoke and the din of null chimneys and factories and whose roadways are traversed by rushing engines dragging numerous cars crowded with men mostly who know not what they are after, who are often absent-minded, and whose tempers do not improve by being uncomfortably packed like sardines in boxes and finding themselves in the midst of utter strangers who would oust them if they could and whom they would in their turn oust similarly. I refer to these things because they are held to be symbolical of material progress. But they add not an atom to our happiness. This is what Wallace, the great scientist, has said as his deliberate Judgement.

In the earliest records which have come down to us from the past, we find ample indications that general ethical considerations and conceptions, the accepted standard of morality, and the conduct resulting from these were in no degree inferior to those which prevail to-day.

In a series of chapters, he then proceeds to examine the position of the English nation under the advance in wealth it has made. He says: "This rapid growth of wealth and increase of our power over nature put too great a strain upon our crude civilization, on our superficial Christianity, and it was accompanied by various forms of social immorality almost as amazing and unprecedented."

1. "Who can be wise, amazed, temperate and furious,/ Loyal and neutral, in a moment?/No man."—*Macbeth*, II, iii.

He then shows how factories have risen on the corpses of men, women and children, how as the country has rapidly advanced in riches, it has gone down in morality. He shows this by dealing with insanitation, life-destroying trades, adulteration, bribery and gambling. He shows how, with the advance of wealth, justice has become immoral, deaths from alcoholism and suicide have increased. the average of premature births and congenital defects has increased, and prostitution has become an institution. He concludes his examination by these pregnant remarks:

The proceedings of the divorce courts show other aspects of the result of wealth and leisure, while a friend who had been good deal in London society assured me that both in country houses and in London various kinds of orgies were occasionally to be met with which would hardly have been surpassed in the period of the most dissolute emperors. Of war, too, I need say nothing. It has always been more or less chronic since the rise of the Roman Empire; but there is now undoubtedly a disinclination for war among all civilized peoples. Yet the vast burden of armaments, taken together with the most pious declarations in favour of peace, must be held to show an almost total absence of morality as a guiding principle among the governing classes.

Under the British aegis, we have learnt much, but it is my firm belief that there is little to gain from Britain in intrinsic morality, that if we are not careful, we shall introduce all the vices that she has been a prey to, owing to the disease of materialism. We can profit by that connection only if we keep our civilization, and our morals, straight, i.e., if instead of boasting of the glorious past, we express the ancient moral glory in our own lives and let our lives bear witness to our past.

Then we shall benefit her and ourselves. If we copy her because she provides us with rulers, both they and we shall suffer degradation. We need not be afraid of ideals or of reducing them to practice even to the uttermost. Ours will only then be a truly spiritual nation when we shall show more truth than gold, greater fearlessness than pomp of power and wealth, greater charity than love of self. If we will but clean town houses, our palaces and temples of the attributes of wealth and show in them the attributes of morality, we can offer battle to any combinations of hostile forces without having to carry the burden of a heavy militia. Let us seek first the kingdom of God and His righteousness and the irrevocable promise is that everything will be added with us. These are real economics. May you and I treasure them and enforce them in our daily life.

An interesting discussion followed in the course of which several students put questions to the lecturer. . . .

Prof. Jevons said . . . . It was necessary for economists to exist. It was not their business to lay down what the end should be. That was the business of philosophers. . . .

Prof. Gidwani, president of the society, thanked the lecturer for his address. . . .

Prof. Higginbottom said that there was no economic problem which could be separated from the moral problem. . . . .

Mr. Gandhi in the course of his remarks referred to Mr. Jevons' remark about the need for economist and said that it was said that dirt was matter misplaced. So also when an economist was misplaced, he was hurtful. He certainly thought that the economist had a place in the economy of nature when he occupied the humble sphere for which he was created. If an economist did not investigate the laws of God and show them how to distribute wealth so that there might not be poverty, he was a most unwelcome intrusion on the Indian soil. He would also suggest for the reflection of their economic students and professors that what might be good for England and America need not necessarily be good for India. He thought that most of the economic laws which were consistent with moral laws were of universal application, but there might be in their restricted application some distinction and difference. So he would utter the note of warning that Indian conditions being in some respects so essentially different from the English and American conditions, it was necessary to bring to bear on the matters that presented themselves to the economists a fresh mind. If they did so, both Indians and the economists would derive benefit.

Mr. Higginbottom, he said, was studying the real economics that were so necessary for India and reducing his studies inch by inch to practice and that was the safest guide to follow, whether they were students or professors. Referring to a question by a student, he said that a man should not hoard money for selfish ends, but if he wished to hoard money as a trustee for the millions of India, he would say that he might have as much riches as he could. Ordinarily, economists prescribed laws for the rich people. It was against those economists that he would always cry out.

As regards another question, whether factories should not be replaced by cottage industries, Mr. Gandhi spoke approvingly of the suggestion but said that the economists should first of all examine with patience their indigenous institutions. If they were rotten, they must be wiped out and if there were remedies which could be suggested for their betterment, they should improve them.

As regards intercourse with other nations, he said that he did not think that they necessarily advanced one little bit in their moral growth by bringing their masses with others into physical contact and pointed to Indians in South Africa as an instance. The rapid locomotion such as steamers, trains and others dislocated so many of their ideals and created a great deal of mischief.

As regards the question what was the minimum and the maximum wealth a man should have—he would answer in the words of Jesus, Ramkrishna and others who said 'none'.

The Hon. Pandit Madan Mohan Malaviya in his concluding remarks offered a cordial vote of thanks to Mr. Gandhi for his excellent address. The ideals which Mr. Gandhi put before them, he said, were so high that he did not expect that all of them would be prepared to subscribe to all of them. But he was sure they would agree with the main object he put before them, namely, that they should go for the welfare of man as the test of all economic questions with which they dealt. . . .

[*The Leader*, 25-12-1916]

12. Education : Ancient and Modern

SPEECH AT ALLAHABAD ON EDUCATION, ANCIENT AND MODERN

[December 23, 1916]

Mr. Gandhi addressed in Hindi a public meeting at Allahabad at Munshi Ram Prasad's garden under the chairmanship of the Hon. Pandit Madan Mohan Malaviya.

The gathering was a record one even for Munshi Ram Prasad's garden where some of the largest public meetings have been held.

Mr. Gandhi, who on rising was greeted with loud and prolonged cheers, said that that he should have felt difficulty—of which he was ashamed—in addressing the meeting in Hindi, was a striking commentary on the system of modern education which was a part of the subject of his lecture that evening. He would, however, prefer to speak in Hindi although he had greater facility of expression in English.

Describing the modern system of education, he said that real education was considered to have begun at the college at the age of 16 or 17. The education received in school was not useful. For instance, an Indian student, while he knew well the geography of England, did not possess a sufficient knowledge of the geography of his own country.

This history of India which they were taught was greatly distorted. Government service was the aim of their education. Their highest ambition was to become members of the Imperial Legislative Council. The boys abandoned their hereditary occupations, and forsook their mother tongue. They were adopting the English language, European ideas and European dress. They thought in English, conducted all their political and social work and all commercial transactions, etc., in English and thought that they could not do without the English language. They had come to think that there was no other road. Education through English had created a wide gulf between the educated few and the masses. It had created a gulf in the families also. An English-educated man had no community of feelings and ideas with the ladies of his family. And, as had been said, the aspirations of the English-educated men were fixed on Government service and at the most on membership of the Imperial Legislative Council. He for one could never commend a system of education which produced such a state of things and men educated under such system could not be expected to do any great service to the country. Mr. Gandhi did not mean that the English-educated leaders did not feel for the masses. On the other hand, he acknowledged that the Congress and other great public movements were initiated and conducted by them.

But, at the same time, he could not help feeling that the work done during all these years would have been much more and much greater progress would have been made if they had been taught in their mother tongue. It was unfortunate, said the speaker, that a feeling had come over them that there was no path to progress other than that which I was being followed. They found themselves helpless. But it was not manliness to assume all attitude of helplessness.

Mr. Gandhi then described the ancient system of education and said that even elementary education imparted by the village teacher taught the student all that was necessary for their occupations. Those who went in for higher education became fully conversant with the science of wealth, *Arthashastra*, ethics and religion, *Dharmashastra*. In ancient times, there were no restrictions on education. It was not controlled by the State but was solely in the hands of the Brahmins who shaped the system of education solely with an eye to the welfare of the people. It was based on restraint and *Brahmacharya*. It was due to such a system of education that Indian civilization had outlived so many vicissitudes through thousands of years, while such ancient civilizations as those of Greece, Rome and Egypt had become extinct. No doubt the wave of a new civilization had been passing through India. But he was sure that it was transitory, it would soon pass away and Indian civilization would be revivified. In ancient times, the basis of life was self-restraint but now it was enjoyment. The result was that people had become powerless cowards and forsook the truth. Having come under the influence of another civilization, it might be necessary to adapt our own civilization in certain respects to our new environment but we should not make any radical change in a civilization which was acknowledged even by some western scholars to be the best. It might be urged that it was necessary to adopt the methods and instruments of western civilization to meet the material forces of that civilization. But the forces born of spirituality, the bedrock of Indian civilization, were more than a match for material forces. India was pre-eminently the land of religion. It was the first and the last duty of Indians to maintain it as such.

They should draw their strength from the soul, from God. If they adhered to that path, *swarajya* which they were aspiring to and working for would become their handmaid.

[*The Leader,* 27-12-1916; also *Mahatma Gandhi: His Life, Writings and Speeches,* pp. 192-95]

13. A National Language for India

SPEECH AT SECOND GUJARAT EDUCATIONAL CONFERENCE, BROACH

[October 20, 1917]

Gandhiji prefaced the speech with an apology to the audience:

As it is already late, reading my speech will proceed beyond the time-limit fixed for it. I read it because I am under pressure from friends here to do so. When preparing the speech, I took the utmost care to see that it briefly expressed all that I wished to say, but it has become longer than I expected. I hope to be excused, therefore, if in reading it I exceed my time.

Gandhiji then read the speech from a printed text.[1]

DEAR SISTERS AND BROTHERS,

You have done me a great honour in selecting me to be the President of this Conference. I know that I do not have the necessary learning for this office. I know, too, that my work in other spheres in the service of our country does not, and cannot, qualify me for the honour you have conferred on me today. I have but one qualification for it, that I would not, I am perfectly sure, be content with anything but the first place in a contest for demonstrating one's love for Gujarati. Indeed, it is because I am confident of this that I have accepted this onerous responsibility. I hope that the generosity which has prompted you to give me this honour will also prompt you to forgive all my shortcomings, and help me in this work—which is as much yours as mine.

This Conference is but a year old. Just as, in the case of a great man, we often find indications of his future greatness even in his infancy, so it is with this Conference. I have read the report of its work for the last year. It is a

1. The translation which follows is reproduced from *True Education*, with some changes intended to bring it into closer conformity with the Gujarati original.

report which would do credit to any institution. The Secretaries are to be congratulated on having prepared and published this valuable report in time. It is our good fortune that we have such able secretaries. To those who have not yet read this report, I suggest that they do so and ponder over it. The death of Shri Ranjitram Vavabhai[1] last year has been a great loss to us.

It is a matter of deep regret that a man of letters like him was snatched away from our midst in the prime of life; this should make us pause and think. May God grant peace to the departed soul. I would request the members of his family to take strength in the thought that we all share their grief.

The organization[2] which has called this Conference has set three aims before itself:

1. To create and give expression to public opinion on questions of education.
2. To carry on propaganda in regard to educational questions in Gujarat.
3. To undertake concrete activities for promoting education in Gujarat.

I shall endeavour to place before you the results of my thinking, such as it has been, on these three aims.

It should be obvious to everyone that the first thing to do in this connection is to come to a definite decision about the medium of instruction. Unless that is done, all other efforts, I fear, are likely to prove fruitless. To impart education without first considering the question of the medium of instruction will be like raising a building without a foundation.

On this point, two views prevail among educationists. Some hold that education should be imparted through the mother tongue; that is, through Gujarati. Others contend that it should be imparted through English. Both parties are honest in their views, for both have the welfare of the country at heart. But mere good intentions are not enough to gain the end we desire. It is the experience of the world that good intentions do occasionally take us to unworthy places We must, therefore, critically examine both these views and, if possible, come to a unanimous decision on this great and important

---

1. Ranjitram Vavabhai Mehta (1882-1916); in appreciation of his active literary interests, a gold medal has been instituted in Gujarat and awarded annually for outstanding achievements in the field of, letters or the art.
2. Broach Kelavani Mandal.

question. There is no doubt whatsoever that the issue is of the utmost importance and we cannot consider it too carefully.

This question concerns the whole of India. But each Presidency or Province may decide this matter for itself. It is erroneous to think that, until unanimity has been reached about it, Gujarat cannot go ahead by itself.

We can, however, solve some of our difficulties by considering what they have done about it in other Provinces. At the time of the Bengal partition[1], when the spirit of *swadeshi* was at its height, an effort was made there to impart education through Bengali. A national school[2] was also started. Money poured forth in plenty. But the experiment failed. In my humble opinion, the sponsors of the movement had no faith in their experiment. The teachers were in the same pitiable condition. In Bengal, the educated classes are blindly in love with English. It has been suggested that the progress made by Bengali literature in recent times is mainly due to the profound knowledge of English language and literature among the Bengalis.

But the facts are against this assumption. The bewitching style of our beloved poet—Rabindranath Tagore[3]—does not owe its excellence to his knowledge of English. Its source lies rather in his love for his own language. *Gitanjali* was originally written in Bengali. This great poet always uses his mother tongue when in Bengal. The great speech he recently made at Calcutta on present-day conditions in India was in Bengali. Among those who went to hear him were some of the most prominent men and women from his part of the country. And I have been told by those who heard him on the occasion that he kept the audience literally spell-bound for an hour-and-a-half with the flow of nectar-like stream of words. He has not borrowed his ideas from English literature. He says, he has acquired them from the atmosphere of this country. He has culled them from the *Upanishads*[4]. It is our glorious Indian sky which has inspired him. I believe it is the same with other Bengali authors.

---

1. In 1905, on grounds of administrative convenience, Bengal was divided into two provinces, one of which was predominantly Hindu and the other, Muslim. The partition, which raised a storm of protest throughout India and let to the movement for boycott of British goods, was finally annulled in 1911.
2. A council and a society for promotion of national education were set up.
3. 1861-1941; was awarded Nobel Prize for Literature in 1913, for *Gitanjali*; founder of Shantiniketan and Visva-Bharati University
4. Concluding portions of the *Veda*, the *Vedanta*; though they do not represent any system, they expound a discernible unity of thought and purpose and bring out a vivid sense of spiritual reality.

When Mahatma Munshiram[1], serene and sublime like the Himalayas, speaks in Hindi, men, women and children alike enjoy listening to him and follow him. He has reserved his English for his English friends. He does not make his [Hindi] speeches with English phrases in his mind.

It is said that the English of the revered Madan Mohan Malaviya[2], who, though a householder, has dedicated his all to the country, shines like silver. Even the Viceroy has to take note of anything that Malaviyaji says. But, if his English is like shining silver, his Hindi, the flow of the Ganga that it is, shines like gold even as the latter does when flowing down from Manasarovar.

These three great speakers have acquired this power of eloquence not from their knowledge of English but from the love of their own language. Swami Dayanand[3] did great service to Hindi not because he knew English but because he loved the Hindi language. English had nothing to do with Tukaram[4] and Ramadas[5] shedding lustre on Marathi. Premananda[6] and Shamal Bhatt[7] and, recently, Dalpatram[8], have greatly enriched Gujarati literature; their glorious success is not to be attributed to their knowledge of English.

The above examples prove beyond doubt that, for the enrichment of the mother tongue, what is needed is not knowledge of English but love for one's own language and faith in it.

We shall arrive at the same conclusion by examining the growth and development of various languages. A language mirrors the character of the people who use it. We acquire information about the manners and customs

---

1. Better known as Swami Shraddhanand, founder of the Gurukul Kangri, near Hardwar, a residential school for imparting education in the traditional Indian style through close communion with a *guru*
2. 1861-1946; edited *Hindustan*, 1887-89; *Indian Union*, 1889-92; *Abhyudaya*, 1907-09; President, Indian National Congress, 1909 and 1918; founded the Benares Hindu University in 1916, and was its Vice Chancellor during 1919-40; Member, Imperial Legislative Council, 1910-20; attended the Round Table Conference in London, 1931-32.
3. Swami Dayanand Saraswati (1824-83); founder of the Arya Samaj.
4. Saint-poets of Maharashtra.
5. Same as footnote No. 10.
6. 1636-1724; Gujarati poet; his narrative poems represent the highest achievement in Gujarati literature during the pre-British period.
7. 1700-1765; Gujarati poet; a stanza from one of his poems became Gandhiji's "guiding principle"; *vide* An *Autobiography*, Part I, Ch. X.
8. Dalpatram Dahyabhai Travadi (1820-1892).

of the Negroes of South Africa by studying their native tongue. A language takes its form from the character and life of those who speak it. We can say without hesitation that the people whose language does not reflect the qualities of courage, truthfulness and compassion are deficient in those virtues. Importing of words expressive of courage or compassion from other tongues will not enrich or widen the content of a language nor make its speakers brave and kind. Courage is not to be had as a gift; if it is there within, covered with rust though it be, it will shine forth when that covering disappears. In our own mother tongue, we find a large number of words denoting an excess of meekness, because we have lived under subjection for many years. Similarly, no other language in the world has as many nautical terms as English. Supposing that an enterprising Gujarati writer were to render books on the subject from English into Gujarati, it would not add one whit to the range and power of our language, nor would it in any way increase our knowledge of ships.

But as soon as we start building ships and raise a navy, the necessary technical phraseology will automatically establish itself. The late Rev. Taylor has expressed this same view in his book on Gujarati grammar. He says: One frequently hears people arguing whether the Gujarati language is perfect or imperfect. There is a proverb saying: "As the King, so the people", and another "As the teacher, so the disciple". In the same way, we might say, "As the speaker, so the language". It does not appear that poets like Shamal Bhatt and others ever felt handicapped in expressing the innumerable thoughts in their minds because of any sense of deficiency in Gujarati. Indeed, they displayed such fine discrimination in the disposing of new and old words that whatever they said or wrote passed into currency and was incorporated in the speech of the people.

In some respects, all the languages of the world are imperfect. When speaking of things beyond man's limited intellect, of God and Eternity, we shall find every language imperfect. Language is but a function of man's intellect. Hence, when the intellect fails to reach out to or fully comprehend a subject, the language [expressing the thought] will be imperfect. The general principle concerning a language is that the ideas which find expression in it reflect the minds of the people who speak it. If the people are courteous, so is their language; if the people are foolish, the language is equally so. All English proverb says: "A bad carpenter quarrels with his tools." Those who complain of the imperfection of their language often do much the same. A student with a smattering of the English language and English learning may feel tempted to think that Gujarati is imperfect, for an accurate translation from English into one's own mother tongue is difficult. The fault does not lie with the language but with the people who use it. Inasmuch as the people do not practise exercising their judgment to follow new expressions, new subjects and new styles, the writer hesitates to use them. Who will be foolhardy enough to sing in front of a deaf man? As long as the people are not ready to discriminate between good and bad, or new and old and evaluate things aright, how can we expect a writer's genius to blossom forth ?

Some of those who translate from English seem to labour under the impression that they have imbibed Gujarati with their mother's milk and learnt English through study and are, therefore, perfect bilinguists. Why, they ask, should they study Gujarati? But surely acquisition of proficiency in one's own language is more important than the effort spent over mastering a foreign one. Look up the works of poets like Shamal and others. Every verse bears evidence of study and labour. Gujarati may seem imperfect before one has struggled with it, but afterwards one will find it mature enough. He whose effort is half-hearted will wield the language but imperfectly; the writer or speaker whose effort is unsparing will likewise command Gujarati that is perfect; nay, it may even be polished. Gujarati, of the Aryan family, a daughter of Sanskrit, related to some of the best languages—who dare call her undeveloped?

May God bless her ! May she speak, till the end of ages, of wisdom and learning ever the best and of true religion. May God, the Creator, grant us that we hear her praises from the mother and the student, for ever and for ever.

Thus, we see that the failure of the movement to impart education through the medium of Bengali in Bengal does not show any inherent imperfection in that language or the futility of such an effort. We have considered the point about imperfection; as for futility, the experiment in Bengal does not prove it. If anything, it only shows the incompetence of those who made the effort, or their lack of faith in it.

In the North, Hindi is certainly making good progress. But a persistent effort to use it as the medium of instruction has been made only by the Arya Samajists in the *Gurukulas*.

In Madras, the movement for using the mother tongue as the medium of education started only a few years ago. The Telugu people are more active in this respect than the Tamilians. The latter are so dominated by the influence of English that they have little enthusiasm for making an effort to use Tamil as the medium of instruction. In the Telugu-speaking region, English education has not yet penetrated to the same extent. Therefore, the people in that part use the mother tongue more than the

Tamilians. The Telugu people are not only carrying on experiments to impart education through their own language but have also started a movement for the redistribution of India on the basis of language. The movement is of recent origin, and is as yet in the initial stage. But so vigorous is their effort that it is not unlikely that we may see the idea being given a practical shape before long. There are rocks on the way, but their leaders have given me the impression that they have the strength all right to break them.

Maharashtra is making the same attempt, sponsored by the great and noble Prof. Karve[1]. Shri Nayak holds the same view. Private schools have taken up the task. With great effort, Prof. Vijapurkar[2] has revived his plan and we shall shortly see his school functioning. He had drawn up a plan for preparing text-books. Some of these have already been printed, others are ready in manuscript. The teachers of that school never wavered in their faith. If, unfortunately, it had not been closed, it would have by now settled the controversy whether or not Marathi can serve as the medium of education even at the highest level.

In Gujarat, too, this movement has got started. We know about it from the essay of R.B. Hargovinddas Kantawala[3]. Prof. Gajjar[4] and the late Diwan Bahadur Manibhai Jasbhai may be regarded as the leaders of this movement. It is now for us to decide whether or not we should help the growth of the seeds sown by these persons. To my mind, there is no doubt that the more we delay, the greater our loss.

It requires a minimum of 16 years to complete one's education through the medium of English. If the same subjects were taught through the mother tongue, it would take ten years at the most. This is the opinion expressed by

---

1. Dhondo Keshav Karve (1858-1962); social reformer and pioneer educationist; established the Shrimati Nathubai Damodar Thakersey University for Women in Poona (1915); was awarded "Bharat Ratna", the highest Indian award in 1958; *vide* also "*Deed Better than Words*", 26-10-1906.
2. V. G. Vijapurkar (1863-1925); pioneer of national education who founded, in collaboration with Lokamanya Tilak, the Samartha Vidyalaya at Talegaon.
3. 1849-1931; was Director of Public Instruction, Baroda State; vide "*Compulsory Education in India*", 7-10-1905.
4. Tribhuvandas Kalyandas Gajjar (1863-1920); an eminent student of Chemistry; founded Kalabhavan, a technical school, in Baroda in 1890 and served as its Principal; he promoted the establishment of the Alembic Chemical Works in Baroda.

many experienced teachers. A saving of six years for each of the thousands of students means a saving of thousands of years for the nation.

Education through a foreign language entails an excessive strain which only our boys could bear, they must needs pay dearly for it, though. To a large extent, they lose the capacity of shouldering any other burden afterwards. Our graduates, therefore, are a useless lot, weak of body, without any zest for work, and mere imitators. They suffer an atrophy of the creative faculty and of the capacity for original thinking, and grow up without the spirit of enterprise and the qualities of perseverance, courage and fearlessness. That is why we are unable to make new plans or carry out those we make. A few who do show promise of these qualities usually die young. An Englishman has said that there is the same difference between Europeans and the people of other countries as between an original piece of writing and its impression on a piece of blotting paper. The element of truth in this statement is not to be attributed to any natural or innate incapacity on the part of the Asians. The reason lies, in a large measure, in the unsuitable medium of instruction. The natives of South Africa are enterprising, strongly built and endowed with character. They do not have such evils as child marriage, etc., which we have, and yet their condition is similar to ours. Why? Because the medium of their education is Dutch. They are able to acquire mastery over the language within a short period as we do [over English], and like us they, too, become weak of body and mind at the end of their education and often turn out to be mere imitators. From them, too, originality disappears along with the mother tongue. It is only we, the English educated people, who are unable to assess the great loss that results. Some idea of it may be had if we estimate how little has been our influence on the general mass of our people. The occasional remarks which our parents are led to make about the worthlessness of our education have some point. We get ecstatic over the achievements of Bose[1] and Ray[2]. But I am convinced that, had we been having our education through the mother tongue for 50 years, a Bose or a Ray would have occasioned no surprise among us.

---

1. Sir Jagdish Chandra Bose (1858-1937); eminent Indian scientist, author of books on plant physiology; founder, Bose Research Institute, Calcutta.
2. Acharya Prafulla Chandra Ray (1861-1944); professor of Chemistry at Presidency College, Calcutta; author of History of Hindu Chemistry, educationist and patriot.

Ignoring for a while the question whether or not the new zeal and energy being exhibited by the Japanese at present is directed into the right channels, we find their enterprise really most remarkable.

They have brought about the awakening of their people through the use of the mother tongue. That is why everything that they do bears the stamp of originality. They are now in a position to teach their teachers. They have belied the comparison [of non-European peoples] with blotting paper. The life of the Japanese is throbbing with vitality and the world looks on in amazement. The system under which we are educated through a foreign language results in incalculable harm.

The continuity that should exist, on the one hand, between the culture the child imbibes along with the mother's milk and the sweet words it receives and, on the other, the training school, is broken when education is imparted through a foreign tongue. Those who are responsible for this are enemies of the people, howsoever, honest their motives. To be a voluntary victim of this system of education is to betray one's duty to one's mother. The harm done by this education received through a foreign tongue does not stop here but goes much further. It has created a gulf between the educated classes and the masses. We do not know them and they do not know us. They regard us as *sahibs* to be feared and may distrust us. If this state of affairs continues very long, the time may come when Lord Curzon's[1] charge that the educated classes do not represent the common people would be true.

Fortunately, our educated classes appear to be awakening from their slumber. Now that they are beginning to come in contact with the people, they themselves realize the handicaps described above.

How may they infect the people with their own enthusiasm? English certainly will not avail us, whereas we have little or no aptitude to do the thing through Gujarati. I always hear people say that they experience great difficulty in expressing themselves in the mother tongue. This barrier dams up the current of popular life. Macaulay's[2] motive in introducing English education was sincere. He despised our literature. His contempt infected us, too, and we also lost our balance.

---

1. 1859-1925; Viceroy and Governor General of India, 1899-1905.
2. Thomas Babington Macaulay (1800-59); President of the General Committee of Public Instruction and Law Member of the Governor General's Executive Council, recommended in his Education Minute of February 2, 1835, the introduction of English education in India. *vide* "*Compulsory Education in India*", 7-10-1905.

Indeed, we have left our masters, the English, far behind us in this matter. Macaulay wanted us to become propagandists of Western civilization among our masses. His idea was that English education would help us to develop strength of character and then some of us would disseminate new ideas among the people. It would be irrelevant here to consider whether or not those ideas were good enough to be spread among the people. We have only to consider the question of the medium of instruction. We saw in English education an opportunity to earn money and, therefore, gave importance to the use of English. Some learned patriotism from it. Thus the original idea became secondary and we suffered much harm from the use of English which extended beyond Macaulay's original intention.

If we had political power in our hands, we would have discovered the error soon enough and would have found it impossible to give up the mother tongue. The officials did not give it up. Many perhaps do not know that our court language is supposed to be Gujarati. The Government gets the laws translated into Gujarati as well. Speeches read at *durbars* are translated into Gujarati simultaneously.

We know that in currency notes Gujarati is used alongside with English. Mathematical calculations which land-surveyors have to learn are difficult. If they had to do so through English, the work of the Revenue Department would have become very expensive. So they evolved Gujarati terminology for the use of the surveyors. These terms will give us a pleasant surprise. If we have a sincere love for our language, we can this very moment put to use the resources at our disposal. If lawyers start using Gujarati for their work, much of the clients' money would be saved. Clients would also get the requisite knowledge of law and come to know their rights. The expenses on the services of interpreters would also be saved. Legal terms would pass into current use. Of course, lawyers would have to put themselves to some trouble to do all this. I believe, and the belief is supported by experience, that this will not harm the interests of the client. There is no reason to fear that arguments in Gujarati would carry less weight with the Court than in English. It is compulsory for Collectors and other Government officials to know Gujarati. But, because of our unreasoning craze for English, we allow their knowledge to rust.

It has been contended that there was nothing wrong in our people learning English and using it for earning money and cultivating a sense of patriotism through it. But the contention has no bearing on the use of English as the medium of instruction. We shall respect a person who learns English for acquiring wealth or for doing good to the country. But we cannot, on this account, assert that English should be used as the medium of instruction. All that is intended here is to bring out the harmful consequences of English having established itself as the medium of education because of these two developments. There are some who hold that English knowing people alone have displayed patriotism. For the past two months, we have been witnessing something very different. We may, however, accept this claim with the modification that others never had the opportunity which the English knowing people had. The patriotism induced by the knowledge of English has not been infectious. Real patriotism is an expanding force which is ever propagating itself. The patriotism of English-knowing people lacks this quality.

It is said that, however, correct these arguments, the idea is not practicable today. "It is a pity that the study of other subjects should have to suffer because of the excessive importance given to English.

And it is to be deplored that much of our mental energy is used up in mastering it. But, in my humble opinion, "the way we are placed in relation to English leaves us no alternative but to accept the present arrangement and then find a way out." This is the view not of any ordinary writer but of one of the foremost scholars of Gujarat and a great lover of our mother tongue. We cannot but take into account anything that Acharya Dhruva[1] says. Few can claim to have the experience that he has. He has rendered great service in the fields of education and literature. He has a perfect right to advise and criticize.

That being so, a man like me has to think twice before expressing a different opinion. Shri Anandshankarbhai has expressed in courteous language the view held by the entire body of the advocates of English. We are in duty bound to give consideration to this point of view. Besides, my position in respect of this is somewhat awkward. I am conducting an experiment in National Education under his guidance and suspension. In this experiment we are using the mother tongue as the medium of education. In view of such close relations between us, I naturally hesitate to write anything in criticism of his views. Fortunately, Acharya Dhruva has considered education through English and that through the mother tongue only as experiments and has not expressed any definite opinion about either. I do not, therefore, feel as much hesitation in voicing my opposition to the above view as I otherwise would.

---

1. Anandshankar Bapubhai Dhruva; Sanskrit scholar and man of letters; Vice Chancellor, Benares Hindu University, 1920-37.

We attach excessive importance to our relationship with English. I am aware that we cannot discuss this question with unrestricted freedom in this Conference. But it is not improper to tell even those who cannot take part in political affairs that the British rule in India should be for the good of our country. There can be no other justification for it. The British rulers themselves admit that for one nation to rule over another is an intolerable situation for both, that it is evil and harms both. This is accepted in principle in discussions which recognize the altruistic point of view. Therefore, if it is proved to the satisfaction of both the rulers and the ruled that education through English saps the mental energy of our people, then, no time should be lost in changing the medium of instruction. The obstacles that lie in the way will then be a challenge to us. If this view is accepted, it should not be necessary to give any further argument to convince those who, like Acharya Dhruva, admit the [present] drain on our mental energy.

I do not think it necessary to consider whether or not the adoption of the mother tongue as the medium of instruction will have any adverse effect on the knowledge of English. It is not essential for all educated Indians to have a mastery of this alien language. Not only that, I even maintain, in all humility, that it is unnecessary to go out of one's way to create the desire for such mastery.

It is true that some Indians will have to learn English. Acharya Dhruva seems to have looked at this question only from the point of view of higher education. If, however, we consider it from all angles, it will be seen that two classes of people will need to learn English:

1. Public-spirited people who possess special aptitude for languages, have time on their hand and want to study English literature in order to put the fruits of their learning before our people, or use them in their contacts with the rulers.
2. Those who want to use their knowledge of English for economic gain.

There is no harm in giving both these groups a thorough knowledge of English as an optional subject. We should even provide the necessary facilities for it. But in this arrangement the medium of instruction will be the mother tongue. Acharya Dhruva fears that, if we do not adopt English as the medium but learn it merely as a foreign language, it will share the fate of Persian, Sanskrit, etc. I must say, with due respect to the Acharya, that this view is not quite correct. There are many Englishmen who know

French well and are able to use it satisfactorily for their work even though they received their education through English. In India, too, there are a number of Indians whose knowledge of French is quite good, though they learned it through the medium of English. The truth is that, when English comes to occupy its own place and the mother tongue has gained its rightful status, our minds which are imprisoned at present will be set free from the prison-house and, for brains which are well cultivated, well exercised and yet fresh, learning English will not be too much of a strain. I even believe that the English we learn under such conditions will be more of a credit to us than it is at present. What is more, with our intelligence vigorous and fresh, we shall be able to use it to better advantage. From the practical point of view of gain and loss, the course proposed will be found effective in promoting all our interests.

When we start receiving education through our own language, our relations in the home will take on a different character. Today, we cannot make our wives real life companions. They have very little idea of what we do outside. Our parents know nothing about what we learn at school. If, however, we were to receive education through our mother tongue, we would find it easy to educate the washerman, the barber, the *Bhangi*[1] and others who serve us. In England, they discuss politics with the hair-dresser while having a hair-cut. Here, we cannot do so even with the members of our own families. The reason is not that they are ignorant. They, too, know as much as the English barber.

We talk with them on the *Mahabharata*, the *Ramayana* and of holy places, because it is these things which our people hear and learn about. But, the knowledge we get at school does not seep down to others, not even to the members of our families, because we cannot impart to them what we learn in English.

At present the proceedings of our Legislative Assemblies are in English. It is the same story with other bodies. Consequently, the riches of our knowledge lie buried in the ground, much like the wealth of the miser. The same thing happens in our courts of law. The judges offer useful counsel. Litigants are eager enough to know what they say, but they get to know nothing except the dry judgment at the end. They cannot even follow the arguments of their lawyers. It is the same with doctors, educated in schools through English. They cannot educate the patients as may be required. They do not even know the Gujarati names for the various parts of the body. In consequence, most of them show no

1. One of the class attending to scavenging work.

interest in their patients except to write out prescriptions for them. It is said that, in our thoughtlessness, we allow huge masses of water flowing down the hills to go waste. In the same way, we produce precious manure worth millions, but, in the result, we get only diseases. Similarly, crushed under the weight of English and wanting in foresight, we fail to give our people what they are entitled to get. This is no exaggeration. It only expresses the intensity of my feeling on this point. We shall have to pay heavily for our disregard of the mother tongue. This has already done us great harm. I consider it the first duty of the educated to save our masses from any further harrn on this account.

There can be no limit to the development of Gujarati, the language of Narasinh Mehta[1], the language in which Nandshankar wrote Karanghelo[2], which has been cultivated by writers like Navalram[3], Narmadashankar[4], Manilal[5], Malabari[6], in which the late poet Rajchandra[7], uttered his immortal words, a language which has Hindu, Muslim and Parsi communities to serve it, which has had, among those who use it, men of holy lives, men of wealth, and daring sailors voyaging across the seas, and in which heroic stories celebrating Mulu Manek and Jodha Manek[8] even today resound in the hills of Kathiawad. What else can one expect of Gujaratis if they do not use such a language for their education? The pity is that the point needs to be argued.

Finally, while bringing this topic to a close, I draw your attention to the articles of Dr. Pranjivandas Mehta on this subject. Gujarati

---

1. 1414-79; Saint poet of Gujarat; one of his poems, *Vaishnava jana to tene kahiye*, describing the character of the true devotee of God, was Gandhiji's favourite hymn.
2. There Pioneer novel in Gujarati about the last independent Hindu king of Gujarat.
3. Navalram Laxmishankar Pandya (1836-1888); Gujarati man of letters.
4. Gujarati poet famed for his patriotic compositions; *vide* "*The Transvaal Strruggle*", 18-5-1907 and 25-5-1907.
5. Son of Revashankar Jhaveri, friend of Gandhiji; Gujarati thinker and writer. Swami Vivekanand refers in one of his letters to a paper by him which was read at one of the sectional meetings of the Parliament of Religions.
6. Bekramji Mervanji Malabari (1854-1912); poet, Journalist and social reformer.
7. Rajchandra Raojibhai Mehta, Jain thinker, poet and jeweller; vide *An Autobiography*, Part II, Ch. I.
8. They fought against the advance of British rule in the manner of medieval outlaws.

translations of these articles have been published and I suggest that you read them. You will find in them many ideas which support these views.

If, now, we are convinced that it is good to adopt the mother tongue as the medium of instruction, the next thing is to consider the steps to implement the decision. Without going into any argument, I set down what these steps should be just in the order in which they occur to me:

1. English knowing Gujaratis should never, intentionally or inadvertently, use English among themselves.
2. Those who possess a sound knowledge of both English and Gujarati should translate into Gujarati good and useful books or ideas in English.
3. Societies for the promotion of education should get text books prepared.
4. The rich among us should start schools in various places for imparting education through Gujarati.
5. At the same time, various Conferences and Educational Associations should petition the Government for using the mother tongue as the sole medium of instruction. Courts and legislatures should carry on their proceedings in Gujarati and people should also use Gujarati in all their work. The prevailing practice of selecting only those who know English for lucrative posts should be changed and the candidates should be selected according to merit and without discrimination on the basis of language. A petition should also go to the Government that schools be opened where Government servants may acquire the necessary knowledge of Gujarati.

Exception may be taken to this programme on one count. It will be said that in the Legislative Assembly[1] there are Marathi, Sindhi and Gujarati members and, may be, from Karnatak as well. The difficulty is serious enough, but not insurmountable. The Telugu speaking people have already raised this question and there is no doubt that some day there will have to be a reorganization of provinces on the basis of language. But, meanwhile, members of the Assembly should have the right to speak either in Hindi or in their mother tongue. If you find this suggestion ridiculous today; I need only say—with due respect to you—

---

1. The reference is to the legislature of the Bombay Presidency, which included Sindh.

that most radical suggestions seem similarly ridiculous in the beginning and on a superficial view. I am of the opinion that the progress of our country will largely depend on our deciding aright the question of the medium of education. I think, therefore, that my suggestion is of great consequence. When the mother tongue is better esteemed and has been restored to its rightful status—that of an official language—it will reveal powers and capacities undreamt of at present.

As we have had to consider the question of the medium of education, so also is it necessary to consider that of the national language. If this is to be English, it must be made a compulsory subject.

Can English become our national language? Some of our learned men, good patriots, contend that even to argue that English should become the national language betrays ignorance, that it is already so. His Excellency the Viceroy[1] in his recent speech merely expressed the hope that it would occupy this place. His zeal did not carry him as far as to say that it had already become our national language and that there could be no question about it. He believes, however, that English will spread in the country day by day, enter our homes, and finally attain the exalted status of a national language. On a superficial consideration, this view appears correct. Looking at the educated section of our population, one is likely to gain the impression that, in the absence of English, all our work would come to a stop. But deeper reflection will show that English cannot, and ought not to, become our national language.

Let us see what are the requirements of a national language:

1. It should be easy to learn for Government officials.
2. It should be capable of serving as a medium of religious, economic and political intercourse throughout India.
3. It should be the speech of large number of Indians.
4. It should be easy for every Indian to learn.
5. In choosing such a language, considerations of temporary or passing circumstances should not count.

English does not fulfil any of these requirements.

The first point ought to have been placed last, but I have purposely reversed the order because it seems as though English fulfils it. Closer examination will, however, show that even at the present moment it is not for officials an easy language to learn or handle. The Constitution, under

1. Lord Chelmsford (1868-1933); Viceroy of India, 1916-21.

which we are being ruled, envisages that the number of British officials will progressively decrease until finally only the Viceroy and a few others are left here. Even now, the majority of people in Government services are Indians and their number will increase as time passes. I think no one will deny that for them English is more difficult than any Indian language.

As regards the second requirement, I think that religious intercourse through English is an impossibility unless our people throughout the land start speaking English. Spreading English among the masses to this extent appears quite impossible.

English simply cannot satisfy the third requirement as it is not the speech of any very large number of Indians.

The fourth also cannot-be met by English because it is not relatively an easy language for all our people to learn.

Considering the fifth point, we see that the status which English enjoys today is temporary; as a permanent arrangement, the position is that the need for English in national affairs will be, if at all, very slight. It will be required for dealings with the British Empire and will remain the language of diplomacy between different countries within the Empire; this is a different matter. It will certainly remain necessary for such purposes. We do not grudge English anything. We only want that it should not overstep its proper limits; this is all that we insist upon. English will remain the imperial language and accordingly we shall require our Malaviyas, our Shastris and our Banerjeas to learn it,[1] confident that they will enhance the glory of India in other lands. But English cannot be the national language of India. To give it that position will be like introducing Esperanto into our country. To think that English can become our national language betrays weakness, as the attempt to introduce Esperanto would betray sheer ignorance.

Which language, then, fulfils all the five requirements? We shall have to admit that it is Hindi.

I call that language Hindi which Hindus and Muslims in the North speak and which is written either in Devanagari or Urdu script.

There has been some objection to this definition.

It is argued that Hindi and Urdu are two different languages.

---

1. Madan Mohan Malaviya, Rt. Hon'ble V. S. Srinivasa Sastri and Sir Surendranath Banerjea were pre-eminent in their masterly use of the English language.

But this is incorrect. Both Hindus and Muslims speak the same language in North India. The difference has been created by the educated classes. That is, educated Hindus Sanskritize their Hindi with the result that Muslims cannot follow it. Muslims of Lucknow Persianize their Urdu and make it unintelligible to Hindus. To the masses both these languages are foreign and so they have no use for them. I have lived in the North and have mixed freely with both Hindus and Muslims, and, though my knowledge of Hindi is limited; I have never found any difficulty in carrying on communication through it with them. Therefore, call it Hindi or Urdu as you like, the language of the people in North India is the same thing—basically. Write it in the Urdu script and call it Urdu, or write it in the Nagari script and call it Hindi.

There now remains the question of the script. For the present, Muslims will certainly use the Urdu script and most of the Hindus the Devanagari. I say "most" because thousands of Hindus even today write in the Urdu script and some even do not know the Devanagari script. In the end, when Hindus and Muslims will have ceased to regard each other with distrust, when the causes for such distrust have disappeared, the script which has greater range and is more popular will be more widely used and thus become the national script. In the intervening period, Hindus and Muslims who desire to write their petitions in the Urdu script should be free to do so and these should be accepted at all Government offices.

No other language can compete with Hindi in satisfying these five requirements. Next to Hindi comes Bengali. But the Bengalis themselves make use of Hindi outside Bengal. The Hindi speaking man speaks Hindi wherever he goes and no one feels surprised at this.

The Hindu preachers and the Mahomedan Moulvis always deliver their religious discourses in Hindi and Urdu and even the illiterate masses understand them. Even an unlettered Gujarati, when he goes to the North, attempts to speak a few Hindi words, but the man from the North who works as gate-keeper for the Bombay businessman declines to speak in Gujarati and it is the latter, his employer, who is obliged to speak to him in broken Hindi. I have heard Hindi spoken even in far-off Dravidian provinces[1]. It is not correct to say that in Madras one needs English. Even there, I have used Hindi for all my work. In the trains, I have heard hundreds of Madrasi passengers speaking to others in Hindi. Besides, the

1. These constitute today the Southern States of Andhra, Kerala, Mysore and Madras, the home of people speaking languages of the Dravidian group.

Muslims of Madras know good enough Hindi. It should be noted that Muslims throughout India speak Urdu and they are found in large number in every province. Thus Hindi has already established itself as the national language of India. We have been using it as such for a long time. The birth of Urdu itself is due to the aptness of Hindi for this purpose.

Muslim kings could not make Persian or Arabic the national language. They accepted the Hindi grammar and, employing the Urdu script, used more Persian words. They could not use a foreign tongue in their dealings with the masses. It is not as if the British are unaware of this position. Those who know anything about military affairs know that they have had to adopt Hindi and Urdu technical terms for use with the sepoys.

Thus, we see that Hindi alone can become our national language, though the matter presents some difficulty to the educated classes of Madras.

For Maharashtrians, Gujaratis, Sindhis and Bengalis, the thing is very easy. In a few months they can acquire enough command of Hindi to be able to use it for all-India intercourse. It is not so easy for Tamil friends. Tamil and other languages of the South belong to the Dravidian group. The structure and the grammar of these languages are different from those of Sanskrit. There is nothing in common between these two groups except certain words. But the difficulty in learning Hindi is confined to the present educated classes only. We are entitled to trust to their patriotic spirit and hope that they will make a special effort to learn Hindi. As for the future, if Hindi attains its due status, it will be introduced in every school in Madras and there will be increased possibilities of contact between Madras and other provinces.

English has failed to reach the Dravidian masses, but Hindi will do so in no time. The Telugu people have already started moving in this direction. If this Conference reaches a decision on the question of the national language, we shall have to think of ways and means of implementing the decision. The measures suggested for the promotion of the mother tongue could, with suitable modifications, be applied to the national language as well. The difference is that the responsibility for making Gujarati the medium of instruction in our province will have to be shouldered mainly by us, whereas, in the movement to popularize the national language, the whole country will play its part.

We have discussed the question of the medium of instruction, the national language and, incidentally, the place of English. We have now to consider whether there are any defects in the present system of education in the schools.

There is no difference of opinion on this point. Both the Government and public opinion condemn the present system. There are, however, differences of view regarding what aspects are fit to be preserved and what to be rejected. I am not competent enough to discuss these differences. I shall only venture to place before this Conference my own conclusions.

Since education is not exactly my sphere of work, I feel diffident in saying anything on this subject. When I see a person talk about a thing of which he has no practical experience and which is, therefore, outside his range, I want to tell him off and grow impatient with him. It would be natural for a lawyer to feel impatient and angry with a physician talking of law. In the same way, I hold that those who have no experience in the field of education have no right to offer criticism on matters connected with it. I should, therefore, like to say a few words about my qualifications to speak on this subject.

I started thinking about modern education[1] twenty-five years ago. I had my children and the children of my brothers and sisters to look after. I was aware of the defects in our schools. I therefore carried out experiments on my children. No doubt, I tossed them about a good deal in the process. Some I sent to one place and some to others. A few I taught myself. My dissatisfaction with the prevailing system remained the same as ever even after I had left for South Africa, and I had to apply my mind further to the subject. The management of the Indian Education Society[2] was in my hand for a long time. I never sent my boys to school. My eldest son was a witness to the different stages through which I passed. He left me in disappointment and studied at a school in Ahmedabad for some time.

But, as he realized later, this did not benefit him particularly. I am convinced that those whom I did not send to school have not stood to suffer and that they have received a good training indeed. I am conscious of their deficiencies, but these are due to the fact that they grew up while my experiments were in their early stages and they were, therefore,

---

1. For Gandhiji's views on the subject, vide *An Autobiography*, Part IV, Chs. XXXII to XXXVI, also "Letter to G. K. Gokhale", 13-1-1905 and "Phoenix School", 9-1-1909 and "Letter to Manilal Gandhi", 25-3-1909.
2. The reference is to the Natal Indian Education Association; and *satyagraha* in South Africa, Ch. VI.

victims of the modifications which the experiments went through despite the continuity of the general pattern. During the *satyagraha* struggle in South Africa, there were fifty boys studying under my supervision.[1] The general line of work in the school was laid down by me. It had nothing in common with the system in vogue in Government or other schools. A similar effort is now being made here and a National School[2] has been started in Ahmedabad with the blessings of Acharya Dhruva and other scholars. It is now five months old. Prof. Sankaleh and Shah, formerly of the Gujarat College, is its Principal. He received his education under Prof. Gajjar and there are many other lovers of the language associated with him. In the main, the responsibility for the scheme is mine, but it has the active approval of all the teachers connected with it. They have dedicated themselves to the work, content to receive a salary just enough to meet their needs. Though circumstances do not permit me to undertake actual teaching work in this school, its affairs constantly engage my attention. Thus, my contribution is more like an amateur's but, I believe, not altogether devoid of thought. I would request you to keep this in mind in considering my criticism of the prevailing system of education.

It has always appeared to me that the present system of education pays no attention to the general pattern of life in our families. Naturally enough, our needs were not taken into account when the scheme was drawn up.

Macaulay despised our literature. He thought we were overmuch given to superstitions. Most of those who drew up this scheme were utterly ignorant of our religion. Some of them thought that it was a false religion. Our scriptures were regarded as mere collections of superstitions. Our civilization seemed full of defects to them.

Because we had fallen on evil times, it was thought that our institutions must be defective. With the best of motives, therefore, they raised a faulty structure. Since a fresh start was being made, the planners could only think of the immediate needs of the situation. The whole thing was devised with this idea in mind, that the rulers would need lawyers, doctors, and clerks to help them and that the people should have the new knowledge. Consequently, books were written without any regard for our way of living. Thus, to use an English proverb, "The cart was placed before the horse".

Shri Malabari said that, if History and Geography were to be taught

1. This was at Phoenix School; *vide* "*Phoenix School*", 2-1-1909; 9-1-1909.
2. The Gujarat Vidyapeeth in Ahmedabad.

to children, a beginning should be made with the history and geography of the home. I remember, however, that I was made to memorize the counties of England, with the result that an interesting subject like geography became poison to me. I found nothing in History to enthuse me. History is a good means of inculcating patriotism. But the way it was taught in the school gave me no reason to take pride in this country. To learn that, I have had to read other books.

In teaching Arithmetic and other allied subjects, too, the traditional method hardly finds any place. It is almost completely abandoned. With the disappearance of the indigenous method of learning tables, we have lost the capacitv for making speedy calculations which our elders possessed.

Science tends to be dry and dull. Our children cannot make much use of what they are taught in this field. A science like astronomy which should be taught to the boys in the open by actually showing them the stars in the sky is taught through books. I do not think many boys remember how to decompose water into its constituent elements once they leave school.

As to Hygiene, it is no exaggeration to say that it is not taught at all. We do not know, after 60 years of education, how to protect ourselves against epidemics like cholera and plague. I consider it a very serious blot on the state of our education that our doctors have not found it possible to eradicate these diseases. I have seen hundreds of homes. I cannot say that I have found any evidence in them of a knowledge of hygiene. I have the greatest doubt whether our graduates know what one should do in case one is bitten by a snake. If our doctors could have started learning medicine at an earlier age, they would not make such a poor show as they do. This is the disastrous result of the system under which we are educated. People in almost all the parts of the world have managed to eradicate the plague.

Here it seems to have made a home and thousands of Indians die untimely deaths. If this is to be attributed to poverty, it would still be up to the Education Department to answer why, even after 60 years of education, there is poverty in India.

Let us now turn our attention to the subjects which are not taught at all. All education must aim at building character. I cannot see how this can be done except through religion. We are yet to realize that gradually we are being reduced to a state in which we shall have lost our own without having acquired the new. I cannot go more into this, but I have met hundreds of teachers and they sighed in pain as they told me of their experiences. This is an aspect which the Conference cannot but deeply ponder over. If pupils in schools lose their character, everything will have been lost.

In our country, 85 to 90 per cent of people are engaged in agriculture. Needless to say that no knowledge of this particular field of work can be too much. And yet it has no place at all in the school syllabus up to the end of the high school education. It is only in India that such an anomalous position can exist.

The weaving industry is also falling into ruin. It provided work to farmers during their free hours. The craft finds no place in the curriculum. Our education can only produce clerks and, its general tendency being what it is, even goldsmiths, blacksmiths and cobblers, once they are caught up in its meshes, become clerks. We desire that everyone should have a good education. But how will it profit us if our education makes us all clerks ?

Military science finds no place in our education. Personally, I am not unhappy over this. I even regard it as an accidental gain. But the people want to learn the use of arms. Those who do so should not be denied the opportunity of learning it. But this science seems to have been completely lost sight of, as it were, in our scheme of education. Nowhere do I find a place given to music. It exercises a powerful influence over us. We do not realize this vividly enough, otherwise we would have done everything possible to teach music to our boys and girls. The Vedic hymns seem to follow musical tunes in their composition. Harmonious music has the power to soothe the anguish of the soul. At times, we find restlessness in a large gathering.

This can be arrested and calmed if a national song is sung by all. That hundreds of boys may sing a poem full of courage and the spirit of adventure and bravery and be inspired with the spirit of heroism is no commonplace fact. We have an example of the power of music in the fact that boatmen and other labourers raise, in unison, the cry of *Harahar* and *Allabeli* and this helps them in their work. I have seen English friends trying to fight cold by singing songs. Our boys learn to sing songs from popular plays in all manner of tunes and without regard to time and place, and try their hands on noisy harmoniums and Other instruments, and this does them harm. If, instead, they were to be correctly trained in music, they would not waste their time singing, or attempting to sing, music-hall songs. Just as a trained singer never sings out of tune or at the wrong time, even so one who has learnt classical music will not go in for street music. Music must get a place in our efforts at popular awakening.

The views of Dr. Ananda Coomaraswami[1] on this subject are worthy of serious study.

I include in the term "physical training" sports, games, etc. These, too, have been little thought of. Indigenous games have been given up and tennis, cricket and football hold sway. Admittedly, these games are enjoyable. If, however, we had not been carried away by enthusiasm for all things Western, we would not have given up our inexpensive but equally interesting games like *gedi-dado, gilli-danda, kho-kho, mag-matali, kabaddi, kharo pat, nava nagelio, sat tali*, etc. Exercises which provided the completest training for every bodily organ and the old style gymnasium where they taught wrestling have almost totally disappeared. I think if anything from the West deserves copying, it is drill. A friend once remarked that we did not know how to walk, particularly when we had to walk in squads and keep step.

Silently to walk in step, by hundreds and thousands of us in twos and fours, shifting the directions from time to time is something we can never do. It is not that such drill is useful only in actual battle. It can be of great use in many other activities in the sphere of public service.

For example, in extinguishing fire, in rescuing people from drowning, in carrying the sick and disabled in a *doli*[2], etc., [previous practice in] drill is a valuable aid. Thus, it is necessary to introduce in our schools indigenous games, exercises and the Western type of drill.

The education of women is as faulty as that of men. No thought has been given to the relations of men and women or to the place of woman in Indian society.

Primary education for the two sexes can have much in common.

There are important differences at all other levels. As Nature has made men and women different, it is necessary to maintain a difference between the education of the two. True, they are equals in life, but their functions differ. It is woman's right to rule the home. Man is master outside it. Man is the earner, woman saves and spends. Woman looks after the feeding of the child. She shapes its future. She is responsible for building its character. She is her children's educator, and hence, mother to the Nation. Man is not father [in that sense].

After a certain period, a father ceases to influence his son; the mother never abdicates her place. The son, even after attaining manhood,

1. 1877-1947; exponent of Oriental art and culture; Curator of Fine Arts Museum, U.S.A; author of *Transformation of Nature in Art*, *Dance of Shiva*, etc.
2. Seat slung from a pole carried by two or more men on shoulders.

will play with the mother even as the child does. He cannot do that with his father.

If this is the scheme of Nature, and it is just as it should be, woman should not have to earn her living. A state of affairs in which women have to work as telegraph clerks, typists or compositors can be, I think, no good, such a people must be bankrupt and living on their capital.

Hence, just as, on the one hand, it is wrong to keep women in ignorance and under suppression, so, on the other, it is a sign of decadence and it is tyrannical to burden them with work which is ordinarily done by men.

There must be provision, therefore, for separate arrangements for the education of women after their attaining a certain age. They should be taught the management of the home, the things they should or should not do during pregnancy, and the nursing and care of children. Drawing up such a scheme presents difficulties. The idea is new. The right course would be to constitute a committee of men and women, of good character and well-informed, who would think further and arrive at conclusions, and ask them to produce a suitable plan for the purpose.

This Committee should consider measures for the education of girls from the time that they cease to be children. There is, however, a very large number of girls who have been married off before puberty, and the number is increasing. Once they are married, they just disappear from the field. I have given my views on this in my foreword to the first book of the "*Bhagini Samaj*" series. I reproduce them here: We shall not solve the problem of women's education merely by educating girls. Victims of child marriage, thousands of girls vanish from view at the early age of twelve. They change into house-wives ! Till this wicked custom has disappeared from among us, the husband will have to learn to be the wife's teacher. A great many of our hopes lie in women being educated on matters mentioned above. It seems to me that unless women cease to be a mere means of pleasure or cooks to us and come to be our life-companions, equal partners in the battle of life, sharers in our joys and sorrows, all our efforts are doomed to failure. There are men to whom their women are no better than animals. For, this sad state, some of the Sanskrit sayings and a well-known *doha*[1] of Tulsidas may be held responsible.

Tulsidas says at one place: "The drum, the fool, the *Sudra*, the animal and the woman—all these need beating."[2]

---

1. Couplet.
2. This is from *Ramacharitamanas*.

I adore Tulsidasji, but adoration is not blind. Either this couplet is an interpolation, or, if it is his, he must have written it without much reflection, following the tradition in his time. As to the Sanskrit sayings, people seem to labour under the impression that every verse in that language was a scriptural precept. We must fight this impression and pluck out from its very root the general habit of regarding women as inferior beings. On the other hand, blinded by passion, many among us regard women as beautiful dolls to be adored as so many goddesses and decorate them with ornaments just as we have Thakorji[1] dressed up in new finery every few hours. We must keep away from this evil also. Ultimately, however, there can be salvation for us only when—and not until—our women become to us what Uma[2] was to Shankar[3], Sita to Rama and Damayanti to Nala, joining us in our deliberations, arguing with us, appreciating and nourishing our aspirations, understanding, with their marvellous intuition, the unspoken anxieties of our outward life and sharing in them, bringing us the peace that soothes. This goal can hardly be achieved in the immediate future merely by starting girls' schools. As long as we have around our necks the noose of child marriage, men have to be teachers to their wives, and that not merely to make them literate. Gradually, it should be possible to introduce women to the subjects of politics and social reform. Literacy is not essential for this. The man, in such a case, will have to change his attitude to his wife. If a girl were treated as a pupil till she came of age, the husband observing *Brahmacharya* the while, if we had not been pressed down by the weight of inertia, we would never subject a girl of twelve or fifteen to the agony of child-bearing. One ought to shudder at the very thought of it.

Classes are now conducted for married women and lectures arranged. All this is good as far as it goes. Those who are engaged in this work make a sacrifice of their time. This is to the credit side. It seems to me, however, that unless men simultaneously discharge the duty indicated above, these efforts will not produce much result. A little reflection will show this to be self evident.

Wherever we look, we find heavy structures raised on weak foundations. Those selected as teachers for primary education may in courtesy be termed so, but in doing this we, in fact, misuse this word. Childhood is the most important period of one's life.

1. The idol or image of God.
2. Parvati, spouse of Shiva.
3. Shiva, one of the Hindu trinity of gods.

Knowledge received during this period is never forgotten. But this is the period during which the child is allowed the least time [for learning] and is held prisoner in no matter what manner of school. I hold that, in our equipping high schools and colleges, we incur expense which this poor land can hardly bear. If, instead, primary education were to be given by well-educated and experienced teachers of high character, in surroundings which would reflect some regard for the beauty of Nature and safeguard the health of the pupils, we would see good results in a short time We would not succeed in bringing about the desired change even if we double the monthly salaries of the present teachers. Big results cannot be brought about through such small changes. The very pattern of primary education must change. I know that this is a difficult proposition and that there are several obstacles in the way. All the same, it should not be beyond the power of the Gujarat Kelavani Mandal to find a solution to this problem.

I should, perhaps, say that it is not my intention to find fault with the teachers in primary schools. That they are able to show results beyond their powers is, in my opinion, to be attributed to our noble culture and traditions. I am sure that, given sufficient training and encouragement, these same teachers will show results of which we can have no conception at present.

I think it would be improper for me to say anything about the question, whether or not education should be free and compulsory.

My experience is limited. Besides, the idea of imposing anything as duty on our people does not appeal to me and so I cannot reconcile myself to this addition to their obligations. It will be more appropriate at present to make education free but optional and make experiments.

I visualize many difficulties in making education compulsory until we have left the days of autocracy behind us. The experience of the Baroda Government may be of some help in coming to a decision on this matter. My own investigation has led me to conclude against the advisability of compulsory education; but the investigation was not thorough and, therefore, no weight can be attached to it. I hope some of the delegates to this Conference will throw helpful light on the point.

I am convinced that petitioning the Government is not the royal road for correcting all the foregoing deficiencies. The Government cannot change things radically in a day. It is for leaders of the people to take the initiative in such ventures. The British Constitution leaves particular scope for such initiative. If we think that anything can be done only if the Government moves, we are not likely to realize our aims for ages. As they do in England, we must first make experiments and show results before asking the Government to adopt new measures. Whoever finds a deficiency in any field can try to correct it by his own efforts and, after he has succeeded, can move the Government for the desired improvement. For such pioneering ventures, it is necessary to establish a number of special educational bodies.

There is one great obstacle in the way—the lure of degrees. We think our entire life depends on success at examinations. This results in great harm to the people. We forget that a degree is useful only for those who want to go in for Government service. But the edifice of national life is not to be raised on the salaried class. We also see that people are able to earn money quite well even without taking up any service. When those who are almost illiterate can become millionaires by their intelligence and shrewdness, there is no reason why the educated cannot do the same. If the educated would only give up their fear, they could be as capable as the unlettered.

If this lure of degrees could be shaken off, any number of private schools could flourish. No government can provide fully for all the education which the people need. In America, education is mostly a private enterprise. In England, too, private enterprise runs a number of institutions. They give their own certificates.

It will require Herculean efforts to put our education on a sound foundation. We shall have to make sacrifices and dedicate ourselves body, mind and soul to the task.

I think there is not much that we can learn from America, but one thing we would do well to copy. Some of the biggest educational institutions there are run by a huge Trust. Wealthy Americans have donated millions to this Trust. It runs a number of private schools. If it has a huge fund, it also has at its disposal the services of a number of learned men who love their country and are well-equipped physically. They inspect all these institutions and help them in maintaining academic standards. They provide help wherever and in whatever measure they think necessary. It is available to any institution which agrees to adopt the approved Constitution. An enthusiastic campaign launched by this Trust carried the results of new researches in the field of agriculture to elderly peasants. We can have a similar plan in Gujarat. There is wealth here and scholarship, too, and love of religion has not altogether disappeared. Children are only waiting to be taught. If we can take up this venture, we may show to the Government in a few years that our efforts are in the right direction. I am sure the Government, then, will not fail to adopt the plan. Actual work will speak to better effect than a thousand petitions

This suggestion covers the other two objects of the Gujarat Kelavani Mandal. The establishment of such a Trust will ensure both a continuous campaign for the spread of education and also practical work in that field. This done, everything else will follow. Evidently, therefore, it will not be easy work. Wealthy people are like the Government, in that they wake up only when we prod them. For this, *tapascharya* is the only means we have. It is the first and last step in *dharma*. I take it that the Gujarat Kelavani Mandal is the embodiment of such *tapascharya*. When its secretaries and members are wholly possessed by the spirit of service and are also men of learning, money will pour forth on its own. Moneyed people are always sceptical. They have reason to be so. Therefore, if we want to please the goddess of wealth, we shall have first to prove our fitness.

Though we shall need plenty of money, we need not stress the matter overmuch. Anyone who would work for the spread of national education will, if uneducated, teach himself as he goes about his daily labour and then, sitting beneath a tree, teach those who want to learn.

This is the way of the Brahmin *dharma*. Anyone who chooses may follow it. When we have such Brahmins, both wealth and power will bow in reverence before them.

I want the Gujarat Kelavani Mandal to have such unshakable faith; may God grant that it have.

In education lies the key to *swaraj*. Let political leaders wait on Mr. Montagu[1], if they want to. It does not matter if politics is out of bounds for this Conference. But the fact remains that all efforts are futile without the right kind of education, which is the special concern of this Conference. If we succeed in this, we succeed in all other things as well.

[*From Gujarati*]
Mahatma Gandhini Vicharsrishti

---

1. Edwin Samuel Montagu (1879-1924); Secretary of State for India, 1917-22; visited India in November 1917, and was responsible, along with Lord Chelmsford, the then Viceroy, for the political reforms of 1918, later embodied in the Government of India Act, 1919.

14. Scheme for National Education[1]

For many years past, several friends and I have felt that our present education is not national and that, in consequence, people do not get from it the benefit they ought to. Our children languish as a result of this education. They become incapable of any great achievement and the knowledge they acquire does not spread among the masses—not even among their families. Nor do the young people have any aim in mind in taking this modern education except to get a job and make money Prof. Anandshankar Bapubhai Dhruva writes:

As, during the last five years or so, India stirred out of her sleep and opened her eyes, she found herself faced with the problem of her education.

The people of India want to have a share in their government and, to be sure, they will get it. Are three-quarters of her population, then, to remain condemned to illiteracy? They are to pledge themselves to the use of *swadeshi* goods. Is their education, then, to remain without due provision for instruction in commerce and industry? India will become conscious of her selfrespect; is she to be content, then, to have her ancient literature and her arts, her religions and her philosophy, expounded always by foreign scholars ?

These and other like aspirations for a fuller life, along with the changed circumstances, have invested the problem of education at the present day with especial importance and till, recognizing the seriousness of this all-important issue, we firmly adhere to certain principles as fundamental to our education, we shall not have done our duty by ourselves and our country, in fact, by the humanity in us.

And again:

Social reform and religion seemed to be quite simple matters to the leaders of that generation, but the threads which go into the making of a religious life are many-coloured and closely inter-twined. Hindu society

1. This article, which appeared as by Mohandas Karamchand Gandhi, is an elaboration of his earlier article: "National Gujarati School", vide "*National Gujarati School*", After 18-1-1917.

derives its vitality from its recognition of these two facts. It is the duty of the new age to understand this truth and order its life accordingly. The system of education in vogue in the last generation was defective as it limited itself to turning out government servants, lawyers and doctors.

Wherever, I have travelled in India, I have discussed this question with the leaders and, without exception, everyone has admitted that our educational system must change. The following extract makes it quite clear that the Government did not consider all the needs of the people in devising this system:

We have, moreover, looked upon the encouragement of education as peculiarly important, because it is calculated not only to produce a higher degree of intellectual fitness, but to raise the moral character of those who partake of its advantages and so to supply you with servants to whose probity you may, with increased confidence, commit offices of trust in India.[1] It is one of the recognized principles of education that it should be planned with a view to the needs of the people. This idea finds no place at all in our schools.

The system of education has to change, but to look to the Government for this will be sheer waste of time. The Government will wait on public opinion and, being foreign, move very timidly; it cannot understand our needs, its advisers may be ill-informed or they may have interests of their own to serve. For a variety of such reasons, it will probably be quite long before there is any serious change in the present system; the time that passes meanwhile, is so much loss to the people. It is, however, not intended to suggest here that we should not try to get the Government to move. Let petitions be made to it and let public opinion be ascertained. But the best petition to the Government will be an actual demonstration by us and this will also be the easiest way of cultivating public opinion. It has accordingly been decided, in consultation with some educated gentlemen, to start a national school.

EDUCATION IN THE SCHOOL

Education in the school will be entirely through the mother tongue. It is surprising that, while among other nations the mother tongue enjoys pride of place, among us this place belongs to English.

---

1. This and the subsequent quotations are English passages as quoted by Gandhiji in footnotes in the original Gujarati version of this article.

This state of affairs is ultimately harmful to the people. The President of the first Gujarat Educational Conference, too, expressed the view that the medium of education should be the mother tongue. The Chairman of the Reception Committee was very emphatic in his speech that education should be through the mother tongue. The matter was specifically mentioned in the Government dispatch of 1854. It is not easy to understand how, in spite of that, the basis of education was altered. The dispatch said:

It is neither our aim nor our desire to substitute the English for the vernacular dialects of the country. We have always been most sensible of the importance of the use of the languages, which alone are understood by the great mass of the population. These languages, not English, have been, put by us in the place of Persian in the administration of justice and in the intercourse between the officers of the Government and the people. It is indispensable, therefore, that in any general system of education, the studio of vernaculars should be assiduously attended to. And any acquaintance with improved European knowledge which is to be communicated to the great mass of the people whose circumstances prevent them from acquiring a high standard of knowledge and who cannot be expected to overcome the difficulty of a foreign language, can only be conveyed to them through one or other of these vernacular languages.

We look, therefore to the English language and the vernacular languages of India together as media for the diffusion of European knowledge, and it is our desire to see them cultivated in all schools in India of a sufficiency high class to maintain a school-master possessing the requisite qualifications.

His Excellency Lord Chelmsford, the Viceroy, also gave an idea, in his address to the Conference of Directors [of Education] held in Delhi on February 22, of the harm that has resulted from English instead of the mother tongue having been assigned the chief place. He asked where the British people would have been if they had had to receive their education through a foreign tongue. His own reply was that many Britons would have given up their studies in sheer despair.

He described the present method of imparting education through English as a "vicious system"[1]. These are his words:

I refer to the relative claims of English and vernacular teaching. At the present moment, we rely on English as the medium of higher instruction.

1. Gandhiji uses the English expression,

This is due mainly to the fact that English is the passport to employment and that vernacular text-books are not available, but the consequence is obvious. Students endeavour to grapple with abstruse subjects through the medium of a foreign tongue and in many cases, thanks to their mediocre acquaintance with that tongue, have perforce to memorize their text-books.

We criticize adversely this tendency to memorize but to my mind it reflects credit on the zeal of the student who, rather than abandon their quest for knowledge, memorize whole pages, whole books which they understand but imperfectly. This is, of course, a mere travesty of education....I would ask you and myself as University men how should we have fared in our education if it had been wholly through the medium of a foreign tongue. I doubt whether we would [not] have abandoned the attempt in despair; and I am lost in admiration for the gift of those boys who made a gallant attempt to surmount the difficulties imposed on them by a vicious system.

An attempt has been made in Poona to impart education through an Indian language, and, in the view of those who run the school, the result has been good. This view is shared by the Government and the public; we, too, aim at providing education through the mother tongue.

The President of the first [Gujarat] Educational Conference had pointed out in his speech that, if the mother tongue was adopted as the medium of instruction, it would require seven years to impart the knowledge which at present requires 11 years in the High School.

This is no insignificant saving. The most important advantage of such a policy would be the reduction in the financial burden on the people.

Hindi has been included in the curriculum of this school for the simple reason that it is spoken by about 220 million people. If a language spoken by such large numbers of our countrymen can be taught [to the rest], they would all find it easy to understand the meaning of the various political movements. I am convinced that, in India, Hindi alone can occupy the position of a national language. It has a fine literature, too, and will therefore enrich our literatures.

The schools under the present dispensation make no provision for teaching the science of religion. It has been given a place in the curriculum of this school.

The pupils here will be trained in two occupations:

(1) agriculture, and (2) weaving. Incidental to these, they will get training in carpentry and smithy. They will also receive instruction in

Physics, Chemistry, Botany and Zoology. In India, the foregoing occupations occupy the most important place and anyone who learns them will never have to go in search of a job.

Every pupil will be taught the means of preserving health and home remedies for common ailments. The pupil's physical training will receive no less attention than the education of his mind.

Every pupil will be taught five languages: (1) Gujarati, (2) Hindi, (3) Marathi, (4) Sanskrit, and (5) English. Mathematics will include Arithmetic, Algebra, Geometry and Trigonometry. In other words, the pupils will be brought up to the level of the present First Year of the College.

History-Geography: The history to be taught will be of Gujarat, India, England, Greece, Rome, and of modern times. During the last year, Philosophy of History and Sociology will also be taught. In Geography, the standard will not be inferior to what obtains in the schools at present.

In Astronomy, the elements of the subjects will be taught.

A study of Economics is also essential and will, accordingly, be provided for. Some knowledge of law is useful to every person and provision will, therefore, be made for teaching it for practical purposes.

Drill has been introduced in the first year to provide recreation and exercise to the pupils.

Music has been introduced as an aid to recitation and also that one may understand something of the subject. All instruction in the first year will be oral. Such general knowledge as will help in the development of the child's mind, it is intended to convey to it as it plays about. Knowledge of colours, shapes, size, etc., can be conveyed in this way and, so conveyed, it will stimulate the child's powers of observation. Hence, this aid to education will also be utilized as an integral part of the method.

India never knew the institution of examinations. The method is of recent introduction. It received no great importance in the dispatch of 1854. The system has lent itself to serious abuse, every subject being taught with an eye on the examination and the conviction firmly planted in the pupil's mind that passing the examination was all that was necessary. The teacher, too, has got into the habit of doing his work in the same spirit, as so much drudgery. Hence any knowledge that is acquired is superficial. Not a single subject is taught with thoroughness. The following passage is worth quoting in this context:

In recent years, they [examinations] have grown to extravagant dimension and their influence has been allowed to dominate the whole system of education in India with the result that instruction is confined to the rigid frame of prescribed courses, that all forms of training which do not admit of being tested by a written examination are liable to be neglected, and that most teachers and pupils are tempted to concentrate their energies not so much on genuine study as upon questions likely to be set by the examiner. Having regard to the view that examinations are quite undesirable, pupils in this institution will be tested periodically from two points of view—whether the teacher has made the right effort and whether the pupil has followed. The pupil will be freed from the fear of examinations. The tests will be held by the teachers of the school and by others familiar with the institution. The expectation is that a pupil who has attended the school for ten years will be as well equipped as the present-day graduate. In addition, he will have a practical knowledge of agriculture and weaving. The use to which the student puts his abilities after leaving school will be the true measure of the worth of his education. Every opportunity will be taken to rid his mind of the fallacious notion that the aim of education is to get employment. At present, it is the general practice among business men to select for the better posts men who know English, and that from among those educated under the Government controlled system. But they will have an alternative field for selection when scholars of this school go out on the completion of their studies. The people will then have some idea of the effectiveness of the method of education followed here. A businessman is not in love with a "degree"; his choice will fall on the efficient man.

If, after ten years of study, anyone wants to pursue a subject further, necessary arrangements for the purpose are left to the future.

EDUCATION FREE

No fees will be charged in this school, the expenses being met from donations received.

TEACHERS

Paid teachers will be engaged and will be, all of them, grown up men who have reached the college level or possess equivalent attainments. The idea is that children should have the best teachers in the early stages.

[*From Gujarati*]
Gujarati, 21-10-1917

15. Need of National Language

CONCLUDING SPEECH AT THE CONFERENCE[1]

[Broach,
October 21, 1917]

I have been thanked already. Never and nowhere could I express all that I feel. It is services such as these which, I believe, lead to *moksha*[2]. For these three days, I have been extremely happy. I am thankful to Mr. Haribhai, for day and night he has been busy serving everyone. If anyone has been dissatisfied with him, I apologize to him on Mr. Haribhai's behalf. From a milch cow you may even bear a kick. I am in love with the mother tongue, crazy over it. I think we just cannot get on without it, can hope for no progress. It is for this reason that I urge its claims wherever I go. Seeing that my pleas have been of some avail here, I offer my thanks to you. Why should you thank me ? If, nonetheless, you do, I shall have no patience to hear what you say. I hope the various committees will carry out what they have been charged with. All obstacles must yield to determined human effort. I am sorry that, for want of time, I have not been able to meet the wishes of the audience for a long speech. I thank you all, sisters and brothers.

Only if I die for India shall I know that I was fit to live.

[*From Gujarati*]
Gujarati, 28-10-1917

---

1. This was delivered on the second day of the Second Gujarat Educational Conference.
2. Liberation as goal of life.

16. Swaraj Being Late

SPEECH AT GUJARATI POLITICAL CONFERENCE—I[1]

[Godhra
November 3, 1917]

Lokamanya B.G. Tilak[2] having arrived late for the opening session, Gandhiji remarked:,

I am not responsible for his being late. We demand *swaraj*. If one does not mind arriving late by three-quarters of an hour at a conference summoned for the purpose, one should not mind if *swaraj* too comes correspondingly late.

Gandhiji then read his speech.[3]

BROTHERS AND SISTERS,

I am thankful to you all for the exalted position to which you have called me. I am but a baby of two years and a half in Indian politics.[4] I cannot trade here on my experience in South Africa. I know that, in these circumstances, acceptance of the position is to a certain extent an impertinence. I have accepted it, all the same, unable to resist the pressure of your overwhelming affection.

I am conscious of my responsibility. This Conference is the first of its kind in Gujarat. The time is most critical for the whole of India.

The Empire is labouring under a strain never before experienced.

---

1. This was Gandhiji's presidential address at the first Political Conference to be held in Gujarat. It lasted three days and was largely attended by cultivators, petty traders and small land-holders.
2. Bal Gangadhar Tilak (1856-1920); great Indian political leader, scholar and writers popularly known as 'Lokamanya'; one of the founders of the Deccan Education Society, Poona and of the newspapers the *Kesari* and the *Mahratta*; suffered six years' deportation for his criticism of the Government; took active part in the Home Rule campaign.
3. The translation which follows is reproduced from Speeches and Writings of Mahatma Gandhi, with some changes intended to bring it into closer conformity with the Gujarati original.
4. Gandhiji had returned to India on January 9, 1915.

My views do not quite take the general course. I feel that some of them run in the opposite direction. Under the circumstances, I am hardly qualified for this privileged position. The president of a meeting is usually its spokesman. I cannot pretend to lay any such claim. It is your kindness that gives me such a unique opportunity of placing my thoughts before the Gujarat public. I do not see anything wrong in these views being subjected to criticism, dissent and even emphatic protest. I would like them to be freely discussed. I will only say with regard to them that they were not formed today or yesterday. But they were formed years ago. I am enamoured of them, and my Indian experience of two years and a half has not altered them.

I congratulate the originators of the proposal to hold this conference as also those friends who have given practical shape to it.

It is a most important event for Gujarat. It is possible for us to make it yield very valuable results. This conference is in the nature of a foundation, and if it is well and truly laid, we need have no anxiety as to the superstructure. Being in the nature of a foundation, it carries a heavy responsibility. I pray that God may bless us with wisdom and that our deliberations will benefit the people.

This is a political conference. Let us pause a moment over the word "political". It is, as a rule, used in a restricted sense, but I believe it is better to give it a wider meaning. If the work of such a conference were to be confined to a consideration of the relations between the rulers and the ruled, it would not only be incomplete, but we should even fail to have an adequate conception of those relations.

For instance, the question of *mahwa* flowers[1] is of great importance for a part of Gujarat. If it is considered merely as a question between the Government and the people, it might have unhappy consequences or we might fail in our aim. If we considered the genesis of the law on *mahwa* flowers and also appreciated our duty as individuals in this matter, we would, very probably, succeed sooner in our fight with the Government than otherwise and easily discover the key to successful agitation. You will more clearly perceive my interpretation of the word "political" in the light of the views I shall place before you.

Conferences do not, as a rule at the end of their deliberations, leave behind them an executive body, and even when such a body is appointed,

1. Used for preparing a sort of country liquor

it is, to use the language of the late Mr. Gokhale[1], composed of men who are amateurs; What we need is men who would make it their business to give effect to the resolutions of such conferences. If such men come forward in great numbers, then and then only will such conferences be a credit to the country and produce lasting results. At present there is much waste of energy. It is desirable that there should be many institutions of the type of the Servants of India Society. Only when men, fired with the belief that service is the highest religion, come forward in great numbers, could we hope to see great results. Fortunately, India is richly endowed with the religious spirit, and if it is realized that in the present age service of the motherland is the best religion, religiously inclined men and women would take part in public life in larger numbers. When sages and saints take up this work, I believe India will achieve her cherished aims quite easily. At all events, it is incumbent on us that, for the purposes of this conference, we form an executive committee whose business it would be to enforce its resolutions.

The air in the country is thick with cries of *swaraj*. It is due to Mrs. Besant[2] that *swaraj* is on the lips of hundreds of thousands of men and women. What was unknown to most men and women only two years ago, has, by her consummate tact and her indefatigable efforts, become common property for them.

There cannot be the slightest doubt that her name will take the first rank in history among those who inspired us with the hope that *swaraj* was attainable at no distant date. *Swaraj* was, and is, the goal of the Congress. The idea did not originate with her.[3] But the credit of presenting it to us as a goal realizable in the immediate future belongs to

---

1. Gopal Krishna Gokhale (1866-1915); Indian leader. patriot and politician; was associated with the Indian National Congress since its inception. and presided over its Benares Session in 1905; founded the Servants of India Society at Poona to train men prepared to dedicate their lives to the cause of the country in a religious spirit; visited South Africa in 1912 at Gandhiji's invitation.
2. Annie Besant (1847-1933); British theosophist, orator and writer; founded the Theosophical Society in 1907; established the Indian Home Rule League in 1916; presided over the Indian National Congress in 1917, edited a daily, *New India*, and The Commonweal, a weekly; author of *The Religious Problem in India* and other books.
3. Gandhiji evidently had in mind, Dadabhai Naoroji who, in 1906, first used the word *swaraj* to define the goal of the Indian National Congress at its Calcutta Session.

that lady alone. For that we could hardly thank her enough. By releasing her and her associates, Messrs Arundale[1] and Wadia[2], Government have laid us under an obligation, and at the same time acknowledged the just and reasonable nature of the agitation for *swaraj*.[3] It is to be wished that the Government extend the same generosity towards our brothers, Mahomed Ali[4] and Shaukat Ali[5]. It is not necessary to inquire how much of what Sir William Vincent[6] has said about them needs to be looked into. It is to be hoped that the Government will accede to the people's desire for their release and leave it to them to see that no untoward results follow. This will place the people under a still greater obligation. The act of generosity will be incomplete so long as these brothers are not released. The grant of freedom to the brothers will gladden the people's hearts and endear the Government to them.[7]

Mr. Montagu will shortly be in our midst. The work of taking signatures to the petition[8] to be submitted to him is going on apace.

The chief object of this petition is to educate the people about *swaraj*.

---

1. G. S. Arundale was the head of the Society for the Promotion of National Education organized by Annie Besant. He took active part in the Home Rule movement and suffered internment.
2. B. P. Wadia organized the Home Rule League and took active part in Home Rule movement.
3. Mrs. Besant and her associates had been interned at Coimbatore and Ootacamand on June 15, 1917. They were released on September 16 in pursuance of the new British policy embodied in the Montagu declaration of August 20.
4. Editor of *The Comrade*, an English weekly; was imprisoned, soon after the out-break of World War, for publishing an article entitled "Evacuate Egypt"; along with his brother, he was interned in October 1914; attended the second Round Table Conference in London.
5. Editor of *Hamdard*, suffered internment along with his younger brother, Mahomed Ali.
6. Sir William Henry Hoare Vincent; distinguished Indian Civil Servant; Member of the Executive Council of the Governor-General of India, 1917; Member of the India Council, 1923-31
7. The Ali brothers were finally released on December 25, 1919, under the amnesty granted by the Royal Proclamation.
8. The reference is to the Home-Rule Petition; *vide* "Petition to E.S.Montagu", Before 13-9-1917 A memorandum was also presented by a joint Congress-League deputation to Montagu and Lord Chelmsford on November 26; vide Appendix "*Congress-League Address*", 26-11-1917.

To say that literacy is essential for achieving *swaraj* betrays ignorance of history. It is not necessary for the purpose of inculcating among people the idea that we ought to manage our own affairs. What is essential is the idea, the desire itself. Hundreds of unlettered kings have ruled kingdoms with great success. To see how far such an idea exists in the minds of the people and to try to create it where it is absent is the object of this petition. It is desirable that millions of men and women should sign it with the fullest understanding of what it means. That such a largely signed petition will naturally have its due weight with Mr. Montagu is its natural result.

No one has the right to alter the scheme of reforms[1] approved by the Congress and the Moslem League, and one need not, therefore, go into the merits thereof. For our present purposes, we have to understand thoroughly the scheme formulated most thoughtfully by our leaders and, putting our faith in them, do whatever is necessary to get it implemented.

This scheme is not *swaraj*, but is a great step towards *swaraj*.

Some English critics tell us that we are not fit to enjoy *swaraj*, because the class that demands it is incapable of defending India. "Is the defence of India to rest with the British alone?" they ask, "and are the reins of Government to be in the hands of the Indians ?" Now this is a question which is both amusing and painful. It is amusing because our British friends fancy that they are not of us, whilst our plan of *swaraj* is based upon retention of the British connection. We do not want the Englishmen who have settled here to leave this country. They will be our partners in *swaraj*. And they will have nothing to complain about if, in such a scheme, the burden of the defence of the country falls on them. They are, however, hasty in assuming that we shall not do our share of defending the country. When India decides to acquire military strength, she will attain it in no time. We have but to harden our feelings to be able to strike. To cultivate a hardened feeling does not take ages. It grows like weeds. The question is painful, because it puts in mind the fact that the

---

1. This scheme of political reforms was originally drawn up and published, towards the end of 1916, by 19 members of the Imperial Legislative Council. Briefly, it sought to subordinate the Executive to the Legislature. The scheme came up for discussion at the sessions of the Indian National Congress and the Muslim League at Lucknow in December 1916. Elaborated and revised, the scheme, as accepted by both bodies in the wake of the Lucknow Pact, provided for the creation of a non-official majority in the Legislative Councils. *Vide* "The Congress-League Scheme",

Government have up to now debarred us from military training. Had they been so minded, they would have had at their disposal today, from among the educated classes, quite a large army. Government have to accept a larger measure of blame than the educated classes for the latter having taken little part in the War. Had the Government policy been shaped differently from the very beginning, they would have today an unconquerable army. But let no one be blamed for the present situation. At the time the British rule was established, it was considered a wise policy for the governance of crores of men to deprive them of arms and military training. But it is never too late to mend, and both the rulers and the ruled must immediately repair the omission.

In offering these views I have assumed the propriety of the current trend of thought. To me, however, it does not appear to be tending altogether in the right direction. Our agitation is based on the Western model. The *swaraj* we desire is of a Western type. As a result of it, India will have to enter into competition with the Western nations. Many believe that there is no escape from this. I do not think so. I cannot forget that India is not Europe, India is not Japan, India is not China. The divine word that "India alone is the land of *karma*[1], the rest is the land of *bhoga* (enjoyment)," is indelibly imprinted on my mind. I feel that India's mission is different from that of other countries. India is fitted for the religious supremacy of the world.

There is no parallel in the world for the *tapascharya* that this country has voluntarily gone through. India has little use for steel weapons; it has fought with divine weapons; it can still do so. Other nations have been votaries of brute force. The terrible war going on in Europe furnishes an irrefutable proof of this. India can conquer all by soul force.

History supplies numerous instances to prove that brute force is nothing before soul-force. Poets have sung of this and men of wisdom have said so. A thirty-year old youth behaves like a lamb before his eighty-year old father. This is an instance of love-force. Love is *atman*[2]: it is the very property of *atman*. If we have faith enough, we can wield that force over the whole world. Religion having lost its hold on us, we are without an anchor to keep us firm amidst the storm of modern

1. Action in pursuance of one's duty.
2. The self unidentifiable with any aspect of human individuality, the soul though growing its own cotton, has to pay crores of rupees to outsiders for its cloth, cannot be otherwise than poor.

civilization, and are, therefore, being tossed to and fro. I shall return to this idea at a later stage.

These views of mine notwithstanding, I have joined the *swaraj* movement, for India is being governed at present under a modern system. The Government themselves believe that the "Parliament" is the best form of that system. Without such a parliament, we should have neither the modern nor the ancient form. Mrs. Besant is only too true when she says that we shall soon be facing a hunger-strike, if we do not have Home Rule. I do not want to go into statistics. The evidence of my eyes is enough for me. Poverty in India is deepening day by day. No other result is possible. A country that exports its raw produce and imports it back as finished goods. A country, in which it is considered extravagance to spend on marriages, etc., can only be described as poor. It must be a terribly poor country that cannot afford to spend enough in carrying out improvements for stamping out epidemics like the plague. In a country whose officials spend most of their earnings outside, the people are bound to grow poorer day by day. What are we to say of the poverty of a country whose people, during cold weather, burn their precious manure for want of woollen clothing in order to warm themselves? Throughout my wanderings in India I have rarely, seen a face exuding strength and joy. The middle classes are groaning under the weight of awful distress. The lowest orders have nothing but the earth below and the sky above. They do not know a bright day. It is pure fiction to say that India's riches are buried underground, or are to be found in her ornaments. What there is of such riches is of no consequence. The nation's expenditure has increased, not so its income. Government have not deliberately brought about this state of things. I believe that their intentions are sincere. It is their honest opinion that the nation's prosperity is daily growing. Their faith in their Blue-books is immovable. It is only too true that statistics can be made to prove anything. The economists deduce India's prosperity from statistics.

People like me who follow rough and ready ways of reckoning shake their heads over Blue-book statistics. If the gods were to come down and testify otherwise, I would insist on saying that I see India growing poorer.

What then would our Parliament do if we had one? When we have it, we would have a right to commit blunders and to correct them.

In the early stages we are bound to make blunders. But, we, being children of the soil, won't lose time in setting ourselves right. We shall, therefore, soon find out remedies against poverty. Then our existence won't be dependent on Lancashire goods. Then we shall not be found spending untold riches on building Imperial Delhi. It will, then, be in keeping with the cottages of India. There will be some proportion observed between that cottage and our Parliament House. The nation today is in a helpless condition; it does not possess even the right to err. He who has no right to err can never go forward. The history of the Commons is a history of blunders. Man, says an Arabian proverb, is error personified. The freedom to err and the power to correct errors is one definition of *swaraj*. Having a parliament means such *swaraj*.

We ought to have Parliament this very day. We are quite fit for it. We shall, therefore, get it on demand. It rests with us to define "this very day".

Swaraj is not to be attained through an appeal to the British democracy, the British people. They cannot appreciate such an appeal

Its reply will be: "We never sought outside help to obtain *swaraj*. We achieved it with our own strength. You have not received it because you do not deserve it. When you do, nobody can withhold it from you."

How then shall we fit ourselves for it? We have to demand *swaraj* from our own people. Our appeal must be to them. When the peasantry of India understands what *swaraj* is, the demand will become irresistible.

The late Sir W.W. Hunters[1] said that, in the British system, victory on the battle field was the shortest way to one's goal. If educated India had, silently, taken its full share in the present War, I am certain that we would not only have reached our goal already, but the manner of it would have been altogether unique.

We often refer to the fact that many sepoys of Hindustan have lost their lives on the battle fields of France and Mesopotamia. The educated classes cannot claim the credit for this. They were not sent out by us, nor did they join up through patriotism. They know nothing of *swaraj*. At the end of the War they will not ask for it. They have gone to demonstrate that they are faithful to the salt they eat. In asking for *swaraj*, I feel that it is not possible for us to bring into account their services. The only thing we can say is that we are not to blame for not being able to take a big part in the prosecution of the War.

---

1. Sir William Wilson Hunter (1840-1900); Indian administrator and member of British Committee of the Indian National Congress ; *vide* Vol . "*Speech at London Farewell* ", 29- 11-1906 and "Letter to Lord Ampthill", 4-8-1909.

That we have been loyal at a time of stress is no test of fitness for *swaraj*. Loyalty is no merit. It is a necessity of national existence all the world over. That loyalty can be no passport to *swaraj* is a self demonstrated maxim.

Our fitness lies in that we now keenly desire *swaraj*, and in our clearly realizing that bureaucracy, although it has served India with best intentions, has had its day. And this kind of fitness is sufficient for our purpose. Without *swaraj* there is now no possibility of peace in India.

But if we confine our activities for advancing *swaraj* only to holding meetings, the nation is likely to suffer harm. Meetings and speeches have their own place and time. But they cannot make a nation.

In a nation fired with the zeal for *swaraj*, we should observe an awakening in all departments of life. The first step to *swaraj* lies in the individual. The great truth, "As with the individual, so with the Universe," is applicable here as elsewhere. If we are ever torn by conflict from within, if we are ever going astray, and if instead of ruling our passions we allow them to rule us, *swaraj* can have no meaning for us. Government of self, then, is the first step.

Then the family. If dissensions reign supreme in our families, if brothers fight among themselves, if members of a family cannot live together; if joint families, i.e., families enjoying self-government, become divided through family quarrels, how can we be considered fit for *swaraj* ?

Now for caste. If caste fellows become jealous of one another, if the castes cannot manage their affairs in an orderly manner, if the elders claim especial importance, if the members become self opinionated and thus show their unfitness for self-government in this limited sphere, how can they be fit for national government ?

After caste, the city. If we cannot regulate the affairs of our cities, if our streets are not kept clean, if our homes are dilapidated and if our roads are crooked, if we cannot command the services of selfless citizens for civic government, and those who are in charge of affairs are neglectful or selfish, how shall we claim larger powers?

The way to national life lies through the cities. It is, therefore, necessary to linger a little longer on this subject. The plague has found a home in India.[1] Cholera has been always with us. Malaria takes an annual toll of thousands. The plague has been driven out from every

1. Plague appeared in a serious form in 1917 and, between July of that year and June 1918, accounted for over 8,00,000 deaths.

other part of the world. Glasgow stamped it out the moment it made its appearance there. In Johannesburg it could appear but once.[1] Its municipality made a great effort and stamped it out within a month, whereas we are able to do nothing about it. We cannot blame the Government for this state of things. To tell the truth, we cannot even blame it on our poverty. None can stand in our way in any remedies that we may wish to adopt. Ahmedabad, for instance, cannot evade responsibility by pleading poverty. I am afraid that in regard to the plague, we must shoulder the entire responsibility. It is very significant that when the plague is working havoc in our rural quarters, cantonments as a rule remain free. The reasons are obvious. In the cantonments the air is pure, houses detached, roads are wide and clean and the sanitary habits of the residents wholesome, whereas ours are as unhygienic as they well could be. Our closets are as filthy as hell. In a country in which ninety per cent of the population go barefoot, people spit anywhere and perform natural functions anywhere and we are obliged to walk on roads and paths thus dirtied. It is no wonder that the plague has found a home in our midst.

Unless we alter the conditions in our cities, rid ourselves of our dirty habits and have improved latrines, *swaraj* can have no value for us.

It will not be out of place here to refer to another matter. We regard men who render us most useful service, *Bhangis*, as untouchables. The result has been that we let them clean only a part of our closets. In the name of religion, we ourselves would not clean the places for fear of pollution and so, despite our reputation for personal cleanliness, a portion of our houses remains the dirtiest in the world, with the result that we grow up in an air which is laden with disease germs. We were safe so long as we kept to our villages. But in the cities we are ever committing suicide by reason of our insanitary habits.

Where large numbers suffer living death, it is very likely that people know neither true religion nor right action and conduct. I believe that it ought not to be beyond us to banish the plague from India, and if we can do so, we shall have so increased our fitness for *swaraj*, as it cannot be by any agitation, howsoever powerful. This is a question meriting the serious consideration of our doctors and *vaidyas*[2].

---

1. In 1904; *vide* "Plague in Johannesburg", 9-4-1904 , "*The Plague*", 2-4-1904 and "*History of the Plague in Johannesburg*", 28-10-1905, Vol. 16 : 1 September, 1917 - 23 April, 1918, 121.
2. Physicians practising Ayurveda, an indigenous system of medicine.

Not far from here is the holy centre of pilgrimage, Dakor. I have visited it. Its unholiness is limitless. I consider myself a devout Vaishnava[1]. I claim, therefore, a special privilege of criticising the condition of Dakorji. The insanitation of that place is so great that one used to hygienic conditions can hardly bear to pass even twenty-four hours there. The pilgrims pollute the tank and the streets as they choose. The keepers of the shrine quarrel among themselves and, to add insult to injury, a receiver has been appointed to take charge of the jewellery and costly robes of the idol. It is our clear duty to set matters right. How shall we, Gujaratis, out to have *swaraj*, fare as soldiers in the army fighting for it, if we cannot put our own house in order?

To think of the state of education in our cities also fills us with despair. It is plainly our duty by our own effort to provide education to the masses. But our gaze is fixed upon Government, whilst thousands of children go without education.

In the cities the drink-evil is on the increase, tea shops are multiplying, gambling is rampant. If we cannot remedy these evils, how can we attain *swaraj* ? *Swaraj* means managing our own affairs.

We are approaching a time when we and our children may have to go without milk altogether. Dairies, here in Gujarat, are doing us infinite harm. They buy out practically the whole milk-supply and produce butter, cheese, etc., for sale. How can a nation whose nourishment is chiefly derived from milk permit itself to be deprived of this important article of food? How can men be so selfish as to be heedless of the national health and think of enriching themselves through commercial exploitation of an article of diet ? Milk and its products are of such paramount value to the nation that they deserve to be controlled by the municipalities. What are we doing about them?

I have just returned from the scene of Bakr-i-Id riots. For a trivial cause, the two communities fell out with each other, mischievous men joined in the fray and a mere spark became a blaze. We found ourselves helpless. We have been obliged to depend entirely upon Government assistance. This shows how crippled we are.

It will not be inopportune to dwell for a moment on the question of cow protection. It is an important question. And yet it is left to be solved by cow protection societies. Protecting the cows seems to be an ancient practice. It originated in the special needs of this country.

---

1. Devotee of Vishnu, one of the Hindu Trinity, and His incarnation, Krishna; a follower of the *bhakti* or devotional cult.

Protection of its cows is incumbent upon a country 90 per cent. Of whose population lives upon agriculture and needs bullocks for it. In such a country, even meat-eaters should abstain from beef-eating.

These natural causes should be enough justification for not killing cows. But here we have to face a peculiar situation. The chief meaning of cow protection seems to be to prevent cows from falling into the hands of our Muslim brethren and being used as food. The rulers need beef. On their account thousands of cows are slaughtered daily.

We do nothing to prevent this slaughter. We hardly make any attempt to prevent the cruel torture of cows by certain Hindus of Calcutta, who subject them to a practice known as "blowing" and make them yield the last drop of milk. In Gujarat, Hindu cart-drivers use sharp goads to drive bullocks. We say nothing about this. The condition of bullocks in our cities is pitiable. Indeed, protection of the cow and her progeny is a very great problem. By making it a pretext for quarrelling with the Muslims, we have only ensured greater slaughter of cows. It is not religion, but want of it, to kill a Muslim brother in order to save a cow. I feel sure that if we were to discuss the matter with our Muslim brethren in the spirit of love, they also would appreciate the peculiar condition of India and readily co-operate with us in the protection of cows. By courtesy and through *Satyagraha*, we can bring them to join that mission. But, in order to be able to do this, we shall have to understand the question in its true bearing. Instead of killing our brethren, we should be ready to die ourselves. But we shall be able to do this only when we understand the real value of the cow and have pure love for her. Success in this will ensure several things simultaneously. Hindus and Muslims will live in peace, the cow will be safe, milk and its products will be available in a pure condition and will be cheaper than now, and our bullocks will become the envy of the world. If our *Tapascharya* is pure, we shall succeed in stopping slaughter of cows, whether by the British, Muslims or Hindus. Even this one achievement will bring *swaraj* nearer.

Many of these issues arise out of civic government. We can clearly see from this that our running the Government of India is dependent upon our upright management of civic affairs.

It will not be incorrect to say that practically there is no *swadeshi* movement in the country. We do not realize that this movement almost holds the key to *swaraj*. If we have no regard for our own language, if we feel aversion to cloth made in our country, if our dress repels us, if we are ashamed to wear the sacred shikha[1], if our food is distasteful to us, even our climate is not good enough, our people uncouth and unfit for our company, our civilization ugly and the foreign attractive, in short, if everything native is bad and everything foreign pleasing to us, I do not know what *swaraj* can mean for us. If everything foreign is to be adopted, surely it will be necessary for us to continue long under foreign tutelage, for so far foreign ways have touched the masses but little. It seems to me that, before we can appreciate *swaraj*, we should have not only love but passion for *swadeshi*. Every act of ours should bear the *swadeshi* stamp. Swaraj can only be built upon the assumption that most of what is national is, on the whole, sound. If the view here put forth be correct, we should have a big movement in our country for *swadeshi*. Every country that has carried on a movement for *swaraj* has fully appreciated the *swadeshi* spirit. Scottish Highlanders hold on to their kilts even at the risk of their lives. We humorously call them the "petticoat brigade".

But the whole world testifies to the strength that lies behind that "petticoat" and the Highlanders of Scotland will not abandon it, even though it is an inconvenient dress, and an easy target for the enemy. I don't wish to suggest that we should treasure our faults, but that what is national, even though not rich in excellences, should be adhered to, and that what is foreign should be avoided though one may succeed well enough in adopting it. That which is wanting in our civilization can be supplied by proper effort on our part. I do hope that the *swadeshi* spirit will possess every member in this assembly; if they all take the vow of *swadeshi* and observe it in the face of any difficulty or inconvenience, *swaraj* will be easy of attainment.

The foregoing illustrations go to show that our movement should be twofold. We may petition the Government, we may agitate in the Imperial Council for our rights; but for a real awakening of the people, the more important thing is activities directed inwards. There is a possibility of hypocrisy and selfishness tainting activities directed outwards. There is very much less danger of this in activities of the other kind. Not only will the former not be justified unless balanced

One sometimes hears it said, "Let us get the government of India in our own hands; everything will be all right afterwards."

---

1. Tuft of hair at the back of the head kept by orthodox Hindus by the latter, they may even be barren of results. It is not my contention that we have no activities at all directed inward, but I submit that we do not lay enough stress upon them.

There could be no greater superstition than this. No nation has gained its independence in this manner. The splendour of the spring is reflected in every tree, the whole earth is then filled with the freshness of youth. Similarly, when the spring of *swaraj* is on us, a stranger suddenly arriving in our midst will observe the freshness of youth in every walk of life and find servants of the people engaged, each according to his own abilities, in all manner of public activities.

If we admit that our progress has not been what it might have been, we should also admit two reasons for this. We have kept our women away from these activities of ours and have thus become victims of a kind of paralysis. The nation walks with one leg only. All its work appears to be only half or incompletely done. Moreover, the educated section, having received its education through a foreign tongue, has become enervated and is unable to give the nation the benefit of such ability as it acquires. I need not reiterate my views on this subject, as I have elaborated them in my address[1] at the Gujarat Educational Conference. It is a wise decision, that of conducting the proceedings of this conference in Gujarati, and I hope that nothing will induce the people of Gujarat to change it.

The educated class, lovers of *swaraj*, must freely mix with the masses. We dare not turn away from a single section of the community or disown any. We shall make progress only if we carry all with us. Had the educated class identified itself with the masses, Bakr-i-Id riots would have been an impossibility. Before coming to the last topic, it remains for me to refer to certain events as a matter of duty and to make one or two suggestions. Every year the god of death exacts his toll from among our leaders. I do not intend to mention the victims claimed by this god all over India during the last 12 months. But it is impossible to omit reference to the sage-like Grand Old Man[2] of India. Who am I to estimate the value of his services to the country? I am no more than one who sat at his feet. I paid my respects to him when I went to London as a mere lad. I came to revere him from the very moment I waited upon him with a letter of introduction.[3] Dadabhai's flawless and uninterrupted service to the country, his impartiality, his spotless character, will always furnish India with an ideal to follow. May God give him peace ! May He

1. *Vide* "Speech at Second Gujarat Educational Conference", 20-10-1917.
2. Dadabhai Naoroji (1825-1917).
3. Gandhiji sought his counsel and help during his public life in South Africa. *Vide An Autobiography*, Part I, Ch. XXV.

grant his family and the Nation the ability to bear the loss. We can immortalize him by making his character our own, by copying his manner of service and by enthroning him forever in our hearts. May the great soul of Dadabhai watch over our deliberations !

It is our duty to express our thanks to His Excellency the Viceroy for having announced the decision of the Government of India to abolish the customs levy on the border [between Saurashtra and British Indian territory] at Viramgam. This step should have been taken earlier. The people were groaning under the weight of this impost. It cost large numbers their trade. It has caused much suffering to many women. The decision does not seem to have been brought into effect. It is to be hoped that it will soon be.

I have submitted through the Press my experiences about the hardships of third class railway passengers.[1] They are, indeed, past endurance. The people of India are docile and trained in silent suffering. Thousands, therefore, put up with the hardships, but they remain unredressed. There is, indeed, merit in such suffering, but it must have its limits. Submission out of weakness is unmanliness. That we tamely put up with the hardships of railway travelling is a sign of our unmanliness. These hardships are of two kinds, those which are due to the remissness of railway administration and those occasioned by the carelessness of the travelling public. The remedies are also, therefore, twofold. Where the railway administration is to blame, complaints should be addressed to it by everyone who suffers. This may be done even in Gujarati. The matter should be ventilated in the Press. Secondly, where the public are to blame, the wiser among passengers should inculcate manners upon their ignorant companions and enlighten them on their carelessness and dirty habits. This will require volunteers. Everyone can do his share according to his ability, and leaders might, in order to appreciate the difficulties of thirdclass travelling, resort to it from time to time without making themselves known and bring their unhappy experiences to the notice of the administration. If these remedies are adopted, we should, in a short time, see great changes.

A committee had been appointed in London to consider certain measures about the supply of indentured labour to Fiji and the other sister islands. The views of that committee have been officially published and the Government of India have invited the opinion of the public upon

---

1. Vide "Letter to the Press on Third Class Travelling on Indian Railways", 25-9-1917.

them. I need not dwell at length upon the matter as I have submitted my views already through the Press. I have given it as my opinion that the recommendations of the committee, if adopted, will result in a kind of indenture. We can, therefore, only come to one conclusion. We do not want to see labourers emigrating under bondage in any shape or form. There is no need for such emigration.

The only thing required is a complete repeal of the law of indenture.

It is no part of our duty to look to the convenience of the Colonies.

I come now to the last subject. There are two methods of attaining one's goal. *Satyagraha*[1] and *Duragraha*[2]. In our scriptures, they have been described, respectively, as divine and devilish modes of action. In *satyagraha*, there is always unflinching adherence to truth. It is never to be forsaken on any account. Even for the sake of one's country, it does not permit resort to falsehood. It proceeds on the assumption of the ultimate triumph of truth. A *Satyagrahi* does not abandon his path, even though at times it seems impenetrable and beset with difficulties and dangers, and a slight departure from that straight path may appear full of promise. Even in these circumstances, his faith shines resplendent like the midday sun and he does not despond. With truth for sword, he needs neither a steel sword nor gunpowder.

Even an inveterate enemy he conquers by the force of the soul, which is love. Love for a friend is not put to the test. There is nothing surprising in a friend loving a friend; there is no merit in it and it costs no effort. When love is bestowed on the so-called enemy, it is tested, it becomes a virtue and requires an effort, and hence it is an act of manliness and real bravery. We can cultivate such an attitude

Love can fight; often, it is obliged to. In the intoxication of power, man fails to see his error. When that happens, a *satyagrahi* does not sit

---

1. Literally, "holding to truth", pursuit of a right cause, a method of political agitation which found expression later in successive civil disobedience campaigns in India.
2. Pursuit of a wrong cause or in a manner unworthy of the cause even towards the Government and, doing so, we shall be able to appreciate their beneficial activities and, as for their errors, rather than feel bitter on their account, point them out in love and so get them rectified. Love does not act through fear. Weakness there certainly cannot be. A coward is incapable of bearing love, it is the prerogative of the brave. Looking at everything with love, we shall not regard the Government with suspicion, nor believe that all their actions are inspired with bad motives. And our examination of their actions, being directed by love, will be unerring and is bound, therefore, to carry conviction with them.

still. He suffers. He disobeys the ruler's orders and his laws in a civil manner, and willingly submits to the penalties of such disobedience, for instance, imprisonment and gallows. Thus is the soul disciplined. In this, one never finds that one's time has been wasted and, if it is subsequently realized that such respectful disobedience was an error, the consequences are suffered merely by the *satyagrahi* and his co-workers. In the event, no bitterness develops between the *satyagrahi* and those in power; the latter, on the contrary, willingly yield to him. They discover that they cannot command the *satyagrahi's* obedience. They cannot make him do anything against his will. And this is the consummation of *swaraj*, because it means complete independence. It need not be assumed that such resistance is possible only against civilized rulers. Even a heart of flint will melt in the fire kindled by the power of the soul. Even a Nero becomes a lamb when he faces love. This is no exaggeration. It is as true as an algebraic equation. This *satyagraha* is India's distinctive weapon. It has had others but *satyagraha* has been in greater use. It is an unfailing source of strength, and is capable of being used at all times and under all circumstances. It requires no stamp of approval from the Congress or any other body. He who knows its power cannot but use it. Even as the eyelashes automatically protect the eyes, so does *satyagraha*, when kindled, automatically protect the freedom of the soul.

But *duragraha* is a force with the opposite attributes. As we saw earlier, the terrible War going on in Europe is a case in point. Why should a nation's cause be considered right and another's wrong because it overpowers the latter by sheer brute force? The strong are often seen preying upon the weak. The wrongness of the latter's cause is not to be inferred from their defeat in a trial of brute strength, nor is the rightness of the strong to be inferred from their success in such a trial. The wielder of brute force does not scruple about the means to be used. He does not question the propriety of means, if he can somehow achieve his purpose. This is not *dharma* but the opposite of it. In *dharma*, there can be no room for even a particle of untruth or cruelty, and no injury to life. The measure of *dharma* is love, compassion, truth. Heaven itself, if attained through sacrifice of these, is to be despised. *Swaraj* is useless at the sacrifice of truth. Such *swaraj* will ultimately ruin the people. The man who follows the path of *duragraha* becomes impatient and wants to kill the so-called enemy.

There can be but one result of this. Hatred increases. The defeated party vows vengeance and simply bides its time. The spirit of revenge thus descends from father to son. It is much to be wished that India never gives predominance to this spirit of *duragraha*. If the members of this assembly deliberately accept *satyagraha* and chalk out its programme accordingly, they will reach their goal all the more easily for doing so. They may have to face disappointment in the initial stages. They may not see results for a time. But *satyagraha* will triumph in the end. The *duragrahi*, like the oilman's ox, moves in a circle. His movement is only motion but it is not progress. The *satyagrahi* is ever moving forward.

A superficial critic of my views may find some contradiction in them. On the one hand, I appeal to the Government to give military training to the people. On the other, I put *satyagraha* on the pedestal.

Surely, there can be no room for the use of arms in *satyagraha*? Of course there is none. But military training is intended for those who do not believe in *satyagraha*. That the whole of India will ever accept *satyagraha* is beyond my imagination. A cowardly refusal to defend the nation, or the weak, is ever to be shunned. In order to protect an innocent woman from the brutal design of a man, we ought to offer ourselves a willing sacrifice and by the force of love conquer the brute in the man. Lacking such strength, we should employ all our physical strength to frustrate those designs. The *satyagrahi* and the *duragrahi* are both warriors. The latter, bereft of his arms, acknowledges defeat, the former never. He does not depend upon the perishable body and its weapons, but he fights on with the strength of the unconquerable and immortal *atman*. Anyone who is neither of the two is not a man, for he does not recognize the *atman*. If he did, he would not take fright and run away from danger. Like a miser his wealth, he tries to save his body and loses all; such a one does not know how to die. But the armoured soldier always has death by him as a companion. There is hope of his becoming one day a *satyagrahi*. The right thing to hope from India is that this great and holy Aryan land will ever give the predominant place to the divine force and employ the weapon of *satyagraha*, that it will never accept the supremacy of armed strength.

India will never respect the principle of might being right. She will ever reserve her allegiance to the principle: "Truth alone triumphs."

On reflection, we find that we can employ *satyagraha* even for social reform. We can rid ourselves of the many defects of our caste system. We can resolve Hindu-Muslim differences and can solve political problems. It is all right that, for the sake of convenience, we speak of these things as separate subjects. But it should never be forgotten that they are all closely inter-related. It is not true to say that neither religion nor social reform has anything to do with politics.

The result obtained by bringing religion into play in the field of politics will be different from that obtained otherwise. When thinking of political matters, we cannot ignore 56,000 ignorant *sadhus* living as wandering mendicants. Our Muslim brethren cannot lose sight of their *fakirs*. Nor can we be unmindful of the condition of our widows and the custom of child marriage and the Muslims of the custom of *purdah*. The two communities cannot, likewise, shut their eyes to scores of questions that arise between them.

Indeed, our difficulties are Himalayan. But we have equally potent means at our disposal for overcoming them. We are children of an ancient nation. We have witnessed the burial of civilizations: those of Rome, Greece and Egypt. Our civilization abides even as the ocean in spite of its ebbs and flows. We have all we need to keep ourselves independent. We have great mountains and rivers. We have the matchless beauty of nature, and the sons and daughters of this land have handed down to us a heritage of deeds of valour. This country is the treasure-house of *tapascharya*. In this country alone do people belonging to different religions live together in amity and the gods of all are venerated. If, despite all this bounty, we fail to work a miracle, bring peace to the world and conquer the British through the play of moral force in our life, we shall have disgraced our heritage. The English nation is full of adventure, the religious spirit guides it, it has unquenchable faith in itself, it is a nation of great soldiers, it treasures its independence; but it has given the place of honour to its commercial instinct, it has not always narrowly examined the means adopted for seeking wealth. It worships modern civilization. The ancient ideals have lost their hold upon it. If, therefore, instead of imitating that nation, we cherish our past and sincerely value our strength, trust firmly in its supremacy, we shall know how to take the best advantage of our connection with the British and so make it profitable to us, to them and to the entire world. I pray to the Almighty that this assembly may play its part in this great work and thereby shed lustre upon itself, upon Gujarat, and upon the whole of India.

[*From Gujarati*]
[*Mahatma Gandhini Vicharsrishti*]

17. Regeneration of Women

SPEECH AT BHAGINI SAMAJ, BOMBAY

[February 20, 1918]

DEAR SISTERS AND BROTHERS OF BHAGINI SAMAJ,

I am thankful to you for asking me to preside over this annual function of the Samaj. Your president, I really feel, should be a woman, though you may seek men's help or advice in your work. The Samaj is dedicated to the noble aim of women's regeneration and, in the same way that another's *tapascharya* does not help one to ascend to heaven, men cannot bring about the regeneration of women. I don't mean to suggest that men do not desire it, or that women would not want to have it through men's help; I merely wish to place before you the principle that it is only through self-help that an individual or a race can rise. This is not a new principle, but we often forget to act upon it.*

1. From Nadiad and Wednesday in the date-line as also from the contents; Gandhiji met the Kheda Collector on February 21, 1918 and was at Nadiad the previous day which was a Wednesday. *Vide* "Chronology".
2. Anasuya Sarabhai.
3. One word is illegible here.
4. Gandhiji presided over the annual gathering of the Bhagini Samaj, a women's welfare organization of Bombay, held in the Morarji Gokuldas Hall. The report of the speech in *The Hindu* is incomplete; the paragraphs not found in it are supplied here from the Gujarati report in *Mahatma Gandhini Vicharsrishti*, and marked by an asterisk.

The Samaj is at present kept going by the enthusiasm of Bhai Karsandas Chitalia. I am looking forward to a time when one of you will take his place and release him from this Samaj for other work.

Having dedicated his life wholly to the service of women, he will find out some work in the same field. The Samaj will come into its own when it elects its office-bearers from among its women members and gives a better account of itself than it does today. I have close associations, as you know, with both men and women, but I find that I can do nothing in the way of service to women without help from women workers. That is why I take every occasion to protest in no uncertain terms that, so long as women in India remain ever so little suppressed or do not have the same rights [as men], India will not make real progress. Hence it will be all to India's honour if this Samaj succeeds completely in its aims.*

It is necessary to understand what we mean when we talk of the regeneration of women. It presupposes degeneration and, if that is so, we should further consider what led to it and how. It is our primary duty to have some very hard thinking on these points. In travelling all over India, I have come to realize that all the existing agitation is confined to an infinitesimal section of our people who are really a mere speck in the vast firmament. Crores of people of both the sexes live in absolute ignorance of this agitation. Full eighty-five per cent of the people of this country pass their innocent days in a state of total detachment from what is going on around them. These men and women, ignorant as they are, do their bit in life well and properly.

Both have the same education or, rather, the absence of education, both are helping each other as they ought to do. If their lives are in any sense incomplete, the cause can be traced to the incompleteness of the lives of the remaining fifteen per cent. If my sisters of the Bhagini Samaj will make a close study of the lives of these 85 per cent of our people, it will provide them ample material for an excellent programme of work for the Samaj.

In the observations that I am going to make, I will confine myself to the 15 per cent above mentioned and, even then, it would be out of place to discuss the disabilities that are common both to men and women. The point for us to consider is the degeneration of our women relatively to our men. Legislation has been mostly the handiwork of men; and man has not always been fair and discriminate in performing that self-appointed task. What the authors of the various *smritis* have said about women can in no wise be defended. Child-marriage, the restrictions on widows and such other evils owe their origin to the injunctions in the *smritis*. Women's being placed on a level with *Sudras* has done unimaginable harm to Hindu society. These statements of mine may have verbal similarity with the occasional attacks of Christians, but, apart from this similarity, there is no other common ground between us. The

Christians, in their attacks, seek to strike at the roots of Hinduism. I look upon myself as an orthodox Hindu and my attack proceeds from the desire to rid Hinduism of its defects and restore it to its pristine glory. The Christian critic, by demonstrating the imperfection of the *smritis*, tries to show that they are just ordinary books. My attempt is to show that the imperfection of the *smritis* comes from interpolated passages, that is to say, verses inserted by persons accepted as *smritikaras*[1] in the period of our degeneration. It is easy to demonstrate the grandeur of the *smritis* minus these verses. I do not have the slightest desire to put up a weak defence of Hinduism, believing out of false pride or in ignorance, and wanting others to believe, that there is no error in the *smritis* or in the other accepted books of the Hindu religion. I am convinced that such an effort will not raise the Hindu religion but will degrade it rather. A religion which gives the foremost place to truth can afford no admixture of untruth.*

The largest part of our effort in promoting the regeneration of women should be directed towards removing those blemishes which are represented in our *shastras* as the necessary and ingrained characteristics of women. Who will attempt this and how ? In my humble opinion, in order to make the attempt we will have to produce women, pure, firm and self-controlled as Sita, Damayanti and Draupadi. If we do produce them, such modern sisters will receive the same homage from Hindu society as is being paid to their prototypes of yore. Their words will have the same authority as the *shastras*. We will feel ashamed of the stray reflections on them in our *smritis* and will soon forget them. Such revolutions have occurred in Hinduism in the past and will still take place in the future, leading to the stability of our faith. I pray to God that this *Samaj* might soon produce such women as I have described above.

We have now discussed the root cause of the degeneration of our women and have considered the ideals by the realization of which the present condition of our women can be improved. The number of women who can realize those ideals will be necessarily very few and, therefore, we will now consider what ordinary women can accomplish if they will try. Their first attempt should be directed towards awakening in the minds of as many women as possible a proper sense of their present condition. I am not among those who believe that such an effort can be made through literary education only. To work on that basis would be to postpone indefinitely the accomplishment of our aims ; I have

---

1. Authors of *smritis*.

experienced at every step that it is not at all necessary to wait so long. We can bring home to our women the sad realities of their present condition without, in the first instance, giving them any literary education.

I am just returning from a district of Bihar. I once met there a large group of women from respectable families of the place. They all observed *purdah*. In my presence, they removed the *purdah* as they would in the presence of a brother. These women had had no education. Just before I went to meet them, an English woman had been to see me. She had called on me where I sat surrounded by a number of men. To meet the Hindu women, on the other hand, I had to go into a room specially set apart. Half seriously, I suggested that we could go to the room where the men were sitting. All enthusiasm, they said that they would be only too happy to do so, but that the custom being what it was, they would need the men's permission.

They did not like the *purdah* at all [they said] and wanted me to see that the custom was ended. While there is tragedy in these words, they also bear out what I have said above. These women had realized their condition without having had any literary education. They were right in asking my help, but I wanted them to have the strength themselves to win their freedom and they admitted, too, that they had such strength. I have come away full of hope that we shall soon hear that these women have flung away the *purdah*. Women who would ordinarily be considered uneducated are doing excellent work in Champaran. They are waking up their extremely backward sisters to the freedom which they themselves enjoy.*

Woman is the companion of man, gifted with equal mental capacities. She has the right to participate in the very minute detail in the activities of man and she has an equal right of freedom and liberty with him. She is entitled to a supreme place in her own sphere of activity as man is in his. This ought to be the natural condition of things and not as a result only of learning to read and write. By sheer force of a vicious custom, even the most ignorant and worthless men have been enjoying a superiority over women which they do not deserve and ought not to have. Many of our movements stop half-way because of the condition of our women. Much of our work does not yield appropriate results ; our lot is like that of the penny wise and pound foolish trader who does not employ enough capital in his business.

If I am right, a good many from among you, members of this Samaj, should go out to educate your ignorant sisters about their real condition. In practical terms, this means that you should spare as much time as you can to visit the most backward localities in Bombay and give the women there what you have yourselves received. If you have joined men in their religious, political and social activities, acquaint them with these. If you have gained any special knowledge about the bringing up of children, impart it to them. If you have studied and realized in your own experience the benefits of clean air, clean water, clean and simple food, and exercise, tell these women about them too. In this way, you will raise yourselves and them.*

But although much good and useful work can be done without a knowledge of reading and writing, yet it is my firm belief that you cannot always do without a knowledge thereof. It develops and sharpens one's intellect and it stimulates our power of doing good. I have never placed an unnecessarily high value on the knowledge of reading and writing. I am only attempting to assign its proper place to it. I have pointed out from time to time [that] there is no justification for men to deprive women or to deny to them equal rights on the grounds of their illiteracy ; but education is essential for enabling women to uphold these natural rights, to improve them and to spread them; again, the true knowledge of self is unattainable by the millions who are without such education. Many a book is full of innocent pleasure and this will be denied to us without education. It is no exaggeration to say that a human being without education is not far removed from an animal. Education, therefore, is necessary for women as it is for men. Not that the methods of education should be identical in both cases. In the first place, our State system of education is full of error and productive of harm in many respects. It should be eschewed by men and women alike. Even if it were free from its present blemishes, I would not regard it as proper for women from all points of view. Man and woman are of equal rank, but they are not identical. They are a peerless pair, being supplementary to one another; each helps the other so that without the one the existence of the other cannot be conceived, and, therefore, it follows as a necessary corollary from these facts that anything that will impair the status of either of them will involve the equal ruin of them both. In framing any scheme of women's education, this cardinal truth must be constantly kept in mind. Man is supreme in the outward activities of a married pair and, therefore, it is in the fitness of things that he should have a greater knowledge thereof. On the other hand, home life is entirely the sphere of woman and, therefore, in domestic affairs, in the upbringing and education of children, women ought to have more knowledge. Not that knowledge should be divided into watertight compartments or that some branches of knowledge should be closed to any one ; but unless courses of instruction are based on a discriminating appreciation of these basic principles, the fullest life of man and woman cannot be developed.

I should say a word or two as to whether English education is or is not necessary for our women. I have come to the conclusion that, in the ordinary course of our lives, neither our men nor our women need necessarily have any knowledge of English. True, English is necessary for making a living and for active association in our political movements. I do not believe in women working for a living or undertaking commercial enterprise. The few women who may require or desire to have English education can very easily have their way by joining the schools for men. Introduction of English education in schools meant for women could only lead to a prolongation of our helplessness. I have often read and heard people saying that the rich treasures of English literature should be opened alike to men and women. I submit in all humility that there is some misapprehension in assuming such an attitude. No one intends to close these treasures against women while keeping them open for men. There is none on earth able to prevent you from studying the literature of the whole world if you are fond of literary tastes. But when courses of education have been framed with the needs of a particular society in view, you cannot supply the requirements of the few who have cultivated a literary taste.

Their needs can be met, after we are fully developed, by separate institutions as in Europe. When, through a well-planned scheme, large numbers of men and women begin to receive education and those who remain without it are looked upon as exceptions, we shall have plenty of writers in our languages to bring to us the pleasures of other literatures. If we seek the pleasure of literature always in English our languages will remain poor, which means that we shall remain a poor people. The habit of deriving enjoyment only from a foreign literature is, I must say, if you will pardon me the simile, like the thief's habit of deriving pleasure from stolen goods. The pleasure which Pope found in the Iliad he placed before the people in English of superb beauty. The pleasure which Fitzgerald derived from the Rubaiyat of Omar Khayyam made him render it in English of such power that millions of Englishmen keep his poem with them as they do the *Bible*. The *Bhagavad Gita* filled Edwin Arnold with transports of joy ; he did not ask the people to learn Sanskrit in order that they may have the same joy, but put the work into English which would stand beside Sanskrit or Pali, pouring his very soul into the language, and thus shared his joy with his people. Our being so very backward is a reason why such work should be undertaken among us on a much larger scale. This will be possible only when a scheme such as I have suggested has been formulated and is firmly adhered to. If only we can give up our infatuation with English and our lack of confidence in ourselves or in the capacity of our languages, the task is not difficult.*

In asking our men and women to spend less time in the study of English than they are doing now, my object is not to deprive them of the pleasure which they are likely to derive from it, but I hold that the same pleasure can be obtained at less cost and trouble if we follow a more natural method. The world is full of many a gem of priceless beauty; but then those gems are not all of English setting. Other languages can well boast of productions of similar excellence; all these should be made available to our common people and that can only be done if our own learned men will undertake to translate them for us in our own languages.

Merely to have outlined a scheme of education as above is not to have removed the bane of child-marriage from our society or to have conferred on our women an equality of rights. Let us now consider the case of our girls who disappear, so to say, from view after marriage. They are not likely to return to our schools. Conscious of the unspeakable and unthinkable sin of the child marriage of their daughters, their mothers cannot think of educating them or of otherwise making their dry life a cheerful one. The man who marries a young girl does not do so out of any altruistic motives, but through sheer lust. Who is to rescue these girls? A proper answer to this question will also be a solution of the woman's problem. The answer is albeit difficult, but it is the only one. There is, of course, none to champion her cause but her husband. It is useless to expect a child wife to be able to bring round the man who has married her. The difficult work must, therefore, for the present at least, be left to man. If I could, I would take a census of child-wives and would find the friends of their husbands and through such friends, as well as through moral and polite exhortations, I will attempt to bring home to them the enormity of their crimes in linking their fortunes with child-wives and will warn them that there is no expiation for that sin unless and until they have by education made their wives fit not only to bear children but also to bring them up properly, and unless, in the meantime, they live a life of absolute celibacy.

Thus there are many fruitful fields of activity before the members of the Bhagini Samaj for devoting their energies to. The field for work is so vast that, if resolute application is brought to bear thereon, the wider movements for reform may, for the present, well be left to themselves and great service can be done to the cause of Home Rule without so much as even a verbal reference to it. When printing presses were non-existent and scope for speech-making very limited, when one could hardly travel twenty-four miles in the course of a day instead of a thousand miles as now, we had only one agency for propagating our ideals and that was our 'acts'; and acts had immense potency. We are now rushing to and fro with the velocity of air, delivering speeches, writing newspaper articles, and yet we fall short of our accomplishments and the cry of despair fills the air. I for one am of opinion that, as in old days, our acts will have a more powerful influence on the public than any number of speeches and writings. It is my earnest prayer to your Association that its members should give prominence to quiet and unobtrusive work in whatever it does.

[*The Hindu*, 26-2-1918, and *Mahatma Gandhini Vicharsrishti*]

18. Value of an Oath

SPEECH TO AHMEDABAD MILL-HANDS

[March 15, 1918][1]

You must have heard what happened this morning. Some were shocked, others wept. I do not feel that there was anything wrong, or anything of which I need be ashamed, in this morning's development. I do not feel angry at the criticism made by the residents of Jugaldas Chawl.[2] Rather, I, and others as well who want to serve India, have much to learn from it. I have always believed that, if our capacity for *tapascharya* or voluntary suffering is real enough, we are bound to reap the fruit. You took an oath relying on my advice. In this age the oath has lost its value. Men break their oath at any time and for any reason and I am grieved to have been instrumental in thus lowering the value of an oath. There is nothing else that will bind a man as effectively as an oath does. The meaning of an oath is that we decide to do a particular thing with God in whom we believe as our witness.

People who are on a higher plane can perhaps do without oaths, but we who are on a lower one cannot. We who fall a thousand times cannot raise ourselves without oaths. You will admit that, had we not taken the oath and repeated it daily, many of us would have fallen long ago. You yourselves have said that never before have you known a strike as peaceful as this. The reason why some have fallen is that they are faced with starvation. I would advice you to keep your oath even if you have to starve, though it is our pledge, mine and my coworkers', that we will not allow you to starve. If we look on unconcernedly while you are starving, you may give up your pledge by all means. There is one more thing we should have mentioned along with these two. It is that if, while not allowing you to starve, we ask you to beg, we would be guilty in the eyes of God and would prove no better than thieves. But what should I do to persuade you

---

1. The speech was delivered on the evening of the day on which the fast commenced.
2. Chhaganlal Gandhi had, the day before, gone to the *chawl* to request the workers to attend the morning meeting and had been rebuffed by them with the remark: "What is it to Anasuyabehn and Gandhiji? They come and go in their car; they eat sumptuous food, but we are suffering death-agonies; attending meetings does not prevent starvation." This was reported to Gandhiji.

to maintain yourselves with manual labour? I can do manual work, I have been doing it, and would do so even now; but I do not get the opportunity for it. I have a number of things to attend to, and can, therefore, do some manual work only by way of exercise. Will it behove you to tell me that you have worked on looms, but cannot do other physical labour ? This notion has taken deep root in India. It is good as a principle that a man should specialize in one type of work only; but it would be improper to use this as an excuse. I have thought much about this. When I came to know of your bitter criticism of me, I felt that, if I wanted to keep you to the path of *dharma* and show you the worth of an oath and the value of labour, I must set a concrete example before you. We are not out to have fun at your cost or to act a play. How can I prove to you that we are prepared to carry out whatever we tell you? I am not God that I can demonstrate this to you in some way [other than by fasting]. I should very much like to do something which would convince you that you would have to be plain with me, that it would not do for you merely to act a part. Nobody can be induced or coerced to keep his oath. Love is the only inducement that can be offered. You must understand that he alone, who loves his religion, loves his honour and country, will refuse to give up his resolve . . . .

I am used to taking such pledges. For fear that people may wrongly imitate me, I would rather not take one at all. But I am dealing with hundreds of thousands of workers. I must, therefore, see that my conscience is clean. I wanted to show you that I was not playing with you.

I have attempted to show you by example that you should value your oath in the same manner as I have done. You have already done one thing. You could have said: "What have we to do with your oath, we cannot continue the fight, we must go back"; but you did not do so. You decided to accept our service. And I thought of you the more highly for that. It seemed a beautiful thing to me to sink or swim with you.[1]

[*From Gujarati*]
Ek Dharmayuddha

---

1. The rest of the speech is not available. Gandhiji's fast became a subject of serious concern. Prof. Anandshankar Dhruva who discussed it with Gandhiji doubted its efficacy for bringing about a real change of heart among the mill-owners. They strove to dissuade him; some offered to concede the demand for a 35 per cent increase for Gandhiji's sake, but, according to Mahadev Desai, he rejected it saying, "Do not give 35 per cent out of pity for me, but do so to respect the workers' pledge, and to give them justice."

19. Fasting for Purity

PRAYER DISCOURSE IN ASHRAM[1]

[March 17, 1918]

The step I have just now taken is a very grave one, but at the back of it there stands a great idea. It is grave because, on hearing of this all those who know me in India will be very much pained, be almost in an agony of grief. But, at the same time, I have here an opportunity to convey to them a beautiful idea, and I should not miss it. This is the motive behind my action. I have been getting quite impatient for the last two days to explain it to you but I could not get enough quiet time for that. It would make me very unhappy to miss the morning and evening prayers in the Ashram. And, besides, yesterday the music maestro dropped in and so I just would not forgo the pleasure of hearing his strains. I have swum past many a lure but many hungers still persist in me. At present I get here all that I long for by way of music and, therefore, although it was Anasuyabehn's express wish yesterday that I should stay on there, I insisted on coming over to the Ashram. At a time like this, the music here has a very soothing effect on me. This is indeed the best occasion for me to unburden my soul to you. At other hours, you are likely to be busy with your work and to make you leave that and assemble here—that won't be proper either.

From the ancient culture of India, I have gleaned a truth which, even if it is mastered by the few persons here at the moment, would give these few a mastery over the world. Before telling you of it, however, I should like to say another thing. At present, there is only one person in India over whom millions are crazy, for whom millions of our countrymen would lay down their lives. That person is Tilak. Maharaj. I often feel that this is a great asset of his, his great treasure.

He has written on the inner meaning of the *Gita*[2]. But I have always felt that he has not understood the age-old spirit of India, has not

---

1. In this Gandhiji has explained at length the reasons for his undertaking a fast in connection with the mill-hands' strike.
2. Gita Rahasya, which he wrote in Mandalay Jail, serving a six-year term.

understood her soul and that is the reason why the nation has come to this pass. Deep down in his heart, he would like us all to be what the Europeans are. As Europe stands on top at present, as it seems, that is, to those whose minds are steeped in European notions—he wants India to be in the same position. He underwent six years' internment but only to display a courage of the European variety, with the idea that these people who are tyrannizing over us now may learn how, if it came to that, we too could stand such long terms of internment, be it five years or twenty-five. In the prisons of Siberia, many great men of Russia are wasting their whole lives, but these men did not go to prison in obedience to any spiritual promptings. To be thus prodigal of one's life is to expend our highest treasure to no purpose. If Tilakji had undergone the sufferings of internment with a spiritual motive, things would not have been as they are and the results of his internment would have been far different. This is what I should like to explain to him. I have often, with great respect, spoken about this to him, as much as I could, though I have not put the thing in so many words orally or in writing. I might have, in what I wrote, watered down my meaning, but *Tilak Maharaj* has so penetrating an intellect that he would understand. This is, however, no matter to be explained orally or in writing. To give him first-hand experience of it, I must furnish a living example. Indirectly, I have spoken to him often enough but, should I get an opportunity of providing a direct demonstration, I should not miss it, and here is one.

Another such person is Madan Mohan Malaviya. Amongst the present leaders of India, he is a man of the holiest character —that is, amongst political personages and amongst those whom we know. Unknown to us, there may be many such indeed. But although he is so holy in his life and so well informed on points of *dharma*, he has not, it seems to me, properly understood the soul of India in all its grandeur. I am afraid I have said too much. If he were to hear this, Malaviyaji might get angry with me, even think of me as a swollen-headed man and take a dislike to me. But I feel no hesitation in saying what I do because it is quite true. I have spoken to him many times. I am bound to him by ties of affection and hence I have even indulged in frequent wranglings with him. At the end of all my arguments, however, he would merely say that all I had said might be true but that he was not convinced of it. I have this opportunity to provide him, too, with a direct demonstration. I owe it to both to show now what India's soul is.

For the last twenty days, I have been mixing with ten thousand mill-hands. In my presence, they took a pledge in the name of God.

At the time, they did so with great enthusiasm. Whatever type of people they are, they all believe at any rate that God exists.

They thought that, when they had observed the pledge for twenty days, God was bound to come to their help. When that did not happen and God prolonged the test, their faith faltered. They felt that, led by this one man, they had suffered all these days but gained nothing whatever, that if they had not allowed themselves to be prevailed upon by him but had turned militant, they would have had their 35 per cent, or even more, in a much shorter time. This is my analysis of how their minds work. I can never bear to be in such a situation. That a pledge once taken, at my instance, should be so lightly broken and that faith in God should decline means certain annihilation of *dharma*. I simply cannot live to be a witness to this in any activity to which I am a party. I must impress upon the minds of the mill-hands what it is to take a pledge. I must show to them what I can do for a pledge; if I did not, I would be a coward. For a man who brags of clearing seven feet, not to clear even one is impotence. Well, then, to keep those ten thousand men from falling, I took this step.

This was why I took the vow and its impact was electrifying. I had never expected this. The thousands of men present there shed tears from their eyes. They awoke to the reality of their soul, a new consciousness stirred in them and they got strength to stand by their pledge. I was instantly persuaded that *dharma* had not vanished from India, that people do respond to an appeal to their soul. If Tilak Maharaj and Malaviyaji would but see this, great things could be done in India.

I am at present overflowing with joy. When, on a former occasion, I took such a vow, my mind did not enjoy the peace it does today. I also felt at that time the pull of the body. This time I experience nothing of the kind. My mind is filled with profound peace. I feel like pouring forth my soul to you all but I am beside myself with joy.

My pledge is directed to making the mill-hands honour theirs and teaching them what value to attach to a pledge. For people in our country to take pledges whenever they fancy and break them at any moment betrays their degraded state. And for ten thousand mill-hands to break faith with themselves would spell ruin for the nation. It would never again be possible to raise the workers' issues. At every turn they would quote this as an example and say that ten thousand mill-hands endured suffering for twenty days with a man like Gandhi to lead them and still they did not win. I was thus forced to consider by what means the mill-hands could be made to remain firm. How could I do this without suffering myself? I saw that it was necessary to show them by example how, for the sake of one's pledge, one had to undergo suffering. So it was that I took this pledge. I am aware that it carries a taint. It is likely that, because of my vow, the mill-owners may be moved by consideration for me and come to grant the workers' [demand for] thirty-five per cent increase. My desire is that they should grant the demand only if they see its justice and not out of charity. But the natural result would be that they would do so out of charity and to that extent this pledge is one which cannot but fill me with shame. I weighed the two things, however, against each other: my sense of shame and the mill-hands' pledge. The balance tilted in favour of the latter and I resolved, for the sake of the mill-hands, to take no thought of my shame. In doing public work, a man must be prepared to put up even with such loss of face. Thus, my pledge is not at all by way of a threat to the mill-owners; on the contrary, I wish they clearly understand this and grant the 35 per cent to the mill-hands only if they think it just to do so. To the mill-hands, too, I would say that they should go to the owners and tell them as much.

[*From Gujarati*]
Mahadevbhaini Diary, Vol. IV

20. Kheda Satyagraha

SPEECH AT NADIAD[1]

[March 22, 1918]

The occasion which has brought us here is so important that it will be enshrined in your memory for ever. For some months past, an agitation has been going on in this district for securing the suspension of land revenue. The crops have been generally less than four annas this year and so the collection of revenue ought to be suspended.

In compliance with the Resolution of the Gujarat Sabha, I toured a number of villages and inquired personally into the matter. My co-workers did the same. The available evidence goes to show that the crops do not exceed four annas in the district as a whole. The Government, too, claims to have made an inquiry, but it is not prepared to give the needed relief to the farmers. It has decided to collect the dues. If people do not pay, it has threatened to adopt coercive measures. Notices have been issued for the collection of *chothai*[2] and for the confiscation of holdings. Complaints of oppression by Talatis are also being received. I have only this to say to the Talatis and chiefs of villages who are present at this meeting:

"Let them by all means be loyal to the Government but that loyalty does not lie in oppressing [the people]." The land revenue must be realized, as ordered, but the Government certainly would not ask them to beat the people. Surely, the law can never authorize such an order.

If there should be any such order, the Talatis are not bound to obey it. Anyone acting in this manner will be committing treason against the country, the State and God. They may execute the orders of superiors loyally, but they have no right to molest the people.

If they are convinced that the crop is below four annas they should say so boldly to their superior officers. There are two reasons why I give

---

1. Gandhiji addressed a meeting of about 5,000 people in connection with the situation in Kheda. The meeting marked the inauguration of Kheda *Satyagraha*. This report of Gandhiji's speech has been collated with the one available in Bombay Secret Abstracts, 1918.
2. One-fourth of the assessment exacted as fine for non-payment of revenue.

you this advice. It has been the system of Government to assert that what they have said is true. In a talk with Lord Willingdon I came to know his opinion that the people of India do not give out their correct views; they are not bold enough to say what they mean; they say anything which pleases the other party; they are lacking in moral courage.[1] What are the people to do in this situation? Those whose crops are less than four annas should tell the Government politely: "It is not possible for us to submit to this injustice; when the crops have, in fact, failed, we cannot pay up our dues and thereby prove ourselves liars. You may realize the dues by force if you choose." It is to give you this advice that this meeting has been called.

This is a very beautiful district. Its people has delightful trees, the like of which I have in this country except in Bihar.

But Bihar has natural beauty, while in this district beauty has been achieved by hard work and perseverance. This is the only district which can boast of intelligent and industrious agriculturists. They have turned their land into a lovely orchard. They can be justly proud of their achievement. It does not, however, follow that they may be called upon to pay land revenue even when their crops have failed.

This industrious section of the district's population is steadily growing poorer and many have been compelled to give up agriculture and take to daily labour. This is a distressing thing for anyone to have to do. A country in which the farmers find this necessary is in for a bad time.

In fact revenue should be paid from the sale value of the crops; it is intolerable, when the crops have failed, that the Government should recover it forcibly. But, in this country, it has become a practice with the Government to insist that it is always in the right. It is intolerable that, however, just the people's case, the Government should have its own way. Justice must prevail and injustice yield. The agriculturists claim, and the evidence collected by those who conducted the inquiry bears them out, that the crops have failed and yet the Government insists that they have been plentiful. In the circumstances, the people have every right to tell the Government that, surely, they could see and judge things as well as the Government, and that they would not submit to injustice done by the officers. That people would tell lies, for the sake of saving at the most a year's interest by asking for a postponement of the assessment, is inconceivable. That the officers should suggest anything of the kind is

1. This additional paragraph is found in Bombay Secret Abstracts.

intolerable. We must show, therefore, that our case is just; placed in the situation that we are, I would tell you that, if the Government does not accept our request, we should declare plainly that we shall not pay land revenue and will be prepared to take the consequences.

All nations which have risen have done so through suffering. If the people have to sacrifice their land, they should be ready to do so and suffer. Some will even argue that this is treason or rebellion; it is nothing of the kind. It means suffering ourselves, no treason. When the crops have failed, to pay up the dues out of fear is cowardice. We are human beings, not animals. To refuse a thing firmly and plainly in the name of truth—that is *satyagraha*.

We have assembled today to do the spade-work for *satyagraha*.

We don't propose to pay up the revenue to the Government; we want to fight it out. We have to prepare ourselves, then, for the suffering that may follow. We must visualize what we shall have to face:

(1) The Government may recover the assessment by selling our cattle and our movable property.
(2) It may impose fines.
(3) It may confiscate *jagirs*.
(4) It may even put people in jail on the ground that they are defiant[1].

The word has been used by the Government and I don't like it. How can they say that you are defiant merely because you speak the truth? Indeed, such a person is brave, not defiant. It is an act of bravery, and no defiance, for a man who, though he can afford to pay, refuses to do so in the interests of the poor. If in the process this man has to leave the village for ever, he will do so; he alone may take the pledge today who is ready for this.

It is very difficult to take the pledge of *satyagraha*; it is still more difficult to carry out one. I cannot bear to think of any one breaking a pledge once taken, forsaking his God. It would cause me very great pain, indeed, if you took a pledge which you did not mean to keep. In the intensity of my suffering, I may take an extreme step. I may have to fast. I don't suffer when I fast; fasting hurts me less than that people should deceive me by breaking their pledge. In *Satyagraha*, a pledge is the most valuable thing of all; it must be kept up to the very end. A pledge taken in

---

1. The Gujarati original has *dandai*.

God's name must never be broken. I would not hesitate to sacrifice my life if that might ensure that thousands would keep their pledge. Those who want to fight must make up their minds once for all. I would not mind very much if people just said that they would hold out as long as possible but that they were not sure of themselves in case of severe repression. I would far rather that they cut my throat than that they break my heart by betraying their pledge. The man who cuts my throat, I would pray to God to forgive, but I would not forgive the other man.

I would tell you, therefore, in all humility, whatever you decide, do so with full thought and consideration. Only those who are determined to carry their decision through are able to raise themselves. When you have so raised yourselves, the Government will respect you, for it will know then, that it was dealing with men who would honour their plighted word and not betray it. A man who breaks his word can do no service to his country, or to his Government or to God.

I want, therefore, to know whether you agree; I ask you: "Are you ready to fight ?" I shall prepare a written pledge. Those friends who wish to take it should come to the Ashram and give their signatures. I have only one request: "Suffer everything and honour the pledge; refuse to pay the revenue and prove to the Government thereby that you are prepared for sacrifices." The Government cannot use force against everyone.[1]

I advise those who have *sanadia* lands to pay the assessment.

Mr. Andrews, who has gone to interview the Governor, sends me a wire to go to Delhi to see him. Mr. Andrews and Mr. Vallabhbhai (Patel) will carry on further work here. I am going to Delhi in connection with the work of Mahomed Ali and Shaukat Ali.

[*From Gujarati*]
[*Kheda Satyagraha*]

1. What follows is as reported in Bombay Secret Abstracts.

21. Question of Language

SPEECH AT HINDI SAHITYA SAMMELAN[1]

[Indore,
March 29, 1918]

BROTHERS AND SISTERS,

Our most venerable and selfless leader Pandit Madan Mohan Malaviya has not found it possible to attend this conference. I had requested him to come if he could and he promised to do so. But though he has not been able to come he has sent us a letter. I was sure that in case he did not come, he would send a letter stating his views, and it would be possible for me to read it out to you. I have received the letter today. I had asked the reception committee to secure views of scholars on two questions in regard to Hindi. Panditji in his letter has replied to these two questions.[2]

The question of language presents a big and indeed a very important problem. Even if all the leaders were to devote themselves entirely to this task turning away from everything else, they well may.

If on the other hand, we were to regard it as of secondary importance only and to direct our attention away from it then all the enthusiasm which people now feel for it and the keen interest they are taking in it at present would be in vain.

Language is like our mother. In fact I have no real interest in this sort of a conference. It will be a three days' pageant after which we shall disperse, go away to our respective places and forget all that we said or heard. What is needed is the urge and the resolve to do things. The president's speech cannot give you that urge. It is something which you have to create for yourselves. One of the charges made against us is that our language lacks spirit. Where, there is no knowledge there is no spirit. We have neither the urge to know nor to do things. It is only when we

---

1. Gandhiji delivered this address in Hindi while presiding over the 8th session of the Hindi Sahitya Sammelan held at the Town Hall, Indore.
2. At this point, Gandhiji read out Pandit Malaviya's letter expressing his conviction that Hindi was the lingua franca of India.

acquire dynamic energy that our people and our language also will acquire it. We cannot get the freedom we want through a foreign language for the simple reason that we are not able to use it effectively. I am pleased to know that in Indore you carry on all your dealings through Hindi. But—excuse me please—the letter I have received from your Chief Minister is in English. The people of Indore perhaps do not know—but I will tell them—that here the courts entertain petitions written in English. I ask why it should be so in Indore. I admit that this movement—the movement for the adoption of Hindi—cannot yet succeed in British India, but there is no reason why it should not succeed in the Indian States. The educated classes, as Pandit Malaviyaji has pointed out in his letter, have unfortunately fallen under the spell of English and have developed a distaste for their own mother tongue,. The milk one gets from the former is adulterated with water and contaminated with poison, while that from the latter is pure. It is impossible to make any advance without this pure milk. But a blind person cannot see and a slave does not know how to break his fetters. We have been living under the spell of the English now for the past fifty years. In the result our people have remained steeped in ignorance. The conference must give special attention to this part of the problem. We should see that within a year conditions are created when not a word of English will be heard in any of our political or social conferences, in the Congress, in the provincial assemblies and the like. Let us abandon the use of English entirely. English has attained the position of a universal language. But that is because the English have spread and established themselves throughout the world. As soon as they lose that position, English will shrink in its extent. We should no more neglect and thus destroy our own language. The English insist on speaking their mother tongue and using it for all their purposes. Let us do the same and thus raise Hindi to the high status of a national language. Only thus shall we discharge our duty to it. Now I will read out my written speech.

MR. PRESIDENT, DELEGATES, BROTHERS AND SISTERS,

You have done me great honour in conferring on me the presidentship of this conference. I know only too well that from the point of view of the knowledge of Hindi, my qualifications for this honour are almost nil. The only thing which may be said to qualify me for it is my boundless love of Hindi. I hope that I would always be able to pass this test of love.

The extent of a particular literature can only be reckoned on the basis of the region where that language is spoken. If the region of Hindi remains confined to the Northern part of India, the extent of its literature must remain limited. But in case it becomes a national language, the expanse of its literature will become as wide as the country. As the people speaking a particular language, so the language. If we want that high-souled men from the East and the West, from the North and the South, should come to take a dip in the sea of this language, it is obvious that the sea must acquire sufficient importance. Therefore the place of Hindi from the point of view of developing a national literature needs to be considered.

It is necessary to give some thought to the definition of the Hindi language. I have often said that Hindi is that language which is spoken in the North by both Hindus and Muslims and which is written either in the Nagari or the Persian script. This Hindi is neither too Sanskritized nor too Persianized. The sweetness which I find in the village Hindi is found neither in the speech of the Muslims of Lucknow nor in that of the Hindu pundits of Prayag. The language which is easily understood by the masses is the best. All can easily follow the village Hindi. The source of the river of language lies in the Himalayas of the people. It will always be so. The Ganga arising with the village Hindi which will flow on for ever, while the Sanskritized and Persianized Hindi will dry up and fade away, as does a rivulet springing from a small hillock.

The distinction made between Hindus and Muslims is unreal. The same unreality is found in the distinction between Hindi and Urdu. It is unnecessary for Hindus to reject Persian words and for Muslims to reject Sanskrit words from their speech. A. harmonious blend of the two will be as beautiful as the confluence of the Ganga and Yamuna and last for ever. I hope that we will not waste our energy and weaken our strength by entering into the Hindi-Urdu controversy.

There is, no doubt, difficulty in regard to script. As things are, Muslims will patronize the Arabic script, while Hindus will mostly use the Nagari script. Both scripts will therefore have to be accorded their due places. Officials must know both scripts. There is no difficulty in this. In the end, the script which is the easier of the two will prevail.

There is no doubt that there ought to be a common language for mutual intercourse between the different parts of India. Once we forget the Hindi-Urdu controversy, we shall realize that for Muslims throughout India Urdu is the lingua franca. This proves that since Moghul times, Hindi or Urdu was well on its way to becoming the national language of India.

Even today, there is no language to rival Hindi in this respect. The question of national language becomes quite easy of solution once we give up the Hindi-Urdu controversy. Hindus will have to learn some Persian words while Muslims will have to learn some Sanskrit words. This exchange will enrich and strengthen the Islamic language and provide a very fruitful means for bringing Hindus and Muslims closer together. in fact we have to work so hard for dispelling the present fascination for the English language that we must not raise the Hindu-Urdu controversy. Nor must we fight over the script.

Why English cannot become our national language, what harm results from the imposition of English on our people, how our people have suffered and their development has been retarded by the adoption of English as the medium of education—I have dealt with in my speeches at Broach and Bhagalpur. I will not therefore repeat myself here. Indeed there is no doubt that Sir Rabindranath Tagore, Smt. Besant, Lokamanya Tilak and other respected and influential persons entertain similar views regarding this question. There will certainly be difficulties in the way of the achievement of our purpose but it will be for this body to tackle them. Lokamanya Tilak has indeed expressed his views in this regard not only in words but also in action by starting a Hindi section in his papers *The Kesari* and *The Mahratta*. The views of *Bharat Ratna* Pandit Madan Mohan Malaviya on this question are well known. Still, unfortunately, some of our learned leaders hold that for at least some years to come English must remain the national language. We will respectfully request these leaders to consider that this unreasonable attraction for English is causing much hardship to our people, as they get little benefit out of the knowledge of their English educated countrymen between whom and them a wide gulf has been created through English.

It is unnecessary to say that I do not hate the English language. I myself have benefited from many of the precious gems of the great treasure of English Literature. We have also to acquire a knowledge of science and such like through the English Language. Knowledge of English is therefore necessary for us. But it is one thing to give it its due place and quite another to make a fetish of it. It is clear that our purpose will not be achieved merely by accepting that Hindi-Urdu should be our national language. We have to consider how we may achieve this goal. The scholars who have graced this assembly by their presence will certainly have something to say on this point. I will make a few suggestions on how we may spread this language. There must first be a handy book—sort of a "Hindi Teacher" which will meet the needs of those who want to learn Hindi. I have seen a small book of this type for those who want to learn Hindi through Bengali. There is one in Marathi also. But I have not seen any such books for other regional languages. This is as easy to do as it is necessary. I hope that this *Sammelan* will soon take up this work. Of course, these books should be written by learned and experienced writers.

The greatest difficulty will be felt in the case of the Southern languages. No effort whatever in this direction has yet been made there. We must train good Hindi teachers to take up the work. There is a great scarcity of such teachers. I have secured one such teacher from Prayag through your popular secretary, Bhai Purushottamdasji Tandon.

Similarly, I have not yet seen a single complete grammar of the Hindi language. Such as exist in English and have been written by foreigners. One of these grammars is by Dr. Kellog. There must be a good Hindi grammar which can compare favourably with similar grammars of other Indian languages. It is my humble request to scholars who love Hindi to make up this deficiency.

In our National Councils Hindi alone should be used. Congress workers and leaders can and should do much in this respect. I would suggest that this Conference should make a request to this effect to the Congress at its next session.

In our legislative bodies too the entire proceedings should be conducted through the national language. Our people cannot have training in political affairs so long as this is not done. Our Hindi newspapers are doing something in this respect but the education we want to be imparted to our people cannot be given through translations. Similarly in our courts too the national and provincial languages must be used. Under the existing set-up people are being deprived of the education which they can easily receive from those who administer justice.

The Princes can promote the national language in a way in which the English Government cannot. In the Holkar State, for example, in the Council and in the courts, Hindi and the provincial language alone can be used. The encouragement they thus give to the national language will go a long way in helping it progress. In the schools of this State the entire education from the beginning to the end should be imparted through the mother tongue. In this way our Princes can render much service to the language. I hope that Maharaja Holkar and his officials will take up this work enthusiastically.[1] It will be a sad delusion to think that we can achieve our objective merely through conferences. Single-minded devotion and constant application alone will bring success. Only when hundreds of selfless scholars regard this work as their own can it be accomplished.

What I regret is that even the provinces which have Hindi for their mother tongue do not seem to show any enthusiasm for its promotion and propagation. The educated classes in these provinces continue to use English for purposes of conversation and correspondence. A friend has written to me that our newspaper proprietors do all their work in English; they keep their accounts, too, in English. Englishmen living in France use their mother tongue in all their dealings. Is it not a pity that we carry on even some of our most important activities in English? It is my humble but firm opinion that unless we give Hindi its national status and the provincial languages their due place in life of the people, all the talk of *swaraj* is useless. It is my fervent hope and prayer to God almighty that this *Sammelan* may be an instrument for the solution of this great question confronting India.

Thoughts on National Language

1. According to a report in the *Bombay Chronicle*, 2-4-1918. Gandhiji thanked Maharaja Holkar for his donation of Rs. 10,000 for propagation of Hindi.

22. Indian Civilization[1]

[Indore,
March 30, 1918[2]]

We often think that changes of the kind that take place in Europe will also occur in India; that when some big transformation comes about, people who know beforehand how to prepare themselves for it win through and those who fail to take account of this are destroyed; that mere movement is progress and that our advancement lies in it. We think that we shall be able to progress through the great discoveries that have been made in the continent of Europe. But this is an illusion. We are inhabitants of a country which has so long survived with its own civilization. Many a civilization of Europe is destroyed, but India, our country, survives as a witness to its own civilization. All scholars agree in testifying that the civilization of India is the same today as it was thousands of years ago. But, now, there is reason to suspect that we no longer have faith in our civilization. Every morning we do our worship and prayer, recite the verses composed by our forbears, but we do not understand their significance. Our faith is turning in another direction.

So long as the world goes on, the war between the Pandavas and the Kauravas will also continue. The books of almost all the religions say that the war between the gods and satan goes on for ever. The question is how we are to make our preparations. I have come here to tell you that you should have faith in your civilization and keep to it steadfastly. If you do this, India will one day hold sway over the entire world. (Applause.)

Our leaders say that, in order to fight the West, we have to adopt the ways of the West. But please rest assured that it will mean the end of Indian civilization. India's face is turned away from your modern trend; that India you do not know. I have travelled much and so come to know the mind of India and I have discovered that it has preserved its faith in

---

1. According to a report in *The Bombay Chronicle*, 2-4-1918, Gandhiji thanked Maharaja Holkar for his donation of Rs. 10,000 for propagation of Hindi.
2. The date is according to the tour itinerary.

its ancient civilization. The *swaraj* of which we hear will not be achieved the way we are working for it. The Congress-League Scheme, or any other scheme which is even better, will not get us *swaraj*. We shall get *swaraj* through the way in which we live our lives.

It cannot be had for the asking. We can never gain it through copying Europe. That European civilization is satanic we see for ourselves. An obvious proof of this is the fierce war that is going on at present. It is so terrible that the *Mahabharata* War was nothing in comparison. This should be a warning to us and we should remember that our sages have given us the immutable and inviolate principles that our conduct should be godly and that it should be rooted in *dharma*. We should follow these principles alone. So long as we do not follow *dharma*, our wish will not be fulfilled, notwithstanding all the grandiose schemes we may devise. Even if Mr. Montagu offers us *swaraj* today we can in no way benefit from that *swaraj*. We must make use of the legacy left us by our *rishis* and *munis*. The whole world knows that the *tapasya* that was practised in ancient India is found nowhere else. Even if we want an empire for India, we can get it through no other method but that of self discipline. We can be certain that once the spirit of discipline comes to pervade our lives, we shall be able to get anything we may want.

Truth and non-violence are our goal. Non-violence is the supreme *dharma*, there is no discovery of greater import than this. So long as we engage in mundane actions, so long as soul and body are together, some violence will continue to occur through our agency.

But we must renounce at least the violence that it is possible for us to renounce. We should understand that the less violence a religion permits, the more is the truth contained in it. If we can ensure the deliverance of India, it is only through truth and non-violence. Lord Willingdon, the Governor of Bombay, has said that he feels greatly disappointed when he meets Indians for they do not express what is in their minds but only what would be agreeable to him, so that he never knows the real position. Many people have this habit of hiding their own sentiments while in the presence of an important person and suiting their talk to his pleasure. They do not realize how cruelly they deceive themselves and harm the truth. One must say what one feels. It is impertinence to go against one's reason. One must not hesitate the least to tell what one feels to anyone, be he a Minister of the Government or even a more exalted person. Deal with all with truth and non-violence.

Love is a rare herb that makes a friend even of a sworn enemy and this herb grows out of non-violence. What in a dormant state is non-violence becomes love in the waking state. Love destroys ill will.

We should love all—whether Englishmen or Muslims. No doubt, we should protect the cow. But we cannot do so by fighting with Muslims. We cannot save the cow by killing Muslims.. We should act only through love; thus alone shall we succeed. So long as we do not have unshakeable faith in truth, love and non-violence, we can make no progress. If we give up these and imitate European civilisation, we shall be doomed. I pray to *Suryanarayan*[1] that India may not turn away from her civilization. Be fearless. So long as you live under various kinds of fears, you can never progress, you can never succeed.

Please do not forget our ancient civilization. Never, never give up truth and love. Treat all enemies and friends with love. If you wish to make Hindi the national language, you can do so in a short time through the principles of truth and non-violence.

[*From Hindi*]
Mahatma Gandhi

---

1. The Lord in the form of the sun.

23. Satyagraha[1]

SPEECH ON SATYAGRAHA, ALLAHABAD[2]

[March 11, 1919]

I am sorry that I am unable to speak to you myself. It is utterly impossible for my voice to reach the farthest end of this meeting. I have therefore to content myself with writing a few lines to be read for me.

It behoves everyone who wishes to take the *Satyagraha* Pledge to seriously consider all its factors before taking it. It is necessary to understand the principles of *satyagraha*, to understand the main features of the Bills known as the Rowlatt Bills and to be satisfied that they are so objectionable as to warrant the very powerful remedy of *satyagraha* being applied and finally to be convinced of one's ability to undergo every form of bodily suffering so that the soul may be set free and be under no fear from any human being or institution. Once in it there is no looking back. Therefore, there is no conception of defeat in *satyagraha*. A *satyagrahi* fights even unto death. It is thus not an easy thing for everybody to enter upon it.

It, therefore, behoves a *satyagrahi* to be tolerant of those who do not join him. In reading reports of *satyagraha* meetings I often notice that ridicule is poured upon those who do not join our movement.

This is entirely against the spirit of the Pledge. In *satyagraha* we expect to win over our opponents by self-suffering, i.e., by love. The process whereby we hope to reach our goal is by so conducting ourselves as gradually and in an unperceived manner to disarm all opposition. Opponents as a rule expect irritation even violence from one another when both parties are equally matched. But when *satyagraha* comes into play the expectation is transformed into agreeable surprise in the mind of the party towards whom *satyagraha* is addressed till at last he relents and recalls the act which necessitated *satyagraha*. I venture to promise that if

---

1. The last paragraph is in Gandhiji's hand.
2. This was read in English by the chairman, Syed Hussain, and in Hindi by Gandhiji's secretary, Mahadev Desai.

we act up to our pledge day after day, the atmosphere around us will be purified and those who differ from us from honest motives, as I verily believe they do, will perceive that their alarm was unjustified. The violationists wherever they may be, will realize that they have in *satyagraha* a far more potent instrument for achieving reform than violence whether secret or open, and that it gives them enough work for their inexhaustible energy. And the Government will have no case left in defence of their measures, if as a result of our activity the cult of violence is notably on the wane if it has not entirely died out. I hope therefore that at *satyagraha* meetings we shall have no cries of shame, and no language betraying irritation or impatience either against the Government or our countrymen who differ from us and some of whom have for years been devoting themselves to the country's cause according to the best of their ability.

[*The Leader,* 13-3-1919]

24. Democracy *vs.* Mobocracy

Looking at the surface there is but a thin dividing line between mob-law and the people's law. And yet the division is complete and will persist for all time.

India is today quickly passing through the mob-law stage. The use of the adverb signifies my hope. It may be our misfortune to have to pass through that process even in slow stages. But it is wisdom to adopt every means at our disposal to have done with that stage as quickly as possible.

There is much tendency on our part to yield to the rule of the mob. There was mob rule at Amritsar on the 10th April 1919. There was mob rule at Ahmedabad on the same fateful day. It represented undisciplined destruction and, therefore, it was thoughtless, profitless, wicked and harmful. War is disciplined destruction, much more bloody than any yet committed by mobs. And yet war has been apostrophized, because we have been deceived by the temporary but brilliant results achieved by some wars. So, if India has to achieve her freedom by violence, it will have to be by disciplined and honourable (insofar as it is possible to associate honour with violence) violence, named war. It will then be an act not of mobocracy but democracy.

But my purpose today is not to write mobocracy of the Ahmedabad type. I intend to deal with the type with which I am more familiar. The Congress is a demonstration for the mob and in that sense and that only. Though organized by thoughtful men and women it may be called a mob demonstration. During the memorable tour of the Khilafat Mission through the Punjab, Sind and Madras, I have had a surfeit of such demonstrations. I have been ashamed to witness at railway stations, thoughtless though unwitting destruction of passengers' luggage by demonstrators who in their adoration of their heroes have ignored every thing else and everybody else. They have made, much to the discomfort of their heroes, unmusical and harsh noises. They have trampled upon one another. They have elbowed out one another. All have shouted, all at the same time, in the holy name of order and peace. Ten volunteers have been heard to give the same order at the same time. Volunteers often become demonstrators instead of remaining people's policemen. It is a task often dangerous, always uncomfortable, for the heroes to be escorted through a broken chain of volunteers from the platform to the coach intended for them.

Often it is a process which although it should occupy no more than five minutes, has occupied, one hour. The crowd instead of pressing back, presses towards the heroes and who therefore require to be protected. The coach is taken possession of by anybody who dares, volunteers being the greatest sinners. The heroes and other lawful occupants have to reason with the intruders that they may not mount the foot-boards in that summary fashion. The hood of the coach is roughly handled by the processionists. It is not often that I have seen hoods of motors left undamaged by crowds. On the route instead of crowds lining the streets, they follow the coach. The result is confusion worse confounded. Every moment there is danger of accidents. That there is rarely any accident at such demonstrations in not due to the skill of the organizers, but the crowd is determined to put up with all jostling and retain its perfect good humour. In spite of everyone jostling everyone else, one has not the slightest wish to inconvenience one's neighbour. To finish the picture, there is the meeting, an ever-growing cause of anxiety. You face nothing but disorder, din, pressing, yelling and shouting there. A good speaker arrests the attention of the audience and there is order such that you can hear a pin drop.

All the same this is mobocracy. You are at the mercy of the mob. So long as there is sympathy between you and the mob, everything goes well. Immediately that cord is broken, there is horror.

An Ahmedabad episode now and then gives you the mob psychology.

We must then evolve order out of chaos. And I have no doubt that the best and the speediest method is to introduce the people's law instead of mob-law.

One great stumbling block is that we have neglected music. Music means rhythm, order. Its effect is electrical. It immediately soothes. I have seen, in European countries, a resourceful superintendent of police by starting a popular song controlling the mischievous tendencies of mobs.[1] Unfortunately like our *shastras*, music has been the prerogative of the few, either the barter of prostitutes or high class religious devotees. It has never become nationalized in the modern sense. If I had any influence with volunteer boy scouts and Seva Samiti organizations, I

1. The reference is to Alexander, who saved Gandhiji in this manner from an attack by the mob.

would make compulsory a proper singing in company of national songs. And to that end I should have great musicians attending every Congress or Conference and teaching mass music.

Much greater discipline, method and knowledge must be exacted from volunteers and no chance comer should be accepted as a full-fledged volunteer. He only hinders rather than helping. Imagine the consequence of the introduction of one untrained soldier finding his way into an army at war. He can disorganize it in a second. My greatest anxiety about non-co-operation is not the slow response of the leaders, certainly not the well-meant and even ill-meant criticism, never unadulterated repression. The movement will overcome these obstacles. It will gain even strength from them. But the greatest obstacle is that we have not yet emerged from the mobocratic stage.

But my consolation lies in the fact that nothing is so easy as to train mobs, for the simple reason that they have no mind, no premeditation.

They act in a frenzy. They repent quickly. Our organized Government does not repent of its fiendish crimes at Jallianwala, Lahore, Kasur, Akalgarh, Ram Nagar, etc. But I have drawn tears from repentant mobs at Gujranwala and everywhere a frank acknowledgment of repentance from those who formed the mob during that eventful month of April. Non-co-operation I am therefore now using in order to evolve democracy. And I respectfully invite all the doubting leaders to help by refusing to condemn, in anticipation of a process of national purification, training and sacrifice.

Next week I hope to give some illustrations[1] of how in a moment order was evolved out of mob disorder. My faith in the people is boundless. Theirs is an amazingly responsive nature. Let not the leaders distrust them. This chorus of condemnation of non-cooperation when properly analysed means nothing less than distrust of the people's ability to control themselves. For the present I conclude this somewhat lengthy article by suggesting some rules for guidance and immediate execution:

1. There should be no raw volunteers accepted for big demonstrations. Therefore, none but the most experienced should be at the head.
2. Volunteers should have a general instructions book on their persons.

---

1. *Vide* "Some Illustrations", 22-9-1920.

3. At the time of demonstrations there must be a review of volunteers at which special instructions should be given.
4. At stations, volunteers should not all be centred at one point, namely, where the reception committee should be. But they should be posted at different points in the crowd.
5. Large crowds should never enter the station. They cannot but inconvenience traffic. There is as much honour in staying out as in entering the station.
6. The first duty of the volunteers should be to see that other passengers' luggage is not trampled upon.
7. Demonstrators ought not to enter the station long before the notified time for arrival.
8. There should be a clear passage left in front of the train for the passengers.
9. There should be another passage if possible half way through the demonstrators for the heroes to pass.
10. There should be no chain formed. It is humiliating.
11. The demonstrators must not move till the heroes have reached their coach or till they receive a pre-arranged signal from an authorized volunteer.
12. National cries must be fixed and must be raised not anyhow, at any time or all the time, but just on the arrival of the train, on the heroes reaching the coach and on the route at fair intervals. No objections need be raised to this on the score of the demonstration becoming mechanical and not spontaneous. The spontaneity will depend upon numbers, the response to the cries above all the general look of the demonstrators, not in the greatest number of noises or the loudest. It is the training that a nation receives which characterizes the nature of its demonstrations. A Mohammedan silently worshipping in his mosque is no less demonstrative than a Hindu temple-goer making a noise either through his voice or his gong or both.
13. On the route the crowd must line and not follow the carriages. If pedestrians form part of the moving procession, they must noiselessly and in an orderly manner take their places and not at their own will join or abstain.
14. A crowd should never press towards the heroes but should move away from them.
15. Those on the last line or the circumference should never press forward but give way when pressure is directed towards them.

16. If there are women in the crowd they should be specially protected.
17. Little children should never be brought out in the midst of crowds.
18. At meetings volunteers should be dispersed among the crowd. They should learn flag and whistle signalling in order to pass instructions from one to another when it is impossible for the voice to carry.
19. It is no part of the audience to preserve order. They do so by keeping motionless and silent.
20. Above all, everyone should obey volunteers' instructions without question.

This list does not pretend to be exhaustive. It is merely illustrative and designed to stimulate thought and discussion. I hope that all the vernacular papers will translate this article.

[*Young India,* 8-9-1920]

25. Non-cooperation

SPEECH ON NON-COOPERATION RESOLUTION, CALCUTTA CONGRESS

[September 8, 1920]

Mr. Gandhi moved his resolution on non-cooperation with the following speech :

I am aware, more than aware, of the grave responsibility that rests on my shoulders in being privileged to move this resolution before this great assembly. I am aware that my difficulties, as also yours, increase if you are able to adopt this resolution. I am also aware that the adoption of any resolution will mark a definite change in the policy which the country has hitherto adopted for the vindication of the rights that belong to it, and its honour. I am aware that a large number of our leaders who have given the time and attention to the affairs of my motherland, which I have not been able to give, are ranged against me. They think it a duty to resist the policy of revolutionizing the Government policy at any cost.

Knowing this I stand before you in fear of God and a sense of duty to put this before you for your hearty acceptance.

THINK IMPARTIALLY

I ask you to dismiss me, for the time being from your consideration. I have been charged of saintliness and a desire for dictatorship. I venture to say that I do not stand before you either as a saint or a candidate for dictatorship. I stand before you to present to you the results of my many years' practical experience in non-cooperation.

I deny the charge that it is a new thing in the country. It has been accepted at hundreds of meetings attended by thousands of men, and has been placed in working order since the first of August by the Mussulmans, and many of the things in the programme are being enforced in a more or less intense form. I ask you again to dismiss personalities in the consideration of this important question, and bring to bear patient and calm judgment on it. But a mere acceptance of the resolution does not end the work. Every individual has to enforce the items of the resolution in so far as they apply to him. I beseech you to give me a patient hearing. I ask you neither to clap nor to hiss. I do not mind them so far as I am concerned, but clapping hinders the flow of thought, clapping and hissing hinder the process of correspondence between a speaker and his audience. You will not hiss out of the stage any single speaker. For non-cooperation is a measure of discipline and sacrifice and it demands patience and respect for opposite views. And unless we were able to evolve a spirit of mutual toleration for diametrically opposite views, non-co-operation is an impossibility. Non-cooperation in an angry atmosphere is an impossibility. I have learnt through bitter experience the one supreme lesson to conserve my anger and as heat conserved is transmuted into energy, even so our anger controlled can be transmuted into a power which can move the world. To those who have been attending the Congress, as brothers in arms I ask what can be better discipline than that, which we should exercise between ourselves.

I have been told that I have been doing nothing but wreckage and that by bringing forward the resolution I am breaking up the political life of the country. The Congress is not a party organization.

It ought to provide a platform for all shades of opinions, and a minority need not leave this organization, but may look forward to translate itself into a majority, in course of time, if its opinion commended itself to the country. Only let no man in the name of the Congress advocate a policy which has been condemned by the Congress. And if you condemn my policy I shall not go away from the Congress, but shall plead with them to convert the minority into majority.

ENFORCE CLEAR REPENTANCE

There are no two opinions as to the wrong done to the *khilafat*.

Mussulmans cannot remain as honourable men and follow their Prophet if they do not vindicate their honour at any cost. The Punjab has been cruelly, brutally treated, and inasmuch as one man in the Punjab was made to crawl on his belly the whole of India crawled on her belly, and if we are worthy sons and daughters of India we should be pledged to remove these wrongs. It is in order to remove these wrongs that the country is agitating itself. But we have not been able to bend the Government to our will. We cannot rest satisfied with a mere expression of angry feeling. You could not have heard a more passionate denunciation of the Punjab wrongs than in the pages of the presidential address. If the Congress cannot wring justice from unwilling hands how can it vindicate its existence and its honour?

How can it do so if it cannot enforce clear repentance, before receiving a single gift, however rich, from those blood-stained hands?

EXTEND THE SPIRIT OF SACRIFICE

I have therefore placed before you my scheme of non-cooperation to achieve this end and want you to reject any other scheme unless you have deliberately come to the conclusion that it is a better scheme than mine. If there is a sufficient response to my scheme, I make bold to reiterate my statement that you can gain *swarajya* in the course of a year. Not the passing of the resolution will bring *swarajya*, but the enforcement of the resolution from day to day in a progressive manner, due regard being had to conditions in the country. There is another remedy before the country, and that is drawing of the sword. If that was possible India would not have listened to the gospel of non-cooperation. I want to suggest to you that even if you want to arrest injustice by methods of violence, discipline and self-sacrifice are necessary. I have not known of a war gained by a rabble, but I have known of wars gained by disciplined armies and if you want to give battle to the British Government and to the combined power of Europe we must train ourselves in discipline and self-sacrifice. I confess I have become impatient, I have seen that we deserve *swarajya* today, but we have not got the spirit of national sacrifice. We have evolved this spirit in domestic affairs, and I have come to ask you to extend it to other affairs. I have been travelling from one end to the other of the country to see whether the country has evolved the national spirit, whether at the altar of the nation it is ready to dedicate its riches, children, its all, if it was ready to make the initiatory sacrifice. Is the country ready? Are the title-holders ready to surrender their titles? Are parents ready to sacrifice literary education of their children for the sake of the country? The schools and colleges are really a factory for turning out clerks for Government. If the parents are not ready for the sacrifice, if titleholders are not ready, *swarajya* is very nearly an impossibility. No nation being under another nation can accept gifts and kick at the responsibility attaching to those gifts, imposed by the conquering nation. Immediately the conquered country realized instinctively that any gift which might come to it is not for the benefit of the conquered, but for the benefit of the conqueror, that moment it should reject every form of voluntary assistance to it. These are the fundamental essentials of success in the struggle for the independence for the country, whether within the Empire or without the Empire. I hold a real substantial unity between Hindus and Mussulmans infinitely superior to the British connection and if I had to make a choice between that unity and the British connection, I would have the first and reject the other. If I had to choose between the honour of the Punjab, anarchy, neglect of education, shutting out of all legislative activity, and British connection, I would choose the honour of the Punjab and all it meant, even anarchy, shutting out of all schools, etc., without slightest hesitation.

If you have the same feeling burning in you as in me for the honour of Islam and the Punjab then you will unreservedly accept my resolution.

BOYCOTT OF COUNCILS

I now come to the burning topic, viz., the boycott of the councils. Sharpest difference of opinion existed regarding this, and if the house has to divide on it, it must divide. If it must divide you will consider that it must divide on one issue, viz., whether *swarajya* has to be gained through the councils or without the councils. If we utterly distrust the British Government and we know that they are utterly unrepentant how can you believe that the councils will lead to *swarajya* and not tighten the British hold on India?

SWADESHI

I now come to *swadeshi*. The boycott of foreign goods is included in the resolution. You have got here, I confess, an anomaly for which I am not originally responsible. But I have consented to it.

I will not go into the history of how it found a place into the resolution, of which the essence is discipline and self-sacrifice.

Swadeshi means permanent boycott of foreign goods. It is therefore a matter of redundancy. But I have taken it in, because I could not reject it as a matter of conscience. I know, however, it is a physical impossibility. So long as we have to rely on the pins and needles—figurative and literal both—we cannot bring about a complete boycott of foreign goods. I do not hesitate to say this clause mars the musical harmony, if I may claim it without vanity, of the programme. I feel that those words do mar the symmetry of the programme. But I am not here for symmetry of the programme as for its workability.

I again ask you not to be influenced by personality. Reject out of your consideration any service that I have done. Two things only I claim. Laborious industry, great thought behind any programme, and unflinching determination to bring it about. You may take only those things from me, and bring them to bear on any programme that you adopt.

[*Young India,* 15-9-1920]

26. The Creed of the Congress[1]

SPEECH ON NEW CONGRESS CREED, NAGPUR[2]

[December 28, 1920]

The resolution which I have the honour to move is as follows:

The object of the Indian National Congress is the attainment of *swaraj* by the people of India by all legitimate and peaceful means.

I do not propose to detain you for any length of time over proposing this resolution to you in a few English words. I am already absolved from that infliction because Lala Lajpat Rai has already arrived and he has undertaken the task of explaining that resolution to you in English. I just want to say a few words, personal words, to those who may not have followed my Hindustani. In my humble opinion, the Congress will have done the rightest thing if it unanimously adopts this resolution.

There are only two kinds of objection, so far as I understand, that will be advanced from this platform. One is, that we may not today think of dissolving the British connection. What I say is that it is derogatory to national dignity to think of permanence of British connection at any cost. (Hear, hear). We are labouring under a grievous wrong which it is the personal duty of every Indian to get redressed. This British Government not only refuses to redress the wrong but it refuses to acknowledge its mistakes, and so long as it retains that attitude it is not possible for us to say that all that we want to get is by retaining the British connection. No matter what difficulties lie in our path, we must make the clearest possible declaration to the world and to the whole of India that we may not possibly have the British connection if the British people will not do this elementary justice. I do not for one moment suggest that we want to end the British connection at all costs unconditionally. If the British

1. The speech was made when Gandhiji heard complaints regarding the election of delegates to the subjects committee, held in the morning. Ultimately fresh elections were ordered by the president.
2. The speech was made at the commencement of the debate on the draft Creed Resolution at the meeting of the subjects committee.

connection is for the advancement of India we do not want to destroy it. But if it is inconsistent with our national self-respect, then it is our bounden duty to destroy it. (Hear, hear). There is room in this resolution for both; those who believe that by retaining the British connection we can purify ourselves and purify the British people and those who have no such belief. As for instance, take the extreme case of Mr. Andrews. He says all hope for India is gone for keeping the British connection. He says there must be complete severance, complete independence. (Hear, hear.) There is room enough in this creed for a man like Mr. Andrews also. Take another illustration—a man like myself or my brother Shaukat Ali. There is certainly no room for us if we have eternally to subscribe to the doctrine that, whether these wrongs are redressed or not, we shall have to evolve ourselves within the British Empire: there is no room for me in that creed. Therefore, this creed is elastic enough to take in both shades of opinion, and the British people will have to beware that, if they do not want to do justice, it will be the bounden duty of every Indian to destroy that Empire.

Then we have some argument as to the means. I will have the right of reply, so I do not want to address myself on that question now.

I want just now to wind up my remarks with a personal appeal drawing your attention to an object-lesson that was presented in the Bengal camp yesterday. If you want *swaraj*, you have got a demonstration of how to get *swaraj*. There was a little bit of skirmish, a little bit of squabble and a little bit of difference in the Bengal camp, as there will always be differences so long as the world lasts. I have known differences between husband and wife because I am still a husband. I have noticed differences between parents and children because I am still a father of four sons and they are all strong enough to destroy their father so far as bodily strength is concerned. So I possess that varied experience of husband and parent. I know that we shall always have squabbles, we shall always have differences. But the lesson that I want to draw your attention to is that I had the honour and privilege of addressing both parties.[1] They gave me their undivided attention and, what is more, they showed their attachment, their affection and their fellowship for me by accepting the humble advice that I had the honour of tendering to them, and I advised them:

"I am not here to distribute justice; the justice that can be awarded is only through our worthy President. But I ask you not to go to the President. You need not worry him. If you are strong, if you are brave, if

1. One led by C. R. Das and the other by Jitendralal Banerjee.

you are intent upon getting *swaraj*, and if you really want to revise the creed, then you will bottle up your rage, you will bottle up all the feelings of injustice that may rankle in your hearts and forget these things here under this very roof." And I told them to forget their differences, to forget the wrongs. I do not want to tell you or go into the history of that incident. Probably most of you know. I simply want to invite your attention to the fact. I do not say they have settled their differences. I hope they have. But I do know that they undertook to forget the differences. They undertook not to worry the President, they undertook not to make any demonstration here or in the subjects committee, and all honour to those who listened to that advice.[1] I only want my Bengal friends and all the other friends, who have come to this great assembly with a fixed determination, to seek nothing but the betterment of their country, to seek nothing but the advance of their respective rights, to seek nothing but the conservation of the national honour. I appeal to everyone of you to copy the example set by those who felt aggrieved and who felt that their heads were broken. I know, before we are done with this great battle on which we have embarked at the special session of the Congress[2], we have to go probably, possibly, through a sea of blood, but let it not be said of us or any of us that we are guilty of shedding blood, but let it be said by generations yet to be born that we suffered, that we shed not somebody's blood but our own; and so I have no hesitation in saying that I do not want to show much sympathy for those who had their heads broken or who were said to be even in danger of losing their lives. What does it matter? It is much better to die at the hands at least of our own countrymen. What is there to revenge ourselves about or upon? So I ask everyone of you that if at any time there is blood boiling within you against some fellow countryman of yours, even though he may be in the employ of the government, even though he may be in the secret service, or he may belong to the detective department, you will take care not to be offended and not to return blow for blow. Understand that the very moment you return the blow from the detective your cause is lost. That is your non-violent campaign and so I ask everyone of you not to retaliate but to bottle up all your rage, to dismiss your rage from you, and you will

1. All Bengal delegates attended the open session of the Congress despite rumours to the effect that the group led by Jitendralal Banerjee would not attend it on account of differences regarding the election to the subjects committee.
2. Held at Calcutta in September 1920.

rise braver men. I am here to congratulate those who have restrained themselves from going to the President and bringing the dispute before him. Therefore I appeal to those who feel aggrieved to feel that they will have done the right thing in forgetting it and if they have not forgotten I ask them to try to forget the thing—and that is the object-lesson to which I wanted to draw your attention.

If you want to carry this resolution do not carry it only by acclamation, though I shall want your acclamation for this resolution.

But I want you to accompany the carrying out of this resolution with a faith and a resolution, which nothing on earth can move, that you are intent upon getting *swaraj* at the earliest possible moment, and that you are intent upon getting *swaraj* by means that is legitimate, that is honourable, and by means that is non-violent, that is peaceful. You have resolved upon this thing: that, so far as we can see today, we cannot give battle to this Government by means of steel but we can give battle by exercising what I have so often called soul-force and soul-force is not the prerogative of one man or a *sannyasi* or even of a so-called saint. Soul-force is the prerogative of every human being, female or male, and therefore I ask my countrymen, if they want to accept this resolution, to accept it with that fixed determination and to understand that it is inaugurated under such good and favourable auspices as I have described to you. I have done. If there is anything which I have got to explain I shall do so in my reply. I thank you very much for giving me this patient hearing. May God grant that you will pass this resolution unanimously. May God grant that you will also have the courage and the ability to carry out the resolution and that within one year. (Loud and continued cheers.)[1]

1. Report of the Thirty-fifth Session of the Indian National Congress.

27. Untouchability — Greatest Blot on Hinduism

SPEECH AT SUPPRESSED CLASSES CONFERENCE, AHMEDABAD[1]

[April 13, 1921]

Mr. Gandhi regretted in the beginning the small attendance,[2] and said that incidents such as the present took away what little faith he had in conferences as an effective agency of social reform. If therefore he occupied the audience shorter than they expected, it would be because his remarks would not reach all he meant to address and not because his enthusiasm for the work was in any way damped. He was also thankful for the fact that the conference had brought him the pleasure of meeting friends on the same platform. It was not usual for him nowadays to meet friends, co-operation with whom used to be a pleasure and privilege but from whom the present conditions had unfortunately cut him off. It was a happy thing, however, that on the question of untouchability he was in the same boat as they.

Coming to the subject, he said:

I do not know how I am to convince those who oppose the reform, of the wrong position they have taken. How am I to plead with those who regard any contact with the members of the suppressed community as entailing defilement and of which they cannot be cleansed without necessary ablutions and who thus regard omission to perform the ablution a sin? I can only place before them my innermost convictions.

I regard untouchability as the greatest blot on Hinduism. This idea was not brought home to me by my bitter experiences during the South

---

1. This fourth conference of the so-called untouchables was held on April 13 and 14, 1921.
2. The report of the speech says: "There was a large attendance of ladies and gentlemen from the town, though the number of the untouchables was much less than expected, a rumour having spread in the town that Government would arrest those of them who attended."

African struggle. It is not due to the fact that I was once an agnostic. It is equally wrong to think—as some people do— that I have taken my views from my study of Christian religious literature. These views date as far back as the time when I was neither enamoured of, nor was acquainted with, the *Bible* or the followers of the *Bible*.

I was hardly yet twelve when this idea had dawned on me. A scavenger named Uka, an untouchable, used to attend our house for cleaning latrines. Often I would ask my mother why it was wrong to touch him, why I was forbidden to touch him. If I accidentally touched Uka, I was asked to perform the ablutions, and though I naturally obeyed, it was not without smilingly protesting that untouchability was not sanctioned by religion, that it was impossible that it should be so. I was a very dutiful and obedient child and so far as it was consistent with respect for parents, I often had tussles with them on this matter. I told my mother that she was entirely wrong in considering physical contact with Uka as sinful.

While at school I would often happen to touch the 'untouchables', and as I never would conceal the fact from my parents, my mother would tell me that the shortest cut to purification after the unholy touch was to cancel the touch by touching any Mussulman passing by. And simply out of reverence and regard for my mother I often did so, but never did so believing it to be a religious obligation.

After some time we shifted to Porbandar, where I made my first acquaintance with Sanskrit. I was not yet put into an English school, and my brother and I were placed in charge of a Brahmin who taught us Ramaraksha[1] and Vishnu Puja[2]. The texts "*Jale Vishnuh sthale Vishnuh*" (there is the Lord present in water, there is the Lord present in earth) have never gone out of my memory. A motherly old dame used to live close by. Now it happened that I was very timid then, and would conjure up ghosts and goblins whenever the lights went out, and it was dark. The old mother, to disabuse me of fears, suggested that I should mutter the Texts whenever I was afraid, and all evil spirits would fly away. This I did and, as I thought, with good effect. I could never believe then that there was any text in the *Ramaraksha* pointing to the conduct of the 'untouchables' as a sin. I did not understand its meaning then, or understood it very imperfectly.

1. Hymns to Rama beseeching protection.
2. Hymns to Vishnu.

But I was confident that *Ramaraksha.* which could destroy all fear of ghosts, could not be countenancing any such thing as fear of contact with the 'untouchables'.

The *Ramayana* used to be regularly read in our family. A Brahmin called Ladha Maharaj used to read it. He was stricken with leprosy, and he was confident that a regular reading of the *Ramayana* would cure him of leprosy, and indeed, he was cured of it. 'How can the *Ramayana*,' I thought to myself, 'in which one who is regarded nowadays as an untouchable took Rama across the Ganges in his boat, countenance the idea of any human beings being 'untouchables' on the ground that they were polluted souls?' The fact that we addressed God as the 'purifier of the polluted' and by similar appellation, shows that it is a sin to regard anyone born in Hinduism as polluted or untouchable— that it is Satanic to do so. I have hence been never tired of repeating that it is a great sin. I do not pretend that this thing had crystallized as a conviction in me at the age of twelve, but I do say that I did then regard untouchability as a sin. I narrate this story for the information of the Vaishnavas and orthodox Hindus:

I have always claimed to be a *sanatani* Hindu. It is not that I am quite innocent of the scriptures. I am not a profound scholar of Sanskrit. I have read the *Vedas* and the *Upanishads* only in translations.

Naturally, therefore, mine is not a scholarly study of them. My knowledge of them is in no way profound, but I have studied them as I should do as a Hindu and I claim to have grasped their true spirit.

By the time I had reached the age of 21, I had studied other religions also.

There was a time when I was wavering between Hinduism and Christianity. When I recovered my balance of mind, I felt that to me salvation was possible only through the Hindu religion and my faith in Hinduism grew deeper and more enlightened.

But even then I believed that untouchability was no part of Hinduism; and, that if it was, such Hinduism was not for me. True Hinduism does not regard untouchability as a sin. I do not want to enter into any controversy regarding the interpretation of the *shastras*. It might be difficult for me to establish my point by quoting authorities from the *Bhagavat*[1] or *Manusmriti*. But I claim to have understood the spirit of Hinduism. Hinduism has sinned in giving sanction to untouchability. It has degraded us, made us the pariahs of the Empire. Even the

1. A *Purana* describing the *avatars* of Vishnu.

Mussulmans caught the sinful contagion from us, and in S[outh] Africa, in E[ast] Africa and in Canada, the Mussulmans no less than Hindus came to be regarded as pariahs. All this evil has resulted from the sin of untouchability.

I may here recall my proposition, which is this: So long as the Hindus wilfully regard untouchability as part of their religion, so long as the mass of Hindus consider it a sin to touch a section of their brethren, *swaraj* is impossible of attainment. Yudhishthira would not enter heaven without his dog. How can, then, the descendants of that Yudhishthira expect to obtain *swaraj* without the untouchables? What crimes for which we condemn the Government as satanic have not we been guilty of towards our untouchable brethren?

We are guilty of having suppressed our brethren; we make them crawl on their bellies; we have made them rub their noses on the ground; with eyes red with rage, we push them out of railway compartments—what more than this has British Rule done? What charge that we bring against Dyer and O'Dwyer may not others, and even our own people, lay at our door? We ought to purge ourselves of this pollution. It is idle to talk of *swaraj* so long as we do not protect the weak and the helpless, or so long as it is possible for a single *swarajist* to injure the feelings of any individual. *Swaraj* means that not a single Hindu or Muslim shall for a moment arrogantly think that he can crush with impunity meek Hindus or Muslims. Unless this condition is fulfilled we will gain *swaraj* only to lose it the next moment. We are no better than the brutes until we have purged ourselves of the sins we have committed against our weaker brethren.

But I have faith in me still. In the course of my peregrinations in India I have realized that the spirit of kindness of which the poet Tulsidas sings so eloquently, which forms the cornerstone of the Jain and Vaishnava religions, which is the quintessence of the *Bhagavat*. and which every verse of the *Gita* is saturated with—this kindness, this love, this charity, is slowly but steadily gaining ground in the hearts of the masses of this country.

Many a fracas between Hindus and Mussulmans is still heard of. There are still many of those who do not scruple to wrong one another. But as to the net result, I feel that kindness and charity have increased. The Hindus and Mohammedans have become god fearing.

We have shaken ourselves free from the hypnotism of law courts and Government schools and no longer labour under any other hallucination.

I have also realized that those whom we regard as illiterate and ignorant are the very people who deserve to be called educated. They are more cultured than we, their lives are more righteous than ours. A little study of the present day mentality of the people will show that according to the popular conception *swaraj* is synonymous with *Ramarajya*—the establishment of the Kingdom of Righteousness on earth.

If it can bring any comfort to you, my untouchable brethren, I would say that your question does not cause so much stir as it used to do formerly. That does not mean that I expect you to cease to have misgivings about the Hindus. How can they deserve to be not mistrusted having wronged you so much? Swami Vivekanand used to say that the untouchables were not depressed, they were suppressed by the Hindus who in turn had suppressed themselves by suppressing them.

I suppose I was at Nellore on the 6th of April.[1] I met the untouchables there and I prayed that day as I have done today. I do want to attain *moksha*. I do not want to be reborn. But if I have to be reborn, should be born an untouchable, so that I may share their sorrows, sufferings, and the affronts levelled at them, in order that I may endeavour to free myself and them from that miserable condition.

I, therefore, prayed that if I should be born again, I should do so not as a Brahmin, Kshatriya, Vaisya, or Sudra, but as an Atishudra[2]. Today is much more solemn than the sixth. It is hallowed by the memory of the massacre[3] of thousands of innocents. And I prayed, therefore, also today that if I should die with any of my desires unfructified, with my service of the untouchables unfinished with my Hinduism unfulfilled, I may be born again amongst the untouchables to bring my Hinduism to its fulfilment.

I love scavenging. In my Ashram, an eighteen-year old Brahmin lad is doing the scavenger's work in order to teach the Ashram scavenger cleanliness. The lad is no reformer. He was born and bred in orthodoxy. He is a regular reader of the *Gita* and faithfully performs *sandhyavandan*[4]. His pronunciation of Sanskrit verses is more faultless than mine. When he conducts the prayer his soft, sweet melodies melt one into love. But he felt that his accomplishments were incomplete until he had become also a

---

1. Gandhiji was at Nellore on April 7, 1921.
2. Shudra of Shudras.
3. At Jallianwala Bagh on April 13, 1919.
4. Morning and evening prayers with a set formula.

perfect sweeper, and that if he wanted the Ashram sweeper to do his work well he must do it himself and set an example.

You should realize that you are cleaning Hindu society. You have therefore to purify your lives. You should cultivate the habits of cleanliness, so that no one may point his finger at you. Use alkali ash or earth if you cannot afford to use soap, to keep yourselves clean.

Some of you are given to drinking and gambling which you must get rid of. You will point your finger at the Brahmins and say even they are given to these vices. But they are not looked upon as polluted, and you are. You must not ask the Hindus to emancipate you as a matter of favour. Hindus must do so, if they want, in their own interests. You should, therefore, make them feel ashamed by your own purity and cleanliness. I believe that we shall have purified ourselves within the next five months. If my expectations are not fulfilled, I will think that although my proposition was fundamentally correct, yet I was wrong in my calculation; and I will again say that I had erred in my calculation.

You claim to be Hindus; you read the *Bhagavat*. If, therefore, the Hindus oppress you then you should understand that the fault does not lie in the Hindu religion but in those who profess it. In order to emancipate yourselves you shall have to purify yourselves. You shall have to get rid of evil habits like drinking.

If you want to ameliorate your condition, if you want to obtain *swaraj*, you should be self-reliant. I was told in Bombay that some of you are opposed to N.C.O. and believe that salvation is only possible through the British Government. Let me tell you that you will never be able to obtain redress by discarding Hindu religion and courting the favour of a third party. Your emancipation lies in your own hands.

I have come in contact with the untouchables all over the country; and I have observed that immense possibilities lie latent in them of which neither they nor the rest of the Hindus seem to be aware. Their intellect is of virginal purity. I ask you to learn spinning and weaving, and if you take them up as a profession, you will keep poverty from your doors. As regards your attitude towards the Bhangis I will repeat what I said at Godhra[1] I cannot understand why you should yourselves countenance the distinction between *Dheds* and *Bhangis*. There is no difference between them. Even in normal times their occupation is as honourable as that of lawyers or Government servants.

---

1. *Vide* "Speech at Social Conference, Godhra" 5-11-1917.

You should now cease to accept leavings from plates, however clean they may be represented to be. Receive grain only—good, sound grain, not rotten grain—and that too only if it is courteously offered. If you are able to do all I have asked you to do, you will secure your emancipation, not in four or five months, but in so many days.

The Hindus are not sinful by nature—they are sunk in ignorance. Untouchability must be extinct in this very year. Two of the strongest desires that keep me in flesh and bone are the emancipation of the untouchables and the protection of the cow. When these two desires are fulfilled, there is *swaraj*, and therein lies my own *moksha*. May God give you strength to work out your salvation.

[*Young India,* 27-4-1921 and 4-5-1921]

28. The Great Trial[1]

[Ahmedabad,
March 18, 1922]

At the Circuit House at Shahi Bag, the trial of Mr. Gandhi and Mr. Banker commenced on Saturday noon.

Sir J.T. Strangman[2] with Rao Bahadur Girdharlal conducted the prosecution while the accused were undefended. The Judge[3] took his seat at 12 noon and said there was a slight mistake in the charges framed, which he corrected. The charges were then read out by the Registrar, the offence being in three articles published in the *Young India* of September 29, December 15, of 1921 and February 23, 1922. The offending articles were then read out; first of them was,"Tampering with Loyalty"; the second, "The Puzzle and its Solution" and the last was "Shaking the Manes".

The Judge said the law required that the charge should not only be read out, but explained. In this case, it would not be necessary for him to say much by way of explanation. The charge in each case was that of bringing or attempting to bring in to hatred or contempt or exciting or attempting to excite disaffection towards His Majesty's Government established by law in British India. Both the accused were charged with the three offences under Section 124 A, contained in the articles read out, written by Mr. Gandhi and printed by Mr. Banker. The words "hatred and

---

1. A verbatim report consisting of a shorthand transcript of the entire Sessions Court proceedings is available in Trial of Gandhiji, pp. 197-212. This report from *Young India* has minor verbal modifications or additions made in it wherever necessary to bring it in line with the Court records. A contemporary report of the trial was published by the Sadaqat Ashram Press, Patna, in 1922, with an 'introduction,' by Mazharul Haque, and reprinted in 1965 by Navajivan Publishing House, Ahmedabad. Also relevant is the book *Two Memorable Trials of Mahatma Gandhi*, edited by R. K. Prabhu, published by Navajivan in 1962. Sarojini Naidu has given a classic description of the memorable trial; *vide Mahatma*, Vol. II, "The Great Trial".
2. Advocate-General, and Special Public Prosecutor.
3. Justice R. S. Broomfield.

contempt" were words the meaning of which was sufficiently obvious. The word "disaffection" was defined under the Section where they were told that disaffection included disloyalty and feelings of enmity and the word used in the Section had also been interpreted by the High Court of Bombay in a reported case as meaning political alienation or discontent, a spirit of disloyalty to Government of existing authority[1].

The charges having been read out, the Judge called upon the accused to plead to the charges. He asked Mr. Gandhi whether he pleaded guilty or claimed to be tried.

MR. GANDHI: I plead guilty on each count of the charge. I merely observe that the King's name is omitted from the charge-sheet and, in my opinion, very properly.

THE JUDGE: Mr. Banker, do you plead guilty, or do you claim to be tried?

MR. BANKER: I plead guilty.

Sir J. Strangman then wanted the Judge to proceed with the trial fully;[2] but the Judge said he did not agree with what had been said by the Counsel. The Judge said that from the time he knew he was going to try the case, he had thought over the question of sentence and he was prepared to hear anything that the Counsel might have to say, or Mr. Gandhi wished to say, on the sentence. He honestly did not believe that the mere recording of evidence in the trial which Counsel had called for would make any difference to them, one way or the other. He, therefore, proposed to accept the pleas.[3]

Mr. Gandhi smiled at this decision.

The Judge said nothing further remained but to pass sentence and before doing so, he liked to hear Sir J.T. Strangman. He was entitled to base his general remarks on the charges against the accused and on their pleas.

SIR J.T. STRANGMAN: It will be difficult to do so. I ask the Court that the whole matter may be properly considered. If I stated what has

---

1. The interpretation of the Judge was: "An attempt to excite disaffection towards Government is equivalent to excite political hatred of Government as established by Law, to excite political discontent and alienate the people from their allegiance."
2. He urged that "the charges should be investigated as fully as possible and also that the Court will be in a better position to pass sentence if it has the whole of the facts"
3. For a fuller version of the judge's observations, vide *Trial of Gandhiji*.

happened before the Committing Magistrate, then I can show that there are many things which are material to the question of the sentence.

The first point, he said, he wanted to make out, was that the matter which formed the subject of the present charges formed a part of the campaign to spread disaffection openly and systematically to render Government impossible and to overthrow it. The earliest article that was put in from *Young India* was dated 25th May, 1921, which said that it was the duty of a non-cooperator to create disaffection towards the Government[1]. The counsel then read out portions of articles written by Mr. Gandhi in the *Young India*.

Court said nevertheless it seemed to it that the Court could accept plea on the materials of which the sentence had to be based.

Sir J. Strangman said the question of sentence was entirely for the Court to decide. The Court was always entitled to deal in a more general manner in regard to the question of the sentence than the particular matter resulting in the conviction. He asked leave to refer to articles before the Court and what result might have been produced if the trial had proceeded in order to ascertain what the facts were. He was not going into any matter which involved dispute.

The Judge said there was not the least objection. Sir J Strangman said he wanted to show that these articles were not isolated. They formed part of an organized campaign, but so far as *Young India* was concerned, they would show that from the year 1921. The Counsel then read out extracts from the paper, dated June 8, on the duty of a non-cooperator, which was to preach disaffection towards the existing government and preparing the country for civil disobedience. Then in the same number there was an article on disobedience. Then in the same number there was an article on Disaffection—a virtue or something to that effect.[2] Then there was an article on the 28th of July 1921,[3] in which it stated that "we have to destroy the system". Again on September 30[4], 1921, there was an

---

1. Commenting that the Government's charge on Sunderlal, student leader of Central Provinces, was not for violence but purely spreading disaffection, Gandhiji had written in *Young India* that "it may be stated to be the creed of the non-cooperator to give voice to the popular disaffection towards the Government and to spread it. Disaffection is the very essence of non-cooperation." Vide "Repression in the G.P", 25-5-1921.
2. Vide ""Notes", 15-6-1921, under the sub-title "Disaffection A Virtue".
3. *Ibid.*
4. This appears to be a slip for September 1; *vide* "Notes", 1-9-1921, under the sub-title "Punjab Prosecutions"

article headed, "Punjab Prosecutions", where it was stated that a non-cooperator worth his name should preach disaffection. That was all so far as *Young India* was concerned. They were earlier in date than the article, "Tampering with Loyalty" and it was referred to the Governor of Bombay. Continuing, he said, the accused was a man of high educational qualifications and evidently, from his writings, a recognized leader. The harm that was likely to be caused was considerable. They were the writings of an educated man, and not the writings of an obscure man and the Court must consider to what the results of a campaign of the nature disclosed in the writings must inevitably lead. They had examples before them in the last few months. He referred to the occurrences in Bombay last November and Chauri Chaura, leading to murder and destruction of property, involving many people in misery and misfortune. It was true that, in the course of those articles, they would find non-violence was insisted upon as an item of the campaign and as an item of the creed. But what was the use of preaching non-violence when he preached disaffection towards Government or openly instigated others to overthrow it ? The answer to that question appeared to him to come from Chauri Chaura, Madras and Bombay. These were circumstances which he asked the Court to make into account in sentencing the accused and it would be for the Court to consider those circumstances which involve sentences of severity.

As regards the second accused, his offence was lesser. He did the publication and he did not write. His offence nevertheless was a serious one. His instructions were that he was a man of means and he asked the Court to impose a substantial fine in addition to such term of imprisonment as might be inflicted upon. He quoted Section 10 of the Press Act as bearing on the question of fine. When making a fresh declaration, he said a deposit of Rs. 1,000 to Rs. 10,000 was asked in many cases.

COURT: Mr. Gandhi, do you wish to make a statement to the Court on question of sentence?

MR. GANDHI: I would like, with the Court's permission, to read a written statement.

COURT: Could you give me the writing to put it on record?

MR. GANDHI: I shall give it as soon as I finish reading it.

Before reading his written statement, Mr. Gandhi spoke a few words as introductory remarks to the whole statement. He said:

Before I read this statement I would like to state that I entirely endorse the learned Advocate-General's remarks in connection with my humble self. I think that he was entirely fair to me in all the statements that he has made, because it is very true and I have no desire whatsoever to conceal from this Court the fact that to preach disaffection towards the existing system of Government has become almost a passion with me, and the learned Advocate-General is also entirely in the right when he says that my preaching of disaffection did not commence with my connection with *Young India*, but that it commenced much earlier and in the statement that I am about to read, it will be my painful duty to admit before this Court that it commenced much earlier than the period stated by the Advocate-General. It is the most painful duty with me, but I have discharge that duty knowing the responsibility that rests upon me, and I wish to endorse all the blame that the learned Advocate-General has thrown on my shoulders in connection with the Bombay, the Madras and the Chauri Chaura occurrences. Thinking over these deeply and sleeping over them night after night, it is impossible to dissociate myself from the diabolical crimes of Chauri Chaura or the mad outrages in Bombay and Madras. He is quite right when he says that, as a man of responsibility, a man having received a fair share of education, having had a fair share of experience of this world, I should know the consequences of every one of my acts. I knew that I was playing with fire. I ran the risk and, if I was set free, I would still do the same[1]. I know that I was feeling it so every day and I have felt it also this morning that I would have failed in my duty if I did not say what I said here just now.

I wanted to avoid violence. I want to avoid violence. Non-violence is the first article of my faith. It is also the last article of my creed. But I had to make my choice. I had either to submit to a system which I considered had done an irreparable harm to my country, or incur the risk of the mad fury of my people bursting forth when they understood the truth from my lips. I know that my people have sometimes gone mad; I am deeply sorry for it. I am, therefore, here to submit not to a light penalty but to the highest penalty. I do not ask for mercy. I do not ask for any extenuating act of clemency. I am here to invite and cheerfully[2] submit to the highest penalty that can be inflicted upon me for what in law is a deliberate crime and what appears to me to be the highest duty of a citizen. The only course open to you, the Judge, is as I am just going to say in my statement, either to resign your post, or inflict on me the severest penalty, if you believe that the system and the law you are assisting to administer

1. These sentences do not occur in the official transcript.
2. *Young India* has this word here.

are good for the people of this country and that my activity is, therefore, injurious to the public weal. I do not expect that kind of conversion, but[1] by the time I have finished with my statement, you will, perhaps, have a glimpse of what is raging within my breast to run this maddest risk[2] that a sane man can run.

The statement was then read out.

STATEMENT

I owe it perhaps to the Indian public and to the public in England, to placate which this prosecution is mainly taken up, that I should explain why, from a staunch loyalist and cooperator, I have become an uncompromising disaffectionist and non-cooperator, To the Court, too, I should say why I plead guilty to the charge of promoting disaffection towards the Government established by law in India.

My public life began in 1893 in South Africa in troubled weather. My first contact with British authority in that country was not of a happy character. I discovered that as a man and an Indian I had no rights. More correctly, I discovered that I had no rights as a man because I was an Indian.

But I was not baffled. I thought that this treatment of Indians was an excrescence upon a system that was intrinsically and mainly good. I gave the Government my voluntary and hearty co-operation, criticizing it freely where I felt it was faulty, but never wishing its destruction. Consequently, when the existence of the Empire was threatened in 1899 by the Boer challenge, I offered my services to it[3], raised a volunteer ambulance corps and served at several actions that took place for the relief of Ladysmith.[4] Similarly in 1906, at the time of the Zulu revolt, I raised a stretcher-bearer party and served till the end of the rebellion.[5] On both these occasions I received medals and was even mentioned in despatches. For my work in South Africa I was given by Lord Hardinge a Kaiser-i-Hind Gold Medal.[6] When the war broke out in 1914 between

---

1. This part of the sentence does not occur in the official report.
2. The official report has "the maddest risks"
3. *Vide* "The Great Trial".
4. *Ibid.*
5. *Vide* "Indian Strectcher-Bearer Corps", 19-7-1906.
6. *Vide* "Natal Indians", 4-4-1908 and "Story of a Soldier of Truth", 4-4-1908.

England and Germany, I raised a volunteer ambulance corps in London consisting of the then resident Indians in London, chiefly students.[1] Its work was acknowledged by the authorities to be valuable. Lastly, in India, when a special appeal was made at the War Conference in Delhi in 1918 by Lord Chelmsford for recruits, I struggled at the cost of my health to raise a corps in Kheda[2] and the response was being made when the hostilities ceased and orders were received that no more recruits were wanted. In all these efforts at service, I was actuated by the belief that it was possible by such services to gain a status of full equality in the Empire for my countrymen.

The first shock came in the shape of the Rowlatt Act, a law designed to rob the people of all real freedom. I felt called upon to lead an intensive agitation against it. Then followed the Punjab horrors beginning with the massacre at Jallianwala Bagh and culminating in crawling orders, public floggings and other indescribable humiliations. I discovered, too, that the plighted word of the Prime Minister to the Mussalmans of India regarding the integrity of Turkey and the holy places of Islam was not likely to be fulfilled. But, in spite of the forebodings and the grave warnings of friends, at the Amritsar Congress in 1919,[3] I fought for co-operation and working the Montagu-Chelmsford reforms, hoping that the Prime Minister would redeem his promise to the Indian Mussalmans, that the Punjab wound would be healed and that the reforms, inadequate and unsatisfactory though they were, marked a new era of hope in the life of India.

But all that hope was shattered. The Khilafat promise was not to be redeemed. The Punjab crime was white-washed and most culprits went not only unpunished, but remained in service and some continued to draw pensions from the Indian revenue, and in some cases were even rewarded. I saw, too, that not only did the reforms not mark a change of heart, but they were only a method of further draining India of her wealth and of prolonging her servitude.

I came reluctantly to the conclusion that the British connection had made India more helpless than she ever was before, politically and economically. A disarmed India has no power of resistance against any aggressor if she wanted to engage in an armed conflict with him.

---

1. *Vide* "Speech at Mass Meeting", 25-1-1914.
2. *Vide* "Apppeal for Enlistment", 22-6-1918.
3. *Vide* "Speech on Reforms Resolution at Amritsar Congress", 1-1-1920.

So much is this the case that some of our best men consider that India must take generations before she can achieve the Dominion status.

She has become so poor that she has little power of resisting famines.

Before the British advent, India spun and wove in her millions of cottages just the supplement she needed for adding to her meagre agricultural resources. This cottage industry, so vital for India's existence, has been ruined by incredibly heartless and inhuman processes as described by English witnesses. Little do town-dwellers know how the semi-starved masses of India are slowly sinking to lifelessness. Little do they know that their miserable comfort represents the brokerage they get for the work they do for the foreign exploiter, that the profits and the brokerage are sucked from the masses. Little do they realize that the Government established by law in British India is carried on for this exploitation of the masses. No sophistry, no jugglery in figures can explain away the evidence that the skeletons in many villages present to the naked eye. I have no doubt whatsoever that both England and the town-dwellers of India will have to answer, if there is a God above, for this crime against humanity which is perhaps unequalled in history. The law itself in this country has been used to serve the foreign exploiter. My unbiased examination of the Punjab Martial Law cases has led me to believe that at least ninety-five per cent of convictions were wholly bad[1]. My experience of political cases in India leads one to the conclusion that in nine out of every ten cases the condemned men were totally innocent. Their crime consisted in the love of their country. In ninety nine cases out of hundred, justice has been denied to Indians as against Europeans in the Courts of India. This is not an exaggerated picture. It is the experience of almost every Indian who has had anything to do with such cases. In my opinion, the administration of the law is thus prostituted consciously or unconsciously for the benefit of the exploiter.

The greatest misfortune is that Englishmen and their Indian associates in the administration of the country do not know that they are engaged in the crime I have attempted to describe. I am satisfied that many English and Indian officials honestly believe that they are administering one of the best systems devised in the world and that India is making steady though slow progress. They do not know that a subtle but effective system of terrorism and an organized display of force on the one hand, and the deprivation of all powers of retaliation or self-defence

1. The original draft has "thing".

on the other, have emasculated the people and induced in them the habit of simulation. This awful habit has added to the ignorance and the self-deception of the administrators. Section 124-A under which I am happily charged is perhaps the prince among the political sections of the Indian Penal Code designed to suppress the liberty of the citizen. Affection cannot be manufactured or regulated by law. If one has no affection for a person or system[1], one should be free to give the fullest expression to his disaffection, so long as he does not contemplate, promote or incite to violence. But the section under which Mr. Banker and I are charged is one under which mere promotion of disaffection is a crime. I have studied some of the cases tried under it, and I know that some of the most loved of India's patriots have been convicted under it. I consider it a privilege, therefore, to be charged under it. I have endeavoured to give in their briefest outline the reasons for my disaffection. I have no personal ill will against any single administrator, much less can I have any disaffection towards the King's person. But I hold it to be a virtue to be disaffected towards a Government which in its totality has done more harm to India than any previous system. India is less manly under the British rule than she ever was before. Holding such a belief, I consider it to be a sin to have affection for the system. And it has been a precious privilege for me to be able to write what I have in the various articles tendered in evidence against me.

In fact, I believe that I have rendered a service to India and England by showing in non-cooperation the way out of the unnatural state in which both are living. In my humble opinion, non-cooperation with evil is as much a duty as is co-operation with good.

But, in the past, non-cooperation has been deliberately expressed in violence to the evil-doer. I am endeavouring to show to my countrymen that violent non-cooperation only multiplies evil and that, as evil can only be sustained by violence, withdrawal of support of evil requires complete abstention from violence. Non-violence implies voluntary submission to the penalty for non-cooperation with evil. I am here, therefore, to invite and submit cheerfully to the highest penalty that can be inflicted upon me for what in law is a deliberate crime and what appears to me to be the highest duty of a citizen. The only course open to you, the Judge, is either to resign your post and thus dissociate yourself from evil, if you feel that the law you are called upon to administer is an evil and that in reality I am innocent; or to inflict on me the severest penalty if you believe that

1. The original draft has "thing".

the system and the law you are assisting to administer are good for the people of this country and that my activity is, therefore, injurious to the public weal.[1]

COURT: Mr. Banker, do you wish to say anything to the Court as regards the sentences?

MR. BANKER: I only want to say that I had the privilege of printing these articles and I plead guilty to the charge. I have got nothing to say as regards the sentence.

The following is the full text of the judgment:

Mr. Gandhi, you have made my task easy in one way by pleading guilty to the charge. Nevertheless what remains, namely, the determination of a just sentence, is perhaps as difficult a proposition as a judge in this country could have to face. The law is no respecter of persons. Nevertheless, it will be impossible to ignore the fact that you are in a different category from any person I have ever tried or am likely to have to try. It would be impossible to ignore the fact that, in the eyes of millions of your countrymen, you are a great patriot and a great leader. Even those who differ from you in politics look upon you as a man of high ideals and of noble and of even saintly life. I have to deal with you in one character only. It is not my duty and I do not presume to judge or criticize you in any other character. It is my duty to judge you as a man subject to the law, who has by his own admission broken the law and committed what to an ordinary man must appear to be grave offences against the State. I do not forget that you have constantly preached against violence and that you have on many occasions, as I am willing to believe, done much to prevent violence, but having regard to the nature of your political teaching and the nature of many of those to whom it is addressed, how you could have continued to believe that violence would not be the inevitable consequence it passes my capacity to understand.

There are probably few people in India who do not sincerely regret that you should have made it impossible for any Government to leave you at liberty. But it is so. I am trying to balance what is due to you against what appears to me to be necessary in the interests of the public, and I propose, in passing sentence, to follow the precedent of a case, in many respects similar to this case, that was decided some 12 years ago, I mean the case against Mr. Bal Gangadhar Tilak under this same section.

1. The signed, handwritten statement is available in photostat in *Trial of Gandhiji*.

The sentence that was passed upon him as it finally stood was a sentence of simple imprisonment for six years. You will not consider it unreasonable, I think, that you should be classed with Mr. Tilak, and that is the sentence, two years' simple imprisonment on each count of the charge, i.e., six years in all, which I feel it my duty to pass upon you and I should like to say in doing so that, if the course of events in India should make it possible for the Government to reduce the period and release you, no one will be better pleased than I.

THE JUDGE (to Mr. Banker): I assume that you have been to a large extent under the influence of your chief. The sentence that I propose to pass upon you is simple imprisonment for six months on each of the first two counts, that is, simple imprisonment for one year and a fine of a thousand rupees on the third count, with six months' simple imprisonment in default.

Mr. Gandhi said:

I would say one word. Since you have done me the honour of recalling the trial of the late Lokamanya Bal Gangadhar Tilak, I just want to say that I consider it to be the proudest privilege and honour to be associated with his name. So far as the sentence itself is concerned, I certainly consider that it is as light as any judge would inflict on me, and so far as the whole proceedings are concerned, I must say that I could not have expected greater courtesy.

Then the friends of Mr. Gandhi crowded round him as the Judge left the court, and fell at his feet. There was much sobbing on the part of both men and women. But all the while Mr. Gandhi was smiling and cool and giving encouragement to everybody who came to him. Mr. Banker also was smiling and taking this in a lighthearted way. After all his friends had taken leave of him, Mr. Gandhi was taken out of the Court to the Sabarmati jail. And thus the great trial finished.

[*Young India,* 23-3-1922]

29. A Scheme for Swaraj

PRESIDENTIAL ADDRESS AT BELGAUM CONGRESS[1]

[December 26, 1924]

FRIENDS,

It was after much misgiving that I accepted the burden of the honour you have done me today. The unique honour for this year should have been bestowed upon Shrimati Sarojini Naidu, who did such wonderful work both in Kenya and South Africa. But it was not to be. The developments both internal and external have necessitated my acceptance of the burden. I know that I shall have your support in my attempt to do justice to the high office to which you have called me.

At the outset, let me note with respectful feelings the deaths during the year of Bi-Amma, Sir Ashutosh Mukherji, Mr. Bhupendra Nath Basu, Dr. Subramania Iyer and Mr. Dalbahadur Giri at home, and of Messrs Rustomjee and P.K. Naidu in South Africa. I tender in your name my respectful condolences to the bereaved families.

RETROSPECTIVE

From the September of 1920 the Congress has been principally an institution for developing strength from within. It has ceased to function by means of resolutions addressed to the Government for redress of grievances. It did so, because it ceased to believe in the beneficial character of the existing system of government. The breach of faith with the Mussalmans of India was the first rude shock to the people's faith in the Government. The Rowlatt Act and O'Dwyerism culminating in the Jallianwala Bagh massacre, opened the eyes of the people to the true nature of the system. At the same time it was realized that the existence of the system depended upon the co-operation, whether conscious or unconscious and whether voluntary or forced, of the people. With the

---

1. This printed address appears to have been prepared before December 18; *vide* "Letter to C. F. Andrews", 18-12-1924.

view, therefore, of mending or ending the system it was decided to try to begin withdrawing voluntary co-operation from the top. At the Special Session of the Congress at Calcutta in 1920, the boycott of Government titles, law courts, educational institutions, legislative bodies and foreign cloth was resolved upon. All the boycotts were more or less taken up by the parties concerned. Those who could not or would not, retired from the Congress. I do not propose to trace the chequered career of the non-cooperation movement. Though not a single boycott was anywhere near completion, every one of them had undoubtedly the effect of diminishing the prestige of the particular institutions boycotted.

The most important boycott was the boycott of violence. Whilst it appeared at one time to be entirely successful, it was soon discovered that the non-violence was only skin-deep. It was the passive non-violence of helplessness, not the enlightened non-violence of resourcefulness. The result was an eruption of intolerance against those who did not non-cooperate. This was violence of a subtler type.

In spite, however, of this grave defect I make bold to say that the propaganda of non-violence checked the outbreak of physical violence which would certainly have broken out, had not non-violent non-cooperation come into being. It is my deliberate conviction that non-violent non-cooperation has given to the people a consciousness of their strength. It has brought to the surface the hidden powers in the people of resistance through suffering. It has caused an awakening among the masses which perhaps no other method could have.

Though, therefore, non-violent non-cooperation has not brought us *swaraj*, though it has brought about certain deplorable results and though the institutions that were sought to be boycotted are still flourishing, in my humble opinion, non-violent non-cooperation as a means of attaining political freedom has come to stay and that even its partial success has brought us nearer *swaraj*. There is no mistaking the fact that the capacity for suffering for the sake of a cause must advance it.

A HALT

But we are face to face with a situation that compels us to cry halt. For, whilst individuals hold firmly to their belief in non-cooperation, the majority of those who are immediately concerned have practically lost faith in it, with the exception of boycott of foreign cloth.

Scores of lawyers have resumed practice. Some even regret having ever given it up. Many who had given up Councils have returned to them and the number of those who believe in Council entry is on the increase. Hundreds of boys and girls who gave up Government schools and colleges have repented of their action and have returned to them. I hear that Government schools and colleges can hardly cope with the demand for admission. In these circumstances, these boycotts cannot be worked as part of the national programme, unless the Congress is prepared to do without the classes directly affected. But I hold it to be just as impracticable to keep these classes out of the Congress as it would be now to keep the non-co-operators out. They must both remain in the Congress, without either party interfering with or hostility criticizing the other. What is applicable to Hindu-Muslim unity is, I feel, applicable to the unity among different political groups. We must tolerate each other and trust to time to convert the one or the other to the opposite belief. We must go further.

We must plead with the Liberals and others who have seceded to rejoin the Congress. If non-cooperation is suspended, there is no reason why they should keep out. Thc advance must be from us Congressmen. We must cordially invite them and make it easy for them to come in.

You are perhaps now able to see why I entered into the agreement with the Swarajists.

FOREIGN CLOTH BOYCOTT

You will observe that one boycott has been retained. Out of regard for the sentiment of an English friend the word "boycott" has been changed in the agreement into "refusal to use foreign cloth".

There is no doubt a bad odour about the word "boycott". It usually implies hatred. So far as I am concerned, I have not intended the word to bear any such meaning. The boycott has reference not to British but to foreign cloth. That boycott is not merely a right but a duty. It is as much a duty as boycott of foreign waters would be if they were imported to substitute the waters of the Indian rivers. This, however, is a digression.

What I wanted to say was that the agreement saves and emphasizes the boycott of foreign cloth. For me it is an effective substitute for violent methods. Just as certain acts such as personal abuse, irritating conduct, lying, causing hurt and murder are symbols of violence, similarly courtesy, inoffensive conduct, truthfulness, etc., are symbols of non-violence. And so to me is boycott of foreign cloth a symbol of non-violence. Revolutionary crime is intended to exert pressure. But it is the insane pressure of anger and ill-will. I contend that non-violent acts exert pressure far more effective than violent acts, for that pressure comes from goodwill and gentleness. Boycott of foreign cloth exerts such pressure. We import the largest amount of foreign cloth from Lancashire. It is also by far the largest of all our imports, sugar being next. Britain's chief interest centres round the Lancashire trade with India. It is the one thing more than any other that has ruined the Indian peasant and imposed partial idleness upon him by depriving him of the one supplementary occupation he had.

Boycott of foreign cloth is, therefore, a necessity if he is to live. The plan, therefore, is not merely to induce the peasant to refuse to buy the cheap and nice looking foreign fabric but also by teaching him to utilize his spare hours in carding and spinning cotton and getting it woven by the village weavers, to dress himself in *khaddar* so woven and thus to save him the cost of buying foreign and, for that matter, even Indian mill made cloth. Thus, boycott of foreign cloth by means of hand spinning and hand weaving, i.e., *khaddar*, not only saves the peasant's money, but it enables us workers to render social service of a first class order. It brings us into direct touch with the villagers. It enables us to give them real political education and teach them to become self-sustained and self-reliant. Organization of *khaddar* is thus infinitely better than co-operative societies or any other form of village organization. It is fraught with the highest political consequence, because it removes the greatest immoral temptation from Britain's way. I call the Lancashire trade immoral, because it was raised and is sustained on the ruin of millions of India's peasants.

And as one immorality leads to another, the many proved immoral acts of Britain are traceable to this one immoral traffic. If, therefore, this one great temptation is removed from Britain's path by India's voluntary effort, it would be good for India, good for Britain and, as Britain, is today the predominant world power, good even for humanity.

I do not endorse the proposition that supply follows demand. On the contrary, demand is often artificially created by unscrupulous vendors. And if a nation is bound, as I hold it is, like individuals to comply with a code of moral conduct, then it must consider the welfare of those whose wants it seeks to supply. It is wrong and immoral for a nation to supply for instance intoxicating liquor to those who are addicted to drink. What is true of intoxicants is true of grain or cloth, if the discontinuance of their cultivation or manufacture in the country to which foreign grain or cloth are exported results in enforced idleness or penury. These later hurt a man's soul and body just as much as intoxication. Depression is but excitement upside down and hence equally disastrous in its results and often more so because we have not yet learnt to regard as immoral or sinful the depression of idleness or penury.

BRITAIN'S DUTY

It is then I hold the duty of Great Britain to regulate her exports with due regard to the welfare of India, as it is India's to regulate her imports with due regard to her own welfare. That economics is untrue which ignores or disregards moral values. The extension of the law of non-violence in the domain of economics means nothing less than the introduction of moral values as a factor to be considered in regulating international commerce. And I must confess that my ambition is nothing less than to see international relations placed on a moral basis through India's efforts. I do not despair of cultivation of limited mass non-violence. I refuse to believe that the tendency of human nature is always downward. The fruition of the boycott of foreign cloth through hand spinning and *khaddar* is calculated not only to bring about a political result of the first magnitude, it is calculated also to make the poorest of India, whether men or women, conscious of their strength and make them partakers in the struggle for India's freedom

FOREIGN *Versus* BRITISH

It is hardly necessary now to demonstrate the futility, not to say the violent nature, of boycott of British cloth or better still British goods as so many patriots have suggested. I am considering the boycott purely from the point of view of India's good. All British goods do not harm us. Some goods such as English books we need for our intellectual or spiritual benefit. As regards cloth, it is not merely British cloth that harms us, but all foreign cloth, and for that matter to a lesser extent even mill made cloth injures us. Boycott brought about anyhow of British cloth cannot yield the same results as such boycott brought about by hand spinning and *khaddar*. This necessitates exclusion at least of all foreign cloth. The exclusion is not intended as a punishment. It is a necessity of national existence.

OBJECTIONS CONSIDERED

But, say the critics, the spinning wheel has not taken, it is not exciting enough, it is an occupation only for women, it means a return to the middle ages, it is a vain effort against the majestic march of scientific knowledge for which machinery stands. In my humble opinion India's need is not excitement but solid work. For the millions solid work itself is excitement and tonic at the same time. The fact is that we have not given the spinning wheel enough trial. I am sorry to have to say that many of us have not given it a serious thought. Even the members of the All-India Congress Committee have failed to carry out the series of resolutions on hand spinning which they themselves have passed from time to time. The majority of us have simply not believed in it. In the circumstances, it is hardly just to say that spinning has failed for want of excitement about it. To say that it is merely an old woman's occupation is to ignore facts.

Spinning mills are a multiplication of spinning wheels. They are managed by men. It is time that we got out of this superstition that some occupations are beneath the dignity of men. Under normal conditions no doubt spinning will be the occupation of the gentle sex.

But the State of the future will always have go keep some men at the spinning wheel so as to make improvements in it within the limitations which as a cottage industry it must have. I must inform you that the progress the mechanism of the wheel has made would have been impossible, if some of us men had not worked at it and had not thought about it day and night.

MACHINERY

I wish, too, you would dismiss from your minds the views attributed to me about machinery. In the first instance, I am no more trying to present for national acceptance all my views on machinery than I am presenting the whole of my belief in non-violence. The spinning wheel is itself an exquisite piece of machinery. My head daily bows in reverence to its unknown inventor. What I do resent is the wanton and wicked destruction of the one cottage industry of India that kept the wolf from the doors of thousands of homes scattered over a surface 1,900 miles long and 1,500 miles broad.

SPINNING FRANCHISE

You will not now wonder at my passion for the spinning wheel, nor will you wonder why I have ventured to present it for introduction in the franchise, and why Pandit Motilal Nehru and Deshbandhu Das have accepted it on behalf of the Swaraj Party. If I had my way, there would be no one on the Congress register who is unwilling to spin or who would not wear *khaddar* on all occasions. I am, however, thankful for what the Swaraj Party has accepted. The modification is a concession to weakness or want of faith. But it must serve as a spur to greater effort on the part of those who have full faith in the wheel and *khaddar*.

NO OTHER MESSAGE

I have thus dilated upon the spinning wheel because I have no better or other message for the nation. I know no other effective method for the attainment of *swaraj* if it is to be by "peaceful and legitimate means". As I have already remarked it is the only substitute for violence that can be accepted by the whole nation. I swear by civil disobedience. But civil disobedience for the attainment of *swaraj* is an impossibility unless and until we have attained the power of achieving boycott of foreign cloth. You will now easily perceive why I should be a useless guide for the Congress if my views about the spinning wheel are not acceptable to you. Indeed you would be justified in regarding me, as some friends do, as a hindrance to national progress, if you consider me to be wrong in my exposition of the doctrine underlying the spinning wheel. If it does not appeal to your heads as well as your hearts, you will be wanting in your duty in not rejecting my lead. Let it no longer be said, as Lord Willingdon very properly once said of us, that we had not the strength and courage to say"No". Indeed your rejection of my proposal, if you do not believe in it, will be a step towards *swaraj*.

HINDU-MUSLIM UNITY

Hindu-Muslim unity is not less important than the spinning wheel. It is the breath of our life. I do not need to occupy much of your time on this question, because the necessity of it for *swaraj* is almost universally accepted. I say "almost" because I know some Hindus and some Mussalmans who prefer the present condition of dependence on Great Britain if they cannot have either wholly Hindu or wholly Mussalman India. Happily their number is small.

I share Maulana Shaukat Ali's robust optimism that the present tension is a mere temporary distemper. The Khilafat agitation in which

Hindus made common cause with their Mussalman brethren and the non-cooperation that followed it caused an awakening among the hitherto slumbering masses. It has given a new consciousness to the classes as well as the masses. Interested persons who were disappointed during the palmy days of non-coopration, now that it has lost the charm of novelty, have found their opportunity and are trading upon the religious bigotry or the selfishness of both the communities. The result is written in the history of the feuds of the past two years. Religion has been travestied. Trifles have been dignified by the name of religious tenets which, the fanatics claim, must be observed at any cost. Economic and political causes have been brought into play for the sake of fomenting trouble. The culminating point was reached in Kohat. The tragedy was aggravated by the callous indifference of the local authority. I must not tarry to examine the causes or to distribute the blame. I have not the material for the task even if I was minded for it. Suffice it to say that the Hindu refugees fled for fear of their lives. There is in Kohat an overwhelming Mussalman majority. They have in so far as is possible under a foreign domination effective political control. It is up to them, therefore, to show that the Hindus are as safe in the midst of their majority as they would be if the whole population of Kohat was Hindu. The Mussalmans of Kohat may not rest satisfied till they have brought back to Kohat every one of the refugees. I hope that the Hindus would not fall into the trap laid for them by the Government and would resolutely decline to go back till the Mussalmans of Kohat have given them full assurances as to their lives and property.

The Hindus can live in the midst of an overwhelming Mussalman majority only if the latter are willing to receive and treat them as friends and equals, just as Mussalmans, if in a minority, must depend for honourable existence in the midst of a Hindu majority on the latter's friendliness. A Government can give protection against thieves and robbers, but not even a *swaraj* government will be able to protect people against a wholesale boycott by one community or another. Governments can deal with abnormal situations. When quarrels become a normal thing of life, it is called civil war and parties must fight it out themselves. The present Government being foreign, in reality a veiled military rule, has resources at its command for its protection against any combination we can make and has, therefore, the power, if it has the will, to deal with our class feuds. But no *swaraj* government with any pretension to being a popular government can possibly be organized and maintained on a war footing. A *swaraj* government means a government established by the free joint-will of Hindus, Mussalmans and others. Hindus and Mussalmans, if they desire *swaraj*, have perforce to settle their differences amicably.

The Unity Conference at Delhi has paved the way for a settlement of religious differences. The Committee of the All Parties Conference is among other things expected to find a workable and just solution of the political differences not only between Hindu and Mussalmans but between all classes and all castes, sects or denominations. Our goal must be removal, at the earliest-possible moment, of communal or sectional representation. A common electorate must impartially elect its representatives on the sole ground of merit. Our services must be likewise impartially manned by the most qualified men and women. But till that time comes and communal jealousies or preferences become a thing of the past, minorities who suspect the motives of majorities must be allowed their way. The majority must set the example of self-sacrifice.

UNTOUCHABILITY

Untouchability is another hindrance to *swaraj*. Its removal is just as essential for *swaraj* as the attainment of Hindu-Muslim unity. This is an essentially Hindu question and Hindus cannot claim or take *swaraj* till they have restored the liberty of the suppressed classes.

They have sunk with the latter's suppression. Historians tell us that the Aryan invaders treated the original inhabitants of Hindustan precisely as the English invaders treat us, if not much worse. If so, our helotry is a just retribution for our having created an untouchable class. The sooner we remove the blot, the better it is for us Hindus. But the priests tell us that untouchability is a divine appointment. I claim to know something of Hinduism. I am certain that the priests are wrong.

It is a blasphemy to say that God set apart any portion of humanity as untouchables. And Hindus who are Congressmen have to see to it that they break down the barrier at the earliest possible moment. The Vykom *satyagrahis* are showing us the way. They are carrying on their battle with gentleness and firmness. They have patience, courage and faith. Any movement in which these qualities are exhibited becomes irresistible.

I would, however, warn the Hindu brethren against the tendency which one sees nowadays of exploiting the suppressed classes for a political end. To remove untouchability is a penance that caste Hindus owe to Hinduism and to themselves. The purification required is not of untouchables but of the so-called superior castes.

There is no vice that is special to the untouchables, not even dirt and insanitation.It is our arrogance which blinds us "superior" Hindus to our own blemishes and which magnifies those of our downtrodden brethren whom we have suppressed and whom we keep under suppression. Religions like nations are being weighed in the balance.

God's grace and revelation are the monopoly of no race or nation.

They descend equally upon all who wait upon God. The religion and that nation will be blotted out of the face of the earth which pins its faith to injustice, untruth or violence. God is Light, not darkness. God is Love, not hate. God is Truth, not untruth. God alone is Great. We His creatures are but dust. Let us be humble and recognize the place of the lowliest of His creatures. Krishna honoured Sudama in his rags as he honoured no one else. Love is the root of religion or sacrifice and this perishable body is the root of self or irreligion, says Tulsidas.

Whether we win *swaraj* or not, the Hindus have to purify themselves before they can hope to revive the Vedic philosophy and make it a living reality.

SWARAJ SCHEME

But the spinning wheel, Hindu-Muslim unity and removal of untouchability are only means to an end. The end we do not know. For me it is enough to know the means. Means and end are convertible terms in my philosophy of life. But I have long professed my conversion to the view pressed upon the public by Babu Bhagwandas that the public must know the end, not vaguely but precisely. They must know the full definition of *swaraj*, i.e., the scheme of *swaraj* which all India wants and must fight for. Happily the Committee appointed by the All Parties Conference is charged with that mission and let us hope that the Committee will be able to produce a scheme that will be acceptable to all parties. May I suggest for its consideration the following points ?

1. The qualification for the franchise should be neither property nor position but manual work, such, for example, as suggested for the Congress franchise. Literary or property test has proved to be elusive. Manual work gives an opportunity to all who wish to take part in the Government and the well-being of the State.
2. The ruinous military expenditure should be curtailed to the proportion necessary for protection of life and property in normal times.

3. Administration of justice should be cheapened and with that end in view the final court of appeal should be not in London but in Delhi. Parties to civil suits must be compelled in the majority of cases to refer their disputes to arbitration, the decisions of these panchayats to be final except in cases of corruption or obvious misapplication of law. Multiplicity of intermediate courts should be avoided. Case law should be abolished and the general procedure should be simplified. We have slavishly followed the cumbrous and work out English procedure. The tendency in the Colonies is to simplify the procedure so as to make it easy for litigants to plead their own cases.
4. Revenues from intoxicating liquors and drugs should be abolished.
5. Salaries of the civil and military service should be brought down to a level compatible with the general condition of the country.
6. There should be redistribution of provinces on a linguistic basis with as complete autonomy as possible for every province for its internal administration and growth.
7. Appointment of a commission to examine all the monopolies given to foreigners and, subject to the findings of the commission, full guarantees to be given for all vested rights justly acquired.
8. Full guarantee of their status to the Indian Chiefs without any hindrance from the Central Government subject to the right of asylum to subjects of these States who, not being offenders against the Penal Code, may seek it in self-governing India.
9. Repeal of all arbitrary powers.
10. The highest post to be open to all who may be otherwise fit. Examination for the civil and military service to be in India.
11. Recognition of complete religious freedom to various denominations subject to mutual forbearance.
12. The official language for provincial governments, legislatures and courts, within a definite period, to be the vernacular of the province of the Privy Council, the final court of appeal, to be Hindustani; the script to be either Devanagari or Persian. The language of the Central Government and of the Central Legislature to be also Hindustani. The language of international diplomacy to be English.

I trust you will not laugh at what may appear to you to be extravagance of thought in the foregoing sketch of some of the requirements of *swaraj* as I would have it. We may not have the power today to take or receive or do the things I have mentioned. Have we the will ? Let us at least cultivate the desire. Before I leave this highly attractive, because speculative, theme, let me assure the Committee in charge of the drafting of a *swaraj* scheme, that I claim for my suggestion no more attention than it should give to any single individual's I have incorporated them in my address only to gain greater currency for them than they would perhaps otherwise receive.

INDEPENDENCE

The above sketch presupposes the retention of the British connection on perfectly honourable and absolutely equal terms. But I know that there is a section among Congressmen who want under every conceivable circumstance complete independence of Britain.

They will not have even an equal partnership. In my opinion if the British Government mean what they say and honestly help us to equality, it would be a greater triumph than a complete severance of the British connection. I would, therefore, strive for *swaraj* within the Empire, but would not hesitate to sever all connection, if severance became a necessity through Britain's own fault. I would thus throw the burden of separation on the British people. The better mind of the world desires today not absolutely independent States warring one against another but a federation of friendly inter-dependent States.

The consummation of that event may be far off. I want to make no grand claim for our country. But I see nothing grand or impossible about our expressing our readiness for universal inter-dependence rather than independence. It should rest with Britain to say that she will have no real alliance with India. I desire the ability to be totally independent without asserting the independence. Any scheme that I would frame, while Britain declares her goal about India to be complete equality within the Empire, would be that of alliance and not of independence without alliance. I would urge every Congressman not to be insistent on independence in each and every case, not because there is anything impossible about it, but because it is wholly unnecessary till it has become perfectly manifest that Britain really means subjugation in spite of her declaration to the contrary.

THE SWARAJ PARTY

So far, then, I have considered the contents of the agreement and the general questions arising from it. Not much need be said about the status of equality given to the Swaraj Party. I wish I could have avoided it, not because the party is not worthy, but because I do not share its views about Council-entry. But if I must remain in the Congress and even lead it, I must recognize facts as they are. It was easy enough for me to go out of the Congress or to decline the honour of presiding. But it was not, so I thought and still think, in the interest of the country for me to take that step. The Swaraj Party represents, if not a majority, at least a strong and growing minority in the Congress. If I was not to divide the Congress on the issue of its status, I was bound to agree to its conditions so long as they were not in conflict with my conscience. They are not in my opinion unreasonable. The Swarajists want to use the name of the Congress for their policy. A formula had to be found for their doing so without their pledging or binding the No-changers to their policy. One of the ways of doing it was to give it the authority and the responsibility both financial and executive with regard to the framing and the prosecution of their policy. The Congress as a whole could not guide that policy without sharing the responsibility. And as I could not take the responsibility, and as I apprehended no No-changer can, I could not be party to shaping the policy, nor could I shape it without my heart in it. And heart can only go where belief is. I know that the sole authority to the Swaraj Party to use the name of the Congress in regard to the Council programme makes somewhat awkward the position of the other parties wishing to join the Congress. But I fear it is inevitable. The Swaraj Party cannot be expected to surrender the advantage it possesses. After all it wants the advantage not for itself but for the service of the country. All parties have or can have that ambition or no other. I hope therefore that the others will join the Congress and work from within to affect the course of the country's politics. Dr. Besant has led the way in that direction. I know that she would have many things done otherwise, but she is content to come in hoping to bring round the electorate to her view by working within the Congress. The No-changers can, in my humble opinion, vote for the agreement with a clear conscience. The only national programme jointly to be worked by all the parties is *khaddar*, Hindu-Muslim unity and, for the Hindus, removal of untouchability. Is not this after all what they want ?

PURELY SOCIAL REFORM ?

It has been suggested that this programme turns the Congress into a purely social reform organization. I beg to differ from that view. Everything that is absolutely essential for *swaraj* is more than merely social work and must be taken up by the Congress. It is not suggested that the Congress should confine its activity for all time to this work only. But it is suggested that the Congress should for the coming year concentrate the whole of its energy on the work of construction, or as I have otherwise described it, the work of internal growth.

Nor does the agreement exhaust the list of constructive items that the Congress must handle. Those I am about to mention are of the highest importance, but they, being non-contentious and not absolutely essential for *swaraj* as the foregoing three items, find no mention in the agreement.

NATIONAL SCHOOLS

One such is the maintenance of national educational institutions. Probably the public do not know that next to *khaddar* the running of national educational institutions has been the most successful. These cannot be given up so long as even a few pupils are left. It must be a point of honour with the respective provinces to keep up their colleges and schools. Suspension of non-cooperation should not have any injurious effect on these institutions. On the contrary, greater effort than ever before should be made to maintain and strengthen them.

Most provinces have their national schools and colleges. Gujarat alone has a national university maintained at an annual cost of Rs. 1,00,000 and having control of three colleges and 70 schools with 9,000 pupils.

It has acquired its own ground at Ahmedabad and has already spent Rs. 2,05,323 in buildings. Throughout the country, finest and silent work has been done by the non-cooperating students. Theirs is a great and noble sacrifice. From a worldly standpoint they have perhaps lost the prospect of brilliant careers. I suggest to them however that from the national standpoint they have gained more than they have lost. They left their schools or colleges, because it was through them that the youth of the nation were insulted and humiliated in the Punjab. The first link in the chain of our bondage is forged in these institutions. The corresponding national institutions, however inefficiently managed they may be, are the factories where the first instruments of our freedom are forged. After all, the hope of the future centres round the boys and girls studying in these national institutions. I, therefore, regard the upkeep of these institutions as a first charge on provincial funds. But these institutions to be truly national must be clubs for promoting real Hindu-Muslim unity, they must be also nurseries for training Hindu boys and girls to regard untouchability as a blot upon Hinduism and a crime against humanity. They should be training schools for expert spinners and weavers. If the Congress retains its belief in the potency of the spinning wheel and *khaddar*, one has a right to expect these institutions to supply the science of the spinning wheel. They should be also factories for *khaddar* production. This is not to say that the boys and the girls are not to have any literary training. But I do maintain that the training of the hand and the heart must go hand-in-hand with that of the head. The quality and the usefulness of a national school or college will be measured not by the brilliance of the literary attainments of its scholars but by the strength of the national character, and deftness in handling the carding bow, the spinning wheel and the loom. Whilst I am most anxious that no national school or college should be closed, I should have not the slightest hesitation in closing down a school or college that is indifferent to the admission of non-Hindu boys or that shuts its door against the entry of untouchables or that has not carding and spinning as an indispensable part of the training. The time is past when we can be satisfied with the word "national" on the signboard of the school and the knowledge that it is not affiliated to any Government university or is not otherwise controlled by the Government. I must also not omit to point out that the tendency in many national institutions still is to neglect the vernaculars and Hindustani. Many teachers have not realized the necessity of imparting instruction through the vernaculars or Hindustani. I rejoice to observe that Sjt. Gangadharrao has arranged a meeting of national educationists to exchange experiences on the several points mentioned by me and to evolve, if possible, a general plan of education and action.

UNEMPLOYED NON-COOPERATORS

This is perhaps the proper place to mention those lawyers who have given up practice, and schoolmasters and other Government employees who have given up Government service at the call of the nation. I know that there are many such men who find it hard to make the two ends meet. They deserve national support. The Khadi Board and the national schools and colleges are the two services that can take in almost an unlimited number of honest and industrious men who are willing to learn and labour and are satisfied with a modest allowance. I observe a tendency not to accept any remuneration for national service. This desire to serve without remuneration is praiseworthy, but all cannot satisfy it. Every labourer is worthy of his hire. No country can produce thousands of unpaid whole time workers. We must, therefore, develop an atmosphere in which a patriot would consider it an honour to serve the country and accept an allowance for such service.

INTOXICANTS

Another item of national importance is the liquor and the opium traffic. Had the wave of enthusiasm that swept across the country in 1921 in the cause of temperance remained non-violent, we would today have witnessed a progressive improvement. But unfortunately our picketing degenerated into violence, veiled when it was not open.

Picketing had, therefore, to be abandoned, and the liquor-shops and opium dens began to flourish as before. But you will be pleased to hear that the temperance work has not died out altogether. Many workers are still continuing their quiet and selfless service in the cause of temperance. We must, however, realize that we would not be able to eradicate the evil till we have *swaraj*. It is no matter of pride to us that our children are being educated out of the revenue derived from this immoral source. I would almost forgive the Council entry by Congressmen, if they would boldly sweep out this revenue even through education may have to be starved. Nothing of the kind should happen if they will insist on a corresponding reduction in the military expenditure.

BENGAL REPRESSION

You will observe that in the foregoing paragraphs I have confined myself to the internal developments. But the external circumstances, and among them chiefly the acts of our rulers, are affecting our destiny no less surely (though it may be adversely) than the internal development. We may turn them to advantage if we will, or we may succumb to them to our disadvantage.

The latest act of the rulers is the repression commenced in Bengal. The All Parties Conference condemned it in no uncertain terms. The Conference had hesitation in saying that the blow was aimed at the Bengal Swaraj Party. But I have none. I have been to Calcutta and had the opportunity of meeting men representing a variety of opinion and I came to the conclusion that the blow was aimed at the Swaraj party.

The opinion is confirmed by the speeches since delivered by Lords Lytton and Reading. The defence they have offered is wholly unconvincing. Such a defence is possible only in a place like India where public opinion counts for little or nothing. Lord Lytton's conditions of release are an insult to our intelligence. Their Excellencies beg the question when they tell us that the situation warranted the Ordinance and the action under the Regulation of 1818.

The national contention is :

1. that the situation they describe has not been proved to exist;
2. that assuming that the situation does exist, the remedy is worse than the disease;
3. that the ordinary law contains enough powers for dealing with the situation; and lastly
4. that even if extraordinary powers were necessary, they should have been taken from the legislature which is of their own creation.

The speeches of Their Excellencies evade these issues altogether. The nation which has had considerable experience of unsupported statements of the Government will not accept them as gospel truth. Their Excellencies know that we cannot and will not believe their statements not because they are wilfully untruthful, but because the sources of their information have often been discovered to be tainted. Their assurances are, therefore, a mockery of the people.

The speeches are almost a challenge to us to do our worst. But we must not be irritated or be impatient. Repression, if it does not cow us down, if it does not deter us from our purpose, can but hasten the advent of *swaraj*; for it puts us on our mettle and evokes the spirit of self-sacrifice and courage in the face of danger. Repression does for a true man or a nation what fire does for gold. In 1921, we answered repression with civil disobedience and invited the Government to do its worst. But today we are obliged to eat the humble pie. We are not ready for civil disobedience. We can but prepare for it. Preparation for civil disobedience means discipline, self-restraint, a non-violent but resisting spirit, cohesion and above all scrupulous and willing obedience to the known laws of God and such laws of man as are in furtherance of God's laws. But unfortunately we have neither discipline nor self-restraint enough for our purpose, we are either violent or our non-violence is unresisting, we have not enough cohesion and the laws that we obey whether of God or man, we obey compulsorily. As between Hindus and Mussalmans we witness a daily defiant breach of laws both of God and man. This is no atmosphere for civil disobedience—the one matchless and invincible weapon at the disposal of the oppressed. The alternative is undoubtedly violence.

We seem to have the atmosphere for it. Hindu-Muslim fights are our training for it. And those who believe that India's deliverance lies through violence are entitled to gloat over the free fights that take place between us. But I say to those who believe in the cult of violence: "You are retarding India's progress. If you have any pity or friendly feeling for the starving millions, know that your violence will do them no service. Those whom you seek to depose are better armed and infinitely better organized than you are. You may not care for your own lives, but you dare not disregard those of your countrymen who have no desire to die a martyr's death. You know that this Government believes in Jallianwala Bagh massacres as a legitimate means of self-defence. Whatever may be true of other countries, there is no chance of the cult of violence flourishing in this country. India is admittedly the best repository and exponent of non-violence. Will you not better devote your lives, if you sacrifice them in the cause of non-violence?"

I know, however, that my appeal to the violent revolutionaries will be just as fruitless as any such appeal to the violent and anarchical Government is likely to be.

We must, therefore, find the remedy and demonstrate to both the violent Government and the violent revolutionaries that there is a force that is more effective than their violence.

REPRESSION A SYMPTOM

I regard this repression as a chronic symptom of a chronic disease. The European dominance and Asiatic subjection is the formula. Sometimes it is stated still more cryptically as White *vs.* Black. Kipling miscalled the white man's yoke as the "white man's burden". In the Malaya peninsula the colour bar that was thought to be temporary has now or almost become a permanent institution. The Mauritius planter must get Indian labour without let or hindrance. The Kenya Europeans successfully lord it over Indians who have a prior right to be there. The Union of South Africa would today drive out every Indian, if it safely could, in total disregard of past obligations.

In all these cases the Government of India and the Imperial Government are not helpless; they are unwilling or not so insistent as they ought to be on the protection of Indian settlers. The Government of India has not shown even the decency to publish the report of its own Commission on Fiji.

The attempt to crush the indomitable spirit of the Akalis is a symptom of the same disease. They have poured their blood like water for the sake of a cause they hold as dear as life itself. They may have erred. If they have, it is they who have 'bled in the process. They have hurt no one else. Nankana Sahib, Guruka-Bagh, and Jaito will bear witness to their courage and their mute sufferings and martyrdom. But the Governor of the Punjab is reported to have vowed that he will crush the Akalis.

One hears that repression is crushing the Burmese spirit. Egypt fares no better than we do. A mad Egyptian kills a British officer—certainly a detestable crime. The punishment is not only a detestable crime, but it is an outrage upon humanity. Egypt has nearly lost all it got. A whole nation has been mercilessly punished the crime of one man. It may be that the murder had the sympathy of the Egyptians. Would that justify terrorism by a power well able to protect its interests without it?

The repression in Bengal is, therefore, not an extraordinary thing. We must treat its periodic eruption in some shape or other, or in some province or other, as our normal condition till we come to our own.

NEED FOR SANCTION

The Congress, therefore, to be worthy of its trust must devise a sanction to back its demands. Before we can forge the sanction, we Hindus, Mussalmans, Christians, Sikhs, Parsis, etc., must unite and so should Swarajists, No-changers, Liberals, Home Rulers, Muslim Leaguers and others. If we can but speak with a united voice and know our own mind, it would be well. If we can develop the power to keep foreign cloth from our land, it would be better. We are ready then for the sanction.

MY FAITH

Let me state my faith; as a Congressman wishing to keep the Congress intact, I advise suspension of non-co-operation for I see that the nation is not ready for it. But as an individual, I cannot—will not—do so as long as the Government remains what it is. It is not merely a policy with me, it is an article of faith. Non-cooperation and civil disobedience are but different branches of the same tree called *satyagraha*. It is my kalpadruma—Jam-i-Jam—the Universal Provider. *Satyagraha* is search for Truth ; and God is Truth. *Ahimsa* or non-violence is the light that reveals that Truth to me. *Swaraj* for me is part of that Truth. This *satyagraha* did not fail me in South Africa, Kheda or Champaran and in a hosts of other cases I could mention. It excludes all violence or hate. Therefore, I cannot and will not hate Englishmen. Nor will I bear their yoke. I must fight unto death the unholy attempt to impose British methods and British institutions on India. But I combat the attempt with non-violence. I believe in the capacity of India to offer non-violent battle to the English rulers. The experiment has not failed. It has succeeded, but not to the extent we had hoped and desired. I do not despair. On the contrary I believe that India will come to her own in the near future, and that only through *satyagraha*. The proposed suspension is part of the experiment. Non-cooperation need never be resumed if the programme sketched by me can be fulfilled. Non-violent non-cooperation in some form or other, whether through the Congress or without it, will be resumed if the programme fails. I have repeatedly stated that *satyagraha* never fails and that one perfect *satyagrahi* is enough to vindicate Truth. Let us all strive to be perfect *satyagrahis*.

The striving does not require any quality unattainable by the lowliest among us. For *satyagraha* is an attribute of the spirit within. It is latent in everyone of us. Like *swaraj* it is our birthright. Let us know it.

[*Young India*, 26-12-1924]

30. Brahmacharya/Celebacy[1]

SPEECH IN REPLY TO SEVA MANDAL ADDRESS, BHADRAN

[February 12, 1925]

I have been asked to say something about *brahmacharya*[2]. This is one of those subjects on which I write in *Navajivan* from time to time. I rarely speak on it, because I think that it is an extremely difficult subject to talk about and one cannot explain one's ideas about it in a speech. You wish to hear my views on ordinary *brahmacharya* and not on *brahmacharya* in the extended definition of the term which connotes the control of all organs of sense. Even ordinary *brahmacharya* is said by the *shastras* to be very difficult to observe. Permit me to say that there is ninety-nine per cent truth in this view, but that it falls short of absolute truth by one per cent. The observance of this ordinary *brahmacharya* is felt to be difficult because we do not strive to control the other organs of sense. The most important of these is the palate. For him who has learnt to control the palate. The observance of *brahmacharya* will be easy enough. Students of zoology tell us that lower creatures observe *brahmacharya* better than man. What they say is true, and if we try to know the reason we shall discover that the lower creatures have the completest control over the palate, which is not the result of an effort of will but is instinctive. They feed on grass and plants, and eat only as much as would satisfy their hunger. They eat to live, and do not live to eat. We do quite the opposite of this. The mother feeds her child all manner of delicacies, believing that only so can she express her love.

By acting in this way, we do not make our food more tasty, but rather less so. Food is made tasty by appetite. A plain rotla[3] is more tasty

1. Presumably the reference is to the "English friend" mentioned in Gandhiji's article "Interrogatories Answered", January 29, 1925.
2. Literally, living in the *Brahman*, the absolute. In ordinary usage, the term has come to signify celibacy.
3. A round, thick, flat cake made of the flour of *bajri*, a coarse millet.

to a hungry person than ladu[1] can be to a person who has no appetite. We actually use all kinds of spices and prepare an endless variety of.

We let our eyes, which God has given us for seeing things, be tainted with lust, and do not learn to observe what we ought to. Why should a mother not learn the *Gayatri* and teach it to her child? It would be enough if, without going into its deeper meaning, she merely understands that it is an invocation to the Sun god and teaches the child to worship the Sun. Sanatanists and Arya Samajists, both may worship the Sun. In explaining the *Gayatri* as worship of the Sun, I have given its most obvious meaning. What is the meaning of this worship? It means that, holding up our heads and looking at the Sun we should cleanse our eyes. The author of the *Gayatri* was a *rishi*, a seer. He tells us that nowhere shall we find anything to equal the drama of sunrise or see beauty and mystery like its. There is no *sutradhara*[2] as skilled as God and no stage grander than the sky. But which mother ever asks her child to look at the sky, for fear that the child might hurt its eyes? Her mind is filled with all manner of worldly thoughts; the education which they give in that big building, she perhaps tells herself, will make her child a well-paid officer. Does she ever ask herself, however, how much the child benefits from what it learns, consciously or unconsciously, from the atmosphere in the home? Parents paid their children with clothes till they feel suffocated, try to make them look smart and handsome, but do the children really look so? Clothes are meant to cover the body, not to beautify it; they are meant to protect us against heat and cold. We should ask a child shivering with cold to go and warm itself at the stove, or sun in the street or go and work on the farm; then alone can we help it build a body as strong as steel.

Anyone who has observed *brahmacharya* ought to have a body of such strength. We, on the contrary, ruin children's bodies. We wish to keep them within the four walls of the home and make them comfortable. This produces a kind of artificial heat in their skin which we can only compare to eczema. We have ruined our bodies by pampering them overmuch, we have been playing with fire.

So much about clothes. Then, through the things we talk about in the home we produce harmful effects on a child's mind. We talk about

1. A sweet ball dishes so that we may be able to load our stomachs to the full, and then we ask why we cannot observe *brahmacharya*.
2. The producer in Sanskrit drama, who appears as a character in the beginning of the play and introduces its theme.

marrying the boy or the girl, and the things which the child sees around it have much the same effect on its mind. What surprises me is that we have not yet become the most uncivilized people on the earth.

Despite everything calculated to destroy decent social restraints, they have survived. God has so made man that, though placed again and again in circumstances which might tempt him to evil, he comes out safe—so profound is His mystery. If we eliminate all such factors which increase the difficulties in the way of *brahmacharya*, we would find it quite easy to observe.

Though this is our condition, we wish to oppose others with physical force. There are two ways in which we can make ourselves fit to do this, a lower and a higher. The lower way is to cultivate strength of body by any means whatever, by eating and drinking anything which may serve our purpose, training ourselves for physical fighting, eating beef, and so on . When I was a boy, a friend used to tell me that we ought to eat meat, that if we did not we would never be as strong and stout as Englishmen. The poet Narmadashanker[1] also gave this advice in a poem of his. The lines, "The Englishman rules and the Indian is content to submit" and "The foreigner is full six feet tall" are intended to suggest this very idea. Narmadashanker has rendered great service to Gujarat but there were two phases in his life, the first of self-indulgence and the second of self-control. This particular poem belongs to the period of self-indulgence. In Japan too, when they found it necessary to fight other countries beef eating became common. If, therefore, we wish to cultivate physical strength the lower way, we shall have to start eating such things.

But *brahmacharya* is the only means for us if we would cultivate *physical* strength the higher way. I feel pity for myself when I hear people describing me as a man of inviolate *brahmacharya*. I have been so described in the address presented to me. I must tell you, therefore, that the person who drafted the address does not know who may be called a man of inviolate *brahmacharya*. Didn't he ask himself how a man like me, married and having several children, could be so described? A man of inviolate *brahmacharya* would never get fever, not even so much as headache, he would never have an attack of bronchitis or appendicitis. Doctors say that appendicitis may even result from an orange seed sticking in the intestines. But the seed will never be retained inside if one's body is clean and healthy. When the intestines have lost their tone, they cannot eliminate such things in the natural course. My

1. Also called Narmad, the first poet of the new age in Gujarat.

intestines also must have lost their tone and so I might have failed to assimilate something which I swallowed. Children often swallow similar things, but their mothers seldom take serious notice of that. The reason [why no harmful effects follow] is that their intestines have the natural strength to eliminate such things. I do not, therefore, want anyone to become a hypocrite by attributing to me the observance of inviolate *brahmacharya* [and following my example].

The power and light of inviolate *brahmacharya* are far greater than what I can boast of. I am not perfect in my *brahmacharya*, though it is true that I strive to be so. I have only placed before you a few observations from my experience which indicate how one may erect a protecting hedge [to preserve one's *brahmacharya*]. Observing *brahmacharya* does not mean that one may not touch any woman, not even one's sister. It means that one's mental state must be such that touching a woman would disturb one no more than touching a piece of paper. If, in order to preserve my *brahmacharya*, I must guard against touching my sister to nurse her when she is ill, that *brahmacharya* is worth no more than the dust under our feet. We would be perfect in our *brahmacharya* if, even when touching a young and extremely beautiful woman, we are disturbed no more than when we touch a corpse. If you wish your children to be capable of such *brahmacharya*, you cannot prescribe their studies but should let a man like me, imperfect though he be in his *brahmacharya*, do that.

A man who observes *brahmacharya* is a sannyasi by nature. The stage of *brahmacharya* is superior to that of sannyasa, but we have corrupted it and in the result the stage of active life as a householder and that of retired life have lost their beauty, to speak nothing of the stage of *sannyasa*—such is our plight.

If we follow the lower path indicated above, we shall not, even after five hundred years, be strong enough to fight the Pathans. If we can follow the higher path today, then we can meet them this very day, for the inward change required by that path can take place in no time, whereas change in our physical constitution will require ages to bring about. We shall be able to follow that higher path only if we have earned holy merit in our previous lives and if our parents equip us for the purpose.

[*From Gujarati*]
Navajivan, 1-3-1925

31. Christianity and Hinduism

SPEECH AT MEETING OF MISSIONARIES

[July 28, 1925]

I had the pleasure of delivering an address before the missionaries in Calcutta at Y.M.C.A. on 28th ultimo. I have been supplied with shorthand notes of that address, and as it was of general interest I reproduce below an abridgement of it. I have omitted on salient thought or expression, but I have omitted some descriptive passages.

M.K.G.

Not many of you perhaps know that my association with Christians, not Christians so called but real Christians, dates from 1889, when as a lad I found myself in London; and that association has grown riper as years have rolled on. In South Africa, where I found myself in the midst of inhospitable surroundings, I was able to make hundreds of Christian friends. I came in touch with the late Mr. Spencer Watton, Director of South Africa General Mission, and, later, with the great divine, Rew. Mr. A. Murray and several others.

My acquaintance, therefore, this evening with so many missionaries is by no means a new thing. There was even a time in my life when a very sincere and intimate friend of mine, a great and good Quaker, had designs on me. (Laughter.) He thought that I was too good not to become a Christian. I was sorry to have disappointed him.

One missionary friend of mine in South Africa still writes to me and asks me, 'How is it with you?' I have always told this friend that so far as I know, it is all well with me. If it was prayer that these friends expected me to make, I was able to tell them that every day the heartfelt prayer within the closed door of my closet went to the Almighty to show me light and give wisdom and courage to follow that light.

In answer to promises made to one of these Christian friends of mine, I thought it my duty to see one of the biggest of Indian Christians, as I was told he was,—the late Kali Charan Banerjee. I went over to him—I am telling you of the deep search that I have undergone in order that I might leave no stone unturned to find out the true path—I went to him with an absolutely open mind and in a receptive mood, and I met him also under circumstances which were most affecting. I found that there was much in common between Mr. Banerjee and myself. His simplicity, his humility, his courage, his truthfulness, all these things I have all along admired. He met me when his wife was on her death-bed. You cannot imagine a more impressive scene, a more ennobling circumstance. I told Mr. Banerjee, 'I have come to you as a seeker,'—this was in 1901—'I have come to you in fulfilment of a sacred promise I have made to some of my dearest Christian friends that I will leave no stone unturned to find out the true light.' I told him that I had given my friends the assurance that no worldly gain would keep me away from the light, if I could but see it. Well, I am not going to engage you in giving a description of the little discussion that we had between us. It was very good, very noble. I came away, not sorry, not dejected, not disappointed, but I felt sad that even Mr. Banerjee could not convince me. This was my final deliberate striving to realize Christianity as it was presented to me. Today my position is that though I admire much in Christianity, I am unable to identify myself with orthodox Christianity. I must tell you in all humility that Hinduism as I know it, entirely satisfies my soul, fills my whole being and I find a solace in the *Bhagavad Gita* and *Upanishads* that I miss even in the *Sermon on the Mount*. Not that I do not prize the ideal presented therein, not that some of the precious teachings in the *Sermon on the Mount* have not left a deep impression upon me, but I must confess to you that when doubts haunt me, when disappointments stare me in the face, and when I see not one ray of light on the horizon I turn to the *Bhagavad Gita*, and find a verse to comfort me; and I immediately begin to smile in the midst of overwhelming sorrow. My life has been full of external tragedies and if they have not left any visible and indelible effect on me, I owe it to the teaching of the *Bhagavad Gita*. I have told you all these things in order to make it absolutely clear to you where I stand, so that I may have, if you will, closer touch with you. I must add that I did not stop at studying the *Bible* and the commentaries and other books on Christianity that my friends placed in my hands; but I said to myself, if I was to find my satisfaction through reasoning, I must study the scriptures of other religions also and make my choice. And I turned to the *Koran*.

I tried to understand what I could of Judaism as distinguished from Christianity. I studied Zoroastrianism and I came to the conclusion that all religions were right, but every one of them imperfect, imperfect naturally and neccssarily, because they were interpreted with our poor intellects, sometimes with our poor hearts, and more often misinterpreted. In all religions, I found to my grief, that there were various and even contradictory interpretations of some texts, and I said to myself, 'Not these things for me. If I want the satisfaction of my soul, I must feel my way. I must wait silently upon God and ask Him to guide me.' There is a beautiful verse in Sanskrit which says 'God helps only when man feels utterly helpless and utterly humble'.

Some of you have come from the Tamil land. When I was studying Tamil, I found in one of the books of Dr. Pope a Tamil proverb which means' God helps the helpless'. I have given you this life story of my own experience for you to ponder over.

You, the missionaries come to India thinking that you come to a land of heathens, of idolators, of men who do not know God. One of the greatest of Christian divines, Bishop Heber, wrote the two lines which have always left a sting with me: "Where every prospect pleases, and man alone is vile." I wish he had not written them. My own experience in my travels throughout India has been to the contrary. I have gone from one end of the country to the other, without any prejudice, in a relentless search after truth, and I am not able to say that here in this fair land, watered by the great Ganges, the Brahmaputra and the Jumna, man is vile. He is not vile. He is as much a seeker after truth as you and I are, possibly more so. This reminds me of a French book translated for me by a French friend. It is an account of an imaginary expedition in search of knowledge. One party landed in India and found Truth and God personified, in a little pariah's hut. I tell you there are many such huts belonging to the untouchables where you will certainly find God. They do not reason but they persist in their belief that God is. They depend upon God for His assistance and find it too. There are many stories told throughout the length and breadth of India about these noble untouchables. Vile as some of them may be, there are noblest specimens of humanity in their midst. But does my experience exhaust itself merely with the untouchables? No. I am here to tell you that there are non-Brahmins, there are Brahmins who are as fine specimens of humanity as you will find in any place on the earth.

There are Brahmins today in India who are embodiments of self-sacrifice, godliness, and humility. There are Brahmins who are devoting themselves body and soul to the service of untouchables, with no expectation of reward from the untouchables, but with execration from orthodoxy. They do not mind it, because in serving pariahs they are serving God. I can quote chapter and verse from my experience. I place these facts before you in all humility for the simple reason that you may know this land better, the land to which you have come to serve. You are here to find out the distress of the people of India and remove it. But I hope you are here also in a receptive mood and, if there is anything that India has to give, you will not stop your ears, you will not close your eyes and steel your hearts, but open up your ears, eyes and, most of all, your hearts to receive all that may be good in this land. I give you my assurance that there is a great deal of good in India. Do not flatter yourselves with the belief that a mere recital of that celebrated verse in St. John makes a man a Christian. If I have read the *Bible* correctly, I know many men who have never heard the name of Jesus Christ or have even rejected the official interpretation of Christianity will, probably, if Jesus came in our midst today in the flesh, be owned by him more than many of us. I, therefore, ask you to approach the problem before you with open-heartedness, and humility.

I was engaged in a friendly conversation with some missionaries this morning. I do not want to relate that conversation. But I do want to say that they are fine specimens of humanity. They did not want to misunderstand me, but I had to pass nearly one hour and a half in my attempt to explain to them that, in writing what I had written, I had not written anything in a spirit of ill will or hatred towards Englishmen. I was hard put to it to carry that conviction. In fact, I do not know whether I carried that conviction to them at all. If salt loseth its savour, wherewith will it be salted? If I could not drive home the truth that was in me to the three friends who certainly came with open minds, how should I fare with others? It has often occurred to me that a seeker after truth has to be silent. I know the wonderful efficacy of silence. I visited a Trappist monastery in South Africa. A beautiful place it was. Most of the inmates of that place were under a vow of silence. I enquired of the Father the motive of it and he said that the motive was apparent. 'We are frail human beings. We do not know very often what we say. If we want to listen to the still small voice that is always speaking within us, it will not be heard if we continually speak.' I understood that precious lesson. I know the secret of silence.

I do not know just now as I speak to you whether it would not have been wise if I had said nothing to those friends beyond saying, 'We shall know each other better when the mists have rolled away.' As I speak to you, I feel humiliated. Why did I argue with these friends?

But I say these things to you, first of all, to make this confession and, secondly, to tell you also that, if you will refuse to see the other side, if you will refuse to understand what India is thinking, then you will deny yourselves the real privilege of service.

I have told my missionary friends, 'Noble as you are, you have isolated yourselves from the people whom you want to serve.' I cannot help recalling to you the conversation I related in Darjeeling at the Missionary Language School. Lord Salisbury was waited upon by a deputation of missionaries in connection with China and this deputation wanted protection. I cannot recall the exact words, but give you the purport of the answer Lord Salisbury gave. He said, "Gentlemen, if you want to go to China, to preach the message of Christianity, then do not ask for assistance of temporal power. Go with your lives in your hands and if the people of China want to kill you, imagine that you have been killed in the service of God". Lord Salisbury was right. Christian missionaries come to India under the shadow, or, if you like, under the protection of a temporal power, and it creates an impassable bar.

If you give me statistics that so many orphans have been reclaimed and brought to the Christian faith, I would accept them, but I do not feel convinced thereby that it is your mission. In my opinion, your mission is infinitely superior to that. You want to find men in India and if you want to do that, you will have to go to the lowly cottages not to give them something, might be to take something from them. A true friend as I claim to be of the missionaries of India and of the Europeans, I speak to you what I feel from the bottom of my heart. I miss receptiveness, humility, willingness on your part to identify yourselves with the masses of India. I have talked straight from my heart. May it find a response from hearts.

At the end of the address questions were invited. The most important questions and their answers are given below :

Q. How do you think should the missionaries indentify themselves with the masses?

A. The question is somewhat embarrassing. But I would venture to say, 'Copy Charlie Andrews.'

Another in the audience asked :

Q. What definite work would you suggest that a missionary should do for and among the masses?

A. Since I have been challenged I must unhesitatingly answer, 'The spinning wheel.' You naturally laugh, but if you knew the masses as I do, you will look upon this very simple instrument of torture (here Mr. Gandhi produced the *takli* he carries with him) with seriousness. You cannot present the hungry and famished masses with God. Their God is their food. General Booth knew what he was doing when at his numerous depots the first thing he did to the hungry men and women who flocked there was to give them a plate of soup.

Before he would give them their next meal, he called upon them to make splinters for his match factory, and then he introduced them to God. The famished millions are famishing not because there is not enough food produced in India, but because they have no work to do.

The only work for the millions is the spinning wheel. I know the Industrial Mission House in Calcutta. It is good in its way, but it does not touch even the fringe of the question. The problem is how to take work to the cottages of these men, cottages which are scattered over a surface 1,900 miles long and 1,500 broad. They will not take the spinning wheel unless they learn the art themselves and unless they spin to set an example to these men who have lost faith in themselves and faith in everything and everybody. And the spinning wheel is useless unless you and I wear *khaddar*. Hence it is that I have not hesitated to say to Lord Reading or to Lord Willingdon that I will not be satisfied unless they and their orderlies are dressed from top to toe in *khaddar*.

A third inquirer asked :

Q Do you definitely feel the presence of the living Christ within you?

A. If it is the historical Jesus, surnamed Christ, that the inquirer refers to, I must say I do not. If it is an adjective signifying one of the names of God, then I must say I do feel the presence of God—call him Christ, call him Krishna, call him Rama. We have one thousand names to denote God, and if I did not feel the presence of God within me, I see so much of misery and disappointment every day that I would be a raving maniac and my destination would be the Hooghli.

[*Young India,* 6-8-1925]

32. Spinning

A CORRECTION

In the issue of 8th October, in my Bihar Notes , I have said: "In Ranchi I was taken to Golcunda." This was a stupid slip on my part.

The Bihari friends are now laughing at my geographical ignorance and tell me that Golcunda is not near Ranchi but near Purulia. I owe an apology to Purulia for the blunder. When, however, several villages and several places in the same village or town have to be visited on the same day and these performances follow in quick succession it is difficult for one to remember all the places accurately. I am, therefore, obliged to omit the mention of the names of many places and persons and simply confine myself to narration of events because at the moment I do not remember either the names of places or persons concerned. When, therefore, people find that the names of persons or places, that in their opinion I should have mentioned, have been omitted, let them understand that often the omission is unintentional and that it is due purely to my weak memory.

SPINNING ESSAY

The reader will remember that early this year[1] Sjt. Rewashanker Jagjivan announced a prize of one thousand rupees to be given to the writer of the best essay on hand spinning, its history and its use. These were the terms:

(1) The essay should be in English in four parts; the first part to contain the history of hand spinning and the *khaddar* (meaning hand spun, including the celebrated *shubnum* of Dacca) trade of India before the British advent, the second part should trace the history of the ruin of hand spinning and the *khaddar* trade, the third part should be an examination of the possibilities of hand spinning and *khaddar* and a comparison between the Indian mill

1. On January 1. For details, *vide* "Notes", 1-1-1925.

industry and hand spinning and hand weaving, the fourth part should examine the possibilities of achieving boycott of foreign cloth through the spinning wheel. The essay should be supported by authoritative statistics and should have an appendix containing a list of all the reference books and authorities used by the author in support of his argument.

(2) The essay may be as brief as the competitors wish to make it, consistently with the giving of a full record of facts and figures.

(3) The essay should be sent to the office of *Young India* by registered book post with the author's name on a separate sheet and should reach the office of *Young India* not later than 15th March next. The judges will be Messrs Shankerlal Banker, Maganlal K. Gandhi and myself. The result will be announced not later than 31st March, 1925. The judges will reserve to themselves the right of rejecting all the essays if they fall below a certain standard. The prize will be paid to the winner on the announcement thereof.

The right of publication will vest in the All-India Khadi Board in accordance with the donor's wishes.

Later Sjt. Ambalal Sarabhai was invited also to act as judge and he kindly consented. The time fixed for the delivery of the essay was 15th March. It was subsequently extended to 30th April and over sixty essays were received within the stipulated time. Each one of the judges carried on an independent examination. Two of us awarded the first prize to one, the third awarded the first prize to another and the fourth to a third. After mutual consultation we decided upon splitting the prize and distributing it between Sjt. S.V. Puntambekar and Sjt. N.S.Varadachari and the judges have proposed that either both of them or, if it is not possible for them to do so, whoever, has the leisure and the inclination should combine the essays and give for publication the result of the combination. I am sorry that means a little more delay. All the delay that has up to now taken place has been unavoidable. The examination had to be and was thorough. That by itself took a great deal of time. The delay that has now taken place is equally inevitable, the idea being to give to the public a thoroughly good compendium on hand spinning. I congratulate the prize winners and I tender my congratulations also to those who have not been able to win the prize, for the effort made by them. For, some of the essays show a great deal of diligence.

SPINNERS, PLEASE NOTE

Those who were in charge of the yarn that was received under the All-India Congress Committee resolution last year ask me to warn the spinners who become members of the A.I.S.A. against sending yarn that is not evenly spun and uniform. A quantity of bad yarn still lies unused. Just as bread that is stodgy and ill baked is no bread, similarly yarn that is not easily woven is no yarn, and the condition of membership is not a thousand yards of self-spun yarn merely but a thousand yards per month of self-spun yarn *well twisted and uniform* for A class and two thousand yards yearly of the same quality of self spun yarn for B class members. Therefore, if the secretaries are to do their duty well, it will be necessary for them not to take yarn that is considered to be below standard, and the standard while it need not be stiff will certainly be stiff enough to meet the elementary requirements of good weavable yarn. In cash subscriptions a bad coin cannot be accepted as a proper tender nor can bad yarn be accepted as proper tender when subscription is payable in yarn.

WHAT HAVE YOU DONE ?

If you are a believer in spinning and if you have faith in the A.I.S.A., have you joined the Association? If you have not, will you write why you have not? If you have already joined, beyond sending your quota of well spun and uniform yarn of your own spinning, what more do you propose to do to make *khaddar* universal? Have you invited the members of your own family and friends to join? Are you asking even the youngsters of your family to labour for the sake of the country? It is no mean training for the youngsters to learn during their childhood the lesson of intelligent self-sacrifice and understand the power of organization. Unorganized half hour's labour may mean nothing but labour given to an organization even from the remotest part of India has a potency that can revolutionize national life. It is no mean thing, again, for little children regularly every day to remember their country in a tangible manner. It will give them priceless discipline. In the act of demonstrating to the children the virtue of the simple little act of labour you will discover for yourself the implications of the *charkha* which you have little thought of. Please do not raise in front of you a mountain of difficulties by asking what use your labour can be when all India is lying supine. It is enough for you to do your little best, the rest will take care of itself.

We have not the governance of the universe in our hands but we have our own in our hands and you will find that that is about all it is possible for us to do. But it is at that same time all in all. There is much truth in the homely English proverb: Take care of the pennies and the pounds will take care of themselves.

LOHANI AT LAST

After I had given up all hope of finding Lohani, I received help from an unexpected quarter and I have now before me full details in the shape of newspaper cuttings. I observe that these cuttings are based upon my first reference to Lohani in the pages of *Young India*.

The writers of these newspaper reports evidently thought that I would see their references. They are obviously unaware of the fact that I do not get the time to read the numerous newspapers which the kind editors and proprietors send me in exchange for *Young India* or *Navajivan*. I have often requested and I repeat the request that those who seek to give me information or correct me or advise me through their writings in newspapers will kindly send me the cuttings in question. The writer in one of the cuttings expresses his surprise and astonishment that I should not know where Lohani is. I share the regret. But why astonishment? I have before now admitted my ignorance of the geography of my own country. In the vernacular school I had the barest outlines of the geography of India and, in the English school, from the very first standard I was called upon, on pain of being caned, to learn by heart the names of all the counties of England and many other foreign names which it gave me headache to pronounce and remember. Nobody taught me, and I am sure my teacher did not know, where Lohani was. Even Bhiwani, near which, I now see, Lohani is situated, was unknown to me before I went to the Punjab. Lohani then according to the cutting in my possession, is a little Hindu village, six miles from Bhiwani. The Hindu *zamindars*, the cutting proceeds, introduced in Lohani some Musalmans. The Hindus and the Mussalmans are now fighting over a piece of land, which the Mussalmans claim, is consecrated and the Hindus claim has never ceased to be their property. The matter is before the courts. And there I must leave it. The writer of the newspaper article invites me to investigate the matter and pronounce my own opinion upon it. If I had the authority which I thought at one time I possessed, I would certainly investigate and prevent the quarrel from being decided in a court of law. But I must now plead my incapacity. I would, however, advise both the parties to approach those in whom they have confidence and seek their intervention.

A TOTAL DENIAL

With regard to the charges of bribery, corruption and intimidation brought against the Swarajists of Madras in connection with the late Municipal elections and recently referred to in these columns, I have a long letter from Sjt. P.S. Doraiswamy Mudaliar totally and specifically denying every one of those charges and on the contrary holding that the defeated party was guilty of the very charges brought against the Swarajists. The correspondent contends that not only the illiterate masses threw in their lot with the Swarajists but so did also "many lawyers, medical practitioners and many eminent men". And he says that they did so because they were disgusted with the tactics of the other party. I am not reproducing the whole of the letter because I have no desire to interest the readers of *Young India* in a local controversy and to open its columns for an interminable correspondence on it.

THE GOANESE UNDER SWARAJ

A Goan friend asks:

What would be your attitude and that of all Indians towards the Goanese who reside and earn their living in this country when *swaraj* is attained?

In briefest terms the answer is, that the attitude towards the Goanese will be exactly the same as towards any other Indian, for the Goanese are as much inhabitants of India as the inhabitants of any other part. That they are under another foreign Government can make no difference in their treatment. If the fear underlying this question is due to difference of religion, then, it has been repeatedly stated in these columns that *swaraj* is not intended for any one religion only but for all, and that those who are not born or domiciled in India would be fully protected, as fully as under the present Government, where they are not unduly favoured. That is the *swaraj* of my conception. What it is ultimately going to be depends upon what thinking humanity in India does in the long run. The Goanese population has the making of the India of the future as much in their hands as any other group. No one need therefore ask what will become of him under *swaraj* because no one but idiots and the imbecile will live on sufferance. Each one will guard his own individual liberty, if the State encroaches upon it. Not until many people acquire that power of resistance will India obtain real freedom.

WHEN CRIME NOT IMMORAL

A fair friend sends me 'crisp sayings' by Dan Griffiths on crime and wants me to find room for them in these pages. Here are some extracts which a *satyagrahi* can readily subscribe to: State law is not necessarily moral. Crime is not necessarily immoral.

There is a world of difference between illegality and immorality. Not all illegalities are immoral and not all immoralities are illegal.

Who can say that, whilst not to crawl on one's belly at the dictation of an officer might be an illegality, it is also an immorality?

Rather is it not true that refusal to crawl on one's belly may be illegal, but it would be in the highest degree moral? An other illuminating passage is the following:

Modern society is in itself a crime factory. The militarist is a relative of the murderer and the burglar is the compliment of the stock jobber.

The third excerpt runs as follows:

The thief in law is merely a person who satisfies his acquisitive instincts in ways not sanctioned by the community. The real thief is the person who takes more out of society than he puts into it. But society punishes those who *annoy* it, not those who *injure* it, the *retail* and not the *wholesale* offenders.

SEVEN SOCIAL SINS

The same fair friend wants readers of *Young India* to know, if they do not already, the following seven social sins:

- Politics without principles
- Wealth without work
- Pleasure without conscience
- Knowledge without character
- Commerce without morality
- Science without humanity
- Worship without sacrifice

Naturally, the friend does not want the readers to know these things merely through the intellect but to know them through the heart so as to avoid them.

[*Young India*, 22-10-1925]

33. Music

SPEECH ON MUSIC, AHMEDABAD[1]

[March 21, 1926][2]

There is a famous classical saying which has now become a proverb that the man "that hath no music in himself" is either an ascetic or a beast. We are far from being ascetics, and to the extent that we are devoid of music we are near allied to beasts. To know music is to transfer it to life. The prevalent discord of today is an indication of our sad plight. There can be no *swaraj* where there is no harmony, no music.

Where there is discord and everyone striking his own tune, there is bad government or anarchy. Work for *swaraj* fails to appeal to us because we have no music in us. When we have millions of people singing together in harmony or taking God's name in unison, making one music, we shall have taken the first step to *swaraj*. If we cannot achieve this simple thing, how can we win *swaraj*?

We have free music classes in Ahmedabad for the last three years conducted by one who is an expert. And yet we have to be satisfied today with a roll-attendance of 10 and regular attendance of four. It is poor consolation indeed; but we live in hope and Dr. Hariprasad, who sees a ray of hope when he finds even one pol out of the hundreds in Ahmedabad clean and tidy, might well feel satisfied that we have at least four regular music lovers.

Where there is filth and squalor and misery there can be no music. It implies an atmosphere quite the contrary. If we put a broad interpretation on music, i.e., if we mean by it union, concord, mutual help, it may be said that in no department of life can we dispense with it.

Music today has been regarded to mean the vocal effort of a singing girl. We fight shy of sending our sisters and daughters to music schools.

---

1. This is Mahadev Desai's translation of Gandhiji's speech at the Second Annual Function of the National Music Association, Ahmedabad. It appeared in *Young India* under the caption "Music in Life"
2. According to the Bombay Secret Abstracts, the function was held at the Ashram on this date.

There seems to be a superstition that their voice is best when it is devoid of sweetness. That explains why Dr. Hariprasad has had to express satisfaction with an attendance of ten students.

Music, truly speaking, is an ancient and sacred art. The hymns of *Samaveda* are a mine of music, and no *ayat* of the *Koran* can be recited unmusically. David's Psalms transport you to raptures and remind you of the hymns from *Samaveda*. Let us revive this art and patronize the school of music.

We see Hindu and Mussalman musicians sitting cheek by jowl and partaking in musical concerts. When shall we see the same fraternal union in other affairs of our life? We shall then have the name of Rama and Rahman simultaneously on our lips.

I am glad some of you here are patronizing music. If many more send their children to the music class it will be part of their contribution to national uplift.

But to go a step further. If we would see music in millions of our poor homes, we should all wear *khadi* and spin. The music we have had today was sweet indeed but it is a privilege of the favoured few. The music of the spinning wheel can be a free gift to all and is, therefore, sweeter, It is the hope and solace and mainstay of the millions, and for me, therefore, the truly good music.

We shall consider music in a narrow sense to mean the ability to sing and play an instrument well while carrying a tune and marking the correct beats of time but, in its wider sense, that is to say that true music is created only when life is attuned to a single tune and a single time beat. Music is born only where the strings of the heart are not out of tune. The experiment with music will be regarded as successful one when the crores of people in the entire country will start speaking with the same voice. In my opinion true music is implict in *khadi* and the spinning-wheel. So long as that has not been made explicit, the country is going to welcome anarchy or misrule and, it will continue to be in a state of bondage.[1]

[*Young India*, 15-4-1926]

1. This paragraph is from Gujarati, 28-3-1926.

34. Unity in Diversity

The Polish professor[1] whose earnest questions I endeavoured to answer a few months back, having read my answer[2], sends me the following further questions:

1. Men are not equal. Do you also admit that there is a vast inequality between nations?
2. If this is true, do you think that representative elective bodies, called parliaments, which have brought Europe to the Great War, are really suitable for India?
3. Do you think that India may become one nation in a similar sense as Italy or France?
4. Is it right to suppose that the future of Asia depends on this unification of India, which alone could overrule the materialistic tendencies of Japan and China?
5. Is this not the real alternative for Asia, either superficial Europeanization as in Japan, or going back to ancient Aryan tradition which seems to be the rule for great Indian masters?
6. Has this recalling of original Aryan tradition also an importance for Europe?
7. Do you not see in European civilization, with all its faults, a new power which goes beyond all Hindu experience?
8. Is there, in all India, a single little town, like many French little towns, in which everybody is really free to follow his aspirations, all people are well-to-do, all have a very high level of education and sociability, and representatives of opposite tendencies meet in friendly intercourse? I know such towns in France and also in England. I wonder whether such a thing exists in India.

My correspondent has stated only a half-truth when he says, "Men are not equal". The other half is that they are equal. For, though they are

1. W. Lutostawski.
2. *Vide* "Truth is One", 21-4-1927.

not all of the same age, the same height, the same skin, and the same intellect, these inequalities are temporary and superficial, the soul that is hidden beneath this earthy crust is one and the same for all men and women belonging to all climes. It would, therefore, be perhaps more accurate to say that there is a real and substantial unity in all the variety that we see around us. The word "Inequality" has a bad odour about it, and it has led to arrogance and inhumanities, both in the East and the West. What is true about men is also true about nations, which are but groups of men. The false and rigid doctrine of inequality has led to the insolent exploitation of the nations of Asia and Africa. Who knows that the present ability of the West to prey upon the East is a sign of Western superiority and eastern inferiority? I know that the East meekly, and all too hastily, submits to this pernicious doctrine, and then makes an ineffectual attempt to imitate the West. There is, after all, a world of truth in the poetic statement, "Things are not what they seem."

The second question does not seem to follow from the first. And seeing that I reject the doctrine of inequality in the sense used by the writer, I am unable to admit that the representative elective bodies are really unsuitable for India. But for the reasons, which I have stated in the Indian Home Rule and which in the main I have found no occasion during the past 20 years to revise, I should be extremely sorry, if India entirely copies the Western model. Representative elective bodies were not unknown to India before the European advent. But the contents of the words "representation" and "election" were, so far as I can see, far different from the European.

In my opinion, India is today one nation, even as Italy or France is; and this I maintain in spite of a vivid and painful knowledge of the fact, that Hindus and Mussalmans are murdering one another, that Brahmins and non-Brahmins are preparing for a similar battle, and that both Brahmins and non-Brahmins exclude from their purview the classes which both have left no stone unturned to suppress. But I have known similar quarrels in families and in other nations. It has often seemed to me that a family connection is necessary to establish a good ground for a quarrel. But it flatters me to be able heartily to endorse the proposition that the future of Asia depends upon a proper and demonstrable unification of India.

I do not, however, think that the alternative to superficial Europeanization consists in a complete reversion to the ancient Aryan tradition. I hold with that great thinker, the late Justice Ranade, that there is no such thing as a literal complete revival of ancient tradition possible, even if it were desirable. In the first place, no one knows authoritatively what the ancient Aryan tradition was or is. It is difficult to state unerringly the period which can be described as the "Golden Age" and then to give a categorical description of that age. And I am humble enough to admit that there is much that we can profitably assimilate from the West. Wisdom is no monopoly of one continent or one race. My resistance to Western civilization is really a resistance to its indiscriminate and thoughtless imitation based on the assumption that Asiatics are fit only to copy everything that comes from the West.

I do believe that if India has patience enough to go through the fire of suffering and to resist any unlawful encroachment upon its own civilization which, imperfect though it undoubtedly is, has hitherto stood the ravages of time, she can make a lasting contribution to the peace and solid progress of the world.

I gladly admit that a new power for good is slowly but surely arising in the West. Whether it will transcend all Hindu experience or not, I do not know. But I should welcome every fresh contribution to the enrichment of humanity, no matter where it comes from.

Lastly, I am unable to say anything about the glowing tribute that the learned professor pays to the self-contained French and English little towns. I know so little about English towns, and still less about the French. I own I have my doubts. But I know that if the professor could stand the almost forbidden exterior of Indian villages, I would undertake to take him to some of them where he would see a culture of a high order, and though he will miss the literary polish he will not miss the human heart and the human touch, and where, if he can accommodate himself to the strange Indian ways about exclusive eating and drinking, he will see amazing tolerance of opposite ideas and friendliest intercourse of the mind and the soul. Let me also remind the professor that the English and the French prosperity and amenities which such prosperity brings depend upon, what I must again repeat and what I would gladly avoid if I could, namely, exploitation.

[*Young India*, 11-8-1927]

35. Prohibition

SPEECH ON PROHIBITION, MADRAS[1]

[September 6, 1927]

FRIENDS,

I am supposed to talk to you this morning about prohibition. I don't remember having talked to a select audience on 'Prohibition' in my life except at one time, although I can claim to be a staunch prohibitionist as I am a staunch khaddarite. My life has been so cast that I get little chance of talking on such matters to a select audience.

The one reason for that flaw in me is that I am a crank or I am supposed to be a crank and, therefore, very often before a select audience I feel like a fish out of water. All cranks are necessarily extremists and where others feel the necessity for caution and moderation and such like about things that matter in life, I feel as if I am nowhere, as if I have no place. When someone says to me that in this practical world I must go slowly, I become impatient and tell him, "How can you go slowly in the matter of prohibition? You won't talk like that to a woman whose husband is drunkard." I have lived in a family where the husband happened to be a drunkard. That was in Pretoria in 1893. The lady tried to make ends meet and was always in dread as to what would happen when her lord and master returned home. If I had told her that "In this practical world we must go slowly", she would not have allowed me to continue as her cotenant.

You may imagine me to be in that plight but not with one husband, not one but thousands of husbands. How can you ask me to wait? I become impatient, angry and, non-violent though I am, you will see fierceness in my eyes. I said the same thing to Mr. Anderson, the Secretary of the Temperance Association. I feel strongly about it.

There are more things about which my feelings are strong and speech becomes useless for me. Those are really sacred things which I keep in my bosom and when opportunity offers itself I express my views strongly which the world cannot possibly mistake.

---

1. At Mani Aiyar Hall, Triplicane.

In this matter of prohibition we have some Englishmen with us, because they happen to be Missionaries or Christians. I do not know whether there are other Englishmen with us in this matter. They are all for some purpose too practical. They say we should realize the difficulties of Government. Why should I realize the difficulties of Government in this matter? The difficulties are purely financial and nothing else. There are three acid tests in this connection.

Not one Englishman has yet told me that prohibition is an impossibility in India except for finance. Everybody says: "Oh yes. You want to make India bear the burden of additional taxation by the introduction of prohibition, for the education of your children, etc." I would like India to become a pauper rather than that India should have lakhs and lakhs of drunkards in her midst in order to educate her children, or I would have Indian children illiterate rather than have drunkenness in the land as the price of their education. But when I am called upon to become a party to additional taxation I say "Hands off"; because there are other ways in which you can make up this financial loss. I think Government made the initial blunder of considering *abkari* as a source of revenue. It should never have been considered a source of revenue and it is not to be a source of revenue.

And my grievance is definite and tangible that this source of revenue should have been left in charge of the transferred departments to meet the charges of education, sanitation, etc., so that our ministers have to fall back upon this immoral, sinful and hideous source of revenue.

There is nothing so sinful as this kind of revenue. It is difficult to contain myself and I have, therefore, to talk to you in a strained language.

I feel that so far as India is concerned she has a complete case for prohibition and not prohibition piece-meal in one or two districts.

I have read the speech of the Madras Excise Minister. I am sorry I have had to write something criticizing that speech in the coming issue of the *Young India*.[1] The method of experimenting in one or two districts does not appeal to me. I shall not be surprised if he makes the experiment in one or two districts and if the experiment fails then it would be said that prohibition can never be tried and it can never be successful. You will try to do the right thing in the wrong manner and then denounce the right thing instead of the wrong manner. The country is in favour of prohibition. If it is a question of lakhs and lakhs of signatures in favour of prohibition it is merely a matter of organization. I have not found a single

1. *Vide* "Total Prohibition", 8-9-1927.

place where there has been really agitation against prohibition except when it is manufactured and financed also. There are States where territorial prohibition has been declared and where not a single man has come forward to say "we want a shop at least here." In one of the States, Europeans, who consumed whisky and brandy, are exempted. But, we are in this matter terribly handicapped; we have as our rulers or Governors those who do not consider drink as a crime or immorality. I have myself English friends who laugh at me when I talk of prohibition. I have great regard for them. They seem to think that if they drink in moderation they would not lose their sense and would not become brutes. I have myself seen these friends not only losing their sense but becoming brutes. I have seen many friends losing self-control when they drink.

They are first-class men. But when they drink they become asses. It may be excusable to have spirituous liquor in countries near the North Pole. There is no need in this country at all for drink. Yet some agitation is going on here against prohibition. I had [from someone] a pile of anti-prohibition pamphlets published anonymously. They constituted a hymn in praise of liquor. Radical, scriptural and all sorts of authorities have been quoted in favour of drinking in moderation and the whole thing has been presented in such an insidiously attractive form that a man who has not his wits about him may easily become a convert to the drink habit. If you are a fierce prohibitionist like myself and if you will agitate from one end of the country to the other for prohibition, you will certainly succeed. Let us not fall into the financial trap that is laid for us. Our position should be absolutely clear. It is not our purpose to find out finances. Those who committed the initial blunder must retrace their steps. There is also a way out of the financial difficulty.

Cut out 25 crores from the crores you spend upon military expenditure. The military expenditure has been jumping from day to day. If you prepare a chart it would show a staggering growth of that expenditure. You can cut out a heavy slice from that expenditure. I must not go into the political history of the question. Whatever, deficit that is found in connection with the *abkari* revenue shculd be made good out of military expenditure and no other. There should be no additional taxation on this score. The result will be that in 10 years' time the revenue of the Government will increase enormously and that is the experience of countries where prohibition has been tried.

Do not believe the interested writings in newspapers that total prohibition has been a failure in America. Scarcely an American who comes to India goes away without seeing me. These Americans and the literature published by the Prohibition League give the testimony that the sum total effect of prohibition is to the good of the country although they have not been able to claim all the brilliant results that they had thought they would be able to have. There is no public opinion in America supporting the removal of prohibition. The Government is their own government and people are satisfied with the state of things there. The labourer leads a sober and honest life there.

Is not that sufficient consideration for loss of revenue? Such a state of things exists in another part of the world, but not in India unfortunately. The experience of countries which have tried prohibition is that the people have become better and that the country has not been financially ruined. No ruin, no financial crisis will befall India if prohibition is introduced in India. It is the solemn duty of every one of us to see the use of drink wiped out of the land altogether if we possibly can. If I had the power and if I could have my way, I would do so today.

I come to picketing. I confess that some pickets were violent; but the real reason for Government not tolerating picketing was the loss of revenue. People in Bihar all on a sudden became teetotallers and they were faithful to the pickets. In Assam the same thing happened. The opium dens were closed for the time being. It was a thing too terrible for Government to contemplate. There was ample evidence to show that picketing was useful and necessary and it conferred immense benefit upon India. It showed the possibility of prohibition. In America prohibition has created a tremendous spiritual upheaval. But the task of creating that spiritual consciousness was great in America. But we in India have not the hundredth part of the difficulty that the Americans had to surmount. They had to surmount the American nature itself. Here it is not so for the atmosphere is favourable to prohibition. Therefore, you need not go here cautiously.

Armchair politicians who have no knowledge of the conditions of India do not distinguish between American and Indian life. They cannot see that we can attain prohibition if only you have the will and courage.

I make a distinction between opium and drink. Opium acts as an opiate and makes a man an idiot, whereas drink makes a man a beast. A woman would rather have her husband an idiot than a drunkard. I am willing to make an exception for the use of liquor or brandy for medicinal purposes. I make also the distinction between England and India. What is good enough for England is not necessarily good enough for India. If we allow this drink problem to continue, our posterity will curse us.

[*The Hindu*, 6-9-1827]

36. The Message of Jesus

SPEECH AT Y.M.C.A., COLOMBO

[November 15, 1927]

Addressing a huge gathering in the hall of Y.M.C.A., Colombo, Gandhiji welcomed the occasion as one more instance of the close touch, he was daily finding himself in, with Christians throughout the world [and said:]. There are some who will not even take my flat denial when I tell them that I am not a Christian.

The message of Jesus, as I understand it, is contained in his *Sermon on the Mount* unadulterated and taken as a whole, and even in connection with the *Sermon on the Mount*, my own humble interpretation of the message is in many respects different from the orthodox. The message, to my mind, has suffered distortion in the West. It may be presumptuous for me to say so, but as a devotee of truth, I should not hesitate to say what I feel. I know that the world is not waiting to know my opinion on Christianity.

One's own religion is after all a matter between oneself and one's Maker and no one else's, but if I feel impelled to share my thoughts with you this evening, it is because I want to enlist your sympathy in my search for truth and because so many Christian friends are interested in my thoughts on the teachings of Jesus. If then I had to face only the *Sermon on the Mount* and my own interpretation of it, I should not hesitate to say, 'Oh yes, I am a Christian'. But I know that at the present moment if I said any such thing I would lay myself open to the gravest misinterpretation. I should lay myself open to fraudulent claims because I would have then to tell you what my own meaning of Christianity is, and I have no desire myself to give you my own view of Christianity. But negatively I can tell you that in my humble opinion, much of what passes as Christianity is a negation of the *Sermon on the Mount*. And please mark my words. I am not at the present moment speaking of Christian conduct. I am speaking of the Christian belief, of Christianity as it is understood in the West. I am painfully aware of the fact that conduct everywhere falls far short of belief. But I don't say this by way of criticism. I know from the treasures of my own experience that although I am every moment of my life trying to live up to my professions, my conduct falls short of these professions. Far, therefore, be it from me to say this in a spirit of criticism. But I am placing before you my fundamental difficulties. When I began as a prayerful student to study the Christian literature in South Africa in 1893, I asked myself, 'Is this Christianity?' and have always got the Vedic answer, *neti neti* (not this, not this). And the deepest in me tells me that I am right.

I claim to be a man of faith and prayer, and even if I was cut to pieces, God would give me the strength not to deny Him and to assert that He is. The Muslim says He is and there is no one else. The Christian says the same thing and so the Hindu, and if I may say so, even the Buddhist says the same thing, if in different words. We may each of us be putting our own interpretation on the word God—God

Who embraces not only this tiny globe of ours, but millions and billions of such globes. How can we, little crawling creatures, so utterly helpless as he has made us, how could we possibly measure His greatness, His boundless love, His infinite compassion, such that He allows man insolently to deny compassion, such that He allows man insolently to deny Him, wrangle about Him, and cut the throat of his fellow man? How can we measure the greatness of God who is so forgiving, so divine? Thus though we may utter the same words they have not the same meaning for us all. And hence I say that we do not need to proselytize or do *shuddhi* or *tabligh* through our speech or writing. We can only do it really with our lives. Let them be open books for all to study. Would that I could persuade the missionary friends to take this view of their mission. Then there will be no distrust, no suspicion, no jealousy and no dissensions.

Gandhiji then took the case of modern China as a case in point. His heart, he said, went out to young China in the throes of a great national upheaval, and he referred to the anti-Christian movement in China, about which he had occasion to read in a pamphlet received by him from the students' department of the Young Women's Christian Association and the Young Men's Christian Association of China. The writers had put their own interpretation upon the anti-Christian movement, but there was no doubt that young China regarded Christian movements as being opposed to Chinese self-expression. To Gandhiji the moral of this anti-Christian manifestation was clear. He said:

"Don't let your Christian propaganda be anti-national, say these young Chinese. And even their Christian friends have come to distrust the Christian endeavour that had come from the West. I present the thought to you that these essays written by young man have a deep meaning, a deep truth, because they were themselves trying to justify their Christian conduct in so far as they had been able to live up to the life it had taught them and at the same time find a basis for that opposition. The deduction I would like you all to draw from this manifestation is that you Ceylonese should not be torn from your moorings, and those from the West should not consciously or unconsciously lay violent hands upon the manners, customs and habits of the Ceylonese in so far as they are not repugnant to fundamental ethics and morality. Confuse not Jesus' teachings with what passes as modern civilization, and pray do not do unconscious violence to the people among whom you cast your lot. It is no part of that call, I assure you, to tear the lives of the people of the East by its roots. Tolerate whatever is good in them and do not hastily, with your preconceived notions, judge them. Do not judge lest you be judged yourselves. In spite of your belief in the greatness of Western civilization and in spite of your pride in all your achievements, I plead with you for humility, and ask you to leave some little room for doubt, in which, as Tennyson sang, there was more truth, though by 'doubt' he no doubt meant a different thing. Let us each one live our life, and if ours is the right life, where is the cause for hurry? It will react of itself."

To you, young Ceylonese friends[1], I say: Don't be dazzled by the splendour that comes to you from the West. Do not be thrown off your feet by this passing show. The Enlightened One has told you in never-to-be-forgotten words that this little span of life is but a passing shadow, a fleeting thing, and if you realize the nothingness of all that appears before your eyes, the nothingness of this material case that we see before us ever changing, then indeed there are treasures for you up above, and there is peace for you down here, peace which passeth all understanding and happiness to which we are utter strangers. It requires an amazing faith, a divine faith and surrender of all that we see before us. What did Buddha do, and Christ do, and also Mahomed? Theirs were lives of self-sacrifice and renunciation.

Buddha renounced every worldly happiness, because he wanted to share with the whole world his happiness which was to be had by men who sacrificed and suffered in search of truth. If it was a good thing to scale the heights of Mount Everest, sacrificing precious lives in order to be able to go there and make some slight observations, it was a glorious

1. The Y.M.C.A. had among its members Buddhist as well as Christian youths.

thing to give up life after life in planting a flag in the uttermost extremities of the earth, how much more glorious would it be to give not one life, surrender not a million lives but a billion lives in search of the potent and imperishable truth? So be not lifted off your feet, do not be drawn away from the simplicity of your ancestors. A time is coming when those who are in the mad rush today of multiplying their wants, vainly thinking that they add to the real substance, real knowledge of the world, will retrace their steps and say:

'What have we done?' Civilizations have come and gone, and in spite of all our vaunted progress I am tempted to ask again and again 'To what purpose?' Wallace, a contemporary of Darwin, has said the same thing. Fifty years of brilliant inventions and discoveries, he has said, has not added one inch to the moral height of mankind. So said a dreamer and visionary if you will—Tolstoy. So said Jesus, and Buddha, and Mahomed, Whose religion is being denied and falsified in my own country today.

By all means drink deep of the fountains that are given to you in the *Sermon on the Mount*, but then you will have to take sackcloth and ashes. The teaching of the *Sermon* was meant for each and every one of us. You cannot serve both God and Mammon. God the Compassionate and the Merciful, Tolerance incarnate, allows Mammon to have his nine days' wonder. But I say to you, youth of Ceylon, fly from that self-destroying but destructive show of Mammon.

[*Young India,* 8-12-1927]

37. Boycott of Foreign Cloth

SPEECH AT THE PUBLIC MEETING, CALCUTTA[1]

[March 4, 1929]

As the Congress has directed we must boycott foreign cloth, not only British cloth but all foreign cloth. It will not do to boycott British cloth alone, for it will find its way into the country along with other foreign cloth. Bengali friends know this from their experience during the *swadeshi* movement.

India is an extremely poor country. I wish to draw strength from having the poor of India with me. That is why I place so much emphasis on the propagation of *khadi*. The author of the *Mahabharata* has dwelt at length on the glory of serving the poor. Buddha has also spoken of this. The people of India sorely need food and clothing. Tormented by the pangs of hunger our countrymen have been known to abandon their children. There is no remedy for their suffering other than propagation of *khadi*. I have reached this conclusion after having travelled all over India. I shall bow to the man who can show an alternative way of removing the distress of the poor millions of India. I shall accept him as my *guru*. The only way is the boycott of foreign cloth. I have the fullest faith in this measure.

I hope you will take off such foreign cloth as you may be wearing and burn it here and now and collect all foreign cloth in your homes and bring it to the spot indicated by the Congress and burn it. And now please take off all your foreign cloth.[2]

(As my speech at the foreign-cloth-burning-demonstration campaign at Calcutta on the 4th instant and the statement made to the Press have a significance beyond the Indian border and as they define the scope of the boycott campaign as also of civil disobedience, I transcribe them below from the daily Press.

M.K. Gandhi)

---

1. The meeting was held in the Shraddhanand Park.
2. The three paragraphs above are a translation of Gandhiji's speech in Hindi as reported in *Aaj*. What follows is the report of his speech in English taken from *Young India*.

FRIENDS,

I do not propose to translate what I have been saying in Hindustani. It is sufficient for me to say that the boycott of foreign cloth, not merely boycott of British cloth, is in my opinion indispensable if we are to attain *swaraj* in terms of the hungry millions.

The Congress accepted this proposition last year. The Working Committee by accepting the scheme drawn up by me at its instance has also set its seal of approval upon the proposition that I have laid down before you. The Working Committee has invited me to shoulder the burden of guiding its deliberations. I have faith in you, my countrymen, I have faith in God. I have faith in the absolute righteousness of this cause and so in fear and trembling and full hope I have shouldered the burden and now ask you to share that burden with me. This meeting is not of my seeking, you have chosen to call this meeting, you have come here well knowing what is to happen here. I hope that this is a sign of your determination to lighten the burden that I have shouldered. I do not want to argue out the pros and cons of the boycott of foreign cloth through *khadi*. Remember, that is, the proposition enunciated in the scheme. Before the Working Committee would accept this scheme it wanted to subject me to a fire of cross-examination. The proceedings lasted for four hours and the Working Committee was fully satisfied that this was the only thing we could possibly do if we were to go through this programme during this year and if need be wake up on the first of January next with the whole country as Independence *wallahs*. If we are to achieve our purpose this is the only effective programme. I want you, therefore, to be true to this programme and to yourselves. No longer deceive yourselves and the country by crowding at meetings of this character, by giving applause and then going away forgetting everything about what might happen at such meetings. I want you to translate every word that you say into effective action. I want you to pledge yourselves not before me but before your God that henceforth you are not going to use any foreign cloth, that you are going to give up foreign clothes in your possession, that you will burn them even as you burn rags in your possession which may require to be disinfected, even as a drunkard suddenly become teetotaller empties his cupboard and destroys every bottle of brandy and whisky in his possession, no matter what it might have cost him. You will count no cost too great against the cause, the liberty and honour of your country.

But there is a fly in the ointment. I have seen a notice served upon the Secretary of the Provincial Congress Committee which proceeds somewhat on these lines: That at this meeting no burning of clothes should take place because it is an offence under the Police Act or Police Regulations, whatever, that may be called. The clause runs after this fashion that no burning of straw or such other things can take place in or near any public street or thoroughfare. Well, I have been taxing my mind as to whether to call this Park a thoroughfare or not. Two lawyers put their heads together—I do not count myself as a lawyer, I am disbarred—they put their heads together and advised me that by no stretch of meaning could this Park be called a thoroughfare. They drew my attention to another section in the Act where a public street, a public thoroughfare and a place of public resort were also mentioned. In this section the place of public resort is specifically omitted. I can well understand this Park being a place of public resort.

In this circumstance what am I to do? I accept this notice as one served upon my humble self. I do not want to avoid the consequences of this law. But today I do not appear before you as a civil breaker of law, I do not appear before you as a civil resister, I do not want you to commit at this moment a breach of any Regulation. I am quite capable of breaking all the Regulations that may hurt my moral sense but that time is not yet for me—that time may come tomorrow, but it is not tonight. But I have got to discharge a public duty in front of you and in interpreting this law as I do or as I am advised to interpret it I venture to submit that this notice has no effect upon me, assuming the argument that the service of that notice upon the Secretary is equal to service upon me. If I am taken before a court of law, I make this definite promise that I shall not raise this issue that the notice was not served upon me. I claim this is not a public thoroughfare, I claim also that I am not doing anything that is dangerous. It is well known that it is the settled policy of the Congress or rather of the Working Committee. The Working Committee has got a duty to discharge. I am a member of that Committee, I am the Chairman of the Boycott Committee and I feel that I shall be running away from my duty if I shirk this issue and avoid a prosecution against me.

If I am allowed to go away, I shall be going away tomorrow and I shall return on the 25th or the 26th of this month to undergo and stand a prosecution against myself for having undertaken to burn foreign cloth in a public park which I claim is not a public thoroughfare. That is, the important statement I wanted to make before you. You are not burning, the act of burning is by me and it will be on my sole responsibility. You are not hurt by being witnesses—I wish you were hurt. But today the campaign is not of civil resistance but one of conducting a boycott, a fierce boycott of foreign clothes, remaining as long as it is possible within the four corners of the law. I do not want you today to be guilty, consciously or unconsciously, of a breach of laws of this kind whatever some of those laws may be. You will get the opportunity if you care to obey the directions of the Working Committee when the proper time comes to break certain laws or all non-moral laws of the country. But as I have said before, the time is not yet and I do not want to precipitate that time and I do not want also to anticipate that time. And if the Government will play the game, if the police will play the game, I promise we shall settle our business with Government without having to resort to civil disobedience, without the public having even to resort to no-tax campaign which is a part of civil disobedience. Believe me I shall strain every nerve to avoid that issue. Speaking with a full sense of responsibility over my shoulders, I know the tremendous consequences of civil disobedience and of no-tax campaign in a vast country like this—a country which has undisciplined masses—but a man who is mad as I am now after freedom, a man who is hungry after freedom—and a real hunger for freedom is infinitely more painful than hunger for mere bread—has got to take tremendous risks, to stake everything that he has in order to gain that precious freedom, and it is because I am hungry for that freedom—although I am on the threshold of death, I want to see *swaraj* whilst I have still breath in me—that I want to take all those risks. But at the same time I want to take every precaution and, therefore, I shall plead with the Government and the powers that be, I shall ask them to come to their senses.

But if you alone will help me we shall be able to avoid all these risks and still find the dawn of freedom breaking upon us before the 31st of December next.

If you will [be truthful, if you will][1] carry out honestly, faithfully and completely the programme that will be set before you from time to time I promise no heroic measures will be necessary to be taken by you. Is boycott of foreign clothes such a heroic measure? Is the putting of the Congress house in order such a heroic measure? Is the registering of thousands upon thousands of members for the Congress or the habitual wearing [of] *khadi* [on the part of the rich and the poor] a heroic act? If you think these are heroic acts I can honestly tell you that you do not

1. Portions in square brackets are taken from *Amrita Bazar Patrika*, 5-3-1929 and *The Hindustan Times*, 7-3-1929.

know what heroic acts are; heroic acts are made of sterner stuff. Do not run away with the idea that the programme before you is heroic stuff. These easy things have been placed before you for the simple reason that you are millions against one hundred thousand men.

If we were not under the spell of hypnotism or if we were not being acted upon by that great force [of] inertia, or want of self confidence, we would find it the most natural thing to breathe the air of freedom which is ours to breathe. If we were not under this hypnotic spell we would not have to go through even these easy stages. [Try and do these things during this year and then come to me and ask me, "Where is *swaraj*?" You will not need coming to me. You will find it within your grasp. The millions of the masses will smile upon you. They will bless you for making a common cause with them by understanding their real grievances. Therefore, I ask you to do this. I have faith in you. This notice from the Commissioner of Police has enabled me to make my appeal to the authorities. I am here to take the risk. I propose to burn the clothes that have been handed to me and I want you before I perform the sacred ceremony to throw all your clothes at me on the platform. Do not make any noise.]

No violence [or force] must be used so long as you want to have me as a participator in this ceremony. I swear by non-violence—that is my creed. I can see no other way open to me to regain my freedom.

[So long as you choose to have me in this campaign, in spite of my creed, so long do I plead with you to observe the law of non-violence, you will find that you have done well.]

The responsibility for this act of burning is entirely on my shoulders—please remember too that we want the boycott of foreign clothes and not merely of British clothes. Let that confusion be dispelled from your minds. Take it from me that the men who have been a party to this scheme are not thoughtless men. They went into the question of foreign clothes *versus* British clothes and they came to the conclusion that the proper thing was boycott of foreign clothes. I do not want to go into the question of the Indian mills; they will take care of themselves if you will take care of *khadi*. [Otherwise the mills will be a halter round your neck.][1]

1. *Aaj*, 8-3-1929, and *Young India*, 14-3-1929.

38. On Bonfire[1]

STATEMENT IN THE COURT[2]

[Calcutta,
March 26, 1929]

Occupying the position I do in public life I owe an explanation to the Court and the public of my conduct which is the subject-matter of this prosecution. I am Chairman of the Foreign Cloth Boycott Committee appointed by the Working Committee of the National Congress. The scheme of boycott sanctioned by the Working Committee includes burning of foreign cloth wherever it is possible.

Therefore, I naturally advised collection and burning of foreign cloth at the meeting that was held at Shraddhanand Park. The notice from the Commissioner of Police came upon me and my colleagues as a disturbing factor. We saw at once that it was not meant for protection of property from danger of fire but it was meant to prevent the demonstration. It was open to us to conduct the burning demonstration at a private place. But two lawyers came to the conclusion that the interpretation sought to be put upon Section 66 of the Police Act was at least open to question, if not altogether wrong.

We, therefore, decided to conduct the full demonstration at the Park as advertised and have the police interpretation tested in a Court of Law.

This boycott is not part of civil disobedience. There was no intention to defy the police notice for the sake of defiance and courting imprisonment.

I made this absolutely clear in English within the hearing of the police at the meeting before I started the burning. I believe that the Deputy Commissioner of Police was present whilst I was speaking. I was therefore surprised and deeply pained to see the police, after the burning was well nigh over, swoop down upon the crowd surrounding the fire, charge it with their big lathis, disperse it and put out the dying embers.

---

1. This letter appears to have been written from Calcutta after Gandhiji's return from Burma. The presence of Rajendrababu is mentioned in the letter of this date to Mirabehn.
2. Of the Chief Presidency Magistrate, Calcutta.

The rest of the painful scene I may not describe here though I should gladly answer questions on it if the Court so desires.

I venture to submit that by taking the law into their own hands, especially in spite of my very clear statement above referred to, the Police put themselves in the wrong and should change places with me.

They should be the accused and my colleagues and I should be the complainants. I have before now in other parts of the world been obliged to differ from police interpretations of laws and act contrary to their notices. But they have recognized the civilized practice of testing the points involved in law courts without in the first instance prejudging the issue and thus running the risk of themselves breaking the law and, what is more, of inviting a disturbance of public peace.

I affirm that the crowd was absolutely peaceful and extremely well behaved. There was no danger to the neighbouring property from the little fire that was lighted. The site chosen for burning was well protected and isolated. It was, therefore, the duty of the police to refrain from interfering with the peaceful and orderly demonstration.

Their interference in my opinion was rudely premature, extremely high-handed and uncalled for. In putting out the fire they usurped the function of the Court and anticipated its judgment. If you believe the statement of facts I have made I ask Your Worship to discharge me and my colleagues and take such notice of the conduct of the police as may be open to you. And this discharge I ask irrespective of the interpretation the Court may put upon the Section under which I am charged.

One word as to the interpretation of the Section. Sjt. Sen Gupta was one of the lawyer friends referred to in my speech at the Shraddhanand Park. After having had another argument with him I am clear in my mind that the Shraddhanand Park is neither a street nor a thoroughfare within the meaning of the Section. Since, it is not the intention, so far as possible, of the Foreign Cloth Boycott Committee to offer civil disobedience in connection with the campaign, an authoritative interpreation of the Section is necessary. But I may not argue the legal point.

As to the three of my colleagues who are charged with the primary offence, I should like to state that the burning was actually started by me. If, therefore, any offence has been committed by any of us, the primary offence has been committed by me and the rest three are but the secondary offenders.[1]

1. *Forward*, 27-3-1929.

39. The Last Fight

SPEECH AT PRAYER MEETING, SABARMATI ASHRAM

[On or before March 11, 1930][1]

Let me, moreover, make one thing clear. Either we shall win the goal for which we are marching or die in the attempt to win it. There can be no turning back for us hereafter. We will keep on our fight till *swaraj* is established in India. This will be the last fight. The soldiers who accompany me must note that there is to be no retreat. Those of them that are married should take leave of their wives, and the wives should congratulate their husbands on their being the first soldiers of the country's freedom battle. We are as good as parting from the Ashram and from our homes. Only with complete victory can we return to this place.

[*From Gujarati*]
[*Gujarati,* 16-3-1930]

1. According to the source the speech was delivered to a large gathering either on the 10th or 11th of March.

40. On the Eve of Dandi March

SPEECH AT PRAYER MEETING, SABARMATI ASHRAM

[March 11, 1930]

In all probability this will be my last speech to you. Even if the Government allow me to march tomorrow morning, this will be my last speech on the sacred banks of the Sabarmati. Possibly these may be the last words of my life here.

I have already told you yesterday what I had to say. Today I shall confine myself to what you should do after I and my companions are arrested. The programme of the march to Jalalpur must be fulfilled as originally settled. The enlistment of volunteers for this purpose should be confined to Gujarat. From what I have seen and heard during the last fortnight I am inclined to believe that the stream of civil resisters will flow unbroken.

But let there be not a semblance of breach of peace even after all of us have been arrested. We have resolved to utilize all our resources in the pursuit of an exclusively non-violent struggle. Let no one commit a wrong in anger. This is my hope and prayer. I wish these words of mine reached every nook and corner of the land. My task shall be done if I perish and so do my comrades. It will then be for the Working Committee of the Congress to show you the way and it will be up to you to follow its lead. That is the only meaning of the Working Committee's resolution. The reins of the movement will still remain in the hands of those of my associates who believe in non-violence as an article of faith. Of course, the Congress will be free to chalk out what course of action commends itself to it. So long as I have not reached Jalalpur, let nothing be done in contravention to the authority vested in me by the Congress. But once I am arrested, the whole general responsibility shifts to the Congress. No one who believes in non-violence, as a creed, need therefore sit still. My compact with the Congress ends as soon as I am arrested. In that case there should be no slackness in the enrolment of volunteers. Wherever possible, civil disobedience of salt laws should be started. These laws can be violated in three ways. It is an offence to manufacture salt wherever there are facilities for doing so. The possession and sale of contraband salt (which includes natural salt or salt earth) is also an offence. The purchasers of such salt will be equally guilty. To carry away the natural salt deposits on the seashore is likewise a violation of law. So is the hawking of such salt. In short, you may choose anyone or all of these devices to break the salt monopoly.

We are, however, not to be content with this alone. Wherever, there are Congress Committees, wherever there is no ban by the Congress and wherever the local workers have self-confidence, other suitable measures may be adopted. I prescribe only one condition, viz., let our pledge of truth and non-violence as the only means for the attainment of *swaraj* be faithfully kept. For the rest, everyone has a free hand. But that does not give a licence to all and sundry to carry on their individual responsibility. Wherever there are local leaders, their orders should be obeyed by the people. Where there are no leaders and only a handful of men have faith in the programme, they may do what they can, if they have enough self-confidence. They have a right, nay, it is their duty, to do so. The history of the world is full of instances of men who rose to leadership by sheer force of self-confidence, bravery and tenacity. We too, if we sincerely aspire to *swaraj* and are impatient to attain it, should have similar self-confidence. Our ranks will swell and our hearts strengthen as the number of our arrests by Government increases.

Let nobody assume that after I am arrested there will be no one left to guide them. It is not I but Pandit Jawaharlal who is your guide. He has the capacity to lead. Though the fact is that those who have learnt the lesson of fearlessness and self-effacement need no leader, but if we lack these virtues, not even Jawaharlal will be able to produce them in us.

Much can be done in other ways besides these. Liquor and foreign cloth shops can be picketed. We can refuse to pay taxes if we have the requisite strength. The lawyers can give up practice.

The public can boycott the courts by refraining from litigation. Government servants can resign their posts. In the midst of the despair reigning all round people quake with fear of losing employment.

Such men are unfit for *swaraj*. But why this despair? The number of Government servants in the country does not exceed a few hundred thousand. What about the rest? Where are they to go? Even free India will not be able to accommodate a greater number of public servants.

A Collector then will not need the number of servants he has got today. He will be his own servant. How can a poor country like India afford to provide a Collector with separate servants for performing the duties of carrying his papers, sweeping, cooking, latrine-cleaning and letter-carrying? Our starving millions can by no means afford this enormous expenditure. If, therefore, we are sensible enough, let us bid good-bye to Government employment, no matter if it is the post of a judge or a peon. It may be difficult for a judge to leave his job, but where is the difficulty in the case of a peon? He can earn his bread everywhere by honest manual labour. This is the easiest solution of the problem of freedom. Let all who are co-operating with the Government in one way or another, be it by paying taxes, keeping titles, or sending children to official schools, etc., withdraw their co-operation in all or as many ways as possible. One can devise other methods, too, of non-co-operating with the Government. And then there are women who can stand shoulder to shoulder with men in this struggle.

You may take it as my will. It was the only message that I desired to impart to you before starting on the march or for the jail. I wish there to be no suspension or abandonment of the war that commences tomorrow morning, or earlier if I am arrested before that time. I shall eagerly await the news that ten batches are ready as soon as my batch is arrested. I believe there are men in India to complete the work begun by me today. I have faith in the righteousness of our cause and the purity of our weapons. And where the means are clean, there God is undoubtedly present with His blessings. And where these three combine, there defeat is an impossibility. A *satyagrahi*, whether free or incarcerated, is ever victorious. He is vanquished only when he forsakes truth and non-violence and turns a deaf ear to the Inner Voice. If, therefore, there is such a thing as defeat for even a *satyagrahi*, he alone is the cause of it. God bless you all and keep off all obstacles from the path in the struggle that begins tomorrow. Let this be our prayer.

[*Young India*, 20-3-1930]

41. Non-violence

MESSAGE TO THE NATION[1]

[Dandi,
April 9, 1930]

At last the long expected hour seems to have come. In the dead of night my colleagues and companions have roused me from deep slumber and requested me to give them a message. I am, therefore, dictating this message, although I have not the slightest inclination to give any.

Messages I have given enough already. Of what avail would this message be if none of the previous messages evoked a proper response? But information received until this midnight leads me to the belief that my message did not fall flat, but was taken up by the people in right earnest. The people of Gujarat seem to have risen in a body as it were. I have seen with my own eyes thousands of men and women at Aat and Bhimrad fearlessly breaking the Salt Act. Not a sign of mischief, not a sign of violence have I seen, despite the presence of people in such large numbers. They have remained perfectly peaceful and non-violent, although Government officers have transgressed all bounds.

Here in Gujarat well-tried and popular public servants have been arrested one after another, and yet the people have been perfectly non-violent. They have refused to give way to panic, and have celebrated the arrests by offering civil disobedience in ever increasing numbers. This is just as it should be.

If the struggle so auspiciously begun is continued in the same spirit of non-violence to the end, not only shall we see *Purna Swaraj* established in our country before long, but we shall have given to the world an object-lesson worthy of India and her glorious past.

---

1. This was published with a note which read: "The following is an English translation of a message dictated by Gandhiji at Dandi on April 9, when there was a strong rumour of his impending arrest. A month has gone by, but the message still holds good. We publish it today as a challenge to the honour and loyalty of India to meet the fiery ordeal that now lies before her."

Swaraj won without sacrifice cannot last long. I would, therefore, like our people to get ready to make the highest sacrifice that they are capable of. In true sacrifice all the suffering is on one side — one is required to master the art of getting killed without killing, of gaining life by losing it. May India live up to this *mantra*.

At present India's self-respect, in fact her all, is symbolized as it were in a handful of salt in the *satyagrahi's* hand. Let the fist holding it therefore be broken, but let there be no voluntary surrender of the salt.

Let the Government, if it claims to be a civilized Government, jail those who help themselves to contraband salt. After their arrest the civil resisters will gladly surrender the salt, as they will their bodies into the custody of their jailors.

But by main force to snatch the salt from the poor, harmless *satyagrahis*' hands is barbarism pure and simple and an insult to India. Such insult can be answered only by allowing our hand to be fractured without loosening the grasp. Even then the actual sufferer or his comrades may not harbour in their hearts anger against the wrongdoer.

Incivility should be answered not by incivility but by a dignified and calm endurance of all suffering in the name of God.

Let not my companions or the people at large be perturbed over my arrest, for it is not I but God who is guiding this movement. He ever dwells in the hearts of all and he will vouchsafe to us the right guidance if only we have faith in Him. Our path has already been chalked out for us. Let every village fetch or manufacture contraband salt. Sisters should picket liquor shops, opium dens and foreign cloth dealers' shops. Young and old in every home should ply the *takli* and spin, and get woven, heaps of yarn every day. Foreign cloth should be burnt. Hindus should eschew untouchability. Hindus, Mussalmans, Sikhs, Parsis, and Christians should all achieve heart unity. Let the majority rest content with what remains after the minorities have been satisfied. Let students leave Government schools and colleges, and Government servants resign their service and devote themselves to service of the people, and we shall find that *Purna Swaraj* will come knocking at our door.

[*Young India,* 8-5-1930]

42. Appeal to the Conscience of the World

BROADCAST TO AMERICA[1]

[September 13, 1931]

In my opinion, the Indian Conference bears in its consequences not only upon India but upon the whole world. India is by itself almost a continent. It contains one-fifth of the human race. It represents one of the most ancient civilizations. It has traditions handed down from tens of thousands of years, some of which, to the astonishment of the world, remain intact. No doubt the ravages of time have affected the purity of that civilization, as they have that of many other cultures and many institutions.

If India is to perpetuate the glory of her ancient past, it can do so only when it attains freedom. The reason for the struggle having drawn the attention of the world, I know, does not lie in the fact that we Indians are fighting for our liberty, but in the fact that the means adopted by us for attaining that liberty are unique and, as far as history shows us, have not been adopted by any other people of whom we have any record. The means adopted are not violence, not bloodshed, not diplomacy as one understands it nowadays, but they are purely and simply truth and non-violence. No wonder that the attention of the world is directed towards this attempt to lead a successful, bloodless revolution. Hitherto, nations have fought in the manner of the brute.

After the address was over, he remarked: "Well that's over." These words also were heard by the listeners. They have wreaked vengeance upon those whom they have considered to be their enemies.

We find in searching national anthems adopted by great nations that they contain imprecations upon the so-called enemy. They have vowed destruction and have not hesitated to take the name of God and seek

---

1. The broadcast was made on the Columbia Broadcasting Service network from Kingsley Hall. According to Louis Fischer's *Life of Mahatma Gandhi*, before beginning his unprepared address, Gandhiji said : "Do I have to speak into that?"

Divine assistance for the destruction of the enemy. We in India have reversed the process. We feel that the law that governs brute creation is not the law that should guide the human race. That law is inconsistent with human dignity.

I, personally, would wait, if need be, for ages rather than seek to attain the freedom of my country through bloody means. I feel in the innermost recesses of my heart, after a political experience extending over an unbroken period of close upon thirty-five years, that the world is sick unto death of blood-spilling. The world is seeking a way out, and I flatter myself with the belief that perhaps it will be the privilege of the ancient land of India to show that way out to the hungering world.

I have, therefore, no hesitation whatsoever in inviting all the great nations of the earth to give their hearty co-operation to India in her mighty struggle. It must be a sight worth contemplating and treasuring that millions of people have given themselves to suffering without retaliation in order that they might vindicate the dignity and honour of the nation. I have called that suffering a process of self-purification. It is my certain conviction that no man loses his freedom except through his own weakness. I am painfully conscious of our own weaknesses.

We represent in India all the principal religions of the earth, and it is a matter of deep humiliation to confess that we are a house divided against itself; that we Hindus and Mussalmans are flying at one another. It is a matter of still deeper humiliation to me that we Hindus regard several millions of our own kith and kin as too degraded even for our touch. I refer to the so-called "untouchables".

These are no small weaknesses in a nation struggling to be free. You will find that, in this struggle through self-purification, we have assigned a foremost [part of our][1] creed to the removal of this curse of untouchability and the attainment of unity amongst all the different classes and communities of India representing the different creeds.

It is along the same lines that we seek to rid our land of the curse of drink. Happily for us, intoxicating drinks and drugs are confined to comparatively a very small number of people, largely, factory hands and the like.

Fortunately for us, the drink and drug curse is accepted as a curse. It is not considered to be the fashion for men or women to drink or to take intoxicating drugs. All the same, it is an uphill fight that we are fighting in trying to remove this evil from our midst.

---

1. These words are found in Entertaining Gandhi by Muriel Lester.

It is a matter of regret, deep regret, for me to have to say that the existing Government has made of this evil a source of very large revenue, amounting to nearly twenty-five crores of rupees. But I am thankful to be able to say that the women of India have risen to the occasion in combating it by peaceful means, that is, by a fervent appeal to those who are given to the drink habit to give it up, and by an equally fervent appeal to the liquor dealers. A great impression has been created upon those who are addicted to these two evil habits.

I wish that it were possible for me to say that in this, at least, we were receiving hearty co-operation of the rulers. If we could only have received the co-operation without any legislation, I dare say that we would have achieved this reform and banished intoxicating drink and drugs from our afflicted land.

There is a force which has a constructive effect and which has been put forth by the nation during this struggle. That is the great care for the semi-starved millions scattered throughout the 700,000 villages dotted over a surface 1,900 miles long and 1,500 miles broad.

It is a painful phenomenon that these simple villagers, through no fault of their own, have nearly six months of the year idle upon their hands.

The time was not very long ago when every village was self sufficient in regard to the two primary human wants: food and clothing. Unfortunately for us, the East India Company, by means I would prefer not to describe, destroyed that supplementary village industry, and the millions of spinners who had become famous through the cunning of their deft fingers for drawing the finest thread, such as has never yet been drawn by any modern machinery. These village spinners found themselves one fine morning with their noble occupation gone. From that day forward India has become progressively poor.

No matter what may be said to the contrary, it is a historical fact that, before the advent of the East India Company, these villagers were not idle, and he who wants may see today that these villagers are idle.

It, therefore, required no great effort or learning to know that these villagers must starve if they cannot work for six months in the year.

May I not, then, on behalf of these semi-starved millions, appeal to the conscience of the world to come to the rescue of a people dying for regaining its liberty ?

[*The New York Times*, 14-9-1931]

43. The National Demand

SPEECH AT FEDERAL STRUCTURE COMMITTEE[1]

[London,
September 15, 1931]

LORD CHANCELLOR, YOUR HIGHNESSES AND FRIENDS,

I must confess at the outset that I am not a little embarrassed in having to state before you the position of the Indian National Congress. I would like to say that I have come to London to attend this Committee, as also the Round Table Conference when the proper time comes, absolutely in the spirit of co-operation, and to strive to my utmost to find

---

1. The second session of the Round Table Conference was held between September 7 and December 1, 1931. There were altogether 112 delegates 20 representing the British Government, 23 Indian States and 69 British India. Gandhiji attended the second session as the sole representative of the Congress. Ramsay MacDonald, Prime Minister, was the Chairman of the Conference. The second session did not open with a meeting of the full Conference. The Federal Structure Committee reassembled on September 7, and the Minorities Committee on September 28, followed by a Plenary Session beginning on November 28, 1931. The other Committees of the Conference did not reassemble. The Federal Structure Committee, over whose deliberations Lord Sankey presided, had the following Heads for discussion :
   1. Strength and Composition of the Federal Legislature.
   2. Questions connected with the Election of Members of the Federal Legislature.
   3. Relations between the two Chambers of the Federal Ligislature.
   4. Distribution of Financial Resources between the Federation and its Units.
   5. The Ministry and its Relations with the Legislature.
   6. Distribution of Legislative powers between the federal and provincial Legislatures, and effect in the States of Legislation relating to Federal Subjects.
   7. Administrative Relations between the Federal Government, the States and the Provinces.
   8. The Federal Court.

points of agreement. I would like also to give this assurance to His Majesty's Government that at no stage is it, or will it be, my desire to embarrass authority and I would like to give the same assurance to my colleagues here, that, however much we may differ about our view-points, I shall not obstruct them in any shape or form.

My position, therefore, here depends entirely upon your goodwill, as also the goodwill of His Majesty's Government. If at any time I found that I could not be of any useful service to the Conference, I would not hesitate to withdraw myself from it. I can also say to those who are responsible for the management of this Committee and the Conference that they have only to give a sign and I should have no hesitation in withdrawing.

I am obliged to make these remarks because I know that there are fundamental differences of opinion between the Government and the Congress, and it is possible that there are vital differences between my colleagues and myself. There is also a limitation under which I shall be working. I am but a poor humble agent acting on behalf of the Indian National Congress. And it might be as well to remind ourselves of what the Congress stands for and what it is. You will then extend your sympathy to me, because I know that the burden that rests upon my shoulders is really very great. The Congress is, if I am not mistaken, the oldest political organizaton we have in India. It has had nearly 50 years of life, during which period it has, without any interruption, held its annual session. It is what it means—national. It represents no particular community, no particular class, no particular interest. It claims to represent all Indian interests and all classes. It is a matter of the greatest pleasure to me to state that it was first conceived in an English brain: Allan Octavius Hume we knew as the father of the Congress. It was nursed by two great Parsis, Pherozeshah Mehta and Dadabhai Naoroji, whom all India delighted to recognize as its Grand Old Man. From the very commencement the Congress had Mussalmans, Christians, Anglo-Indians—I might say all the religions, sects, creeds—represented upon it more or less fully. The late Badruddin Tyabji identified himself with the Congress. We have had Mussalmans as Presidents of the Congress, and Parsis undoubtedly. I can recall at least one Indian Christian at the present moment, W.C. Bonnerji, Kalicharen Bannerji, than whom I have not had the privilege of knowing a purer Indian, was also thoroughly identified with the Congress. I miss, as I have no doubt all of you miss, the presence in our midst of Mr. KT. Paul. Although—I do not know, but so far as I know—he never officially belonged to the Congress, he was a nationalist to the full. As you know, the late Maulana Mohammed Ali, whose presence also we miss today, was a President of the Congress, and at present we have four Mussalmans as members of the Working Committee, which consists of 15 members. We have had women as our Presidents : Dr. Annie Besant was the first, and Mrs. Sarojini Naidu followed; we have her as a member of the Working Committee also. And so, if we have no distinctions of class or creed, we have no distinctions of sex either.

The Congress has, from its very commencement, taken up the cause of the so-called untouchables. There was a time when the Congress had at every annual session as its adjunct the Social Conference, to which the late Ranade dedicated his energies, among his many other activities. Headed by him you will find, in the programme of the Social Conference, reform in connection with the untouchables taking a prominent place. But in 1920, the Congress took a large step and brought in the question of the removal of untouchability as a plank on the political platform, making it an important item of the political programme. Just as the Congress considered Hindu-Muslim unity–thereby meaning unity amongst all the classes–to be indispensable for the attainment of *swaraj*, so also did the Congress consider the removal of the curse of untouchability as an indispensable condition for the attainment of full freedom. The position the Congress took up in 1920 remains the same today; and so you will see the Congress has attempted from its very beginning to be what it described itself to be, namely, national in every sense of the term. If Your Highnesses will permit me to say so, in the very early stages the Congress took up your cause also. Let me remind this Committee that it was the Grand Old Man of India who sponsored the cause of Kashmir and Mysore; and these two great Houses, I venture in all humility to submit, owe not a little to the efforts of Dadabhai Naoroji and the Congress. Even up to now the Congress has endeavoured to serve the Princes of India by refraining from any interference in their domestic and internal affairs.

I hope, therefore, that this brief introduction that I thought fit to give will serve to enable the Committee, and those who are at all interested in the claims of the Congress, to understand that it has endeavoured to deserve the claim that it has made. It has failed, I know, often to live up to the claim but I venture to submit that, if you were to examine the history of the Congress, you would find that it has more often succeeded, and progressively succeeded than failed.

Above all, the Congress represents, in its essence, the dumb, semistarved millions scattered over the length and breadth of the land in its 700,000 villages, no matter whether they come from what is called British India or what is called Indian India. Every interest which, in the opinion of the Congress, is worthy of protection, has to subserve the interests of these dumb millions; and so you do find now and again apparently a clash between several interests. But, if there is a genuine real clash, I have no hesitation in saying on behalf of the Congress that the Congress will sacrifice every interest for the sake of the interests of these dumb millions. It is, therefore, essentially a peasant organization, and it is becoming so progressively. You will—even the Indian members of the Committee—perhaps be astonished to find that today the Congress, through its organization, the All India Spinners' Association, is finding work for nearly 50,000 women in nearly 2,000 villages, and these women are possibly 50 per cent Mussalman women. Thousands of them belong to the so-called untouchable class.

We have thus, in this constructive manner, penetrated these villages, and effort is being made to cover every one of the 700,000 villages. It is a super human task; but if human effort can do so, you will presently find the Congress covering all of these villages and bringing to them the message of the spinning wheel.

That being the representative character of the Congress, you will not be astonished when I read to you the Congress mandate. I hope that it may not jar upon you. You may consider that the Congress is making a claim which is wholly untenable. Such as it is, I am here to put forth that claim on behalf of the Congress in the gentlest manner possible, but also in the firmest manner possible. I have come here to prosecute that claim with all the faith and energy that I can command.

If you can convince me to the contrary and show that the claim is inimical to the interests of these dumb millions, I shall revise my opinion. I am open to conviction, but even so I should have to ask my principals to consent to that revision before I could usefully act as the agent of the Congress.

At this stage I propose to read to you this mandate so that you can understand clearly the limitations imposed upon me. This was a resolution passed at the Karachi Congress:

> This Congress, having considered the Provisional Settlement between the Working Committee and the Government of India, endorses it, and desires to make it clear that the Congress goal of

purna swaraj, meaning complete independence, remains intact. In the event of a way remaining otherwise open to the Congress to be represented at any Conference with the representatives of the British Government, the Congress Delegation will work for this goal; and in particular, so as to give the nation control over the army, external affairs, finance, fiscal and economic policy, and to have scrutiny by an impartial tribunal of the financial transactions of the British Government in India, and to examine and assess the obligations to be undertaken by India or England and the right to either party to end the partnership at will: provided, however, that the Congress Delegation will be free to accept such adjustments as may be demonstrably necessary in the interests of India.

Then follows the appointment.

I have in the light of this mandate endeavoured, as carefully as I was capable, to study the provisional conclusions arrived at by the several Sub-committees appointed by the Round Table Conference. I have also carefully studied the Prime Minister's statement giving the considered policy of His Majesty's Government. I speak as subject to correction; but, so far as I have been able to understand this document, it falls far short of what is aimed at and claimed by the Congress. True, I have the liberty to accept such adjustments as may be demonstrably necessary in the interests of India, but they have all to be consistent with the fundamentals stated in this mandate. I remind myself at this stage of the terms of what is to me a sacred settlement—the settlement arrived at Delhi between the Government of India and the Congress. In that Settlement the Congress has accepted the principle of federation, the principle that there should be responsibility at the Centre, and has accepted also the principle that there should be safeguards in so far as they may be necessary in the interests of India.

There was one phrase used yesterday. I forget by which Delegate, but it struck me very forcibly. He said, "We do not want a mere political constitution". I do not know that he gave that expression the same meaning that it immediately bore to me; but I immediately said to myself, this phrase has given me a good expression. It is true the Congress will not be—and, personally speaking, I myself would never be—satisfied with a mere political Constitution, which to read would seem to give India all it can possibly politically desire, but in reality would give her nothing. If we are intent upon complete independence, it is not from any sense of arrogance; it is not because we want to parade before the universe that we have now severed all connection with the British people. Nothing of the kind. On the contrary, you find in this mandate itself that the Congress contemplates a partnership—the Congress contemplates a connection with the British people—but that connection to be such as can exist between two absolute equals. Time was when I prided myself on being, and being called, a British subject. I have ceased for many years to call myself a British subject; I would far rather be called a rebel than a subject. But I have aspired—I still aspire—to be a citizen, not of the Empire, but in a Commonwealth; in a partnership if possible—if God wills it, an indissoluble partnership but not a partnership superimposed upon one nation by another. Hence, you find here that the Congress claims that either party should have the right to sever the connection, to dissolve the partnership. It has got to be necessarily, therefore, of mutual benefit.

May I say—it may be irrelevant to the consideration, but not irrelevant to me—that, as I have said elsewhere, I can quite understand the responsible British statesmen today being wholly engrossed in domestic affairs, in trying to make two ends meet. We could not expect them to do anything less; and I wondered, even as I was sailing towards London, whether we in the Committee at the present moment would not be a drag upon the British Ministers—whether we would not be interlopers. And yet I said to myself: It is possible that we might not be interlopers; it is possible that the British Ministers themselves might consider the proceedings of the Round Table Conference to be of primary importance even in terms of their domestic affairs.

India, yes, can be held by the sword ! I do not for one moment doubt the ability of Britain to hold India under subjection through the sword. But what will conduce to the prosperity of Great Britain, the economic freedom of Great Britain—an enslaved but rebellious India, or an India an esteemed partner with Britain to share her sorrows to take part side by side with Britain in her misfortunes? Yes ! if need be, but at her own will, to fight side by side with Britain—not for the exploitation of a single race or a single human being on earth, but it may be conceivably for the good of the whole world ! If I want freedom for my country, believe me, if I can possibly help it, I do not want that freedom in order that I, belonging to a nation which counts one-fifth of the human race, may exploit any other race upon earth or any single individual. If I want that freedom for my country, I would not be deserving of that freedom if I did not cherish and treasure the equal right of every other race, weak or strong, to the same freedom.

And so I said to myself whilst I was nearing the shores of your beautiful island, per chance it might be possible for me to convince the British Ministers that India as a valuable partner, not held by force but by the silken cord of love—an India of that character might conceivably be of real assistance to you in balancing your Budget, not for one occasion but for many years. What cannot two nations do—one a handful, but brave, with a record for bravery perhaps unequalled, a nation noted for having fought slavery, a nation that has at least claimed times without number to protect the weak—and another a very ancient nation, counted in millions, with a glorious and ancient past, representing at the present moment two great cultures, the Islamic and Hindu cultures; if you will, also containing not a small but a very large number of Christian population; and certainly absorbing the whole of the splendid Zoroastrian stock, in numbers almost beneath contempt, but in philanthropy and enterprise almost unequalled and certainly unsurpassed. We have got all these cultures concentrated in India. And supposing that God fires both Hindus and Musslmans represented here with a proper spirit, so that they close ranks and come to an honourable understanding—take that nation and this nation together, and I again ask myself and ask you whether, with an India free, completely independent as Great Britain is, whether an honourable partnership between these two cannot be mutualy beneficial, even in terms of the domestic affairs of this great nation. And so, in that dreamy hope, I have approached the British Isles, and I shall still cherish that dream.

And when I have said this perhaps I have said all; and you will be able to dot the i's and to cross the t's, not expecting me to fill in all the details, and tell you what I mean by control over the Army, what I mean by control over external affairs, finance, fiscal and economic policy, or even the financial transactions which a friend yesterday considered to be sacrosanct. I do not take that view. If there is a stocktaking between incoming and outgoing partners, their transactions are subject to audit and adjustment; and the Congress will not be guilty of any dishonourable conduct or crime in saying that the nation should understand what it is to take over and what it should not take over.

This audit, this scrutiny, is asked for not merely in the interests of India; it is asked for in the interests of both. I am positive that the British people do not want to saddle upon India a single burden which it should not legitimately bear; and I am here to declare, on behalf of the Congress, that the Congress will never think of repudiating a single claim or a burden that it should justly discharge. If we are to live as an honourable nation worthy of commanding credit from the whole world, we will pay every farthing of legitimate debt with our blood.

I do not think that I should take you any further through the clauses of this mandate and analyse for you the meaning of these clauses as Congressmen give them. If it is God's will that I should continue to take part in these deliberations, as the deliberations proceed, I shall be able to explain the implications of these clauses. As the deliberations proceed, I would have my say in connection with the safeguards also. But I think I have said quite enough in having, with some elaboration and with your generous indulgence, Lord Chancellor, taken the time of this meeting. I had not intended really to take that time, but I felt that I could not possibly do justice to the cause that I have come to expound to you, the Committee, and to the British nation of which we, the Indian Delegates, are at present the guests, if I did not give you out of the whole of my heart my cherished wish even at this time. I would love to go away from the shores of the British Isles with the conviction that there was to be an honourable and equal partnership between Great Britain and India. I cannot do anything more than say that it will be my fervent prayer, during all the days that I live in your midst, that this consummation may be reached.

I thank you, Lord Chancellor, for the courtesy that you have extended to me in not stopping me, although I have taken close upon forty-five minutes. I was not entitled to all that indulgence, and I thank you once more.

[*Indian Round Table Conference (Second Session) : Proceedings of Federal Structure Committee and Minorities Committee, Vol. I*, pp. 41-7]

44. What I Want[1]

The Editor has kindly asked me to say in these columns "what I want". The title is a misnomer. I am here merely as an agent for the Indian National Congress, and I can want nothing apart from the Congress. "What I want", therefore, means what the Indian National Congress wants.

Let me then introduce my principal, the Indian National Congress, to the reader. It is perhaps the oldest political organizaton in India and claims to represent the whole of India. I know that some people would deny this claim. I can only say that it is made by right of service.

The Indian National Congress is over forty-seven years old. It was conceived by an Englishman, Allan Octavius Hume. It has had, besides Hindus, Mohammedan, Parsi and Christian presidents. It had two women as presidents, Dr. Annie Besant and Mrs. Sarojini Naidu. It has zamindars, too, as its members.

The Indian National Congress is no respector or persons. It knows no distinction between classes or creeds of the sexes. It has always championed the cause of the so called untouchables, and has of recent years appointed an anti-untouchability committee for hastening the destruction of untouchability.

But the unchallenged and unchallengeable claim of the Indian National Congress consists in its representing the millions of dumb paupers living in the seven hundred thousand Indian villages who constitute over 85 per cent of the population.

It is in the name of this great organization that I claim :

(1) Complete independence for India.

(2) This does not exclude partnership at will and on terms of absolute equality.

(3) Nor does this exclude Federation or such safeguards as may be demonstrably necessary in the interest of India.

---

1. Editor of the *Tea and Coffee Trade Journal* of New York. In a letter dated September 18 he had asked how Gandhiji's plans of a free India were likely to affect the tea industry.

I hope the readers of *The Daily Mail* will not be frightened by the claim boldly put forth on behalf of the Congress. "Do unto others as you would that others should do unto you." On the strength of the wise saying nineteen hundred years old, I hope that Englishmen and English women will not grudge India the freedom which she has remained without by reason of British rule.

No reason should be necessary for a self-evident truth. Independence is every nation's birthright.

It is India's also. But it may not be out of place to mention here that the people of India under British rule have become progressively poor and emasculate. The village industry has been killed and a whole nation has been disarmed. Nothing less than complete freedom in every sense of the term can make India happy and strong.

—M.K. GANDHI

[*The Daily Mail,* 19-9-1931]

45. Voluntary Poverty[1]

SPEECH AT GUILDHOUSE CHURCH[2]

[London,
September 23, 1931]

You will be astonished to hear from me that, although to all appearances my mission is political, I would ask you to accept my assurance that its roots are—if I may use that term—spiritual. It is commonly known, though perhaps not believed, that I claim that at least my politics are not divorced from morality, from spirituality, from religion. I have claimed—and the claim is based upon extensive experience—that a man who is trying to discover and follow the will of God cannot possibly leave a single field of life untouched. I came also, in the course of my service, to the conclusion that if there was any field of life where morality, where truth, where fear of God, were not essential, that field should be given up entirely.

But I found also that the politics of the day are no longer a concern of kings, but that they affect the lowest strata of society. And I found, through bitter experience that, if I wanted to do social service, I could not possibly leave politics alone.

Do not please consider that I want to speak to you tonight about politics and somehow or other connect voluntary poverty with politics.

That is not my intention. I have simply given you an introduction how I came to believe in the necessity of voluntary poverty for any social worker or for any political worker who wanted to remain untouched by the hideous immorality and untruth that one smells today in ordinary politics. The stench that comes from that life has appeared to some to be so suffocating that they came to the conclusion that politics were not for a god fearing man.

---

1. Gandhiji made the statement after his meeting with the Aga Khan at the Ritz Hotel late in the night. No report of the interview is available.
2. The meeting was held under the auspices of the Franciscan Society with Dr. Maude Royden in the chair. The subject was "Voluntary Poverty".

Had that been really so, I feel that it would have been a disaster for mankind. Find out for yourselves, in the light of what I am now saying, whether directly or indirectly every activity of yours today in this one of the greatest cities of the world is not touched by politics.

Well, then, when I found myself drawn into the political coil, I asked myself what was necessary for me in order to remain absolutely untouched by immorality, by untruth, by what is known as political gain.

In the course of my search, I made several discoveries which I must, for tonight, leave alone. But, if I am not mistaken, this necessity for poverty came to me first of all.

I do not propose to take you through all the details of that act or performance—interesting and, to me, sacred though they are—but I can only tell you that it was a difficult struggle in the beginning and it was a wrestle with my wife and—as I can vividly recall—with my children also.

Be that as it may, I came definitely to the conclusion that, if I had to serve the people in whose midst my life was cast and of whose difficulties I was witness from day to day, I must discard all wealth, all possessions.

I cannot tell you with truth that, when this belief came to me, I discarded everything immediately. I must confess to you that progress at first was slow. And now, as I recall those days of struggle, I remember that it was also painful in the beginning. But, as days went by, I saw that I had to throw overboard many other things which I used to consider as mine, and a time came when it became a matter of positive joy to give up those things. And one after another then, by almost geometric progression, the things slipped away from me. And, as I am describing my experiences, I can say a great burden fell off my shoulders, and I felt that I could now walk with ease and do my work also in the service of my fellowmen with great comfort and still greater joy. The possession of anything then became a troublesome thing and a burden.

Exploring the cause of that joy, I found that, if I kept any thing as my own, I had to defend it against the whole world. I found also that there were many people who did not have the thing, although they wanted it; and I would have to seek police assistance also if hungry, famine-stricken people, finding me in a lonely place, wanted not merely to divide the thing with me but to dispossess me. And I said to myself : if they want it and would take it, they do so not from any malicious motive, but they would do it because theirs was a greater need than mine.

And then I said to myself : possession seems to me to be a crime. I can only possess certain things when I know that others, who also want to possess similar things, are able to do so. But we know—every one of us can speak from experience—that such a thing is an impossibility. Therefore, the only thing that can be possessed by all is non-possession, not to have anything whatsoever. In other words, a willing surrender.

You might then well say to me : but you are keeping many things on your body even as you are speaking about voluntary poverty and not possessing anything whatsoever ! And your taunt would be right, if you only superficially understood the meaning of the thing that I am speaking about just now. It is really the spirit behind. Whilst you have the body, you will have to have something to clothe the body with also. But then you will take for the body not all that you can get, but the least possible, the least with which you can do. You will take for your house not many mansions, but the least cover that you can do with. And similarly with reference to your food and so on.

Now you see that there is here a daily conflict between what you and we understand today as civilization and the state which I am picturing to you as a state of bliss and a desirable state. On the one hand, the basis of culture or civilization is understood to be the multiplication of all your wants. If you have one room, you will desire to have two rooms, three rooms, the more the merrier. And similarly, you will want to have as much furniture as you can put in your house, and so on, endlessly. And the more you possess the better culture you represent, or some such thing. I am putting it, perhaps, not as nicely as the advocates of that civilization would put it, but I am putting it to you in the manner I understand it.

And, on the other hand, you find the less you possess the less you want, the better you are. And better for what? Not for enjoyment of this life, but for enjoyment of personal service to your fellow beings; service to which you dedicate yourselves, body, soul and mind.

Well, here you find there is ample room for hypocrisy and humbug, because a man or a woman may easily deceive himself or herself and deceive his or her neighbours also, by saying : In spirit I have given up all possessions, and yet externally I am possessing these things; you must not examine my deed, you must examine my intention; and of my intention only I must remain the sole witness.

That is a trap, and a death trap. How are you then to justify the possession even of a piece of cloth two or three or four yards, say, in length and a yard in width ? How can you justify even the possession of that piece of cloth in order to cover your body somewhat, when you know that, if you left that piece of cloth alone, even that would be taken over by someone—not maliciously again—but because he would want it for he has not even so much as that piece of cloth? I am witness, eyewitness, of millions of human beings who have not even so much as that piece of cloth. How are you then to justify your act of possessing this thing with your intention not to possess anything at all?

Well, there is a remedy provided for this dilemma, this difficulty, this contradiction in life—that if you must possess these things, you must hold them at the disposal of those who want them. What happens is that, if somebody comes and wants your piece of cloth, you are not going to keep it from him, you are not going to shut any doors, you are certainly not going to the policeman to ask him to help you to keep these things.

And you have also got to be content with what the world will give you. The world may give you that piece of cloth or may not because, if you do not possess anything, naturally you do not possess the token coin with which you may buy clothing or food. You have got then to live purely on the charity of the world. And even when charitable people give you something, that something does not become your possession. You simply retain it with the fullest intention of that thing being surrendered to anybody who wishes to take it. If somebody comes and uses force against you to dispossess you, you may not go and report to the next policeman you meet and say you have been assaulted. You will not have been assaulted.

Well, that, to my mind, is the meaning of voluntary poverty. I have given you an ideal. Dr. Royden has claimed that I am the greatest exponent of voluntary poverty in the world. I must, in all humility, disown any such claim whatsoever. And this I say to you not because of false modesty, but I say it to you sincerely, believing it to be true. I have given you but a little of my conception of voluntary poverty. And I must own to you that I am far from having realized that ideal in its fullness. In order to realize that ideal in its fullness, there must be a definite intention and conviction in my mind that I do not want to, I must not, possess anything on this earth as my property, not even this body, because this body also is a possession.

If you believe with me—as you must believe with me if you are church-goers, that is, if you believe in God—you believe that body and soul are not one and the same thing, but that the body is a house only, a temporary residence for a soul or a spirit within; and if you believe that, as you do believe, I take it—then it follows that even the body is not yours. It has been given to you as a temporary possession, and it can also be taken from you by Him who has given it to you.

Therefore, having that absolute conviction in me, such must be my constant desire, that this body also may be surrendered at the will of God, and while it is at my disposal, must be used not for dissipation, not for self-indulgence, not for pleasure, but merely for service and service the whole of our waking hours.

And if this is true with reference to the body, how much more with reference to clothing and many other things that we use ?

Having got that conviction and held it for so many years, I am here to give you my evidence against myself, that I have not reached that perfect state of voluntary poverty. I am a poor man, in the sense you understand of struggling to reach that ideal, not poor in the sense in which we ordinarily use the word poor.

As a matter of fact, when I was once challenged by someone, I was able to claim that to my neighbours, and people in the world I seemed to be the richest man on earth, for the richest man is really one who, possessing nothing, has everything at his disposal.

And those who have actually followed out this vow of voluntary poverty to the fullest extent possible (to reach absolute perfection is an impossibility, but the fullest possible extent for a human being) those who have reached the ideal of that state, they testify that, when you dispossess yourself of everything you have, you really possess all the treasures of the world. In other words, you really get all that is in reality necessary for you, everything. If food is necessary, food will come to you.

Many of you are men and women of prayer, and I have heard from very many Christian lips that they got their food in answer to prayer, that they get everything in answer to prayer. I believe it. But I want you to come with me a step further, and believe with me that those who voluntarily give up everything on earth, including the body, that is to say, have readiness to give up everything (and they must examine themselves critically, rigidly, and give always an adverse judgment against themselves)—those who will follow this out will really find that they are never in want.

And I will confess to you that, when I felt God had given me some portion of the riches of the earth and when I had many possessions, I had not the facilities for possessing things that I have at this time. I had not certainly one-millionth part of the ability to command money and everything that I need for service.

A spirit of service had come to me even when I was practising and earning money and was in possession of several things, but at that time I had certainly not the capacity for getting whatever I wanted for service. But today (whether it is good for me or bad for me I do not know, God alone knows) I can give you this evidence, that I have never been in want.

After a period when I had really dispossessed myself by intention and had no hankering after anything that I could call my own, and began to share everything I possessed in common with my neighbours (I cannot share everything with the whole world; if I share with my neighbours, I do share with the whole world, my neighbours also doing likewise; if we do that, it is all a limited human being can do) but immediately I came to that state to a fair extent, I found that I was never in want.

Want must not, again, be taken literally. God is the hardest taskmaster I have known on this earth, and He tries you through and through. And when you find that your faith is failing or your body is failing you and you are sinking, He comes to your assistance somehow or other and proves to you that you must not lose your faith and that He is always at your beck and call, but on His terms, not on your terms. So I have found. I cannot really recall a single instance when, at the eleventh hour, He has forsaken me. And I have got this reputation, which I can repeat to you, a reputation for being one of the best beggars in India. And, as my critics will tell you, at one time I collected one crore of rupees; in pounds, shillings and pence I cannot count it for you, but it is some horribly large sum (about £ 750,000), but I had no difficulty in collecting it. And since then, whenever any emergency has arisen, not for any consideration, not in the soul of my fundamental being, can I recall a single instance of my failing to obtain whatever was necessary for service.

But you will say: this is in answer to prayer. It is not just an answer to prayer, it is a scientific result of this vow of non-possession or vow of voluntary poverty. You do not want to possess anything whatever: and the more therefore you simplify your life, dispossess yourself, the better it is for you. Immediately you come to that, you can command anything. You can command vanities, but if you only once take possession of these, this power will immediately be gone; you must not take for yourself. If you do, you are done for. I have known this happen in so many instances. Many a man has said: " Oh yes, God has now answered my prayer for money or possessions. I will now keep this—this Koh-i-noor diamond, or whatever it may be." That will be the last time. He won't be able to defend that diamond.

Thereore, all I am just now holding out before you as a grand thing is that you can command all the resources of the world for service. To one who does not believe, that may seem an arrogant statement to make. But, as I believe, it is not an arrogant thing to say that you can command all the resources of the earth for service—to the extent of your ability to serve. If you want to command the whole services of the world, it is not enough to go down to some of those houses in the East End, find out the distress of those who live there and fling in their faces a few coppers; you will not have all the resources of the world for that; God will fling in your face also a few coppers.

But if you surrender yourself, body, soul and mind, and give yourself up to the world, then I say : the treasures of the world are at your feet, not for your enjoyment, but for the enjoyment of that service, only yours for that service.

The moral that I would have us to draw from this talk that I have given to you is really very opposite at this time. I want you to believe me when I tell you that my whole heart goes out to this nation in its distress. I cannot possibly present my solution of your financial difficulty. You are great enough, resourceful enough, to find out your own remedies. But I would ask you to elaborate this thought in your own minds in connection with the present distress.

Mr. C.F. Andrews brought to my notice a letter that was written by the Prime Minister to a correspondent and which he told me yesterday was being used as an advertisement throughout the District Railway, probably in the Tubes also; it runs somewhat like this : "You must buy only British goods; must employ only British labour, and try to buy as much as you can." That is one remedy I know. But I want to suggest to you that, in order to solve the problem of distress in the world, this idea of voluntary poverty is a root idea. No doubt, with your resourcefulness, you will tide over the difficulty and feel that there was nothing wrong. If you will permit me to say so, that would be perhaps short-sighted, for a time perhaps has come for a revision of values.

But again I must not go into deep waters. I can only throw out this hint to those who can appreciate the necessity of voluntary poverty for service. I have not tonight presented this blessed thing for the acceptance of all : though let me add that, in the innermost recesses of my heart, I feel that the world would not go all wrong, would not become a world of idiots, if all of us took the vow of voluntary poverty. But I know that this is almost an impossible thing.

Everything is possible for God but, humanly speaking, it is wise to say that it is an impossible thing. But it is not an impossible thing; indeed, I hold it to be absolutely indispensable that those who give themselves wholly to the service of their fellow-beings must take the vow of voluntary poverty.

Try to find out for yourself whether you are not thereby assisting very materially in solving this great national problem that today faces you.

You will not have solved the problem if the people, who do not want to give up their salaries or whatever they are required to give up, are compelled to give them up by law. While they say: "What can we do ? We do not want to resist; we cannot resist," their minds are still hankering after these things.

But imagine that, in the midst of this hankering, there is a body of servants arising, who will themselves become voluntarily poor.

They would be like lighthouses to guide the paths of those who do not know what voluntary poverty is because they know only involuntary poverty. I do not go among my fellows who starve and talk of voluntary poverty; I do not tell them how blessed they would be if they changed that involuntary poverty into voluntary. There is no such thing as magic of that character on this earth. It is a painful process, and these men have first of all to have the necessities of life before I can talk to them of voluntary poverty.

What does happen is this: that a man like me going among them, living in their midst as best he can their life, can bring a ray of hope into their hearts. They will accept remedies that a man like me may suggest to them. At least, if I cannot suggest any immediate remedy, they would find in a man like me a friend. They would say : "He is happy although he possesses nothing; how is it?" I do not need to argue with them; they begin to argue for themselves.

How can I share these richest treasures from my experience with everybody on earth ? I could not. But today, having undertaken to speak on voluntary poverty, I am sharing, to a certain extent only, these treasured experiences of mine not amongst a few hundred people here but amongst millions of people. I tell you that it is beyond description, the bliss, the happiness, and the ability that this voluntary poverty gives one. I can only say: try it and experiment with it, test it for yourselves.

I thank you for giving me your undivided attention. There are still exactly ten minutes left before the hour of prayer, and if any of you wish to ask me any questions, I shall be glad. You need not hesitate to ask anything that is in your mind; you will never offend me by asking any questions, let them be as awkward as they may be.

Q. Can the Mahatma tell us how he can justify collecting large sums of money when Jesus, the Buddha and other great religious teachers who have practised voluntary poverty have never asked for or received large sums of money ? I cannot reconcile this with the rest of what he told us.

A. Did these great teachers never ask for or receive moneys?

After Jesus many Christians, who believed in poverty also, took moneys and used them for service. And I can speak with better confidence about the Buddha who is reported in his own lifetime to have founded institutions. He could not possibly found institutions without money. And it is said that they who gave themselves body, soul and mind gave their riches also and placed them at the feet of the Buddha, who gladly accepted them—but not for himself.

Q. Why should we serve our fellow-beings ?

A. In order that we may see a glimpse of God through them; because they have got the same spirit as we have, and unless we learn that, there is a barrier drawn between God and ourselves; if we want to demolish that barrier, the beginning is made by complete identification with our fellow-beings.

[*The Guildhouse*, 23-9-1931]

46. Self-sacrifice

SPEECH AT INDIAN STUDENTS' MEETING[1]

[London,
October 13, 1931]

Gandhiji, after reiterating India's fundamental claims, said he knew before starting that these were not likely to be granted because no nation ever yet obtained its lost freedom by mere appeal to reason. Something much more serious had always been required. He did not suppose India would be an exception. It was now plainer than ever that only through suffering would victory be won, but his hope was that the suffering already endured might have created a sufficient impression on the British mind favourable to reason and negotiation.

I must confess that, as I go on, I feel the task Herculean. Probably nothing would come out of it, but being an optimist, I would not give up hope in its entirely until I find nothing more can be done.

Still I pray the seed being sown now will bear fruit in the conscience of this country and the Ministers will feel compelled to come to terms with the nation of sufferers.[2]

It may be that the seed which is being sown now may result in softening the British spirit and that it may result in the preventing of the brutalization human beings. I have known the English nature in its hideous form in the Punjab. I have known it elsewhere also, during these fifteen years of experience and through history, I have known the same thing happening. It is my purpose by every means at my command to prevent such a catastrophe occurring again. I am more concerned in preventing the brutalization of human nature than in preventing the sufferings of my own people.

I have often gloated over the sufferings of my own people. I know

1. The meeting took place in Gower Street Hostel, Bloomsbury. Sir Ewart Greaves of the Indian Y.M.C.A. was in the chair.
2. What follows is extracted from Mahadev Desai's "London Letter" in *Young India*.

that people, who voluntarily undergo a course of suffering raise themselves and the whole of humanity, but I also know that people who become brutalized in their desperate efforts to get victory over their opponents or to exploit weaker nations or weaker men, not only drag down themselves but mankind also. And it cannot be a matter of pleasure to me or anyone else to see human nature dragged in the mire. If we are all sons of the same God and partake of the same divine essence, we must partake of the sin of every person whether he belongs to us or to another race. You can understand how repugnant it must be to invoke the beast in any human being, how much more so in Englishmen, amongst whom I count numerous friends ! I invite you to give all the help you can in the endeavour that I am making.

To the Indian students my appeal is to study this question in all thoroughness and, if you really believe in the power of non-violence and truth, then, for God's sake express these two things in your daily life—not merely in the political field—and you will find that whatever you do in this direction will help me in the struggle. It is possible that Englishmen and Englishwomen who come into close touch with you will assure the world that they have never seen students so good, so truthful, as Indian students. Don't you think that that would go a long way towards vindicating our nation ? The words "self-purification" occurred in a Congress Resolution in 1920. From that moment the Congress realized that we were to purify ourselves. We were by self-sacrifice to purify ourselves so that we would deserve liberty and so that God would also be with us. If that is the case, every Indian whose life bears testimony to the spirit of self-sacrifice helps his country, without having to do anything more. Such, in my opinion, is the strength of the means which the Congress adopted.

Therefore, in the battle for freedom, every student here need do nothing more than that he should purify himself and present a character above reproach and above suspicion.

Q. Lord Irwin is reported to have said in a speech at the Central Hall that he knew you would not insist on Complete Independence. Is this true?

A. Well: In the first instance, I do not know that Lord Irwin made the speech which is imputed to him. Secondly, I must not speak for Lord Irwin. That would be a question well addressed to him. But I never told Lord Irwin that I would not press for Complete Independence. On the contrary, so far as my memory serves me right, I told him that I would press for Complete Independence, and, for me that does not mean ruling

India through deputies, i.e., Indian agents rather than English agents. Complete independence to me means National Government.

Q. How do you reconcile Complete Independence with the retention of British troops.

A. British troops may remain in India and that would depend upon the arrangement that the partners came to. This, for a limited period, would be to the interests of India because India has become emasculated and it is necessary to retain some portion of British troops or some portion of British officers under the National Government and in the employ of the National Government. I shall defend the partnership and yet defend the retention of those troops.

Q. Do you envisage a Viceroy when you speak of an Independent India ?

A. Whether the Viceroy remains is a question to be decided by both the parties. Speaking for myself, I cannot conceive a Viceroy remaning. But I can conceive a British Agent remaining there because there would be so many interests which the British have brought into being there which I personally do not seek to destroy and, in order to represent those interests and if there is also an army consisting of British troops and officers, I could not possibly say, 'No, there will not be a British Agent.' And since there are also the Princes concerned I cannot vouchsafe for what the Princes will do and, therefore, I do not expect that under the scheme I have in mind there will be no British Agent there—whether he is called a Viceroy or a Governor-General.

But I would defend it as a partnership having the condition that it is to be terminated at the will of either on terms of absolute equality. I am writing on a slate from which I have to rub out many things.

Q. What are the common objects that such a partnership would advance ?

A. The common object that the partnership is going to advance is to cease the exploitation of the races of the earth. If India becomes free from this curse of exploitation, under which she has groaned for so many years, it would be up to India to see that there is no further exploitation. Real partnership would be of mutual benefit. It would be a partnership between two races the one having been known for its manliness, bravery, courage and its unrivalled powers of organization, and the other an ancient race possessing a culture perhaps second to none, a continent in itself. A partnership between these two peoples cannot but result in mutual good and be to the benefit of mankind.[1]

Dealing lengthily with the communal problem, he said he was incapable of bargaining away the rights of minorities and insisted again that the Congress was predominantly representative of the dumb millions.

The golden rule is: Believe just the contrary of what the newspapers say on such matters. What I have been trying to do is to persuade Hindus and Sikhs to give Muslims what they want and persuade Muslims to so frame their demands as to make them acceptable to other communities.

Regarding smaller minorities, he pointed out the part played by the Parsis in Bombay as an example of what numerically insignificant communities could do without special advantages and what great opportunities adult suffrage would provide all alike.

The most determined opposition to the claims of untouchables and other minorities except Muslims and Sikhs was expressed by Mr. Gandhi. He said: "I shall resist those claims at the cost of my life and I appeal to you to join me in shaming the delegates into withdrawing them."

He denied that he had offered to accept the demands of Mussalmans if they would join him in resisting the demands of untouchables. He said he was forced to agree to Muslim and Sikh demands for historical reasons, but he would not agree to the grant of special representation to any other community in any circumstances.

The manifestations of goodwill by people in England had convinced him that the English people would never again tolerate repression in India. If it became necessary for Indians to resume passive resistance and non-cooperation, he appealed to the students to behave themselves and win the respect of the English people.

[*The Hindu*, 14-10-1931, and *Young India*, 29-10-1931]

1. What follows is from *The Hindu*.

47. Educating Children

SPEECH AT MONTESSORI TRAINING COLLEGE[1]

[London,
October 28, 1931][2]

Madame, you have overwhelmed me with your words.[3] It is perfectly true, I must admit it in all humility, that, however, indifferently it may be, I endeavour to represent love in every fibre of my being. I am impatient to realize the presence of my Maker, Who to me embodies Truth, and in the early part of my career I discovered that if I was to realize Truth I must obey, even at the cost of my life, the law of love. And having been blessed with children, I discovered that the law of Love could be best understood and learned through little children. Were it not for us, their ignorant poor parents, our children would be perfectly innocent. I believe implicitly that the child is not born mischievous in the bad sense of the term. If parents would behave themselves whilst the child is growing, before it is born and after, it is a well-known fact that the child would instinctively obey the law of Truth and the law of Love. And when I understood this lesson in the early part of my life, I began a gradual but distinct change in life.

I do not propose to describe to you the several phases through which this stormy life of mine has passed, but I can only, in truth and in perfect humility, bear witness to the fact that to the extent that I have represented Love in my life, in thought, word and deed I have realized the "peace that passeth understanding". I have baffled many of my friends when they have noticed in me peace that they have envied, and they have asked me for the cause of that priceless possession. I have not been able to explain the cause by saying that, if my friends found that peace in me, it was due to my attempt to obey this, the greatest law of our being.

---

1. Extracted from Mahadev Desai's report; "At Montessori Training College".
2. According to Gandhiji's diary, he visited the institution on this date.
3. Madame Montessori had welcomed Gandhiji "as a soul rather than a man".

It was in 1915 when I reached India, that I first became acquainted with your activities. It was in a place called Amreli that I found that there was a little school being conducted after the Montessori system. Your name had preceded that first acquaintance.

I found no difficulty in finding out at once that this school was not carrying out the spirit of your teaching; the letter was there. But whilst there was an honest—more or less honest—effort being made, I saw too that there was a great deal of tinsel about it.

I came in touch, then, with more such schools, and the more I came in touch, the more I began to understand that the foundation was good and splendid, if the children could be taught through the laws of nature—nature, consistent with human dignity, not nature that governs the beast. I felt instinctively from the way in which the children were being taught that, whilst they were being indifferently taught, the original teaching was conceived in obedience to this fundamental law. Since then, I have had the pleasure of coming across several of your pupils, one of whom had even made a pilgrimage to Italy and had received your personal blessings. I was looking forward to meeting the children here and you all and it was a great pleasure to me to see these children. I had taken care to learn something about these little children. I had a foretaste of what I saw here, in Birmingham, where there is a school between which and this there is a difference. But I also saw that there also human nature was struggling to express itself. I see the same thing here and it was a matter of inexpressible joy to me that from their childhood the children were brought to understand the virtue of silence, and how, in response to the whisper from their teacher, the children came forward one after another in that pin-drop silence. It gave great joy to see all those beautiful rhythmic movements and, as I was watching those movements of the children, my whole heart went out to the millions of the children of the semi-starved villages of India, and I asked myself as my heart went out to those children, "Is it possible for me to give them those lessons and the training that are being given under your system, to those children"? We are conducting an experiment amongst the poorest of the children in India. I do not know how far the experiment will go. We have the problem of giving real vital education to these children of India's hovels, and we have no material means.

We have to fall back upon the voluntary assistance of teachers, but when I look for teachers, they are very few, especially, teachers of the type wanted, in order to draw the best from the children through understanding, through studying their individuality and then putting the child on its own resources, as it were, on its own honour. And believe me from my experience of hundreds, I was going to say thousands, of children–I know that they have perhaps a finer sense of honour than you and I have. The greatest lessons in life—if we would but stoop and humble ourselves, we would learn not from grown up learned men, but from the so called ignorant children. Jesus never uttered a loftier or a grander truth than when he said that wisdom cometh out of the mouths of babes. I believe it, I have noticed it in my own experience that, if we would approach babes in humility and in innocence, we would learn wisdom from them.

I must not take up your time. I have simply given you what is, at the present moment, agitating me, namely, the delicate problem, considered in human terms, of drawing out the best from these millions of children of whom I have told you. But I have learned this one lesson—that what is impossible with man is child's play with God and, if we have faith in that Divinity which presides over the destiny of the meanest of His creation, I have no doubt that all things are possible and in that final hope I live and pass my time and endeavour to obey His will. Therefore, I repeat that even as you, out of your love for children, are endeavouring to teach those children, through your numerous institutions, the best that can be brought out of them, even so I hope that it will be possible not only for the children of the wealthy and the well-to-do, but for the children of paupers to receive training of this nature. You have very truly remarked that if we are to reach real peace in this world and if we are to carry on a real war against war, we shall have to begin with children and if they will grow up in their natural innocence, we won't have the struggle, we won't have to pass fruitless idle resolutions, but we shall go from love to love and peace to peace, until at last all the corners of the world are covered with that peace and love for which, consciously or unconsciously, the whole world is hungering.

[*Young India,* 19-11-1931]

48. Partnership[1]

SPEECH AT FRIENDS' HOUSE[2]

[London,
October 31, 1931]

1. I should shortly say it[3] is intended to bear the dictionary meaning, but in the Congress mandate it is said it does not exclude termination of partnership at will by either party; in order not to create any confusion and not to be uncertain, mandate mentions that.

It includes the three controls, subject to such adjustment as are absolutely necessary in the interest of India. A nation which has been a subject nation and another which has been an exploiting nation cannot easily become partners. But for the fact that our struggle is non-violent, independence and partnership are incompatible and complete severance would have been necessary.

2. Canada is not considered to be in partnership with Great Britain. It is a daughter State. They represent the same civilization—same mode of life—of course all humanity meets in the end, otherwise ours is a distinct civilization. Independence was mentioned so that there may be no idea lingering in our mind of a subject nation. Then it is used to distinguish Dominion Status. I was for it once, but when lawyers contended against me and said it was a higher status, I said to myself that I was certainly for no lower status. I said if Dominion Status is lower, I was for independence.

3. Separate not from British Commonwealth—if India means to be independent in reality it must be complete severance from the Empire. It is an Empire because there are Princes, vassal States. Great Britain

1. This was in reply to the addressee's cable of 30-10-1931 saying : "Thanks letter wife. Burdwan arrived launching vigorous anti-Gandhi campaign supported interested parties with practical appreciation importance American opinion. If my God same God guiding you then search inner conscience and realize with me way clear your visit. . ." S.N. 18208.
2. Mahadev Desai also reported briefly this meeting with the Quakers in his "London Letter", published in *Young India*, 19-11-1931.
3. "Partnership"

should cease to subjugate all these Princes. It means extinction of the Empire and the Empire spirit. I should not associate with any nation which believed in exploitation and sustained its commerce by force. A tremendous principle is at stake. We are eager not only to get rid of exploitation but to prevent India from becoming a highly industrialized nation and becoming a menace to the world. We want the masses to feel that they do not want any dominion on any nation or any groups of individuals even. There should be vital equality between nations, and even if it took years to make this idea mature, we would wander in the wilderness to get them. This is no verbal jugglery, but a fundamental yearning of human nature.

Q. For some years Britain would continue certain subject territories like Gold Coast. Would Mr. Gandhi object?

A. I would certainly object. India would certainly aspire after influencing British policy. Supposing there came a cry from West Coast or Swaziland, India would feel that it was a partner . . . .[1] I do not want India to be an engine of oppression. I am dreaming of a time when India would be a check on aggrandizement by other nations.

But I should not immediately sever the connection, though I know that Zulus, Swazis are being corrupted and exploited. It is a policy which is radically wrong. To be able to call these dominions should be no matter for pride. There is no use your saying that, whilst they were Crown Colonies, you do for them everything, and when they become responsible, you would do nothing.

Q. Partnership means economic alliance or does it presuppose a common British Crown?

A. That question has been agitating me. There is a Crown, but how far I should be linked with the Crown I do not know. I should argue it out with friends. It is a solid and good question as to what connection India would have with the Crown. How the Council would be defined is more a matter of phraseology than of moral difficulty.

Q. Termination of partnership like termination of alliances between nations—on what terms?

A. If it is not profitable for Britain, it must retire. I would wish it to be in perpetuity. Common relations would be contractual relations.

For constitutional partnership I have not fixed any terms. It does involve giving of a notice for dissolution.

4. I have agreed yet to no safeguards. When I have been cornered, I

---

1. A few words here are not clear.

have said safeguards for such I.C.S. members as you will keep, such military officers as you keep. For we want to go before the world as a solvent nation. We should be sure of what we take over. . . . .[1]

I have been cruelly misrepresented as repudiating liabilities. A lurid picture of widows being ruined who had taken loans, etc., was cruelly untruthful. That party could not be harmed in any shape or form.

Great Britain's honour, prestige and everything is concerned as partner in all these liabilities. All that happens in a commercial business should happen between Britain and India also. We should satisfy creditors that the liabilities we take over should be discharged.

There is a third safeguard—existing interests of Europeans in India. . . . .[2] Every legitimate interest will be legally and lawfully protected.

There is no desire for racial discrimination. We have been fighting it in South Africa and elsewhere. But it is one thing and guarding the nation against ruinous competition is another thing. There is a Swedish match factory combine which has descended upon India as a blight and threatens ruin of match factories. They have secured handsome terms from Government. They have acquired fine land and have even penetrated the Andamans. I do not object to this because it is a Swedish combine. I should have objected to it if it was an Indian combine. Under the partnership there would be a favoured nation clause, without being charged with racial discrimination.

5. The adjustment would be adjustment naturally due between outgoing and incoming firms. . . . .[3] If Britain wants to do the thing it must do it decently. Safeguards do not in any way derogate from complete independence.

Horace Alexander: Schuster suggested assurance of establishment of a Reserve Bank and raising a new internal loan.

6. Gandhiji : We would have to do it. We want the Reserve Bank ourselves, but there are no reserves to fall back upon. No gold reserve. I have given you an inkling. Partnership at will. Period I do not know.

7. No one came by right of election—none by invitation. If the Prime Minister wanted to bar my entry he could do so. An M.P. cannot be put out. No procedure is necessary to put one out. It is an embarrassing position. I have come as a guest of the nation and must walk warily and I

1. A few words here are not clear.
2. Some portions here are not clear.
3. *Ibid*

cannot tell you how warily I am walking. . . . .[1] I have a tremendous moral problem before me. I have an invitation to attend the King's party. I am feeling so heart-sick and sore upon happenings in India that I should not like to go. If I had come as an elected representative, I should have had no hesitation. Here is the function which is social [but] has a political nature, but I am doing nothing hastily. I put myself in touch with Whitehall. I am a man who every moment considers the morality of the thing, not its legality.

The Conference is packed. The other representatives have been chosen by the Viceroy. His conception was faulty. The selection was his and it was not possible for him to come to an unerring judgment. I can demonstrate to you how wicked some of these things have been, how much wire-pulling has been done. We would certainly have captured the Mahasabha. I would have been the only elected representative of the untouchables. I would be selling their birthright if I lent myself to this vile scheme of separate representation. Moonje is a friend of mine, but he is a reactionary. Would Congress have allowed the Native States' subjects' rights to be sold away? It is a diabolical thing for them to say that they represent their own people also. It is a fatal flaw in the formation of the Conference that Princes should come here in a double capacity. There is a States' People's Conference and it is held back under my iron rule. I have been holding them back and though they are men of great status and ability. I have asked them to be satisfied with their present position.

But this shows to you that it is wholly unrepresentative. Today the communalists occupy the front pages of newspapers. I would at once say to Mussalmans and Sikhs : take what you can. It is today the dream of a visionary. Therefore, I have suggested three things : (1) I have put before the R.T.C. the Congress Scheme framed by a Committee of Hindus, Mussalmans and Sikhs. They met all leading Mussalmans and leading Sikhs. (2) Otherwise private arbitration. (3) Failing that, a judicial tribunal. The fourth thing is one with which I cannot associate myself, viz., Asking Government to suggest a solution.

It would be selling the country. For no Government in the nature of things would suggest a solution unfavourable to themselves. The utmost I said that could be done is to go to British Courts of Law, Non-Hindu, Non-Muslim Judges or Members of Judicial Committee of the Privy

1. A few words here are not clear.

Council. These are concrete alternative proposals. If Government cannot summon courage, it is doomed to failure.

Government put themselves into a tight corner by suggesting that nothing can be done without settlement. What has Defence to do with communal settlement? No favoured minorities but pampered minorities. Congress foolishly lent itself to a communal settlement and it cannot be easily undone. How can I go out of an express train and jump into an aeroplane? I shall only be falling to my destruction. . . . .[1]

I have given you an outline of what is agitating me. You may think the Congress incapable of bargaining away any minorities' rights to win *swaraj*. The Congress considers it bad for Mussalmans, Sikhs, Hindus and bad for the nation to give them separate electorates.

But it is worst for untouchables. Untouchables are above this. For me who feels with them and knows their life, it is equal to killing them if separate electrorates are given them. They are in the hands of superior classes. They can suppress them completely and wreak vengeance upon the untouchables who are at their mercy.

I may be opening out my shame to you. But, in the existing circumstances, how can I invite utter destruction for them? I would not be guilty of that crime. Dr. Ambedkar, able as he is, has unhappily lost his head over this question. He sees blood wherever Hinduism is.

If he was a real representative, I should have withdrawn. Today he cannot coherently think of the problem. I repudiate his claim to represent them. I am the representative of the depressed classes. Get a mandate and I may not [*sic*] be elected but Ambedkar cannot be returned. The Congress Scheme covers the interest of minorities completely. One line or clause I would insert—Judicial Tribunal. I said I proposed this clause and I would see that it was carried.

I must take the other end. I should resist separate representation for Europeans on other grounds. They are the ruling race, they were able to shadow an Indian Governor and make his life a hell.

Sinha's Secretariat shadowed him. His very servants were acting as his spies. He died of a broken heart. I had seen him at the height of his power. I saw him when he was utterly broken. I said smilingly to Sir Hubert Carr, "why not come to us for votes? You may be sure that a man like Mr. Andrews would always be returned by an Indian electorate."[2] Carr said Andrews would not be a fit representative of Englishmen, Mr. Andrews no more represents the English mind than an Indian does. "Well, if the

1. A few words that follow are not clear.
2. This sentence is from *Young India*.

Englishman must stay there, he must represent the Indian mind. Lord Salisbury's black man Dadabhai Naoroji was elected by the suffrage of Central Finsbury."

Then Anglo-Indians. I know them much better than Col. Gidney does. I have seen them weep before me. They come to me and say, "We are bastards. Englishmen do not recognize us; Indians would not adopt us." I say, "Come to us, discard your tinsel and we will adopt you." I saw a fat man—an Anglo-Indian—he could not bear the idea that his mother was an Indian woman. They would be pariahs and untouchables with a separate electorate under Nationl Government. Sir Henry Gidney may be all right but others won't be knighted. But if they would come and claim the suffrage of our people they are quite welcome—Kumarappa—Joseph Kumarappa[1] — can turn Gujarat round his fingers by dint of service.

Horage Alexander : You would have constituted the Conference by election.

Just how tell us?

An orientation should have been defined. There are telegrams from Jains—also Lingayats. If you are to humour these so-called manufactured orientation, how can you do so?

The Congress Scheme recognizes (1) Weightage; (2) Sind [as a] separate province if it can be economically sustained; (3) Joint electorates and adult suffrage; (4) Reservations for minorities and weightage; (5) Guarantees-cum-rights and civic liberties for all communities;

Q. Is it not a fact that the majority of Mussalmans [do not] consent to have responsibility in Centre if the majority question cannot be settled?

A. I say whether they attend or not, the Conference must finish deliberations. If British Government wants to part with power, its progress must not be allowed to be blocked by even the Congress. If a proper scheme is prepared, what is the meaning of a party resisting the thing? After all, the Congress represents Mussalmans also. Judicial tribunal composed of Parsis, Christians or all of them but not of Hindus or Muslims. It is foolish, tantalizing, humiliating—this playing a waiting game.

SIR Francis Younghusband : Would a formula in Act of Parliament, indicating wish of the people of India to be separated, or not separated, do?

A. Yes; but the partnership must be a strong bond and not subject to be torn to pieces by disruptive forces.

[*From the manuscript of Mahadev Desai's Diary,* 1931]

---

1. Dr. J. C. Kumarappa.

49. Fundamental Change

SPEECH AT PEMBROKE COLLEGE[1]

[Cambridge,
November 1, 1931][2]

The partnership has to be on equal terms. It should not be 'subjection' in glorified language. That means that the present relationship must be completely transformed though the connection may be retained, and that connection should be wholly and solely for the benefit of mankind. India by herself has no capacity to exploit the nations of the earth, but with Great Britain's assistance she can do it.

Now the partnership must mean that exploitation shall cease, and, if Great Britain should not desist from it, India should sever the connection. All that is wanted is a fundamental change in the British policy of exploitation. Britain cannot thereafter boast that she has a strong navy guarding the maritime highways and all her overseas commerce.

What about the South African possession? I would not insist on a transformation of Britain's relations with them, as a condition precedent to our partnership. But I should certainly strive to work for the deliverance of those South African races which, I can say from experience, are ground down under exploitation. Our deliverance must mean their deliverance. But, if that cannot come about, I should have no interest in a partnership with Britain, even if it were of benefit to India. Speaking for myself, I would say that a partnership, giving the promise of a world set free from exploitation, would be a proud privilege for my nation and I would maintain it for ever. But India cannot reconcile herself in any shape or form to any policy of exploitation and, speaking for

---

1. Extracted from Mahadev Desai's "London Letter". According to Desai this is a condensation of the talk which lasted several hours. Present at the meeting were Ellis Barker, Lowes Dickinson, Dr. John Murray, Dr. Baker and Evelyn Wrench.
2. The date is according to Gandhiji's diary, which also says that the meeting was held in the morning.

myself, I may say that, if ever the Congress should adopt an imperial policy, I should sever my connection with the Congress.

But would not the Congress be satisfied with a status equal to South Africa or Canada, for the time being at any rate? I see the danger of saying 'yes'. If you visualize a higher or superior status towards which we have then to work, I should say 'no'. But if it is a status beyond which we have not to aspire, I should say 'yes'. It should be a status which the ordinary man in the street should understand to be a radically different status from the present. I would, therefore, not accept a transition period during which we may have to be satisfied with a lower status. The Congress will not be satisfied with a state lower than the best.

But what about the Princes ? They do not want independence. I know they don't, and they cannot, as they are the mouthpiece of the British Government. But there are others too who think that they cannot live except under the protection of British arms. For me, I cannot accept anything short of a complete control of the army. If all other leaders of the land were to accept a compromise on the army question, I would say I would rather stay out, but would not resist it and make a call to the people to suffer. If there were such a large step taken which would ultimately and quickly lead to the final thing, I would tolerate it, though I would not endorse it.

But, if you say the British units will never serve under the national Government, it would mean to me a fatal objection to any connection with Great Britain. We do not want, we cannot possibly tolerate, an army of occupation. No scheme of Indianization can serve any useful purpose inasmuch as, until the last moment, the command will be British, and the same doubts about our capacity to take over charge will be expressed as are expressed today. The real responsible Government can come when Britishers begin to trust India and her ability. Chaos can be got over only when Britain has a living conviction that it has done wrong to India and should now, by way of undoing the wrong, keep British troops at the disposal of Indian ministers. You are afraid that British soldiers may be cut to pieces under the foolish orders of Indian ministers. Well, I ask you not to forget that, during the Boer War, there came a time when British generals were described in England as asses and British soldiers as heroes. If British generals erred, Indian ministers too may err. The Indian ministers would certainly discuss everything with the Commander-in-Chief and other military experts, but the final authority and responsibility will certainly have to be the ministers'.

Let the Commander-in-Chief then resign or obey. The idea of my paying for freedom by blood startles you.

Well, I who claim to know the conditions of India through and through, know that India is dying by inches. The land revenue exactions mean morsels forcibly taken out of the mouths of the peasants' children. It is an indescribable agony through which the peasant is passing. In order to put that condition right, a transition stage is not the remedy. Do the British Government understand transition as I mean it? Would they keep the British soldiers to help us, i.e., only in our interests? If so, we would have them and pay them according to our means. But, if the position honestly held is that we are incapable, and the control should not be relaxed, then, if God wills it, we must go through the purgatory. I have not talked of rivers of other people's blood flowing, for I know that the party of violence is dying out. But I have talked of Ganges ful of our own blood—a pure voluntary act of self-immolation to face the situation. It would be good for India to go through that purgatory if it must. Personally, I do not think there can be such communal riots as you fear. Ninety per cent of the population of India is rural and the strife is confined only to the ten per cent urban population. I would count that bloodshed as of no consequence beside this slow ignominious death which carries no glory with it. This, of course, assumes that India is being starved to death by having to pay the phenomenal expenditure for a foreign army of occupation and the most expensive civil service in the world.

Even Japan, which is armed to the teeth, does not pay for her army to the extent that we have to do. My quarrel with you is this. I know that every honest Englishman wants to see India free, but is it not tragic for them to feel that the moment British arms are removed there would be invasions and internecine strife? Well, as against that, my contention is that it is the British presence that is the cause of internal chaos, because you have ruled India according to the principle of divide and rule.

Because of your benevolent intentions you feel that the harrow does not hurt the toad. In the nature of things, it cannot but hurt. It is not that you are in India in response to our invitation. You must realize that there is sullen discontent everywhere and everyone says, "We do not want foreign rule." And why this over-anxiety about how we would fare without you? Go to the pre-British period. History does not record a larger number of Hindu-Muslim riots. In fact, the history of my own times shows a darker record. The fact is that the British arms are powerless to prevent riots, though they are powerful enough to punish the guilty and the innocent. We hear of no riots in the reign of even Aurangzeb. As for the invasions, the worst invasion left the villages untouched. There were periodic visitations of the plague. If to avoid that kind of plague, which after all may be a cleansing process, we should have to maintain an army of doctors and starve ourselves to pay for them, we would far rather have the cleansing process. Take the occasional inroads of tigers and lions.

Would we submit to the erection of castles and fortresses at the expense of millions of rupees rather than fight the beasts straight and take the risks? Pardon me, we are not such a nation of absolute cowards who would always run away from risk. Better that we were wiped off the face of the earth than remain alive sustained by foreign bayonets. No, you must trust us to know how to patch up our quarrels and to deal with invasions. India, which has survived many invasions, and showed a culture and a civilization unsurpassed by any on earth, need not be pitied and kept in cotton-wool.

[*Young India,* 19-11-1931]

50. Responsibility[1]

SPEECH AT FRIENDS' HOUSE[2]

[LONDON,
November 9, 1931]

You have asked me whether, though there was a voice crying in India for freedom, there were enough people ready to shoulder the responsibility of the country. To me the question is quite reasonable. I shall endeavour, as brielfy as I can, to answer this important question. Let me tell you that the real point at issue is the Congress demand on the one hand and, if I can so put it, reluctance on the part of responsible men to respond to that demand on the other. The Congress wants independence which in other words means it wants control over Defence, External Relations and Finance, i.e., partnership at will, terminable by either party. That is the substance of the Congress demand, because the Congress honestly believes that the country has got capable hands to take over charge from the foreign Government.

But on the part of responsible men I have been seeing nothing during my wanderings and talks. On the other hand, I find they are raising considerable difficulties in conceding what is the legitimate claim of the Congress. I shall tell you without any modesty that the Congress seeks and claims to represent the whole mass of India. Its claim cannot be disputed. You know India is in villages and not in cities like Bombay, Calcutta or Madras. The Congress claims to represent also even the Princes in spite of themselves. Of course, it does not want to usurp their rights, but does justice to them also so long as their claims do not become inconsistent with those of the teeming millions. At the same time, the Congress offers the least resistance to them because it engages itself in putting forth the claims on behalf of the masses.

---

1. It being his Silence Day, Gandhiji made the statement in writing at 11 a.m. on his return from his visit to Oxford.
2. The meeting, held in the evening, was organized by the Fellowship of Reconciliation. The hall was filled to capacity and a large crowd had to go back disappointed.

As you are devoted to seeking avenues for peace, you should have no difficulty in recognizing the claim of the Congress. The history of the past fifteen months before the Delhi Pact tells you that these masses were at war with Government, but it was a peaceful war for the simple reason that the masses had taken the pledge to win freedom without shedding a drop of blood. In this struggle, thousands upon thousands of women and children received lathi blows. Tens of thousands were sent to jail. Women of India rose as if by magic.

There was a phenomenal awakening on their part. Thousands of villages responded to the Congress message. I myself do not know why and how I was not prepared for such a splendid response to me.

There must have been the hand of God behind. These villages and villagers were all unarmed, because remember, there is compulsory disarmament in my country.

But those who wielded lathis and used bayonets did not realize that these women and villagers had with them an instrument which was not perishable and which was far more effective. That instrument was in the form of love, non-violence and truth against heir force of arms and other brutal methods.

Though the work 'independence' has a specific meaning in the English disctionary, to these masses it has also a larger and deeper meaning. They do not understand what 'Parliament', 'Responsible Government', or 'Councils' mean, but the word *swaraj* gives them the meaning in the twinkling of an eye. Today they are paying the land revenue but they do not know why and how much is spent for the country's purposes. They do not even know that 55 crores are spent over the military. At the same time, remember they have no fear from the frontiers, or the Afghans or any other place. As a matter of fact, the invasions never bother Indian villagers because invasions in India did not begin with the East India Company. We had them even before that period. These invaders did not go beyond the cities. They did not go beyond Delhi and, as you know from the geography of India, a vast number of its people living in villages were unaffected by the invasions. Moreover, internal quarrels do not affect by the villagers. They, therefore, need no protection. Today the vast masses are living in abject starvation. They do not know what it is to have two meals a day. They have no bread and butter for themselves, nor a drop of milk for their children. We have added dignity to their life and they have gained confidence that they will be able to make both ends meet and keep the wolf away from their doors.[1]

The Congress has purified politics. It has almost spiritualized it, though personally I do not like that word. We are out to win freedom with non-violence and truth, by removal of untouchability, and by recognition of every villager as a human being. Our non-co-operation fight signifies that no man can possibly tyrannize over another. Our whole movement is based on morality. We do not believe in the theory of the sweet will of our rulers. You know what we do in India. When authorities say do this, which we know is a wrong order, we say, thank you, we will not do it. We say we won't do anything which injures our self-respect, hurts our human dignity, and in such a struggle even millionaires have discarded their wealth and have ultimately become trustees of their wealth for the betterment of Indian villagers.

If British Ministers do not recognize my claim and want to keep the yoke on our neck, we may once again go through the fiery ordeal because, perhaps, we still need to suffer. Your Government has brought no benefit to my country. It has only emasculated it. It is a shame that we are made incapable of defending ourselves against foreign yoke, and even in our internal affairs. That is terribly disgraceful, but what have we done? We have today created selfless workers in every village. They are our civil servants and they will do anything that he Congress asks them to do.

They are capable of governing the country. They know, as I do know, that we have already burnt our boats and are marching with our backs to the wall, because we are working for freedom of the teeming villagers.

[*The Bombay Chronicle*, 12-11-1931]

1. Gandhiji here was referring to the work done by the All-India Spinners' Association.

51. Freedom and Slavery

SPEECH AT LONDON SCHOOL OF ECONOMICS[1]

[London,
November 10, 1931]

The main obstacle to my mission is—myself. So many people tell me that the Congress demand is pitched too high. When I come to grips, they begin to listen to me. Those responsible are equally guilty inasmuch as they are in no mood to listen. There does not seem to be that atmosphere which is responsive and receptive. Some of the best Englishmen and Englishwomen feel that something has got to be done to define freedom. . . . .[2] I have come here out of prison; with me there were thousands. The avowed object of the Settlement with the Viceroy was that Congress should be represented at the Round Table Conference. I and many Congressmen were trying to negotiate this. Generally at a round table people sit who are elected; who have got there is their own right. I do not sit in my own right, I am there on sufferance: our of nominated members you do not expect brilliant results. I have never known a conference with nominated members which has decided on principles.

We have set out to give our own blood. But the attitude here [is]: 'Look at these ungrateful fellows, they do not see the blessings of British rule.' It is not only the official mind, but those capable of shaping public mind. It was Sir Henry Campbell-Bannerman who said that good government was no substitute for self-government. Those who are concerned do not feel that British rule has done good. Gokhale said it has emasculated us. How has that nation suddenly become conscious of its strength? The obstacle is the colossal ignorance of the best of Englishmen.

---

1. According to a Press Report "the theatre of the London School of Economics did not suffice to accommodate the members of the School's Students' Union who assembled to hear Mahatma Gandhi. The audience consisted mostly of English students and was perhaps the largest English audience Mahatma Gandhi had addressed in England".
2. Some words are not clear here.

The ignorance is nearly appalling. It is misinformation, false history. The Press contains nothing of what happens in India. Chittagong is a black page in history. Officers ran amok and created havoc on unarmed population. In Hijli innocent men were shot down; 16 were seriously injured. I would condemn attempts on lives of Englishmen in the severest language possible.

But what does this mean? There is a vital connection between Chittagong, Hijli and these attacks.

The whole of India is seething with unrest for which there are definite causes, and in which British rule is involved. Moral and material progress of India? The sum total is nil. See what a hurdle race I have to run. I give you absolute assurance that day and night I am trying my very best to reach a solution and am putting no obstacle in the way. We have burnt our boats and we have our backs to the wall. I want freedom in the name of untouchables, poor masses. I would sacrifice a million lives, and that freedom would be cheaply bought. Voluntary sacrifice of a million lives is infinitely preferable to the death millions are undergoing by inches. I cannot tolerate this .....[1] The only restriction is that we shall not soil our fingers with the blood of our opponents and we will not descend to untruth.

We won't have the tremendous weight of an army of occupation...[2] We pay the bulk of our savings to our door-keepers.

You have no door-keepers, only unequalled matchless policemen. The difference between freedom and slavery. The axe would descend upon the military budget. When Mir Alam Khan attacked me, an Englishman saved my life and his daughter sang "Lead Kindly Light". Are the ten thousand Mussalmans who went to jail going to be traitors?...[3] Immediately the wedge is withdrawn we shall close our ranks. If the God of the Afghans tells them that they should take our lives, we shall invoke that very God—though they are taking the name of that God five times a day. If God wants it , we will challenge Him too. Let us shed the fear of man.

A NEGRO STUDENT: You love an Englishman as much as an Indian and yet you dislike British Government. Now British people make up the Government.

---

1. Some words are not clear here.
2. *Ibid.*
3. *Ibid.*

GANDHIJI : Man is superior to his method. A man's method may be vile, and yet you may not aptly apply the adjective to the man himself....[1] British system is Satanic. But, in spite of British system being Satanic, I love the British like my brothers. I have a boy who has rebelled against me. Yet I love that boy equally as I do the other brothers. I detest his methods and ways. I have learnt from domestic law that, if I have humanity in me, I should love the Britisher whom God has made. And yet I detest his method and am doing my best to destroy his method... .[2]

In the war of non-violence we walk in the fear of God, give no secret information, brook no treacherousness.

[*From the manuscript of Mahadev Desai's Diary. Courtesy: Narayan Desai.*]

1. Some words are not clear here.
2. *Ibid.*

52. Minorities

SPEECH AT MINORITIES COMMITTEE MEETING

[London,
November 13, 1931]

PRIME MINISTER AND FELLOW DELEGATES,

It is not without very considerable hesitation and shame that I take part in the discussion on the minorities question. I have not been able to read with the care and attention that it deserves the memorandum[1] sent to the Delegates on behalf of certain minorities and received this morning.

Before I offer a few remarks on that memorandum, with your permission and with all the deference and respect that are your due, I would express my dissent from the view that you put before this Committee, that the inability to solve the communal question was hampering the progress of Constitution-building, and that it was an indispensable condition prior to the building of any such Constitution. I expressed at an early stage of the sittings of this Committee that I did not share that view. The experience that I have since gained has confirmed me in that view; and, if you will pardon me for saying so, it was because of the emphasis that was laid last year and repeated this year upon this difficulty, that the different communities were encouraged to press with all the vehemence at their command their own respective views.

---

1. The memorandum, submitted "on behalf of the Mohammedans, the Depressed Classes, the Anglo-Indians, the Europeans and a considerable section of Indian Christian groups", demanded *inter alia* that these communities "shall have representation in all legislatures through separate electorates. . . provided that, after a lapse of ten years, it will be open to Muslims in the Punjab and Bengal and any minority communities in any other provinces to accept joint electorates. . . With regards to the Depressed Classes no change to joint electorates... shall be made until after 20 years. . . ." Special claims were advanced on behalf of Mussalmans, the Depressed Classes, the Anglo-Indians and the Europeans. The document was signed by the Agha Khan, Dr. Ambedkar, Rao Bahadur Pannirselvam, Sir Henry Gidney and Sir Hubert Carr.

It would have been against human nature if they had done otherwise. All of them thought that this was the time to press forward their claims for all they were worth, and I venture to suggest again that this very emphasis has defeated the purpose which I have no doubt it had in view. Having received that encouragement, we have failed to arrive at an agreement. I, therefore, associate myself entirely with the view, expressed by Sir Chimanlal Setalvad, that it is not this question which is the fulcrum, it is not this question which is the central fact, but the central fact is the Constitution-building.

I am quite certain that you did not convene this Round Table Conference and bring us all six thousand miles away from our homes and occupations to settle the communal question, but you convened us, you made deliberate declarations that we were invited to come here, to share the process of Constitution-building, and that, before we went away from your hospitable shores, we should have the certain conviction that we had built up an honourable and a respectable framework for the freedom of India, and that it awaited only the imprimatur of the approval of the House of Commons and the House of Lords.

Now, at the present moment, we are face to face with a wholly different situation, namely, that, because there is no communal settlement agreed to by us, there is to be no building of the Constitution, and that, as a last resort and as the last touch, you will announce the policy of His Majesty's Government in connection with the Constitution and all the matters that may arise from it. I cannot help feeling that it would be a sorry ending to a Conference which was brought into being with so much trumpeting and with so much hope excited in the minds and in the breasts of many people.

Coming to this document, I accept the thanks that have been given to me by Sir Hubert Carr. Had it not been for the remarks that I made when I shouldered that burden, and had not it been for my utter failure to bring about a solution, Sir Hubert Carr rightly says he would not have found the very admirable solution that he has been able, in common with the other minorities, to present to this Committee for consideration and finally for the consideration and approval of His Majesty's Government.

I will not deprive Sir Hubert Carr and his associates of the feeling of satisfaction that evidently actuates them, but, in my opinion, what they have done is to sit by the carcass, and they have performed the laudable feat of dissecting that carcass. As representing the predominant political organization in India, I have no hesitation in saying to His Majesty's Government, to those friends who seek to represent or who think they represent the minorities mentioned against their names, and indeed to the whole world, that this scheme is not one designed to achieve responsible government, but is undoubtedly a scheme designed to share power with the bureaucracy.

If that is the intention—and it is the intention running through the whole of that document—I wish them well, and the Congress is entirely out of it. The Congress will wander no matter how many years in the wilderness rather than lend itself to a proposal under which the hardy tree of freedom and responsible government can never grow.

I am astonished that Sir Hubert Carr should tell us that they have evolved a Scheme which, being designed only for a temporary period, would not damage the cause of nationalism, but, at the end of ten years. we would all find ourselves hugging one another and throwing ourselves into one another's laps. My political experience teaches me a wholly different lesson. If this responsible government, whenever it comes, is to be inaugurated under happy auspices, it should not undergo the process of vivisection to which this scheme subjects it; it is a strain which no government can possibly bear.

There is the coping-stone to the structure, and I am surprised, Mr. Prime Minister, that you allowed yourself to mention this as if it was an indisputable fact, namely, that the proposals may be taken as being acceptable to well over one hundred and fifteen millions of people, or about 46 per cent of the population of India. You had a striking demonstration of the inaccuracy of this figure. You have had, on behalf of the women, a complete repudiation of special representation, and as very happen to be one-half of the population of India, this 46 per cent is somewhat reduced, but not only that: the Congress may be a very insignificant organization, but I have not hesitated to make the claim, and I am not ashamed to repeat the claim, that the Congress claims to represent 85 per cent of the population not merely of British India but of the whole of India.

Subject to all the questions that may be raised, I repeat the claim with all the emphasis at my command that the Congress, by right of service, claims to represent that population which is called the agricultural population of India, and I would accept the challenge, if the Government were to issue the challenge, that we should have a referendum in India, and you would immediately find whether the Congress represents them or whether it does not represent them. But I go a step further. At the present moment if you were to examine the register of the Congress, if you were to examine the records of the prisons of India, you would find that the Congress represented and represents on its register a very large number of Mohammedans. Several thousand Mohammedans went to jail last year under the banner of the Congress. The Congress today has several thousand Mohammedans on its register. The Congress has thousands of untouchables on its register. The Congress has Indian Christians also on its register. I do not know that there is a single community which is not represented on the Congress register. With all deference to the Nawab Sahib of Chhatari, even landlords and even mill-owners and millionaires are represented there. I admit that they are coming to the Congress slowly, cautiously, but the Congress is trying to serve them also. The Congress undoubtedly represents Labour. Therefore, this claim that the proposals set forth in this memorandum are acceptable to well over one hundred and fifteen millions of poeple needs to be taken with a very great deal of reservation and caution.

One word more and I shall have done. You have had presented to you and circulated to the members, I hope, the Congress proposal in connection with the communal problem[1]. I venture to submit that, of all the schemes that I have seen, it is the most workable scheme, but I may be in error there. I admit that it has not commended itself to the representatives of the communities at this table, but it has commended itself to the representatives of these very classes in India.

It is not the creation of one brain, but it is the creation of a Committee on which various important parties were represented.

Therefore, you have got on behalf of the Congress that scheme; but the Congress has also suggested that there should be an impartial arbitration. Through arbitration all over the world people have adjusted their differences, and the Congress is always open to accept any decision of an arbitration court. I have myself ventured to suggest that there might be appointed by the Government a judicial tribunal which would examine this case and give its decision. But if none of these things are acceptable to any of us, and if this is the *sine qua non* of any Constitution building, then I say it will be much better for us that we should remain without so called responsible Government than that we should accept this claim.

I would like to repeat what I have said before, that while the Congress will always accept any solution that may be acceptable to the Hindus, the Mohammedans and the Sikhs, Congress will be no party to special reservation or special electorates for any other minorities. The Congress will always endorse clauses or reservations as to fundamental

---

1. *Vide* "Speech at Minorities Committee Meeting", 8-10-1931.

rights and civil liberty. It will be open to everybody to be placed on the voters' roll and to appeal to the common body of the electorates.

In my humble opinion, the proposition enunciated by Sir Hubert Carr is the very negation of responsible Government, the very negation of nationalism. If he says that, if you want a live European on the legislature, then he must be elected by the Europeans themselves, well, Heaven help India if India has to have representatives elected by these several, special, cut-up groups. That European will serve India as a whole, and the European only, who commands the approval of the common electorate and not the mere Europeans. This very idea suggests that the responsible Government will always have to contend against these interests which will always be in conflict against the national spirit—against this body of 85 per cent of the agricultural population. To me it is an unthinkable thing. If we are going to bring into being responsible Government and if we are going to get real freedom, then I venture to suggest that it should be the proud privilege and the duty of every one of these so-called special classes to seek entry into the Legislatures through this open door, through the election and approval of the common body of electorates. You know that Congress is wedded to adult suffrage, and under adult suffrage it will be open to all to be placed on the voters' list. More than that nobody can ask.

One word more as to the so-called untouchables. I can understand the claims advanced by other minorities but the claims advanced on behalf of the untouchables, that to me is the "unkindest cut of all". It means the perpetual bar-sinister. I would not sell the vital interests of the untouchables even for the sake of winning the freedom of India. I claim myself in my own person to represent the vast mass of untouchables. Here I speak not merely on behalf of the Congress, but I speak on my own behalf, and I claim that I would get, if there was a referendum of the untouchables, their vote, and that I would top the poll. And I would work from one end of India to the other to tell the untouchables that separate electorates and separate reservation is not the way to remove this bar-sinister, which is the shame, not of them, but of orthodox Hinduism.

Let this Committee and let the whole world know that today there is a body of Hindu reformers who are pledged to remove this blot of untouchability. We do not want on our register and on our census untouchables classified as a separate class. Sikhs may remain as such in perpetuity, so may Mohammedans, so may Europeans. Will untouchables remain untouchables in perpetuity? I would far rather that Hinduism died than that untouchability lived. Therefore, with all my regard for

Dr. Ambedkar, and for his desire to see the untouchables uplifted, with all my regard for his ability, I must say in all humility that here the great wrong under which he has laboured and perhaps the bitter experiences that he has undergone have for the moment warped his judgment. It hurts me to have to say this, but I would be untrue tc the cause of the untouchables, which is as dear to me as life itself, if I did not say it. I will not bargain away their rights for the kingdom of the whole world. I am speaking with a due sense of responsibility, and I say that it is not a proper claim which is registered by Dr. Ambedkar when he seeks to speak for the whole of the untouchables of India. It will create a division in Hindusim which I cannot possibly look forward to with any satisfaction whatsoever. I do not mind untouchables , if they so desire, being converted to Islam or Christianity. I should tolerate that, but I cannot possibly tolerate what is in store for Hinduism if there are two divisions set forth in the villages. Those who speak of the political rights of untouchables do not know their India, do not know how Indian society is today constructed, and, therefore, I want to say with all the emphasis that I can command that, if I was the only person to resist this thing, I would resist it with my life.

[*Indian Round Table Conference (Second Session): Proceedings of the Federal Structure Committee and Minorities Committee,* Vol. I, pp. 543-44]

53. Vegetarianism

SPEECH AT MEETING OF LONDON VEGETARIAN SOCIETY

[London,
November 20, 1931]

When I received the invitation to be present at this meeting, I need not tell you how pleased I was, because it revived old memories and recollections of pleasant friendship formed with vegetarians. I feel especially honoured to find on my right Mr. Henry Salt. I was Mr. Salt's book, A Plea for Vegetarianism, which showed my why, apart from a hereditary habit, and apart from my adherence to a vow administered to me by my mother , it was right to be a vegetarian. He showed me why it was a moral duty incumbent on vegetarians not to live upon fellow animals. It is, therefore, a matter of additional pleasure to me that I find Mr. Salt in our midst.

I do not propose to take up your time by giving you my various experiences of vegetarianism, nor do I want to tell you something of the great difficulty that faced me in London itself in remaining staunch to vegetarianism, but I would like to share with you some of the thoughts that have developed in me in connection with vegetarianism.

Forty years ago I used to mix freely with vegetarians. There was at that time hardly a vegetarian restaurant in London that I had not visited. I made it a point, out of curiosity, and to study the possibilities of vegetarian restaurants in London, to visit every one of them. Naturally, therefore, I came into close contact with many vegetarians. I found at the tables that largely the conversation turned upon food and disease. I found also that the vegetarians who were struggling to stick to their vegetarianism were finding it difficult from health point of view. I do not know whether, nowadays, you have those debates, but I used at that time to attend debates that were held between vegetarians and vegetarians, and between vegetarians and non-vegetarians. I remember one such debates, between Dr. Densmore and the late Dr. T.R. Allinson. Then vegetarians had a habit of talking of nothing but food and nothing but disease. I feel that is the worst way of going about the business. I notice also that it is those persons who become vegetarians because they are suffering from some disease or other—that is, from purely the health point of view–it is those persons who largely fall back. I discovered that for remaining staunch to vegetarianism a man requires a moral basis.

For me that was a great discovery in my search after truth. At an early age, in the course of my experiments, I found that a selfish basis would not serve the purpose of taking a man higher and higher along the paths of evolution. What was required was an altruistic purpose. I found also that health was by no means the monopoly of vegetarians.

I found many people having no bias one way or the other, and that non-vegetarians were able to show, generally speaking, good health. I found also the several vegetarian found it impossible to remain vegetarians because they had made food a fetish and because they thought that by becoming vegetarians they could eat as much lentils, haricot beans, and cheese as they liked. Of course, those people could not possibly keep their health. Observing along these lines, I saw that a man should eat sparingly and now and then fast. No man or woman really ate sparingly consumed just that quantity which the body requires and no more. We easily fall a prey to the temptations of the palate, and, therefore, when a thing tastes delicious,we do not mind taking a morsel or two more. But you cannot keep health under thsose circumstances. Therefore, I discovered that in order to keep health, no matter what you ate, it was necessary to cut down the quantity of your food and reduce the number of meals. Become moderate; err on the side of less, rather than on the side of more. When I invite friends to share their meals with me, I never press them to take anything except only what they require. On the contrary, I tell them not to take a thing if they do not want it.

What I want to bring to your notice is that vegetarians need to be tolerant if they want to convert others to vegetarianism.

Adopt a little humility. We should appeal to the moral sense of the people who do not see eye to eye with us. If a vegetarian became ill, and a doctor prescribed beef-tea, then I would not call him a vegetarian. A vegetarian is made of sterner stuff. Why? Because it is for the building of the spirit and not of the body. Man is more than meat. It is the spirit in man for which we are concerned.

Therefore, vegetarians should have that moral basis—that a man was not born a carnivorous animal, but born to live on the fruits and herbs that the earth gorws. I know we must all err. I would give up milk if I could but I cannot. I have made that experiment times without number. I could not , after a serious illness, regain my strength unless I went back to milk. That has been the tragedy of my life. But the basis of my vegetarianism is not physical, but moral. If anybody said that I should die if I did not take beef-tea or mutton, even under medical advice, I would prefer death. That is the basis of my vegetarianism. I would love to think that all of us who called ourselves vegetarians should have that basis. There were thousands of meat eaters who did not stay meat-eaters. There must be a definite reason for our making that change in our lives, for our adopting habits and customs different from society, even though sometimes that change may offend those nearest and dearest to us. Not for the world should you sacrifice a moral principle. Therefore the only basis for having a vegetarian society and proclaiming a vegetarian principle is, and must be, a moral one. I am not to tell you, as I see and wander about the world, that vegetarians, on the whole, enjoy much better health than meat-eaters. I belong to a country which is predominantly vegetarian by habit or necessity. Therefore, I cannot testify that that shows much greater endurance, much greater courage, or much greater exemption from disease. Because it is a peculiar, personal thing. It requires obedience, and scrupulous obedience, to all the laws of hygiene.

Therefore, I think that what vegetarians should do is not to emphasize the physical consequences of vegetarianism, but to explore the moral consequences. While we have not yet forgotten that we share many things in common with the beast, we do not sufficiently realize that there are certain things which differentiate us from the beast. Of course, we have vegetarians in the cow and the bull—which are better vegetarians than we are—but there is something much higher which calls us of vegetarianism. Therefore, I thought that during the few minutes which I give myself the privilege of addressing you, I would just emphasize the moral basis of vegetarianism. And I would say that I have found from my own experience, and the experience of thousands of friends and companions, that they find satisfaction, so far as vegetarianism is concerned, from the moral basis they have chosen for sustaining vegetarianism.

In conclusion, I thank you all for coming here and allowing me to see vegetarians face to face. I cannot say I used to meet you forty or forty-two years ago. I suppose the faces of the London Vegetarian Society have changed. There are very few members who, like Mr. Salt, can claim association with the Society extending over forty years. Lastly, I would like you, if you want to, to ask me any questions, for I am at your disposal for a few minutes.

Mr. Gandhi was then asked to give his reasons for limiting his daily diet to five articles only, and he replied:

That has no connection with vegetarianism. . . . There was another reason. I had been a pampered child of nature. I had acquired then that notoriety that when I was invited by friends, they placed before me ample dishes of food. I told them, I had come there to serve, and personally, I should find myself dying by inches if I allowed myself to be pampered like that. So, in limiting myself to five ingredients of food, I served a double purpose. And I must finish all my eating before sundown. I have been saved many pitfalls by that. There are many discoveries about that in regard to health reasons.

Dietists are saying that we are more and more tending towards simplifying diet, and that, if one must live for health one must have one thing at a time and avoid harmful combinations. I like the process of exclusion better than that of inclusion because no two doctors have the same opinion.

Then I think the restriction to five articles of food has helped me morally and materially—materially because, in a poor country like India, it is not always possible to procure goat's milk, and it is a hard thing to produce fruit and grapes. Then, I go to visit poor people, and if I expected hothouse grapes, they would banish me. So, by restricting myself to five articles of food, it also serves the law of economy.

[*Harijan*, 20-2-1949]

54. Round Table Conference

SPEECH AT PLENARY SESSION OF ROUND TABLE CONFERENCE

[London,
December 1, 1931][1]

PRIME MINISTER AND FRIENDS,

I wish that I could have done without having to speak to you, but I felt that I would not have been just to you or just to my principles if I did not put in what may be the last word on behalf of the Congress. I live under no illusion. I do not think that anything that I can say this evening can possibly influence the decision of the Cabinet. Probably the decision has been already taken. Matters of the liberty of practically a whole continent can hardly be decided by mere argumentation, even negotiation. Negotiation has its purpose and has its play, but only under certain conditions. Without those conditions negotiations are a fruitless task. But I do not want to go into all these matters. I want as far as possible to confine myself within the four corners of the conditions that you, Prime Minister, read to this Conference at its opening meeting. I would, therefore, first of all, say a few words in connection with the Reports that have been submitted to this Conference. You will find in these Reports that generally it has been stated that so and so is the opinion of a large majority, some, however, have expressed an opinion to the contrary, and so on. Parties who have dissented have not been stated. I had heard when I was in India, and I was told when I came here, that no decision or no decisions will be taken by the ordinary rule of majority, and I do not want to mention this fact here by way of complaint that the Reports have been so framed as if the proceedigns were governed by the test of majority. But it was necessary for me to mention this fact, because to most of these Reports you will find that there is a dissenting opinion, and in most of the cases that dissent unfortunately happens to belong to me. It was not a matter of joy to have to dissent from

1. The session began on November 30 and, after adjourning at 11.50 p.m., was resumed at 12.5 a.m.

fellow Delegates, but I felt that I could not truly represent the Congress unless I notified that dissent.

There is another thing which I want to bring to the notice of this Conference, namely: what is the meaning of the dissent of the Congress? I said at one of the preliminary meetings of the Federal Structure Committee that the Congress claimed to represent over 85 per cent of the population of India, that is to say, the dumb, toiling, semi-starved millions. But I went further: that the Congress claimed also by right of service to represent even the Princes, if they would pardon my putting forth that claim, and the landed gentry, the educated class. I wish to repeat that claim and I wish this evening to emphasize that claim.

All the other parties at this meeting represent sectional interests. Congress alone claims to represent the whole of India, all interests. It is no communal organization; it is a determined enemy of communalism in any shape or form. Congress knows no distinction of race, colour or creed; its platform is universal. It may not always have lived up to the creed. I do not know a single human organization that lives up to its creed. Congress has failed very often to my knowledge. It may have failed more often to the knowledge of its critics. But the worst critic will have to recognize, as it has been recognized, that the National Congress of India is a daily-growing organization, that its message penetrates the remotest village of India; that on given occasions the Congress has been able to demonstrate its influence over and among these masses who inhabit 700,000 villages.

And yet here I see that the Congress is treated as one of the Parties. I do not mind it; I do not regard it as a calamity for the Congress; but I do regard it as a calamity for the purpose of doing the work for which we have gathered together here. I wish I could convince all the British public men, the British Ministers, that the Congress is capable of delivering the goods. The Congress is the only all-India-*wide* national organization, bereft of any communal basis; that it does represent all the minorities which have lodged their claims here and which, or the signatories on their behalf, claim I hold unjustifiably to represent 46 per cent of the population of India. The Congress, I say, claims to represent all these minorities.

What a great difference it would be today if this claim on behalf of the Congress was recognized. I feel that I have to state this claim with some degree of emphasis on behalf of peace, for the sake of achieving the purpose which is common to all of us, to you Englishmen who sit at this table, and to us the Indian men and women who also sit at this table. I say so for this reason. Congress is a powerful organization; Congress is an organization which has been accused of running or desiring to run a parallel Government; and in a way I have endorsed the charge. If you could understand the working of the Congress, you would welcome an organization which could run a parallel Government and show that it is possible for an organization, voluntary, without any force at its command, to run the machinery of Government even under adverse circumstances. But no.

Although you have invited the Congress, you distrust the Congress. Although you have invited the Congress, you reject its claim to represent the whole of India. Of course it is possible at this end of the world to dispute that claim, and it is not possible for me to prove this claim; but, all the same, if you find me asserting that claim, I do so because a tremendous responsibility rests upon my shoulders.

The Congress represents the spirit of rebellion. I know that the word 'rebellion' must not be whispered at a Conference which has been summoned in order to arrive at an agreed solution of India's troubles through negotiation. Speaker after speaker has got up and said that India should achieve her liberty through negotiation, by argument, and that it will be the greatest glory of Great Britian if Great Britain yields to India's demands by argument. But the Congress does not hold that view, quite. The Congress has an alternative which is unpleasant to you. I heard several speakers—and let me say I have endeavoured not to miss a single sitting; I have tried to follow every speaker with the utmost attention and with all the respect that I could possibly give to these speakers—saying what a dire calamity it would be if India was fired with the spirit of lawlessness, rebellion, terrorism and so on. I do not pretend to have read histroy, but as a schoolboy I had to pass a paper in history also, and I read that the page of history is soiled red with the blood of those who have fought for freedom. I do not know an instance in which nations have attained to their own without having to go through an incredible measure of travail. The dagger of the assassin, the poison bowl, the bullet of the rifleman, the spear and all these weapons and methods of destruction have been up to now used by what I consider blind lovers of liberty and freedom, and the historian has not condemned him. I hold no brief for the terrorists.

Mr. Ghuznavi brought in the terrorists and he brought in the Calcutta Corporation. I felt hurt when he mentioned an incident that took place at the Calcutta Corporation. He forgot to mention that the Mayor of that

Corporation made handsome reparation for the error into which he himself was betrayed and the error into which the Calcutta Corporation was betrayed through the instrumentality of those members of the Corporation who were Congressmen. I hold no brief for Congressmen who directly on indirectly would encourage terrorism. As soon as this incident was brought to the notice of the Congress, the Congress set about putting it in order. It immediately called upon the Mayor of the Calcutta Corporation to give an account of what was done and the Mayor, the gentleman that he is, immediately admitted his mistake and made all the reparation that it was then legally possible to make. I must not detain this Assembly over this incident for any length of time. He mentioned also a verse which the children of the forty schools conducted by the Calcutta Corporation are supposed to have recited. There were many other misstatements in that speech which I could dwell upon, but I have no desire to do so. It is only out of regard for the great Calcutta Corporation and out of regard for truth and on behalf of those who are not here tonight to put in their defence that I mention these two glaring instances. I do not for one moment believe that this was taught in the Calcutta Corporation schools with the knowledge of the Calcutta Corporation. I do know that in those terrible days of last year, several things were done for which we have regret, for which we have made reparation. If our boys in Calcutta were taught these verses which Mr. Ghuznavi has recited, I am here to tender an apology on their behalf, but I should want it proved that the boys were taught by the schoolmasters of these schools with the knowledge and encouragement of the Corporation.

Charges of this nature have been brought against the Congress times without number, and times without number these charges have also been refuted, but I have mentioned these things at this juncture. It is again to show that for the sake of liberty people have fought, people have lost their lives, people have killed and have sought death at the hands of those whom they have sought to oust. The Congress then comes upon the scene and devises a new method not known to history, namely, that of civil disobedience, and the Congress has been following that method up. But again I am up against a stone wall and I am told that that is a method that no Government in the world will tolerate. Well, of course, the government may has not tolerate, no government has tolerated open rebellion.

No government may tolerate civil-disobedience, but governments have to succumb even to these forces, as the British Government has done before now, even as the great Dutch Government after eight years of trial had to yield to the logic of facts. General Smuts is a brave

General, a great statesman, and a very hard taskmaster also, but he himself recoiled with horror from even the contemplation of doing to death innocent men and women who were merely fighting for the preservation of their self-respect and the things which he had vowed he would never yield in the year 1908, reinforced as he was by General Botha, he had to do in the year 1914, after having tried these civil resisters through and through. And in India Lord Chelmsford had to do the same thing; the Governor of Bombay had to do the same thing in Borsad and Bardoli. I suggest to you, Prime Minister, it is too late today to resist this, and it is this thing which weighs me down, this choice that lies before them, the parting of the ways probably. I shall hope against hope, I shall strain every nerve to achieve an honourable settlement for my country if I can do so without having to put the millions of my countrymen and countrywomen and even children through this ordeal of fire. It can be a matter of no joy and comfort to me to lead them on again to a fight of that character, but if a further ordeal of fire has to be our lot. I shall approach that with the greatest joy and with the greatest consolation that I was doing what I felt to be right, the country was doing what it felt to be right, and the country will have the additional satisfaction of knowing that it was not at least taking lives, it was giving lives; it was not making the British people directly suffer, it was suffering .

Professor Gilbert Muray told me–I shall never forget that—I am paraphrasing his inimitable language. He said: You do not consider for one moment that the Englishmen do not suffer when thousands of your countrymen suffer, that we are so heartless? I do not think so. I do not know that you will suffer; but I want you to suffer because I want to touch your hearts; and when your hearts have been touched will come the psychological moment for negotiation.

Negotiation there always will be; and if this time I have travelled all these miles in order to enter upon negotiation, I thought that your countryman, Lord Irwin, had sufficiently tried us through his ordinances, that he had sufficient evidence that thousands of men and women of India and that thousands of children had suffered; and that, ordinance or no ordinance, lathis or no lathis, nothing would avail to stem the tide that was onrushing and to stem the passions that were rising in the breasts of the men and women of India who were thirsting for liberty.

Whilst there is yet a little sand left in the glass, I want you to understand what this Congress stands for. My life is at your disposal.

The lives of all the members of the Working Committee, the All-India Congress Committee, are at your disposal. But remember that you have at your disposal the lives of all these dumb millions. I do not want to sacrifice those lives if I can possibly help it. Therefore please remember that I will count no sacrifice too great if by chance I can pull through an honourable settlement. You will find me always having the greatest spirit of compromise if I can but fire you with the spirit that is working in the Congress, namely, that India must have real liberty. Call it by any name you like; a rose will smell as sweet by any other name, but it must be the rose of liberty that I want and not the artificial product. If your mind and the Congress mind, the mind of this Conference and the mind of the British people, mean the same thing by the same word, then you will find the amplest room for compromise, and will find the Congress itself always in a compromising spirit. But so long as there is not that one mind, that one definition, not one implication for the same word that you and I and we may be using, so long there is no compromise possible. How can there be any compromise so long as we each one of us has a different definition for the same words that we may be using. It is impossible, Prime Minister, I want to suggest to you in all humility that it is utterly impossible then to find a meeting ground, to find a ground where you can apply the spirit of compromise. And I am very grieved to have to say that up to now I have not been able to discover a common definition for the terms that we have been exchanging during all these weary weeks.

I was shown last week the Statute of Westminster by a sceptic, and he said: "Have you seen the definition of 'Dominion'?" I read the definition of 'Dominion', and naturally I was not at all perplexed or shocked to see that the word 'Dominion' was exhaustively defined, and it has not a general definition but a particular definition.

It simply said: the word 'Dominion' shall include Australia, South Africa, Canada and so on, ending with the Irish Free State. I do not think I noticed Egypt there. Then he said: "Do you see what your Dominion means?" It did not make any impression upon me. I do not mind what my Dominion means or what Complete Independence means. In a way I was relieved. I said I am now relieved from having to quarrel about the word 'Dominion', because I am out of it. But I want Complete Independence, and even so, so many Englishmen have said: "Yes, you can have Complete Independence, but what is the meaning of 'complete independence'?" And again we come to different definitions. Therefore, I say the Congress claim is registered as Complete Independence.

One of your great statesmen[1]—I do not think I should give his name—was debating with me, and he said: "Honestly, I did not know that you meant this by Complete Independence." He ought to have known, but he did not know, and I shall tell you what he did not know. When I said to him, "I cannot be a partner in an Empire," he said, "Of course, that is logical." I said, "But I want to become that.

It is not as if I shall be if I am compelled to, but I want to become a partner with Great Britain. I want to become a partner with the English people; but I want to enjoy precisely the same liberty that your people enjoy, and I want to seek this partnership not merely for the benefit of India, and not merely for mutual benefits; I want to seek this partnership in order that the great weight that is crushing the world to atoms may be lifted from off its shoulders."

This took place ten or twelve days ago. Strange as it may appear, I got a note from another Englishman whom also you know and whom also you respect. Among many things he writes: "I believe profoundly that the peace and happiness of mankind depend on our friendship," and as if I would not understand that, he says, "your people and mine." I must read to you what he also says, "And of all Indians you are the one that the real Englishman likes and understands."

He does not waste any words on flattery, and I do not think he has intended this last expression to flatter me. It will not flatter me in the slightest degree. There are many things in this note which, if I could share them with you, would perhaps make you understand better the significance of this expression, but let me tell you that, when he writes this last sentence, he does not mean me personally. I personally signify nothing, and I know I would mean nothing to any single Englishman; but I mean something to some Englishman because I represent a cause, because I seek to represent a nation, a great organization which has made itself felt. That is the reason why he says this.

But then, if I could possibly find that working basis, Prime Minister, there is ample room for compromise. It is friendship I crave. My business is not to throw overboard the slave-holder and tyrant. My philosophy forbids me to do so, and today the Congress has accepted that philosophy not as a creed, as it is to me, but as a policy, because the Congress believes that it is the right and best thing for India, a nation of three hundred and fifty millions, to do. A nation of 350 million people does not

---

1. Presumably, Lloyd George who met Gandhiji on November 18; *vide* "*Diary, 1931*".

need the dagger of the assassin, it does not need the position bowl, it does not need the sword, the spear or the bullet. It needs simply a will of its own, an ability to say "No", and that nation is today learning to say "No".

But what is it that that nation does ? Summarily, or at all, dismiss Englishmen? No. Its mission is today to convert Englishmen. I do not want to break the bond between England and India, but I do want to transform that bond. I want to transform that slavery into complete freedom for my country. Call it 'complete independence' or whatever you like, I will not quarrel about that word, and even though my countrymen may dispute with me for having taken some other word, I shall be able to bear down that opposition so long as the content of the word that you may suggest to me bears the meaning.

Hence I have times without number to urge upon your attention that the safeguards that have been suggested are completely unsatisfactory.

They are not in the interests of India. Three experts from the Federation of Commerce and Industry have in their own manner, each in his different manner, told you out of their expert experience how utterly impossible it is for anybody of responsible Ministers to tackle the problem of administration when 80 per cent of India's resources are mortgaged irretrivably. Better than I could have shown to you they have shown, out of the amplitude of their knowledge, what these financial safeguards mean for India.

They mean the complete cramping of India. They have discussed at this table financial safeguards, but that includes necessarily the question of Defence and the question of the Army. Yet, while I say that the safeguards are unsatisfactory as they have been presented, I have not hesitated to say, and I do not hesitate to repeat, that the Congress is pledged to giving safeguards endorsing safeguards which may be demonstrated to be in the interests of India.

At one of the sittings of the Federal Structure Committee, I had no hesitation in amplifying the admission and saying that these safeguards must be also of benefit to Great Britain. I do not want safeguards which are merely beneficial to India and prejudicial to the real interests of Great Britain. The fancied interests of India will have to be sacrificed. The fancied interests of Great Britain will have to be sacrificed. The illegitimate interests of India will have to be sacrificed.

The illegitimate interests of Great Britain will also have to be sacrificed. Therefore, again I repeat, if we have the same meaning for the same word, I will agree with Mr. Jayakar, with Sir Tej Bahadur Sapru, and other distinguished speakers who have spoken at this Conference. I will agree with them all, that we have after all, after all these labours, reached a substantial measure of agreement, but my despair, my grief, is that I do not read the same words in the same light. The implications of the safeguards of Mr. Jayakar, I very much fear, are different from my implications, and the implications of Mr. Jayakar and myself are perhaps only different from the implications that Sir Samuel Hoare, for instance, has in mind; I do not know. We have never really come to grips. We have never come to brass tacks as you put it, and I am anxious—I have been pinning to come to real grips and to brass tacks all these days and all these nights, and I have felt: 'Why are we not coming nearer and nearer together, and why are we wasting our time in eloquence, in oratory, in debating, and in scoring points?' Heaven knows I have no desire to hear my own voice. Heaven knows I have no desire to take part in any debating. I know that liberty is made of sterner stuff, and I know that the freedom of India is made of much sterner stuff. We have problems that would baffle any statesman. We have problems that other nations have not to tackle. But they do not baffle me; they cannot baffle those who have been brought up in the Indian climate. Those problems are there with us. Just as we have to tackle our bubonic plague, we have to tackle the problem of malaria. We have to tackle, as you have not, the problem of snakes and scorpions, monkeys, tigers and lions. We have to tackle these problems because we have been brought up under them. They do not baffle us. Somehow or other we have survived the ravages of these venomous reptiles and various creatures. So also shall we survive our problems and find a way out of these problems. But today you and we have come together at a Round Table and we want to find a common formula which will work. Please believe me that, whilst I abate not a title of the claim that I have registered on behalf of the Congress, which I do not propose a repeat here, while I withdraw not one word of the speeches that I had to make at the Federal Structure Committee, I am here to compromise; I am here to consider every formula that British ingenuity can prepare, every formula that the ingenuity of such constitutionalists as Mr. Sastri, Sir Tej Bahadur Sapru, Mr. Jayakar, Mr. Jinnah, Sir Muhammad Shafi, and a host of other constitutionalists can weave into being. I will not be baffled. I shall be here as long as I am required because I do not want to revive civil disobedience. I want to turn the truce that was arrived at, at Delhi, into a permanent settlement. But for heaven's sake give me, a frail man, 62 years gone, a little bit of a chance. Find a little corner for him and the organization that he represents. You distrust that organization though you may seemingly trust me. Do not for one moment differentiate me from the organization of which I am but a drop in the ocean. I am no greater than the organization to which I belong. I am infinitely smaller than that organization; and if you find me a place, if you trust me, I invite you to trust the Congress also. Your trust in me otherwise is a broken reed. I have no authority save that I dervie from the Congress. If you will work the Congress for all it is worth, then you will say goodbye to terrorism; then you will not need terrorism. Today you have to fight the school of terrorists which is there with your disciplined and organized terrorism, because you will be blind to the facts or the writing on the wall. Will you not see the writing that these terrorists are writing with their blood ? Will you not see that we do not want bread made of wheat, but we want bread of liberty; and without that liberty there are thousands today who are sworn not to give themselves peace or to give the country peace.

I urge you then to read that writing on the wall. I ask you not to try the patience of a people known to be proverbially patient. We speak of the mild Hindu, and the Mussalman also by contact, good or evil, with the Hindu, has himself become mild. And that mention of the Mussalman brings me to the baffling problem of minorities.

Believe me, that problem exists here, and I repeat what I used to say in India—I have not forgotten those words—that without the problem of minorities being solved there is no *swaraj* for India, there is no freedom for India. I know that, I realize it; and yet I came here in the hope, perchance, that I might be able to pull through a solution here.

But I do not despair of some day or other finding a real and living solution in connection with the minorities problem. I repeat what I have said elsewhere, that so long as the wedge in the shape of foreign rule divides community from community and class from class, there will be no real living solution, there will be no living friendship between these communities. It will be after all and at best a paper solution. But immediately you withdraw that wedge, the domestic ties, the domestic affections, the knowledge of common birth—do you suppose that all these will count for nothing?

Were Hindus and Mussalmans and Sikhs always at war with one another when there was no British rule, when there was no English face seen there? We have chapter and verse given to us by Hindu historians and by Mussalman historians to say that we were living in comparative peace even then. And Hindus and Mussalmans in the villages are not even today quarrelling. In those days they were not known to quarrel at all. The late Maulana Muhammad Ali often used to tell me, and he was himself a bit of an historian, he said, "If God"—'Allah', as he called

God—"gives me life, I propose to write the history of Mussalman rule in India; and then I will show through documents that British people have erred, that Aurangzeb was not so vile as he has been painted by the British historian; that the Mogul rule was not so bad as it has been shown to us in British history," and so on. And so have Hindu historians written. This quarrel is not old; this quarrel is coeval with this acute shame. I dare to say it is coeval with the British advent, and immediately this relationship, the unfortunate, artificial, unnatural relationship, between Great Britain and India is transformed into a natural relationship, when it becomes, if it does become, a voluntary partner ship to be given up, to be dissolved at the will of either party,when it becomes that you will find that Hindus, Mussalmans, Sikhs, Europeans, Anglo-Indians, Christians, untouchables, will all live together as one man.

I want to say one word about the Princes, and I shall have done. I have not said much about the Princes, nor do I intend to say much to-night about the Princes, but I should be wronging them, and I should be wronging the Congress if I did not register my claim, not with the Round Table Conference, but with the Princes. It is open to the Princes to give their terms on which they will join the Federation.

I have appealed to them to make the path easy for those who inhabit the other parts of India, and, therefore, I can only make these suggestions for their favourable consideration, for their earnest consideration. I think that if they accepted, no matter what they are, but some fundamental rights as the common property of all India, and if they accepted that position and allowed those rights to be tested by the Court, which will be again of thier own creation, and if they introduced elements—only elements—of representation on behalf of their subjects, I think that they would have gone a long way to conciliate their subjects. They would have gone a long way to show to the world and to show to the whole of India that they are also fired with a democratic spirit, that they do not want to remain undiluted autocrats, but that they want to become constitutional monarchs even as King George of Great Britain is.

Sir, a note has been placed in my hands by my friend Sir Abdul Qaiyum, and he says, will not I say one word about the Frontier Province ? I will, and it is this. Let India get what she is entitled to and what she can really take, but whatever she gets, whenever she gets it, let the Frontier Province get complete autonomy today. That Frontier will then be a standing demonstration to the whole of India, and therefore, the whole vote of the Congress will be given in favour of the Frontier

Province getting Provincial autonomy tomorrow. Prime Minister, if you can possibly get your Cabinet to endorse the proposition that from tomorrow the Frontier Province becomes a full-fledged autonomous Province, I shall then have a proper footing amongst the Frontier tribes and convene them to my assistance when those over the border cast an evil eye on India.

Last of all, my last is a pleasant task for me. This is, perhaps, the last time that I shall be sitting with you at negotiations. It is not that I want that. I want to sit at the same table with you in your closets and to negotiate and to plead with you and to go down on bended knees before I take the final leap and final plunge. But whether I have the good fortune to continue to tender my co-operation or not does not depend upon me. It largely depends upon you. But it may not even depend upon you. It depends upon so many circumstances over which neither you nor we may have any control whatsoever. Then let me perform this pleasant task of giving my thanks to all—from Their Majesties down to the poorest men in the East End, where I have taken up my habitation.

In that settlement which represents the poor people of the East End of London I have become one of them. They have accepted me as a member, and as a favoured member of their family. It will be one of the richest treasures that I shall carry with me. Here, too, I have found nothing but courtesy and nothing but a genuine affection from all with whom I have come in touch. I have come in touch with so many Englishmen. It has been a priceless privilege to me. They have listened to what must have often appeared to them to be unpleasant, although it was true. Although I have often been obliged to say these things to them, they have never shown the slightest impatience or irritation. It is impossible for me to forget these things. No matter what befalls me, no matter what the fortunes may be of this Round Table Conference, one thing I shall certainly carry with me—that is, that from high to low I have found nothing but the utmost courtesy and the utmost affection. I consider that it was well worth my paying this visit to England in order to find this human affection. It has enhanced, it has deepened my irrepressible faith in human nature that although Englishmen and Englishwomen have been fed upon lies so often that I see disfiguring your Press, that although in Lancashire, the Lancashire people had perhaps some reason for becoming irritated against me, I found no irritation, no resentment even in the operatives. The operatives, men and women, hugged me. They treated me as one of their own. I shall never forget that.

I am carrying with me thousands upon thousands of English friendships. I do not know them, but I read that affection in their eyes as early in the morning I walk through your streets. All this hospitality, all this kindness will never be effaced from my memory no matter what befalls my unhappy land. I thank you for your forbearance.

[*Indian Round Table Conference (Second Session) : Proceedings of the Plenary Sessions,* pp. 265-75]

55. A Manifesto[1]

[On or before December 5, 1931]

The Congress demands Complete Independence, including full control of defence forces, External Affairs and Finance, not excluding equal partnership with Britain determinable at the instance of either party, subject to the discharge or adjustment of mutual obligtions.

SAFEGUARDS

The Congress will accept safeguards necessary in the interests of India and is willing to take over all legitimate obligations, subject to examination by an impartial tribunal. The Congress is committed to a purely national solution of the question of minorities but will, if necessary, accept the principle of special reservation of seats in legislature for Muslims and Sikhs as a necessary evil for historical reasons.

UNTOUCHABLES

The cause of untouchables will be the special care of the Congress, and it would be unjust to treat them separately and thus give untouchablity a legal status when every attempt is being made to abolish the evil altogether.

NO RACIAL DISCRIMINATION

No political disability will be placed on anyone on the ground of race, creed or colour and, the Congress being wedded to adult franchise, there

1. The source says that this was a parting manifesto by Gandhiji issued by the Commonwealth of India League. Since no other version is available, it cannot be ascertained whether this was the complete text or only portions taken from the document.

should be no difficulty in representatives of any adult minority getting elected to the legislatures on the strength of national service.

[*The Hindustan Times*, 9-12-1931]

56. East and West

ANSWERS TO QUESTIONS[1]

[Lausanne,
December 8, 1931]

Q. How can East and West be brought together to work for peace?

A. This question was asked me some 5 years ago. And this was my answer: I, who belong to a subject nation, did not know how I could work for peace except by working for freedom, and if India could be helped to win freedom through peaceful means, it would be a very good combination for peace. I have said this after having attempted the deliverance of my country through absolutely non-violent and truthful means.

Q. Must we admit that, parallel to the use of non-violence in India, there should be a movement here also for use of non-violence for political ends?

A. If you are convinced that the means adopted in India are day by day bringing about the results we desire, and if you are convinced that India is doing so through spiritual means, then do so here too. Though there is greater difference in Europe. Friends have told me there were special difficulties in Europe to adopt non-violent means. Europe consists of martial races unlike India. Here all know how to wield arms. All the male population has at one time or another wielded arms. It is difficult for you to understand the efficacy and beauty of non-retaliation. Why not punish the wrongdoer—and in an exemplary manner?—that is what is asked everywhere here. Thus non-violence is quite foreign to Europe. For people belonging to such a country it is difficult to strike out a new path. Your economic life is so constructed that it is not possible, generally speaking, for an ordinary man to get out of the ordinary rut unless he

1. Although the source does not mention the occasion of the questions, these were presumably put at the very first meeting Gandhiji addressed at Lausanne.

faces poverty. And the fourth difficulty is that in Catholic Europe the iron discipline allows very little free play to the intellect. These are the four difficulties we have not to face in India which you have to face. If India becomes free through non-violent means, it won't enter upon war. But if she does, God will give me strength to fight India single-handed.

Q. What do you think of Einstein's call to military people not to take part in war?

A. My answer can only be one. That, if Europe can take up this method enthusiastically like me, I can only say Einstein has stolen the method from me. But if you want me to elaborate the thing, I would like to elaborate the method a little deeper. To refuse to render military service when a particular individual's time comes is to do the thing after all the time for combating the evil is practically gone. The disease is deeper. I suggest to you that those who are not on the Register for military service are equally participating in the crime. He or she, therefore, who supports a State so organized is, whether directly or indirectly, participating in the sin. It is fraught with immediate danger. Seeing that each man, old or young, takes part in this sin by contributing to the State (by paying the tax to the State) I said so long as I ate wheat supplied by the Navy, whilst I was doing everything short of being a soldier, it was best for me to be shot; otherwise I should go to the mountains and eat food grown by nature.

Similarly, all those who want to stop military service can do so by withdrawing all military cooperation. Refusal of military service is much more superficial than non-cooperation with a whole system which supports the State. But then your opportunity becomes so swift and so effective that you run the risk of not only being marched to jail, but of being thrown on the street. This was the position of Tolstoy.

Q. Are we not allowed to accept the State? Should we even refuse local self-government (including public works, schools, etc.)?

A. Now you have touched the tenderest spot in human nature.

This question touched me as author of non-cooperation in the initial stage. And before I could make up my mind, I said to myself: I co-operate with the State in two ways. There is no State, run either by Nero or Mussolini, which has no good points about it. We have in India what is called the Grand Trunk Road. It provides facility for millions of travellers; well-equipped hospitals, grand palaces built for schools. These we may consider to be good points. But I said, if the whole thing crushes the nation, I should not have anything to do with them. They are like the snake with a jewel but with poison fangs. So I came to the conclusion that British rule in India had stunted the nation and so I denied myself all the privileges. The gentlemanly way was to deny them.

The plea of self-defence is a wretched plea. You organize your country and society to prey upon ill-organized communities and nations. It is a bad thing. . . . .[1] What Einstein has said would occur only once in a year and only with a very few people. But your first duty is to non-cooperate with the State.

Q. Is there so deep a difference between a man in India and subjects of other countries which are free? Could not we say that our position is different from yours before we can quarrel with our State ?

A. Difference there undoubtedly is. As a member of a subject nation I could best help by shaking rid of my subjection. Here, I am asked how best to get out of military mentality. You are enjoying amenities on condition that you render military service to the State.

There you have to rid the State of military mentality. But you are in a hopeless minority. A State that rests on military violence is a bad State. You will then say that a majority of people are like that. They are. In examining the efficacy of the method I am able to draw a distinction between a free State and a subject State. If you want the minority to become a majority, you will have to deny the privileges.

[*From the manuscript of Mahadev Desai's Diary.*
Courtesy: Narayan Desai]

1. Some words here are not clear in the source.

57. God is Truth

SPEECH AT MEETING IN LAUSANNE[1]

[December 8, 1931]

FRIENDS,

Let me say how overwhelmed I have felt by the kindness of which I have been the recipient ever since I have been in your beautiful city. If earthly beauty can make a paradise, you are indeed living in a paradise. I come from a land where God has showered His choicest gift in the shape of earthly beauty. There is nothing grander you can find in all the earth than the beauty you can find in the uttermost extremity of India—Travancore—and yet as the train was slowly gliding by your beautiful lake and as we passed the villages so beautifully clean, I could not but be entranced by the sublimity of the beauty. And when I came here, I enjoyed and drank deep the beauty of your affection. I could trace your affection in the many searching and relevant questions put to me, where I had heart-to-heart talks and, now to crown all in this house of God, you have commenced your bombardment by a question which has been occupying me—the whole of my being—for nearly 50 years.

You have asked me why I consider that God is Truth. In my early childhood or youth, I was taught to repeat what in Hindu scriptures is one thousand names of God. Among the several little things one of the religious teachers my family had was a little pamphlet which contained these thousand names of God. But these thousand names of God were by no means an exhaustive list. We believe—and I think it is the truth—that God has as many names as there are creatures and, therefore, we also say that God is nameless and since God has many forms we also consider him formless, and since he speaks to me through many tongues we consider him to be speechless and so on. And so when I came to study

1. The source does not specify which meeting this was. But Mahadev Desai in his "Letter from Europe", published in *Young India*, 31-12-1931, says that this was the Conscientious Objectors' meeting organized by Pierre Ceresole and his friends and was held in a church. The speech and the answers to questions that followed were translated by Edmond Privat and Prof. Bovet.

Islam, I found that Islam too had many names, but I had not come to recognize God for my personal satisfaction as Truth. I would say for those who say God is love, God is love. But deep down in me I say God may be love, but God is Truth. If it is possible for the human tongue to give the fullest description of God, for myself I have come to the conclusion that God is Truth. But two years ago I went a step further and said Truth is God. You will see the fine distinction between the two statements: God is Truth and Truth is God. And that conclusion I came to after a continuous, relentless search after Truth which began so many years ago. I found that the nearest approach to Truth is through love. But I found also that love has many meanings, in the English language at least, and human love in the sense of passion becomes a degrading thing also. I found too that love in the sense of *ahimsa* and non-violence has only a limited number of votaries in the world. And as I made progress in my search, I made no dispute with "God is love". It is very difficult to understand "God is love" (because of a variety of meanings of love) but I never found a double meaning in connection with Truth and not even atheists have denied the necessity or power of Truth. Not only so. In their passion for discovering Truth, they have not hesitated even to deny the very existence of God— from their own point of view rightly. And it was because of their reasoning that I saw that I was not going to say "God is Truth", but "Truth is God". Therefore, I recall the name of Charles Bradlaugh—a great Englishman who lived 50 years ago. He delighted to call himself an atheist. But knowing as I do something of his life. I never considered him an atheist. I would call him a godfearing man although he would reject the claim, and I know his face would redden. I would say: No Mr. Bradlaugh, you are a truth-fearing man, not a god-fearing man, and I would disarm his criticisms by saying "Truth is God" as I have disarmed criticisms of many a young man.

Add to this the great difficulty that millions have taken the name of God and have committed nameless atrocities in the name of God. Not that scientists do not very often commit cruelties in the name of Truth.

I know today in the name of Truth and science inhuman cruelties are perpetrated on animals when men perform vivisection. To me it is a denial of God whether you recognize Him as Truth or by any other name. So I know that there are these difficulties in one's way no matter how you describe God. But human mind is a limited thing, and you have to labour under limitation when you think of a being or entity who is beyond the power of man to grasp. But we have another thing in Hindu philosophy viz., God alone is and nothing else exists.

Now the same truth you find emphasized and exemplified in the *Kalama* of Islam. There you find it clearly stated—a Mussalman has to recite it at all his prayers—that God alone is and nothing else is and that is the same about Truth. And the name that Sanskrit has for Truth literally means that which is—*Sat*. For these and several other reasons that I can give you I have come to the conclusion that the definition. "Truth is God" gives me the greatest satisfaction. And when you want to find Truth is God, the only inevitable means is love, non-violence—and since I believe that ultimately means and ends are convertible terms I should not hesitate to say that God is love.

Q. What is Truth ?

A. A difficult question, but I have solved it for myself by saying that it is what the voice within tells one. How then, you ask, different people think of different and contrary truths?

Seeing that the human mind works through innumerable media and that evolution of the human mind is not the same for all, it follows that what may be truth for one may be untruth for another and hence those who have made these experiments have come to the conclusion that there are certain conditions to making experiments. Just as for science there is an indispensable course common for all, even so it is true for persons who would make experiments in the spiritual realm—they must submit to certain conditions. And since everybody says it is his inner voice which speaks, you must listen to the voice, and you will then find out your limitations as you go along the path. Therefore, we have the belief based upon uninterrupted experience that those who would make diligent search after Truth—God—must go through these vows: the vow of truth—speaking and thinking of truth, the vow of *brahmacharya*, of non-violence, poverty and non-possession. If you do not take these five vows you may not embark on the experiments.

There are several other things which were prescribed, but I must not take you through all those. But those who have made these experiments know that it is not proper for everyone to claim to hear the voice of conscience and it is because we have at the present moment everybody claiming the right of conscience without going through any discipline whatsoever that there is so much untruth being delivered to a bewildered world. All, therefore, that I can in all humility present to you is that Truth is not to be found by anybody who has not got an abundant sense of humility. If you would swim on the bosom of the ocean of Truth, you must reduce yourself to a zero.

Further than this I may not tonight go along this fascinating path.

Q. What do you think of Christianity?

A. A delicate question. Christianity is very good; many Christians are very bad.

The economic crisis can be relieved if people love poverty. I would ask you to emphasize the word 'love' here. There would be no economic crisis if they really loved poverty. Economic crises arise because our eyes lust after the property of our neighbour. Forced poverty is to be found on earth simply because many have more than they are entitled to. There would bo no poverty on earth if we made a sacred resolution that we would have no more than we need for our creature comforts. And it would not do for a millionaire to sluggishly say that he owns millions because he needs those for his creature comforts. On the contrary, a man who is poor will continually examine himself and find out what are the superfluous things he keeps for himself and, if you conduct yourself in a sportsmanlike spirit from day to day, you will be astounded at the fewness of things you require.

I would like very much, being in the House of God, to say: cast out the beam from your eye before you dare to see a mote in your neighbour's eye. If we would but be good enough to take care of ourselves, I have very little doubt that the world would take care of itself.

Q. What is your message to the women of Europe ?

A. I do not know if I have the courage to give the message without incurring their wrath. I would direct their steps to the women of India who rose in one mass last year and I really believe, if India would drink in the nectar of non-violence, Europe would do it through women. Woman I hold is the personification of self-sacrifice, but unfortunately today women do not realize what a tremendous advantage they hold over men. As Tolstoy would say, they are labouring under the hypnotic influence of man. If they would realize the nobility of non-violence, they would not consent to be called the weaker sex.

Tolstoy and Ruskin renewed my faith in things which I had only darkly felt.

Q. What is the difference between non-resistance and your resistance without violence ?

A. It has been often said that the doctrine of non-violence I owe to Tolstoy. It is not the whole truth, but there again I derive the greatest strength from his writings. But as Tolstoy himself admitted, the non-resistance method I had cultivated and elaborated in South Africa was different from the non-resistance Tolstoy had written upon and recommended. This I say in no derogation of Tolstoy's fame. He is not an apt pupil who will not build upon foundations laid by his teacher for him. He only deserves a good teacher who would add to the legacy that teacher would leave for him. I should be an unworthy son to my father if I should not add to my inheritance, and so I have always regarded it as a matter of pride that, thanks be to God, what I had learned from Tolstoy has fructifiez a hundredfold. Tolstoy talked of passive resistance largely, but non-resistance elaborated in Transvaal was a force infinitely more active than resistance that an armed man can devise and, I am glad to recall the fact that in a long letter he wrote to me unsolicited he said that his eyes were fixed upon me wherever I was. And if you will study the movements in South Africa and India, you will find how this thing is capable of infinite expansion.

Q. Is not non-resistance submission ?

A. Passive resistance is regarded as the weapon of the weak but the resistance for which I had to coin a new name altogether for want of a phrase in the English language and not to have this mixed up with non-resistance, namely, '*satyagraha*', is not conceived in any shape or form as a weapon of the weak but as a weapon of the strongest. But its matchless beauty is that it can be wielded by the weak in body, [by the] oldest and even by children if they have strong hearts and, since resistance through *satyagraha* is offered through self-suffering, it is a weapon open pre-eminently to women. And we found in actual experience in India last year that women in many instances surpassed men in suffering. And children also—thousands—played a noble part in this campaign. For the idea of self-suffering became contagious and they embarked upon amazing acts of self-denial. Supposing that women of Europe and children of Europe became fired with love of humanity and said our men are doing wrong by arming, they would take them by storm and reduce militarism to nothingness in an incredibly short time. And the underlying idea is that children, women and others have the same identical soul, same potentiality. The question is of drawing out the limitless power of Truth. But I must again call a halt to this fascinating subject.

Q. What is the value of vegetarian diet?

A. Priceless value for me, not for beef-eating Europe. But I do feel that spiritual progress does demand at some stage—an inexorable demand—that we should cease to kill our fellow-creatures for satisfaction of our bodily wants. The beautiful lines of Goldsmith occur to me as I tell you of my vegetarian fad: No flocks that range the valley free. To slaughter I condemn; Taught by the Power that pities me I learn to pity them.

Q. What about liquor?

A. Liquor is as we say in invention of the devil. In Islam it is said that when satan began to beguile men and women, he dangled before them this red water. I have seen that it has not only robbed men of their money but of reason; they have for the time being forgotten the distinction between wife and mother, lawful and unlawful. See barristers rotting in gutters, taken home by the police. I have found on two occasions captains of steamers dead drunk, incapable of keeping charge of their boats, and someone else had to take charge before they came to their senses. For both flesh and liquor the sovereign rule is: we must not live in order to eat and drink and be merry but eat in order to make our bodies temples of God and to use them for the service of man. Liquor may be a medical necessity; when life is extinct, it may be possible to prolong it. It is possible to keep perfect health without flesh or meat. If you want to develop cruelty in a soldier, he would not have it unless he takes flesh or meat. You may not know that Japan, when she took to imitating Western civilization, made beef-eating compulsory.

Q. Is non-cooperation in military matters balanced by service in non-military matters?

A. That must be the last question. It is a good question. This was very exhaustively dealt with at the first meeting of a few friends.

Briefly, I entirely agree that both these services go hand in hand. Non-cooperation in military service and service in non-military matters is not compatible. Friendly relations may be cultivated. Definitely military service is an ill-chosen word. Because you are all the while giving military service by deputy because you are supporting a State which is based on military service. In the Transvaal we had this law.

There were some who were debarred—Indians, Bantus, Zulus—by law.

But they were obliged to pay money. They were commuting that service. You will have to extend the scope of non-cooperation, how I shall not say. There is no limit to extending service to our neighbours across our State-made frontiers. God never made those frontiers.

[*From the manuscript of Mahadev Desai's Diary. Courtesy:* Narayan Desai]

58. Organization and Traning for Workers

SPEECH AT CENTRAL BOARD MEETING OF HARIJAN SEVAK SANGH

[Benares[1]
July 29, 1934]

There are two questions on which I have to speak to you—one in connection with the nature of the whole organization and the other in connection with the idea of having a training institution for workers for a period or for life. To take up the first question, I know there is a general desire to introduce an element of democracy—voting, election, etc.—into our organization. I was torn between two opposites; but, after having gone through this nine months' tour, I have come to the conclusion that in an organization like ours there is no room for election, democracy or anything of that sort. Ours is a different kind of institution. It is not a people's organization in the ordinary sense. We handle money merely as self-appointed trustees, using it solely for the benefit of the Harijans, and in such a manner that it finds its way directly into their pockets. Ours is an organization formed with a view to doing our duty by those whom we have despised. We are an organization to give effect to the pledge given to Harijans at Bombay by the great meeting[2] held under the chairmanship of Pandit Madan Mohan Malaviyaji. The people who pay to the Harijan Fund do so, we assume, in a penitent spirit, and all we have to do is to utilize it for the Harijans. To run an elective institution means expense and delay. Our aim is to distribute the funds among the Harijans with as little expenditure and delay as possible. We do not want any intervening medium between Harijans and ourselves. We are mere trustees, and the trust descends to those whom we appoint. There are people who say the donors ought to have a voice in the administration. I should say, they do

1. Published under the title "A Talk to the Workers", this appeared as "a condensed summary" of Gandhiji's speech "at the conclusion of the proceedings" at Kashi Vidyapith on July 28 and 29.
2. *Vide* "Resolution at The Hindu Leaders Conference, Bombay", 25-9-1932.

not know. To me, he who pays a pie is as much a donor as, say, Ghanshyamdas Birla, who pays ten to fifty thousand. May be, the value of that pie is greater than the ten thousand rupees that Ghanshyamdas may give. I have seen in Orissa poor people untying their knots and parting with their coppers. That has given me more hope and greater pleasure than the thousands, however, willingly given. The thousands without the coppers would be of little use in this cause of self-purification. But the thousands of the poor donors will never receive the vote. We do not even know their names. And still we are as much responsible to them as to the big donors, or even more. We are a charitable institution, depending for its existence upon honest and efficient management. And if we are to have the highest amount of efficiency, we have to select the best and the most honest workers.

Having said this, I leave it entirely to you to decide. I look at the movement as purely religious, moral or humanitarian. It is to me purely one of reparation and penitence. I do not know to what extent all the lakhs of donors share with me the belief in the penitential character of the work. But so far as I am concerned, I would declare that there is nothing in my mind save the desire to expiate for sins we have been guilty of all these years. Therefore, I cannot think of the movement in terms of any political end. Not that it will not have political results, but we need not give a moment's thought to them.

The results will be surer, our relation with Mussalmans and other communities will be infinitely purer, if we keep only the larger end in view, and no other, as a result of this movement. I want everyone to dismiss the thought from his mind that our aim has been to raise an army of six crores of *goondas*. That certainly is not how I would think of defending Hinduism. I am sure that it can stand against the whole world, if it is purged of the curse of untouchability. This is no narrow movement; it is, I hope, the broadest of movements of our times.

The second question is easier. As a matter of fact, it follows from what I have said. I believe in the ideal of life-service. I want servants whose sole ambition is to devote themselves body, mind and soul to the *Harijan* cause. If we had ten thousand such workers—I make bold to say even if we had a thousand, we should have startling results. I would welcome a training institution for such workers. In Pinetown, near Durban in South Africa, there is a Trappist monastery[1].

1. *Vide* "A Band of Vegetarian Missionaries".

The rigour observed at the time, now more than thirty years ago, when I visited the place, was very great. They had nothing like privacy for themselves; they had one long hall in which they stretched themselves; they had to get up at 2.30 a.m.; they had purely vegetarian food; they strictly observed the vow of silence. Only two or three who had to go to the market or to speak to visitors could speak.

All others had to work silently. They were giving instruction to the Zulus. Their proselytization consisted in working among the Zulus and giving them the best of their life. They were workers for life.

They were all learned *sannyasins*. They added to their learning a calling. They were carpenters, smiths, porters, shoemakers. They made all sorts of experiments. Their monastery was a model of beauty, a veritable garden, with not a particle of dust anywhere, and there was a sweet silence pervading the whole atmosphere. Zulu students were taken as raw youths and discharged as accomplished artisans. My idea is to have a training institution of this type. If anything, I would do better. But we are today fallen from grace. We used to have this rigorous discipline in our country but we have not progressed, while they have progressed. They have made researches and increased their heritage. If we can make anything like an approach to them, I should be satisfied. If we can get even five persons who are prepared to forget father, mother and children, and to devote themselves to Harijan service, I would have them. They would form the nucleus. But if we cannot aim so high, we may conduct an industrial home or a Harijan hostel or some other thing. Sheth Shivratan Mohatta has an industrial school in Karachi out of an endowment made by his brother. He had got two teachers from Dayalbagh (Agra), which has its own aroma and its own Western finish. The students are kept well, there is a good boarding-house and a good dormitory. There are two departments—boot-making and tailoring. It is not a training institution but an industrial home. The Harijans there are conscious that they will not be discharged without being taught some handicraft, so that, when they come out, they will not be thrown on the streets. We may multiply such institutions.

We, Harijan workers, have not done justice to ourselves. Many of us are not workers even to a passable type. They have not given their whole time to their work; they do it in a leisurely fashion. I have often asked them, 'Do you read Harijan?' They have said, 'No'. Out of the three editions of this weekly—English, Gujarati and Hindi—English and Gujarati are self-supporting; Hindi is not. Sufficient reception has not been given to these journals, though much labour is put forth in the preparation of these. Even in this preparation, sufficient help is not coming forth. Workers do not send information, facts. They do not go in for a discussion of problems as they occur from day to day. For, problems occur to workers and not to thinkers.

If our workers were alive to their work, they would flood the editors with matter from which poor editors might find it difficult to make selections. Today they are starved. *Harijan* is a workers' journal, for their guidance and for the interchange of their thoughts. I do not want for it essays. I have been pained to be asked questions by workers who should find the answers in the journal, if they were reading it carefully. But many do not read it at all. If you do not read the budget of news collected in these pages, how are you going to hold the movement together? You must know what is being done by sister organizations. We have not got itinerant messengers who will take the story of the vicissitudes of institutions from place to place. That would be a costly medium. But we have Harijan. It is full of information, but it can still be filled with more accurate information and greater variety.

Please do not run away with the idea that I am not capable of recognizing what little has been done. Nice things are there, but they do not need to be recounted. Virtue is its own reward. But I am an inspector. I must show you the blemishes and not tickle your ears with praise for the good things that you have done.

A word about the Harijan Ashram at Sabarmati. It is a big thing. It is not being made full use of. It is nobody's fault. Poor Parikshitlal is there, but it is beyond his capacity to conduct it. He has also to look to the work of the whole of Gujarat. To utilize this institution fully would be an immense task for anybody. The burden of conducting and maintaining it will be on trustees specially appointed. Many baffling problems arise there from day to day. You can now understand why we want men of the Trappist type before we can make the fullest use of the big Ashram at Sabarmati.

[*Harijan,* 24-8-1934]

59. *Gita*—The Mother

SPEECH AT BENARES HINDU UNIVERSITY

[August 1, 1934]

The Hindu University is not new to me. Since its inception[1] Malaviyaji had me associated with it and it remains exactly so to this day. If there has been any change, the association has been strengthened and my regard for this University is increasing. With the progress of this University there should be progress in *dharma* as well; this is Pandit Malaviyaji's idea. I hope students will acquire learning and will make good use of it and not accept a narrow view of religion.

A broad-minded religion accepts all other religions in its fold. This is the auspicious occasion of Lokamanya Tilak's anniversary and I have come to tell you what we should do about one aspect of religion. I shall not speak of Lokamanya's political strength; I have also no freedom to touch upon that subject. I wish to tell you at this time what Tilak Maharaj said about religion. You should know that Lokamanya had great sympathy in his heart for the Harijan brothers.

In our exchange of thoughts and ideas with each other, he said that in the *dharmashastra* there is no sanction for untouchability and there cannot be because truth ranks highest in the Hindu religion. If truth was put in one scale of the balance and all the rest in the other, even then the scale with truth in it will go down. No *pundit* can find anywhere in the *Vedas*, *Puranas* or history things said contrary to the principles of religion. There is no mention of untouchability in other religions. Hinduism alone seems to have taken a monopoly. There are several things mentioned in our religion which are not found elsewhere. If the *varna* system is abolished in our country, then Hinduism will also disappear. There is no connection between the *varnashrama* and the present-day concept of untouchability. My faith in this is growing stronger and after nine months of this tour I can avow it with greater

---

1. For Gandhiji speech on the occasion, *vide* "Speech at Benares Hindu University", 6-2-1916.

conviction...[1] I have been asked by Acharya Anandshankar Dhruva to say a few words on the *Gita* to the students of the Kashi Vishvavidyalaya.

It is not without hesitation that I have accepted the invitation. What right can a layman like myself have to discourse on a theme like this in the presence of a savant like him? I have neither his profound scholarship, nor the deep study of our ancient religious lore which Pandit Malaviyaji, for instance, has. Sardar Vallabhbhai, in his characteristic manner, asked me this morning whether scavengers, cultivators, and weavers like him and me were not altogether out of court in a city of *pundits* like Kashi and in the presence of such learned *pundits* as Malaviyaji and Acharya Dhruva, and in a way he was right. But I have come here, not with any pretence to learning, but only to tell you what reaction the *Gita* had on lay natures like mine and the Sardar's. I wonder Whether you have even a distant idea of how profoundly it affected the Sardar during his imprisonment. I am here to bear witness to the fact that in the Yeravda Prison it gave him more strength and sustenance than meat and drink. To read the *Gita* in the original he set about learning Sanskrit with the help of Pandit Satavalekar's Sanskrit self-instructor, and once he had started on it, the book seldom left his hands. It occupied him from morning till night. It was not an obsession of an unoccupied mind, as you might be tempted to think, but the result of deep thought. 'Which is the one book that can be to the Hindus what the *Bible* is to the Christians or the *Koran* to the Maussalmans?' We asked ourselves. Is it the *Vedas*? No. The *Bhagavata*? No. *Devipurana*? No. Early in my childhood I had felt the need of a scripture that would serve me as an unfailing guide through the trials and temptations of life. The *Vedas* could not supply that need, if only because to learn them would require fifteen to sixteen years of hard study at a place like Kashi, for which I was not ready then. But the *Gita*, I had read somewhere, gave within the compass of its 700 verses the quintessence of all the *Shastras* and the *Upanishads*. That decided me. I learnt Sanskrit to enable me to read the *Gita*. Today the *Gita* is not only my *Bible* or my *Koran*; it is more than that—it is my mother. I lost my earthly mother who gave me birth long ago; but this eternal Mother has completely filled her place by my side ever since. She has never changed, She has never failed me. When I am in difficulty or distress, I seek refuge in Her bosom. Often in the course of my struggle against untouchability, I am confronted with conflicting opinions delivered by

1. This paragraph is translated from the Hindi report in *Harijan Sevak*. What follows in reproduced from *Harijan*. It appeared under the title "*Gita*—The Mother".

doctors of learning. Some of them tell me that untouchability as it is practised today has no sanction in Hinduism and they bless my efforts to eradicate it; but there are some others who maintain that untouchability has been an essential part of Hinduism from the very beginning. Which authority should I follow under the circumstances ? I feel absolutely at sea. The *Vedas* and the *Smritis* are of no avail to me. I then approach the Mother and say, "Mother, these learned *pundits* have put me in a predicament. Help me out of my perplexity." And the Mother, with a smile, says in reply: "The assurance[1] held out by me in the ninth chapter is not meant for the Brahmins only, but for the sinner and the outcaste, the downtrodden and the disinherited, too.' But in order to be worthy of that promise, we must be obedient and devoted children of the Mother and not disobedient and disloyal children, who only make a pretence of devotion.

It is sometimes alleged against the *Gita* that it is too difficult a work for the man in the street. The criticism, I venture to submit, is ill founded.

The *Gita* enabled the late Lokamanya, out of his encyclopaedic learning and study, to produce a monumental commentary. For him it was a store-house of profound truths to exercise his intellect upon. But that need not scare away a lay reader.

If you find all the eighteen chapters too difficult to negotiate, make a careful study of the first three chapters only. They will give you in a nutshell what is propounded in greater detail and from different angles in the remaining fifteen chapters. Even these three chapters can be further epitomized in a few verses that can be selected from these chapters. Add to this the fact that at three distinct[2] places the *Gita* goes even further and exhorts to us to leave alone all 'isms' and take refuge in the Lord alone, and it will be seen how baseless in the charge that the message of the *Gita* is too subtle or complicated for lay minds to understand. The *Gita* is the universal Mother. She turns away nobody. Her door is wide open to anyone who knocks. A true votary of the *Gita* does not know what disappointment is. He ever dwells in perennial joy and peace that passeth understanding. But that peace and joy come not to the sceptic or to him who is proud of his intellect or learning. It is reserved only for the humble in spirit who brings to Her worship a fullness of faith and an undivided singleness of mind.

There never was a man who worshipped Her in that spirit and went back disappointed.

---

1. *Bhagavad Gita*, IX. 32.
2. *Bhagavad Gita*, III. 30, VIII. 7 and XVIII. 66.

Our students are prone to be upset by trifles. A trivial thing like failure in an examination plunges them into the darkest despair. The *Gita* inculcates upon them the duty of perseverance in the face of seeming failure. It teaches us that we have a right to action only but not to the fruit thereof and that success and failure are one and the same thing at bottom.[1] It calls upon us to dedicate ourselves, body, mind and soul, to pure duty, and not to become mental voluptuaries at the mercy of all chance desires and undisciplined impulses. As a *satyagrahi*, I can declare that the *Gita* is ever presenting me with fresh lessons. If somebody tells me that this is my delusion, my reply to him would be that I shall hug this delusion as my richest treasure.

I would advise the students to begin their day with an early morning recitation of the *Gita*. I am a lover and devotee of Tulsidas. I adore the great spirit that gave to an aching world the all healing *mantra* of *Ramanama*. But I am here today, not to present Tulsidas to you, but to ask you to take up the study of the *Gita*, not in a carping or critical spirit, but in a devout and reverent spirit. Thus approached, She will grant your every wish. It is no joke, I admit, remembering by heart all the eighteen chapters but it is worthwhile to make the attempt. Once you have tasted of its sweet nectar, you attachment to it will grow from day to day. The recitation of the *Gita* verses will support you in your trials and console you in your distress, even in the darkness of solitary confinement. And, if with these verses on your lips you receive the final summons and deliver up your spirit, you will attain *Brahmanirvana*—the Final Liberation. What that blessed state is, I leave it for your learned Acharyas to explain to you.

[*Harijan Sevak*, 10-8-1934; also *Harijan*, 24-8-1934]

---

1. *Bhagavad Gita*, II. 47 and 48.

60. A Restatement of Faith

SPEECH AT EXHIBITION GROUND, FAIZPUR

[December 27, 1936]

This speech was scheduled for 8.30. I a m sorry that it is being delivered so late at 9.15. But there was no alternative. People have turned up here in such large numbers and as our exhibition has only screens of unseasoned bamboo for walls, if everyone makes a rush for it they would collapse. Hence, arrangements had to be made to protect things and the organizers took some time in doing this. They were not prepared for such an onrush. You will feel that there has been a trick in putting my speech on the programme. This was deliberate. If for no other reason, people would come to hear me and give two annas for the exhibition. While doing so if they by accident or mistake purchase some *khadi* and have a glimpse of rural art, they will earn some merit without any particular effort and so will I.

You must have seen that the whole of Tilaknagar is like an exhibition. The credit for this goes to Shri Nandalal Bose. It was he who decided that the plan for both the exhibition and the Congress should be the same. Only a paltry sum has been spent in doing so. I do not know of any Congress session which has been organized at such a low cost. Of course, in my opinion, some expenses have been unnecessarily incurred, but, then, is this not the first Congress to be held in a village? A fair amount had to be spent in obtaining land. But we have done something which will encourage us to hold the future sessions of the Congress in villages. You can see the crowd is increasing. There are many volunteers, but they seem to get lost in the crowd. There are so many persons who have to be fed that it has become difficult to make arrangements for them. .[1]

I am going to say nothing new today. The cult of the spinningwheel

---

1. This is taken from the Gujarati version published in Harijanbandhu. What follows is reproduced from Mahadev Desai's report in *Harijan*, "A Restatement of Faith". The report was revised by Gandhiji.

is 18 years old. I said in 1918 that we could win *swaraj* through the spinning wheel. My faith in the ability of the spinning wheel is as bright today as when I first declared it in 1918. It has become richer for the experience and experiment of all these years.

But you should know the implications of the wheel or *khadi*, its product. It is not enough that one wears *khadi* on ceremonial occasions or even wears it to the exclusion of all other cloth if he surrounds himself with *videshi* in everything else. *Khadi* means the truest *swadeshi* spirit, identification with the starving millions.

Let there be no mistake about my conception of *swaraj*. It is complete independence of alien control and complete economic independence. So at one end you have political independence, at the other the economic. It has two other ends. One of them is moral and social, the corresponding end is *dharma*, i.e., religion in the highest sense of the term. It includes Hinduism, Islam, Christianity, etc., but is superior to them all. You may recognize it by the name of Truth, not the honesty of expedience but the living Truth that pervades everything and will survive all destruction and all transformation.

Moral and social uplift may be recognized by the term we are used the term we are used to, i.e., non-violence. Let us call this the square of *swaraj*, which will be out of shape if any of its angles is untrue. In the language of the Congress we cannot achieve this political and economic freedom without truth and non-violence, in concrete terms without a living faith in God and hence moral and social elevation.

By political independence I do not mean an imitation of the British House of Commons, or the Soviet rule of Russia or the Fascist rule of Italy or the Nazi rule of Germany. They have systems suited to their genius. We must have ours suited to ours. What that can be is more than I can tell. I have described it as *Ramarajya* i.e., sovereignty of the people based on pure moral authority. The Congress constitutions of Nagpur and Bombay for which I am mainly responsible are an attempt to achieve this type of *swaraj*.

Then take economic independence. It is not a product of industrialization of the modern or the Western type. Indian economic independence means to me the economic uplift of every individual, male and female, by his or her own conscious effort. Under that system all men and women will have enough clothing—not the mere loin-cloth, but what we understand by the term necessary articles of clothing and enough food including milk and butter which are today denied to millions.

This brings me to socialism. Real socialism has been handed down to us by our ancestors who taught: "All land belongs to *Gopal*, where then is the boundary line? Man is the maker of the line and he can therefore unmake it."[1] *Gopal* literally means shepherd; it also means God. In modern language it means the State, i.e., the people.

That the land today does not belong to the people is too true. But the fault is not in the teaching. It is in us who have not lived up to it.

I have no doubt that we can make as good an approach to it as is possible for any nation, not excluding Russia, and that without violence. The most effective substitute for violent dispossession is the wheel with all its implications. Land and all property is his who will work it. Unfortunately, the workers are or have been kept ignorant of this simple fact.

Let us now see how India came to be utterly impoverished. History tells us that the East India Company ruined the cotton manufacture and by all kinds of means made her dependent upon Lancashire for her cloth, the next great necessity of man. It is still the largest item of import. It thus created a huge army of partially unemployed men and women counted in millions and gave them no other employment in return. With the destruction of hand-ginning, carding, spinning and weaving to a certain extent, perished the other industries of India's villages. Continuous unemployment has induced in the people a kind of laziness which is most depressing. Thus whilst the alien rule is undoubtedly responsible for the growing pauperism of the people, we are more responsible for it. If the middle class people, who betrayed their trust and bartered away the economic independence of India for a mess of pottage, would now realize their error and take the message of the wheel to the villagers and induce them to shed their laziness and work at the wheel, we can ameliorate the condition of the people to a great extent. It would be a terrible thing if laziness replaces industry and despair triumphs over hope.

The parliamentary programme is in the air. It has come to stay and rightly. But it cannot bring us independence. Its function is strictly limited though quite necessary. Its success will prevent the Government from claiming that Ordinance rule or any measure restricting our progress to the goal was sanctioned by popular representatives. Hence, the necessity for voters voting for the Congress candidates who dare not vote for unpopular measures without being liable to Congress discipline.

---

1. सबै भूमि गोपाल की वामें अष्ठक कहां ?
फाके मनमें अयक है, सोई अश्क रहा ।

The success of that programme may also bring some relief in individual cases such as the release of Shri Subhash Bose or the detenus. But that is not independence, political or economic.

Then look at it in another way. Only a limited number of men and women can become members of legislatures, say 1,500. How many from this audience can become legislators? And just now no more than $3\frac{1}{2}$ crores can vote for these 1,500 members. What about the remaining $31\frac{1}{2}$ crores? In our conception of *swaraj* they are the real masters and the $3\frac{1}{2}$ crores are the former's servants who in their turn are masters of the 1,500. Thus the latter are doubly servants, if they will be true to their trust.

But the $31\frac{1}{2}$ crores have also a trust to discharge towards themselves and the nation of which they as individuals are but tiny parts. And if they remain lazy, know nothing of *swaraj* and how to win it, they will themselves become slaves of the 1,500 legislators. For my argument the $3\frac{1}{2}$ crores of voters here belong to the same category as the $31\frac{1}{2}$ crores. For if they do not become industrious and wise, they will be so many pawns in the hands of 1,500 players, it is of little consequence whether they are Congressmen or otherwise. If the voters wake up only to register their votes every three years or more and then go off to sleep, their servants will become their masters.

The only way I know to prevent such a catastrophe is for the 35 crores to be industrious and wise. This they can only be if they will take up the spinning wheel and the other village industries. They will not take to them unintelligently. I can tell you from experience that the effort means adult education of the correct type and requires possession of patience, moral fibre and a scientific and practical knowledge of the industry the worker seeks to introduce in the village of his choice.

In such a scheme the spinning wheel becomes its centre. If you call it the solar system, the wheel becomes the golden disc and the industries the planets revolving round it in obedience to the inviolable law of the system. When the sun lost its illuminating power by the action of the East India Company, the planets lost their power and became invisible or almost so. The sun is being reinstated in his past status now and the planets are regaining their motion in exact proportion to the strength of the sun.

Now perhaps you will understand the meaning and the message of the *charkha*. I said in 1920 that if the Congress truly and successfully worked the programme laid down in 1920 including the fourfold constructive programme of *khadi*, communal unity, prohibition of intoxicants and removal by Hindus of untouchability, the attainment of *swaraj* within a year was a certainty. I am neither sorry for nor ashamed of having made that declaration. I would like to repeat that declaration before you today. Whenever, the fourfold programme is achieved in its fulness, you can have *swaraj* for the asking. For you will then have attained the power to take it. Just think for a moment where the *charkha* stands today in your faith or action.

Is the mutual secret assassination of Bombay a sign of communal unity? Where is total prohibition? Have the Hindus rid themselves of untouchability root and branch? One swallow does not make a summer. Travancore's great Proclamation may be the beginning of the end, but it is not the end. If we remove the untouchability of Harijans, but treat Mussalmans or others as such, we have not removed the blot. "All land belongs to God" has a deeper meaning. Like the earth we, of it, also belong to God, and hence we must all feel like one and not erect boundary walls and issue prohibition decrees against one another.

This is the non-violent way in action. If we could fulfil this programme, there would be no need to offer civil disobedience, there would certainly be no need to do violence. Thirty-five crores of people conscious of their numerical strength as one man would be ashamed of doing violence to 70,000 white men in India, no matter how capable they are of dealing destruction and administering poison gas to millions in a moment. The *charkha* understood intelligently can spin not only economic salvation but can also revolutionize our minds and hearts and demonstrate to us that the non-violent approach to *swaraj* is the safest and the easiest. Though the progress may seem slow, it will prove quickest in the long run.

Believe me if Jawaharlal Nehru is not in jail today, it is not because he is afraid of it. He is quite capable of walking into prison doors as of mounting the gallows with a smile on his lips. I do not think I have lost the power or faith in the efficacy of such suffering. But there is no issue for it today as far as I can see. But what I feel is that all that suffering can be avoided if by united faith and will we achieve the constructive programme. If we can, I promise that we won't need to struggle with or against the British nation, but Lord Linlithgow will come to us and own that he was mistaken in his disbelief of our non-violence and truth and will undertake on behalf of his nation to abide by our decisions. Whether he does or not, I am working towards that and no other. "All belong to God".

[*Harijanbandhu,* 3-1-1937, *and Harijan,* 2-1-1937]

61. Religious Revival

SPEECH AT EZHAVAS' MEETING, TRIVANDRUM

[January 13, 1937]

I wish I were able to speak to you in your own mother tongue. I am sorry that I have not yet been able to learn the very musical language that you speak, and it is a matter of equal sorrow to me that you do not understand the national language of India—Hindi-Hindustani. Therefore, we have to fall back on the cumbrous process of translation. But it is inevitable if I am at all to reach your hearts somewhat. I assure you I do not want to make here an idle speech, nor am I fond of hearing my own voice. I know that silence is often better than speech. But I know also from experience that there are occasions when speech becomes a necessity, and probably this is one of those occasions.

I thank you very much for having asked me to preside over this celebrations meeting. I thank you also for presenting me with this address. You have already tendered your hearty congratulations to His Highness the Maharaja and Maharani and Sachivottama Sir C.P. Ramaswami Iyer. I want to associate myself fully with the expression of your joy and congratulations. The joy is written on the numerous faces of this assembly over the restoration of a right which was taken away from you, no one knows how many years ago. You have done well also in tracing the historical sequence of the agitation for opening all the temples to the *avarna* Hindus in Travancore, and I again associate myself with you in the praise you have bestowed upon His Holiness the late Narayanaguru Swami and also upon that brave soul Madhavan. You will also let me recall in this connection two names—I mean the late Krishnaswami who at the time of the Vykom *Satyagraha* used to lead the prayer in his own inimitable manner with recitations of verses from *Gita Govinda*. Though a staunch Brahmin and lover of his religion, he made common cause with all the *avarnas*. And I may not forget also one who is still in our midst—Sjt. Kelappan Nair.

These brave men laid the foundation of the thing we see today in our midst.

But I think that we may not forget the orthodoxy which has come to our assistance at this hour, and in this connection I suppose I may not omit to mention the Namboodiri orthodox people whom I had found to my great regret very difficult to convert to the obvious truth. If they and the other orthodox people had not recognized the spirit of the times, it might be that they would have rendered the task of their Highnesses well nigh impossible or, at least, ineffective.

In this connection let me recall also a meeting I had with the Senior Maharani years ago. That meeting took place when the Vykom *Satyagraha* was going on, and I appealed to her, with all the earnestness at my command, to come to the assistance of all those who were fighting a forlorn battle, to issue a new *Smriti* and to declare all the temples open. She and her husband, who was present at the interview, expressed their sympathy with this movement. They both welcomed the movement that was going on in Travancore for the liberation of *avarnas*. But they felt burdened with the responsibility of a great State and told me that the time had not come for taking that great step. She then thought that it was still necessary to sound *savarna* opinion and to convert it to the reform. Several years have passed by since that interview. Thanks be to God that you did not remain idle during all these years, and but for the sustained efforts on your part to arouse both *avarna* and *savarna* public opinion, even the Maharaja with all the goodwill in the world would have found it impossible to issue the Proclamation. I hope that the Senior Maharani is today rejoicing over the great change that has come over Travancore and over the fact that the Proclamation is being welcomed by all and sundry—both *avarnas* and *savarnas*. I am hoping also that with the incoming of this great change over the State of Travancore the *savarna* Hindus are as enthusiastic in visiting temples as the *avarna* Hindus. I want to tell all *savarnas*, men and women, who have from day to day gone to these temples in search of blessings and in the hope that their prayers will be answered; I want to assure them that the temples have gained in efficacy and not lost one whit from the efficacy they enjoyed. Our *Shastras* teach us—I am not giving you any new truth—that efficacy lies in our hearts, not in stone however well carved it may be, and I do hope that your faith will not fail you because a large part of your co-religionists have had an ancient right restored to them of offering their prayers in the same manner and on the same conditions as you have offered them.

I would like to mention one sorrow that has oppressed me ever since I came here. I have wondered why you have called this celebration

Ezhava Temple-entry Proclamation Celebrations. I wonder if presently we shall have All-Travancore Pulaya and Pariah Celebrations ! I know and I grant that Ezhavas are a great and growing and important community in Travancore, but have I not seen the Pulayas and Pariahs of Travancore? When I have met them I have not been able to stare them straight in their faces. I have felt deeply humiliated. I shall never forget the sight of an old Pulaya man shaking with fear, as he was brought to me, and as he tried to hand me a sheet of paper which had been put into his hands. He was brought to me in Cochin as I was passing through the crowds in the streets. I was told that he held in his hand an address to be given to me on behalf of the Pulayas. His withered hands, as they were shaking, could not deliver that address in my hands. There was no lustre in his eyes. I do not know that I saw even a ray of hope in those deep sunken eyes. He did not know what he was being called upon to do. I do not know that he could understand the choice Malayalam which the Namboodiri volunteer was speaking. I seized the situation at a glance. I hung my head in shame and sorrow, and I felt it my duty to snatch that precious paper from his hands. Why is he not a member of today's Celebration Committee ? I know that he is nameless. Most probably he is dead. If he is alive perhaps he does not know what is happening in Travancore today. And also I asked myself whether you members of this Celebration Committee, you members of this vast gathering, do or do not represent such men. And I must tell you with all respect and humility that if this vast assembly does not represent these Pulayas, then I am certain that there is no place in your midst for me. If this is a purely religious movement, if this is a purely religious revival, if it has no taint of base 'self' in it, then you will be denying yourselves and nullifying the effect of this great Proclamation if you do not represent the lowest and the least in our midst. You heard with what force Sir C.P. Ramaswami Iyer spoke to this meeting. The Maharaja has given you a *Smriti*, but it is for you to carry it out and breathe life into it , and you will hopelessly fail to do that unless you rise to the occasion and see to it that this religious spirit pervades the whole of Travancore—both *avarnas* and *savarnas*.

I tell you if you approach this great step, each with his own mental reservation, and not give effect to it whole-heartedly, you will find this Proclamation a nine days' wonder. Therefore I want you to understand, whilst you are properly rejoicing over this Proclamation and celebrating it with the joy and zeal that I see on your faces, that you will not be doing your duty if you do not realize your responsibility to the whole of the community that had been so far excluded.

I see that you are now getting restless. I do not propose to keep you longer than is absolutely necessary. I am speaking to you from the fulness of my heart, and when heart is speaking to hearts, it expects to find a lodgment in those hearts. I do not want to keep you more than perhaps ten minutes now. I shall try to omit many of the things I wanted to say this evening, and shall seek another occasion for doing so.

I must mention what I saw at the great Padmanabha Temple. It will perhaps best illustrate what I am saying about the pure and spiritual revival. In the days of my youth I went to so many temples with the faith and devotion with which my parents had fired me. But of late years I have not been visiting temples, and ever since I have been engaged in anti-untouchability work I have refrained from going to temples unless they were open to everyone called untouchable. So what I saw this morning at the temple dawned upon me with the same newness with which it must have dawned upon so many *avarna* Hindus who must have gone to the temple after the Proclamation. In imagination my mind travelled back to the prehistoric centuries when they began to convey the message of God in stone and metal. I saw quite clearly that the priest who was interpreting each figure in his own choice Hindi did not want to tell me that each of those figures was God. But without giving me that particular interpretation he made me realize that these temples were so many bridges between the Unseen, Invisible and Indefinable God and ourselves who are infinitesimal drops in the Infinite Ocean. We the human family are not all philosophers. We are of the earth very earthy, and we are not satisfied with contemplating the Invisible God.

Somehow or other we want something which we can touch, something which we can see, something before which we can kneel down. It does not matter whether it is a book, or an empty stone building, or a stone building inhabited by numerous figures. A book will satisfy some, an empty building will satisfy some others, and many others will not be satisfied unless they see something inhabiting these empty buildings.

Then I ask you to approach these temples not as if they represented a body of superstitions. If you will approach these temples with faith in them, you will know each time you visit them you will come away from them purified, and with your faith more and more in the living God.

Anyway, I have looked upon this Proclamation as a pure religious act. I have regarded this visit to Travancore in the spirit of a pilgrimage, and I am going to these temples as an untouchable suddenly made touchable. If all of you will approach this Proclamation in this spirit, you will abolish all distinctions between *savarnas* and *avarnas* as also all those distinctions which unfortunately still exist between *avarnas* and *avarnas*. Finally, you will not be satisfied until you have lifted up your brothers and sisters who are supposed to be the least and the lowest, to heights which you have attained yourselves. True spiritual regeneration must include economic uplift and the removal of ignorance and everything that goes to retard human progress.

May God enable you to realize to the full the possibilities that are embedded in this Proclamation of the Maharaja. I thank you for giving me this patient hearing.

[*Harijan*, 23-1-1937]

62. What is Khadi Science ?

I have often said that if *khadi* is a sound economic proposition it is also a science and a romance. I believe there is a book called *The Romance of Cotton* wherein the origin of cotton has been traced and an attempt made to show how its discovery altered the course of civilization. Everything can be turned into a science or a romance if there is a scientific or a romantic spirit behind it. Some people scoff at *khadi* and betray signs of impatience or disgust when one talks of hand-spinning. But it ceases to be an object of disgust or ridicule immediately you attribute to it the power of removing India-wide idleness, unemployment and consequent pauperism. It need not be, as a matter of fact, a panacea for the three ills. To be absorbingly interesting, the mere honest attributing of the power is enough. But you cannot attribute that potency to *khadi* and pursue it, as some do, in the manner of an ignorant needy artisan who gins, cards, spins or weaves because he must for his bread. A believer in its potency will pursue it in a deliberate, wise, methodical manner and in a scientific spirit, taking nothing for granted, testing every proposition, checking facts and figures, undaunted by defeats, unelated by petty successes, never satisfied till the goal is reached. The late Maganlal Gandhi had a living faith in the potency of *khadi*. It was for him a thrilling romance. And he wrote the elements of the science of *khadi*. No detail was too trifling for him, no scheme was too big for him. Richard Gregg had and has the same fire in him. He has given it a universal meaning. His Economics of *Khaddar* is an original contribution to the movement. He recognizes the spinning wheel as the symbol par excellence of non-violence. It may or may not be all that. But their belief gave Maganlal Gandhi and gives Richard Gregg all the joy and pleasure derivable from any fascination theme. A science to be science must afford the fullest scope for satisfying the hunger of body, mind and soul. Sceptics have wondered how *khadi* can afford such satisfaction or, in other words, what I mean when I use the expression "Science of Khadi". I cannot better answer the question than by copying below the questions framed by me hurriedly for a *khadi* worker who offered to be examined by me. The questions were not framed in their logical sequence nor were they exhaustive. They admit of rearrangement and addition. But I reproduce a translation made for me by a friend from the original in Hindi.

PART I

1. How much cotton is produced in India and where? Name the varieties. How much remains in India, how much is spun by hand, how much goes to England and other lands?
2. (a) What quantity of cloth is manufactured in Indian mills? How much of it is used in India and how much is exported?
   (b) Of the above how much is manufactured from *swadeshi* mill yarn and how much from foreign mill yarn?
   (c) How much cloth is imported?
   (d) What quantity of *khadi* is produced in India?

Note: Give your answers in square yards and in terms of money.

3. Discuss the merits and demerits of the three kinds of cloth above mentioned.
4. Some say *khadi* is dear, coarse and not lasting. Give your answers to these complaints, and where there is foundation for any of them offer your solution.
5. In the (AISA) *khadi* work how many spinners are engaged? How much have they earned during all these years? Give the number of mill spinners and their total annual earnings.
6. (a) How is the work of the AISA carried on? How much is spent by them in administration?
   (b) What staff is employed in the running of a *swadeshi* mill, and what proportion of wages do such persons get in comparison with the mill hands?
7. (a) What place in your opinion does clothing occupy in the necessaries of life?
   (b) Name the chief necessaries of life and give their proportionate percentages.
8. If everyone in India gave up wearing mill-made cloth, whether foreign or Indian, how much money would remain in India and to whom would it go?
9. What does India export in place of the cloth she imports? What loss, if any, does India sustain through this exchange?
10. What percentage of the population is able to buy cloth?
11. What is the percentage of those who have the leisure to make their own cloth? And how?

12. "*Khadi* will establish perfect economic balance." Is this statement really correct? Give reasons for your answer.
13. If *khadi* became universal, what effect would this have on trade, occupation and transport, and in what manner?
14. Assuming that for another 50 years *khadi* does not become universal, what is likely to be the effect on the economic condition of our people?

PART II

1. Give a description of current Indian spinning wheels. Which is the best amongst them? Give drawings of any four spinning wheels and the correct measurement of each constituent part. State the species of wood employed, the length and the girth of the spindle and the thickness of the *mal*.
2. Compare the current *charkhas* with the Yeravda wheel in the matter of speed, cost and general advantages.
3. How would you ascertain the variety of cotton, the strength of the yarn, and the count of spun yarn?
4. Of what count and strength is the yarn you spin? What is your speed on the *takli* and the wheel? Which wheel do you generally use?
5. How much cloth does a man and a woman require respectively for his or her clothing? How much yarn is required for making the same, and how much time is necessary for spinning it?
6. How much yarn is required to clothe one family? How much cotton is needed to produce the above? How much land is required for growing the necessary amount of cotton? (A family consists of a father, mother and three children—one girl and two boys, 7, 5 and 3 years old.)
7. Compare the current carding-bow with the new ones. How much do you card per hour? How can you judge whether the cotton is properly carded or not? How long does it take you to make one pound of slivers? How many slivers do you make from one tola of cotton?
8. How much cotton can you gin in one hour? Compare ginning by hand with ginning by machine, giving the respective merits and demerits of either process. Describe and give a drawing of the current hand-ginning machine.

9. Give the length of the yarn of 20 counts required to weave one yard of cloth 36 inches wide. How many hands are required to weave the same?
10. Compare the pit loom with the shuttle loom.

[*Harijan*, 16-1-1937]

63. Notes for Khadi Organization

The year 1936 is just over and all *khadi* organizations would do well to examine promptly and carefully the results of the year's work and submit their statements to the A.I.S.A. office. I have asked the latter to produce a brief but full report of the work of the Association during the last year, particularly with reference to the working of the new scheme of increased spinning wages. Such a report can be had only if all the branches and the various organizations affiliated to the Association readily co-operate and send without delay accurate particulars regarding work done and results achieved by them to the Central Office. The plans and programme for the current year have to be prepared at once, and for this, too, full information regarding the previous year's working is indispensable. I hope, therefore, that *khadi* organizations will realize the urgency and supply all available information to the A.I.S.A. office at the earliest moment. Let them remember that time is of the essence in this matter.

SPINNERS' WAGES

The council of the A.I.S.A. has decided that the A.I.S.A. branches and its certified organizations should give spinning wages on the basis of a scale sufficient to enable the spinner to have, besides minimum clothing requirements, adequate nutritive diet for eight hours' efficient work. The various branches and organizations have, in accordance with this decision, fixed suitable standards of spinning rates which are calculated to enable the spinner to earn a daily wage of Rs. 2 to $2\frac{1}{2}$. This wage is, however, related to efficient work and can be actually earned only if the requisite standard of output and quality of yarn is attained by the spinner. The standard fixed, though high, is not difficult to attain, but it must be admitted that at the present time only a small percentage of the spinners has come up to it, partly because of the crudeness of the spinning wheels and slivers they use and partly because of their lack of skill. The real objective of the scheme is, however, not merely to lay down a reasonable scale for wage basis but to enable the bulk of the spinners to actually earn the same. It, therefore, becomes the duty of all workers engaged in production activity to do all that they can to help the spinners to attain the requisite skill besides securing satisfactory wheels and slivers so as to ensure the actual earning of the desired wage by them. It is hoped the *khadi* workers will not rest content until the majority of the spinners on their registers actually earn the amount aimed at. Let them also realize that the higher scale is not the highest aimed at. The real aim in terms of present values is to ensure eight annas for eight hours' attentive and skilled spinning. That may be a far-off event. But it will never come unless very early ten pice become as natural as three are today. Let it be also remembered that in the new scale the increase is roughly distributed half-and-half between the effort of the spinner and the rise given by the A.I.S.A.

AN IMPORTANT CORRECTION

I know there are readers of *Harijan* who study many articles that appear from time to time in *Harijan*. The weekly is not published for providing momentary amusement or pleasure for the reader. It is designed to be a serious contribution to the *Harijan* cause in the widest sense of the term. It, therefore, often contains writings of more than transitory value. Hence, serious errors need to be corrected. Such an error was detected in the *Harijan* of the 9th inst. at page 382, 2nd column, line 2. Read 'sub-human' for 'human'.

[*Harijan*, 16-1-1937]

64. Message of Hinduism

SPEECH AT HARIPAD

[January 17, 1937]

At this meeting I would love to detain you for a few minutes on the message of Hinduism I gave to the meeting in Quilon last night. I ventured at that meeting to say that the whole of Hinduism could be summed up in the first verse of *Ishopanishad.* I suggested then that if all other Hindu scriptures happened to be reduced to ashes and to go out of the memory of men and if only that one verse were to abide with us, the destruction would be no loss. Hinduism would even then remain with us. The original Sanskrit of the *mantra* is perhaps as easy as anybody learning Sanskrit could possibly wish. This *Upanishad* enjoys the reputation of being part of the original *Vedas*. It is the shortest *Upanishad* known to us. But, as I have said, if we had only the first verse of that *Upanishad* remaining with us, it would be enough to supply all our wants. Let me repeat that *mantra* in my faulty Sanskrit pronunciation:

Those who know a little bit of Sanskrit will find that there is nothing abstruse there that you find in other *Vedic mantras,* and its meaning is simply this: All that there is in this Universe, great or small, including the tiniest atom, is pervaded by God, known as Creator or Lord. *Isha* means the Ruler, and He who is the Creator naturally by very right becomes the Ruler, too. And here in this verse the seer has chosen no other epithet for the Deity but that of the Ruler, and he has excepted nothing from His jurisdiction. He says everything that we see is pervaded by the Deity, and from that naturally the other parts of the *mantra* follow. Thus he says: Renounce everything, i.e., everything that is on this Universe, the whole of the Universe, and not only this tiny globe of ours, renounce it. He asks us to renounce it as we are such insignificant atoms that if we had any idea of possession it would seem ludicrous. And then, says the *rishi,* the reward of renunciation is, i.e., enjoyment of all you need. But there is a meaning about the word 'enjoy'—you might as well say use, eat, etc.,—but it means that you may not take more than is necessary for your growth. Therefore this enjoyment or use is limited by two conditions. One is the act of renunciation or, as the author of the *Bhagavata* would say, enjoy in the spirit And every day in the morning everyone who believes in *Bhagavata Dharma* has to dedicate his thoughts, words and deeds to Krishna, and not until he has performed that daily act of renunciation or dedication has he the right of touching anything or drinking even a cup of water. And when a man has performed that act of renunciation and dedication, he derives from that act the right of eating, drinking, clothing, and housing himself to the extent necessary for his daily life. Therefore, take it as you like, either in the sense that the enjoyment or use is the reward or renunciation, or that the renunciation is the condition of enjoyment, renunciation is essential for our very existence, for our soul. And as if that condition given in the *mantra* was incomplete, the *rishi* hastened to complete it by adding: 'Do not covet what belongs to another'. Now I suggest to you that the whole of the philosophy or religion found in any part of the world is contained in this *mantra*, and it excludes everything contrary to it. According to the canons of interpretation, anything that is inconsistent with *Shruti*—and the *Ishopanishad* is a *Shruti*—is to be rejected altogether.

Now I should like to apply this *mantra* our own condition in virtue of the Proclamation. Whilst I have unstintingly associated myself with your rejoicings over this great Proclamation and in tendering my thanks and congratulations to His Highness, Her Highness and their Dewan, in terms of this *mantra* I am obliged also to say that this Proclamation is a tardy carrying out of the behest contained in this verse of the *Ishopanishad* that I have recited. Only yesterday we were unfit to call ourselves Hindus. For if all that there is in the Universe is pervaded by God, that is to say, if the Brahmin and the Bhangi, the learned man and the scavenger, the Ezhava and the Pariah, no matter what caste they belong to—if all these are pervaded by Lord God, in the light of this *mantra*, there is none that is low, all are absolutely equal, equal because all are the creatures of that Creator. And this is not a philosophical thing to be dished out to Brahmins or Kshatriyas, but it enunciates an eternal truth which admits of no reduction, no dilution[1]. Therefore, the Maharaja himself and the Maharani are not one whit superior to the lowliest being in Travancore. We are all creatures and servants of one God. If the Maharaja is the first among equals, as he is, he is so not by right of overlordship but by right of service. And, therefore, how nice, how noble it is that that very Maharaja is called '*Padmanabhadas*'. It is a proud title and I congratulate those who bestowed that title on the Maharaja of

1. The source has "palliation".

Travancore. Therefore, when I told you that the Maharaja or the Maharani were not one whit superior to any one of us I told you what was the actual truth accepted by their Highnesses themselves.

And if that is so, how can anyone here dare to arrogate superiority to himself or herself over any other human being? I tell you, therefore, that if the *mantra* holds good, if there is any man or woman here who believes that the temples are defiled by those called *avarnas*, that person I declare would be guilty of a grave sin. I tell you that the Proclamation has purified our temples of the taint that had attached to them.

I would like the *mantra* I have recited to be enshrined in the hearts of all our men and women and children, and if this contains, as I hold, the essence of Hinduism, it should be inscribed on the portals of every temple. Don't you then think that we should be belying that *mantra* at every step if we excluded anyone from those temples?

Therefore, if you will prove yourselves deserving of the gracious Proclamation and if you will be loyal to yourselves and to those who preside over your destinies, you will carry out the letter and spirit of this Proclamation I regard it as such a great spiritual act that it ought to remove scepticism from the hearts of sceptics or doubt from the hearts of those who doubted the truth of Hinduism or religion itself.

Rightly understood this Proclamation should dispel the ignorant atheism of so called atheists. From the date of the Proclamation the Travancore temples, which, as I once said, were not abodes of God, have become abodes of God, since no one who used to be regarded as untouchable is any more to be excluded from them. I therefore hope and pray that throughout Travancore there may be no man or woman who will abstain from going to the temples for the reason that they have been opened to those who were regarded as Pariahs of society.

[*Harijan*, 30-1-1937]

65. Ramgarh Congress

SPEECH AT SUBJECTS COMMITTEE[1]

[Ramgarh,
March 18, 1940]

Since I went out of the Congress at Bombay[2], there has been an understanding between me and the Working Committee that I should not be asked to speak at the A.I.C.C. or the Subjects Committee or the open session and[3] should be allowed to conserve the little strength that is left in me. I have usually been attending the meetings of the Working Committee. On this occasion, I myself suggested that I should address the Subjects Committee and also the delegates. The Working Committee agreed to this and, although I wanted to address you before the resolution[4] was adopted, the Committee suggested that I do so after the resolution was disposed of.

It was my desire to see the faces of you all, and also to give you an opportunity of looking at me and finding out if there had been any change in me since my retirement in Bombay. Fifty years of public life have given me the capacity to read your faces. I have during these years created many institutions, met thousands and tens of thousands of people. Besides, I have been in contact with the Working Committee and many of you have been in correspondence with me....[5] And it should not therefore, be difficult for me to get at the back of your minds. .[6] But my desire to see you was in order to find out where I was.

You have, I see, made considerable progress in the art of debate and I congratulate you, for in a democratic organization powers of persuasion and a high level of debate are essential. I have also seen that the number

1. Gandhiji spoke in Hindi.
2. In October 1934.
3. *Congress Bulletin* here has : "I should be allowed to serve the country in my own way with whatever strength is left to me."
4. *Vide* "A Resolution", 1-3-1940.
5. This sentence is from *Congress Bulletin.*
6. *Congress Bulletin* has : "It should, therefore, not be difficult for me to remember you."

of amendments you move has also increased, and it is well that you should all be anxious to press new points of view[1], though I cannot congratulate you on some of the amendments which were either frivolous or absurd.

You have adopted the resolution practically unanimously as there were only seven or eight dissentients.[2] That adds to my responsibility, for I have been witness to debate. If I had so desired, I should have warned you before voting, but I accepted the suggestion of the Working Committee that I should not address the house before the resolution was passed.

I do not want to reply to what has been said by some of you in the course of the debate. But I do want to say that, though there was a time in my life when I launched movements even if some of my conditions had not been fulfilled, I am now going to be hard, not for the sake of being hard, but because a General who has to lead the army must let the army know his conditions beforehand.

Let me then tell you that I do not see at the present moment conditions propitious for an immediate launching of campaign. We are hemmed in with difficulties greater than those we had to face in the past. They are external and internal. The external difficulties are due to the fact that we have declared unmistakably what we want and the Government have also declared their intentions as clearly as possible.

Then there is the fact that the British Government are engaged in a world war and naturally, if we engage them in a fight, we ask for enough trouble. This is the first difficulty. .[3] What, however, appals me is our internal difficulties. I have often said that external difficulties need never frighten a *satyagrahi*. On the contrary, he flourishes on external difficulties and faces them with redoubled zeal and vigour. Today the situation is almost the reverse.

Our external difficulties do not find us stronger and more united. Our internal difficulties are increasing. Our Congress registers are full of bogus members and members who have swelled them because they know that getting into the Congress means getting to power. Those who, therefore, never before thought of entering the Congress have come into it and corrupted it. And how can we prevent people from coming into a

1. *Congress Bulletin* here adds: "So that any point that is not accepted today may be accepted tomorrow."
2. *Congress Bulletin* here adds: "They had every right to do so."
3. This sentence is from Congress Bulletin.

democratic organization because they come from selfish motives? We have not that discipline, and not the strength and purity of public opinion which would compel such people to stay out.

And this strength and purity cannot come so long as we approach the primary members only once in a year for the vote.

There is no discipline in our ranks, they have been divided up into groups which strive to gain more and more power. Non-violence as between ourselves does not seem to us to be necessary.[1] Wherever, I go I hear the same complaint. My conception of democracy is not the formation of groups quarrelling with one another to such an extent as would destroy organization itself. There may be groups, but they should strengthen and not weaken and destroy the organization.

Ours has been both a democratic organization and a fighting one, ever since we reorganized it in 1920...[2] We have used even military language, though in a non-violent sense. Well then, I want to repeat what I have said times without number that, if you will be soldiers in my army understand that there is no room for democracy in that organization. The army may be a part of a democratic organization, but there can be no democracy in it, as there can be none in its ranks, as there is none in our various organizations A.I.S.A., A.I.V.I.A. and so on. In an army the General's word is law, and his conditions cannot be relaxed.

I am supposed to be your General,[3] but I do not know a more feeble General in history. I have no sanctions...[4] My only sanction is the love and affection in which you hold me. But it has its weakness as it has its strength. I know that you love me. Does your love translate itself into action?[5] If it does not, if it does not mean ever-increasing discipline and ever-increasing response to what I say, let me declare to you that I cannot launch civil disobedience, and you must select another General. You cannot make me your General on your terms.[6]

You must fulfil the conditions set down in the Independence Pledge.

---

1. The following two sentences are from *Congress Bulletin.*
2. Congress Bulletin here adds: "Our fight is not yet over".
3. *Congress Bulletin* here adds : "It should not mean that I should keep you in the dark regarding my feelings."
4. This sentence is from Congress Bulletin.
5. *Congress Bulletin* here has : "In one way it is a great thing but in another sense it can also be worthless, I can say I cherish love for all in my heart. Perhaps you also do so but your love must be active."
6. The following five sentences are from *Congress Bulletin.*

You must allow me to tell you that if you do not fulfil those conditions it will not be possible for me to launch a struggle. . . . You cannot compel me to lead you against my will. When you appoint me as your General, you must obey my command. There can be no argument about it. Know, therefore, that I will insist on my conditions.

They are inexorable, and if you do not observe them, I will automatically withdraw.

The General of a military army insists on strict discipline. I go on arguing with you, because my only sanction is love. I say to you, therefore, that unless you accept my condition, unless you have faith in them as you have in me, you should not think of going to jail. If you will go to jail, you have to pay the price.[1] Ours is a civil fight, and imprisonment as a civil prisoner has got to be earned by strict observance of the programme. For thieves and dacoits also fill the jails but they do not carry the country to freedom.

Well, then, I laid down the conditions in 1920 and have never ceased to repeat them. You may not believe in the programme, you may have grown wiser since then, but I have not. My faith in it has increased with the years. I see more virtues in it than I saw before.[2]

I turned a rebel against this Government in 1919, but before that I was as loyal to it as any Britisher.[3] It is that unique loyalty that gave me the unique power of civil disobedience, and the unquenchable spirit of search. I therefore go on making my experiments and also go on declaring my mistakes whenever I discover them. I am an erring mortal like you.[4] I have never even in my dream thought that I was a *maha-atma* (great soul) and that others were *alpa-atma* (little souls).

---

1. *Congress Bulletin* here has : "For love must be characterized by patience. I have heard friends criticizing the *charkha*. I know you are all ready to go to jail but you must earn the right and pay the price for going to jail. You will not be going to jail as criminals."
2. *Congress Bulletin* here has: "The more I think about non-violence, the greater the virtues I find in it."
3. *Congress Bulletin* here reports: "I have been an outlaw since 1918. Before that I was so loyal to the Empire that I wrote to Lord Chelmsford that I longed to have the same loyalty towards the Empire as a Britisher has in his heart. I wrote those words because I am a believer in truth. Truth is my God and I could not have written anything else I wanted to be true to myself."
4. *Congress Bulletin* here has: "You may have other ways than truth and nonviolence but mine is the same old path and, being just a human being like you, I also commit mistakes."

We are all equal before our Maker—Hindus, Mussalmans, Parsis, Christians, worshippers of one God. Why then do we fight among ourselves?

We are all brothers—even the Quaid-e-Azam is my brother. I have meant all that I have said about him, never has a frivolous word escaped my lips, and I say that I want to win him over. A speaker said that I would not fight until I had won him over, and he was right.[1]

There was a time when there was not a Muslim whose confidence I did not enjoy. Today I have forfeited that confidence and most of the Urdu Press pours abuse on me.[2] But I am not sorry for it. It only confirms me in my belief that there is no *swaraj* without a settlement with the Mussalmans.

You will perhaps ask, in that case, why I am talking of a fight. I do so in order to have a Constituent Assembly which means agreement and settlement. But if the Mussalmans will have nothing to do with it, I will understand that there is no settlement.[3] I am also a reader of the *Koran* like them, and I will tell them that the *Koran* makes no distinction between the Hindus and the Mussalmans.[4] But if they feel that they should have the Heaven without the Hindus, I will not grudge it to them.

I have no ill will towards Englishmen. When I heard that Lord Zetland was wounded, my heart was wounded. That is my temperament.[5] I, therefore, always work with and for goodwill for them. That I want to destroy British imperialism in another matter, but I want to do so by converting those who are associated with it.[6] If non-violence has the

1. *Congress Bulletin* here adds: "I would be happy indeed if he could keep me in his pocket."
2. *Congress Bulletin* here reports: "I do not read all that appears in the Urdu Press ; but perhaps I get a lot of abuses there."
3. *Congress Bulletin* here has: "If Muslims who came to the Constituent Assembly through Muslim votes declare that there is nothing common between Hindus and Muslims, then alone would I give up hope, but even then I would argue with them because they read the *Koran* and I have also studied something of that holy book.
4. *Congress Bulletin* here reports: "I will tell them that God makes no distinction between Hindus and Muslims".
5. *Congress Bulletin* here adds: "These are my ways. You may call them weakness. If you want me you must understand this."
6. *Congress Bulletin* here has: "I fight British imperialism but I have no quarrel with those who run the imperialist machine. I do not want to destroy them but I want to bring about a change in them."

power that I attribute to it, it is sure to react on the opponent. If it does not, the fault will be mine, not that of non-violence.

You must, therefore, understand that you have to deal with a dangerous man who will land you in unexpected situations. Compromise is part and parcel of my nature. I will go to the Viceroy fifty times, if I feel like it. I went to Lord Reading whilst non-cooperation was going on.[1] I would not only go to the Viceroy when invited, but I would seek opportunities to go to him, if necessary. You must know that, if I do so, I do it in order to strengthen our cause and not weaken it. It happened so with General Smuts. At the last moment I telephoned to him.[2] He put the receiver down in anger, but I thrust myself on him. As a result he relented and I was in stronger position.

Today we are friends. The basis of my fight is love for the opponent.[3]

I could not have fought the Dutch and the English[4] without love in my heart for them, and without a readiness for compromise. But my compromise will never be at the cost of the cause or of the country.

One of the amendments was to the effect that the word 'mass' be inserted before 'civil disobedience'. Well, if it is not mass civil disobedience is it to be the civil disobedience of a handful? In that case I should not have come to you.[5] You might perhaps not be taking these things seriously, but in my mind there is no other thought. My mind is wholly concentrated on trying this great experiment with your help and support, because it will not only benefit India but the whole world. It is the thought of mass civil disobedience that keeps my mind awake all the twenty-four hours. Why should a man of 70 trifle with a thing of this kind ?

Therefore, let me tell you that there is no civil disobedience until I feel that you are ready. You have therefore to purify every Congress Committee and make it a *satyagrahi* unit. To that extent it will have to cease to be a democracy, because my word will be law. But if it does not become such a unit, millions of our dumb countrymen will be sacrificed. None of my campaigns has crushed or ruined the masses.

---

1. On May 13 and 14, 1921; *vide* "Notes", 4-8-1921.
2. *Congress Bulletin* here adds : "to try and see if the fight could be abandoned."
3. This sentence is from *Congress Bulletin.*
4. *Congress Bulletin* here adds : "In South Africa".
5. The following two sentences are from *Congress Bulletin.*

They have increased their stature, and it is in order to take it still higher that I want to live. There was in the earlier campaigns enough of violence of thought and word, but there was non-violence in act and, therefore, the masses were saved. I would not light-heartedly imperil those masses today, and that is why I insist on strictest non-violence and the fulfilment of my conditions. For that is the only link that binds them and me.[1] I may have to lay down my life for preserving the power that has accrued to India. You may not be able to analyse that power but it is there. It is the power of *ahimsa*.

If I am your General, your pulse should be in my hands. Otherwise I cannot fight through you. I can fight single-handed, but for that fight I need not come and argue with you.

One last word before I close. I do not want to stand in the way of those who want to fight at once. But if they have any sense of honour, I should advise them to do so after getting out of the Congress. Let me assure them that, if they put up a non-violent fight and carry it through, I shall follow their lead. Of course it is open to them to remain in the Congress and to defy it, but it will not be *satyagraha*[2]. Those who are impatient today do not know the power of *satyagraha*.

The resolution does not bind you. If you do not accept the conditions, you can still say you do not accept them, and you can have the resolution reversed. That will free you and me both. But if you accept the conditions and will all observe them, you may be sure that it need not take me a month to launch the struggle.[3]

[*Harijan*, 30-3-1940, and *Congress Bulletin*, 12-4-1940,
Vol. No. 1, pp 10-6]

---

1. The rest of the paragraph is from Congress Bulletin.
2. *Congress Bulletin* here adds : "which never harms the man who uses the weapon."
3. *Congress Bulletin* here reports: "You may have other methods, but so far as I am concerned I have only the same old programme. I know that that method has never harmed anyone who has followed it and even now if I can get your whole-hearted support and co-operation. I can show you what can be achieved within even a month."

66. We are Not Ready

SPEECH AT CONGRESS SESSION[1]

[Ramgarh,
March 20, 1940]

I am pleased to have been here to hear all these discussions today. When I see that all those who have spoken had the word 'civil disobedience' on their tongue, I am reminded of the Biblical saying :

"Not everyone that sayeth to me Lord, Lord, shall enter into the Kingdom of Heaven : but he that doeth the will of my Father who is in Heaven, he shall enter the Kingdom of Heaven."[2] (cheers) I do not need your cheers, I want to win your hearts and your intellects, and cheers and acclamations stand in the way of winning them.[3] It is not those who shout the word civil disobedience that can launch civil disobedience. It is only those who work for civil disobedience that are capable of launching the movement. Real civil disobedience makes it binding on those who join it to do what they are enjoined to do and avoid what is prohibited. Civil disobedience properly launched and conducted is bound to lead to freedom.

I feel you are not prepared.[4] Therefore, when I saw you acclaiming the speakers who said that we are ready I was shocked. For I know that we are not ready. It is true that we all know and realize that we are slaves in our own land. We also realize that freedom is essential for us. Further we all realize that we will have to fight for freedom. I may also join you in applauding the speakers who have demanded immediate launching of civil disobedience. A thief has come and turned me out of my house. I will have to fight him and get if back, but before I can do this, I must be prepared. (*Applause*) Your claps only demonstrate that you do not understand what this preparation means. Your General finds that you are

1. Gandhiji spoke in Hindi.
2. St. Matthew, VII. 21.
3. This sentence is from *Harijan.*
4. The following two sentences are from *Harijan.*

not ready, that you are not real soldiers and that if we proceed on the lines suggested by you, we are bound to be defeated.[1] And knowing this, how can I ask you to fight? I know that with such as you I can only have defeat.

I must make it clear that I am not prepared to do anything for which I will have to repent. I have never acknowledged defeat throughout all these years in any of my struggles. Though some people may point out to Rajkot, I maintain that it was not a defeat for me. Future history alone can make this clear.[2] The word 'defeat' is not to be found in my dictionary, and everyone who is selected as a recruit in my army may be sure that there is no defeat for a *satyagrahi*.

I can assure you and I promise you and publicly announce it, that when you are ready I shall march forth and then I [shall] have no doubt about victory. I said this before the Subjects Committee and I repeat it again here. Purify your mind and heart. Some people here have been asserting that it is not necessary for us to concentrate on the *charkha* before launching a fight. I do not doubt their sincerity and bravery, but, as Pandit Jawaharlal Nehru has told you, they betray certain weakness of mind.[3] Well, I tell you, as I have been telling you these 20 years, that there is a vital connection between *satyagraha* and the *charkha*, and the more I find that belief challenged the more I am confirmed in it. Otherwise I am no fool to persist in turning the *charkha*, day in and day out, at home and even on trains, in the teeth of medical advice. Doctors want me to leave the *charkha*. But I am devoting greater attention to it, because I have to prepare myself.[4] I want you too to be turning the *charkha* with the same faith. And unless you do it and unless you habitually use *khadi* you will deceive me and deceive the world. No one who does not believe in the *charkha* can be a soldier under me.

With me there is no other alternative than non-violence.[5] I shall of course die with non-violence on my lips, but you are not wedded to it in the sense I am, and so it is open to you to have another programme and to make our country free. But if you will not do this, nor turn the *charkha*, and want me to fight, it will be an impossible situation. If you feel that you are to fight, and you must fight now, and immediately, and feel

1. The following two sentences are from *Harijan*.
2. This sentence is from *Harijan*.
3. The following two sentences are from *Harijan*.
4. *Ibid.*
5. *Ibid.*

convinced that there is some other method of winning the fight, I would ask you to go ahead and I shall be the first to applaud your victory. But if you do not want to leave me and yet are not prepared to follow my methods and instructions, then I would like to know what kind of generalship is this that you offer me.

Those who clamour for immediate launching of civil disobedience want to have me with them. Why? Because they are conscious that the masses are with me. I unhesitatingly say that I am a people's man.

Every moment of my life I feel for the starving millions. I live and am prepared to lay down my life to relieve their sufferings and mitigate their miseries. I claim to have some influence with the millions, because I have been a faithful servant of theirs.[1] My loyalty to them is greater than any other loyalty, and it is for them that I would not give up the *charkha* even if you were to forsake me or kill me. For I know that, if I were to relax the condition of the *charkha*, I should bring ruin upon those dumb millions for whom I have to answer before God. If, therefore, you do not believe in the *charkha* in the sense I believe in it, I implore you to leave me. Even if you stone me to death I will still work for the masses. This is my way. If you think there is any other way please leave me alone.

Without the *charkha* I cannot lead you to jail in the course of the fight for freedom. I will not have anyone under me who does not believe in the *charkha*. I shall go ahead only when I am satisfied that you have faith in the *charkha*. Remember if we, who are assembled here, blunder [we] shall cause untold suffering to the dumb millions by our mistake. The delegates to the Congress bear a heavy responsibility and as your General my responsibility is still greater. As a General I have to be a sort of beacon-light to you and warn you against possible disaster. Therefore, I have to proceed cautiously.

Many speakers dilated on the evils of British imperialism. I do not wish to elaborate that point except to state that we must get rid of it. I have told you the cue. Before I agree to launch *satyagraha* I must be convinced that you have understood my remedy.

It is no use going to a doctor and asking for a medicine if you do not propose to take it according to his instructions. I would much rather ask you to seek another doctor for your ailment. All the sermons you have heard today against British imperialism will not help you to remove it. They will only make you angry. This will not solve our problem. Anger is opposed to *satyagraha*. We have no quarrel with the British people. We

1. The following three sentences are from *Harijan*.

want to be their friends and retain their goodwill, not on the basis of their domination, but on the basis of a free and equal India.

As a free country India will bear no malice to anyone, nor attempt to enslave any people. We shall march with the rest of this world, just as we shall desire the rest of the world to march with us.[1] Remember, therefore, that you have to fulfil both the internal and external conditions. If you fulfil the internal condition, you will cease to hate your opponent, you will not seek or work for his destruction, but pray to God to have mercy on him. Do not, therefore, concentrate on showing the misdeed of the Government, for we have to convert and befriend those who run it. And after all no one is wicked by nature. And if others are wicked, are we the less so? That attitude is inherent in *satyagraha*, and if you do not subscribe to it, even then I would ask you to leave me. For without a belief in my programme and without an acceptance of my condition you will ruin me, ruin yourselves and ruin the cause.

Satyagraha is the path of truth at all cost. If you are not prepared to follow this path please leave me alone. You can pronounce me worthless and I shall not resent it. If I do not make this clear here and now, I shall be ruined and along with me the country.

Truth and *ahimsa* are the essence of *satyagraha*, and the *charkha* is their symbol. Just as the General of any army insists that his soldiers should wear a particular uniform, I as your General must insist on your taking to the *charkha* which will be your uniform. Without full faith in truth, non-violence and the *charkha*, you cannot be my soldiers. And I repeat again that if you do not believe in this, you must leave me alone and you can try your own methods.

[*The Indian Annual Register,* 1940, Vol. I, pp. 230-1, and *Harijan,* 30-3-1940]

1. The rest of the paragraph is from *Harijan*.

67. Freedom Here and Now

SPEECH AT A.I.C.C. MEETING[1]

[Bombay,
August 8, 1942]

I congratulate you on the resolution that you have just passed. I also congratulate the three comrades on the courage they have shown in pressing their amendments to a division, even though they knew that there was an overwhelming majority in favour of the resolution, and I congratulate the thirteen friends who voted against the resolution. In doing so, they had nothing to be ashamed of. For the last twenty years we have tried to learn not to lose courage even when we are in a hopeless minority and are laughed at. We have learned to hold on to our beliefs in the confidence that we are in the right. It behoves us to cultivate this courage of conviction, for it ennobles man and raises his moral stature. I was, therefore, glad to see that these friends had imbibed the principle which I have tried to follow for the last fifty years and more.

Having congratulated them on their courage, let me say that what they asked this Committee to accept through their amendments was not the correct representation of the situation. These friends ought to have pondered over the appeal made to them by the Maulana to withdraw their amendments; they should have carefully followed the explanations given by Jawaharlal Nehru. Had they done so, it would have been clear to them that the right which they now want the Congress to concede has already been conceded by the Congress.

Time was when every Mussalman claimed the whole of India as his motherland. During the years that the Ali Brothers were with me, the assumption underlying all their talks and discussions was that India belonged as much to the Mussalmans as to the Hindus. I can testify to the fact that this was their innermost conviction and not a mask; I lived with them for years. I spent days and nights in their company. And I make

---

1. Gandhiji spoke first in Hindi and then in English. This is a translation of his Hindi speech. For the English speech, *vide* the following item.

bold to say that their utterances were the honest expression of their beliefs. I know there are some who say that I take things too readily at their face value, that I am gullible. I do not think I am such a simpleton, nor am I so gullible as these friends take me to be. But their criticism does not hurt me. I should prefer to be considered gullible rather than deceitful.

What these Communist friends proposed through their amendments is nothing new. It has been repeated from thousands of platforms. Thousands of Mussalmans have told me that if the Hindu-Muslim question was to be solved satisfactorily, it must be done in my lifetime.

I should feel flattered at this; but how can I agree to a proposal which does not appeal to my reason? Hindu-Muslim unity is not a new thing. Millions of Hindus and Mussalmans have sought after it. I consciously strove for its achievement from my boyhood. While at school, I made it a point to cultivate the friendship of Muslim and Parsi fellow students. I believed even at that tender age that the Hindus in India, if they wished to live in peace and amity with the other communities, should assiduously cultivate the virtue of [good] neighbourliness. It did not matter, I felt, if I made no special effort to cultivate the friendship with Hindus, but I must make friends with at least a few Mussalmans. It was as counsel for a Mussalman merchant that I went to South Africa. I made friends with other Mussalmans there, even with the opponents of my client, and gained a reputation for integrity and good faith. I had among my friends and co-workers Muslims as well as Parsis. I captured their hearts and when I left finally for India, I left them sad and shedding tears of grief at the separation.

In India, too, I continued my efforts and left no stone unturned to achieve that unity. It was my life-long aspiration for it that made me offer my fullest co-operation to the Mussalmans in the Khilafat movement. Muslims throughout the country accepted me as their true friend.

How then is it that I have now come to be regarded as so evil and detestable? Had I any axe to grind in supporting the Khilafat movement? True, I did in my heart of hearts cherish a hope that it might enable me to save the cow. I am a worshipper of the cow. I believe the cow and myself to be the creation of the same God, and I am prepared to sacrifice my life in order to save the cow. But, whatever my philosophy of life and my ultimate hopes, I joined the movement in no spirit of bargain. I co-operated in the struggle for the Khilafat solely in order to discharge my obligation to my neighbour who, I saw, was in distress. The Ali Brothers, had they been alive today, would have testified to the truth of this assertion. And so would many others bear me out in that it was not a bargain on my part for saving the cow. The cow, like the Khilafat, stood on her own merits. As an honest man, a true neighbour and a faithful friend, it was incumbent on me to stand by the Mussalmans in the hour of their trial.

In those days I shocked the Hindus by dining with the Mussalmans, though with the passage of time they have now got used to it. Maulana Bari told me, however, that though he would insist on having me as his guest, he would not allow me to dine with him, lest some day he should be accused of a sinister motive. And so, whenever, I had occasion to stay with him, he called a Brahmin cook and made special arrangements for separate cooking. Firangi Mahal, his residence, was an old styled structure with limited accommodation; yet he cheerfully bore all hardships and carried out his resolve from which I could not dislodge him. It was the spirit of courtesy, dignity and nobility that inspired us in those days. The members of each community vied with one another in accommodating members of sister communities. They respected one another's religious feelings, and considered it a privilege to do so. Not a trace of suspicion lurked in anybody's heart. Where has all that dignity, that nobility of spirit, disappeared now? I should ask all Mussalmans, including Qaid-e-Azam Jinnah, to recall those glorious days and to find out what has brought us to the present impasse. Qaid-e-Azam Jinnah himself was at one time a Congressman. If today the Congress has incurred his wrath; it is because the canker of suspicion has entered his heart. May God bless him with long life, but when I am gone, he will realize and admit that I had no designs on Mussalmans and that I had never betrayed their interests. Where is the escape for me if I injure their cause or betray their interests? My life is entirely at their disposal. They are free to put an end to it, whenever they wish to do so. Assaults have been made on my life in the past, but God has spared me till now, and the assailants have repented for their action.

But if someone were to shoot me in the belief that he was getting rid of a rascal, he would kill not the real Gandhi, but the one that appeared to him a rascal.

To those who have been indulging in a campaign of abuse and vilification I would say, 'Islam enjoins you not to revile even an enemy. The Prophet treated even enemies with kindness and tried to win them over by his fairness and generosity. Are you followers of that Islam or of any other? If you are followers of the true Islam, does it behove you to distrust the words of one who makes a public declaration of his faith?

You may take it from me that one day you will regret the fact that you distrusted and killed one who was a true and devoted friend of yours.' It cuts me to the quick to see that the more I appeal and the more the Maulana importunes, the more intense does the campaign of vilification grow. To me, these abuses are like bullets. They can kill me, even as a bullet can put an end to my life.

You may kill me. That will not hurt me. But what of those who indulge in abusing? They bring discredit to Islam. For the fair name of Islam, I appeal to you to resist this unceasing campaign of abuse and vilification.

Maulana Saheb is being made a target for the filthiest abuse. Why? Because he refuses to exert on me the pressure of his friendship. He realizes that it is a misuse of friendship to seek to compel a friend to accept as truth what he knows is an untruth.

To the Qaid-e-Azam I would say: 'Whatever is true and valid in the claim for Pakistan is already in your hands. What is wrong and untenable is in nobody's gift, so that it can be made over to you. Even if someone were to succeed in imposing an untruth on others, he would not be able to enjoy for long the fruits of such coercion. God dislikes pride and keeps away from it. God would not tolerate a forcible imposition of an untruth.'

The Qaid-e-Azam says 'that he is compelled to say bitter things but that he cannot help giving expression to his thoughts and his feelings'. Similarly I would say: I consider myself a friend of the Mussalmans. Why should I then not give expression to the things nearest to my heart, even at the cost of displeasing them? How can I conceal my innermost thoughts from them? I should congratulate the Qaid-e-Azam on his frankness in giving expression to his thoughts and feelings, even if they sound bitter to his hearers. But even so why should the Mussalmans sitting here be reviled, if they do not see eye to eye with him ? If millions of Mussalmans are with you, can you not afford to ignore the handful of Mussalmans who may appear to you to be misguided ? Why should one with the following of several millions be afraid of a majority community, or of the minority being swamped by the majority ? How did the Prophet work among the Arabs and the Mussalmans ? How did he propagate Islam ? Did he say he would propagate Islam only when he commanded a majority ? I, therefore, appeal to you for the sake of Islam to ponder over what I say. There is neither fair play nor justice in saying that the Congress must accept a thing even if it does not believe in it and even if it goes counter to principles it holds dear.

Rajaji said: 'I do not believe in Pakistan. But Mussalmans ask for it, Mr. Jinnah asks for it, and it has become an obsession with them. Why not then say 'yes' to them just now? The same Mr. Jinnah will later on realize the disadvantages of Pakistan and will forgo the demand.' I said: 'It is not fair to accept as true a thing which I hold to be untrue and ask others to do so in the belief that the demand will not be pressed when the time comes for settling it finally. If I hold the demand to be just, I should concede it this very day. I should not agree to it merely in order to placate Jinnah Saheb. Many friends have come and asked me to agree to it for the time being to placate Mr. Jinnah, disarm his suspicions and to see how he reacts to it. But I cannot be party to a course of action with a false promise. At any rate, it is not my method.'

The Congress has no sanction but the moral one for enforcing its decisions. It believes that true democracy can only be the outcome of non-violence. The structure of a world federation can be raised only on a foundation of non-violence, and violence will have to be totally abjured from world affairs. If this is true, the solution of the Hindu-Muslim question, too, cannot be achieved by resort to violence.

If the Hindus tyrannize over the Mussalmans, with what face will they talk of a world federation? It is for the same reason that I do not believe in the possibility of establishing world peace through violence as the English and American statesmen propose to do. The Congress has agreed to submitting all the differences to an impartial international tribunal and to abide by its decisions. If even this fairest of proposals is unacceptable, the only course that remains open is that of the sword, of violence. How can I persuade myself to agree to an impossibility? To demand the vivisection of a living organism is to ask for its very life. It is a call to war. The Congress cannot be party to such a fratricidal war. Those Hindus who, like Dr. Moonje and Shri Savarkar, believe in the doctrine of the sword may seek to keep the Mussalmans under Hindu domination. I do not represent that section.

I represent the Congress. You want to kill the Congress which is the goose that lays golden eggs. If you distrust the Congress, you may rest assured that there is to be a perpetual war between the Hindus and the Mussalmans, and the country will be doomed to continue warfare and bloodshed. If such warfare is to be our lot, I shall not live to witness it.

It is for that reason that I say to Jinnah Saheb, 'You may take it from me that whatever in your demand for Pakistan accords with considerations of justice and equity is lying in your pocket; whatever in the demand is contrary to justice and equity you can take only by the sword and in no other manner.'

There is much in my heart that I would like to pour out before this assembly. One thing which was uppermost in my heart I have already dealt with. You may take it from me that it is with me a matter of life and death. If we Hindus and Mussalmans mean to achieve a heart unity, without the slightest mental reservation on the part of either, we must first unite in the effort to be free from the shackles of this Empire. If Pakistan after all is to be a portion of India, what objection can there be for Mussalmans against joining this struggle for India's freedom? The Hindus and Mussalmans must, therefore, unite in the first instance on the issue of fighting for freedom. Jinnah Saheb thinks the war will last long. I do not agree with him. If the war goes on for six months more, how shall we be able to save China?

I, therefore, want freedom immediately, this very night, before dawn, if it can be had. Freedom cannot now wait for the realization of communal unity. If that unity is not achieved, sacrifices necessary for it will have to be much greater than would have otherwise sufficed.

But the Congress must win freedom or be wiped out in the effort. And forget not that the freedom which the Congress is struggling to achieve will not be for the Congressmen alone but for all the forty crores of the Indian people. Congressmen must forever remain humble servants of the people.

The Qaid-e-Azam has said that the Muslim League is prepared to take over the rule from the Britishers if they are prepared to hand it over to the Muslim League, for the British took over the Empire from the hands of the Muslims. This, however, will be Muslim *raj*. The offer made by Maulana Saheb and by me does not imply establishment of Muslim *raj* or Muslim domination. The Congress does not believe in the domination of any group or any community. It believes in democracy which includes in its orbit Muslims, Hindus, Christians, Parsis, Jews—every one of the communities inhabiting this vast country. If Muslim *raj* is inevitable, then let it be; but how can we give it the stamp of our assent? How can we agree to the domination of one community over the others ? Millions of Mussalmans in this country come from Hindu stock.

How can their homeland be any other than India ? My eldest son embraced Islam some years back. What would his homeland be—Porbander or the Punjab? I ask the Mussalmans: 'If India is not your homeland, what other country do you belong to ? In what separate homeland would you put my son who embraced Islam?' His mother wrote him a letter after his conversion, asking him if he had on embracing Islam given up drinking which Islam forbids to its followers. To those who gloated over the conversion, she wrote to say: 'I do not mind his becoming a Mussalman so much as his drinking. Will you, as pious Mussalmans, tolerate his drinking even after his conversion? He has reduced himself to the state of a rake by drinking. If you are going to make a man of him again, his conversion will have been turned to good account. You will, therefore, please see that he as a Mussalman abjures wine and women. If that change does not come about, his conversion goes in vain and our non-cooperation with him will have to continue.'

India is without doubt the homeland of all the Mussalmans inhabiting this country. Every Mussalman should therefore cooperate in the fight for India's freedom. The Congress does not belong to any one class or community; it belongs to the whole nation. It is open to Mussalmans to take possession of the Congress. They can, if they like, swamp the Congress by their numbers, and can steer it along the course which appeals to them. The Congress is fighting not on behalf of the Hindus but on behalf of the whole nation, including the minorities. It would hurt me to hear of a single instance of a Musslman being killed by a Congressman. In the coming revolution, Congressmen will sacrifice their lives in order to protect the Mussalman against a Hindu's attack and *vice versa*. It is a part of their creed, and is one of the essentials of non-violence. You will be expected on occasions like these not to lose your heads. Every Congressman, whether a Hindu or a Mussalman, owes this duty to the organization to which he belongs. The Mussalman who will act in this manner will render a service to Islam. Mutual trust is essential for success in the final nation-wide struggle that is to come. I have said that much greater sacrifices will have to be made this time in the wake of our struggle because of the opposition from the Muslim League and from Englishmen. You have seen the secret circular issued by Sir Frederick Puckle. It is a suicidal course that he has taken. It contains an open incitement to organizations which crop up like mushrooms to combine to fight the Congress. We have thus to deal with an Empire whose ways are crooked. Ours is a straight path which we can tread even with our eyes closed. That is the beauty of *satyagraha*.

In *satyagraha*, there is no place for fraud or falsehood, or any kind of untruth. Fraud and untruth today are stalking the world. I cannot be a helpless witness to such a situation. I have travelled all over India as perhaps nobody in the present age has. The voiceless millions of the land saw in me their friend and representative, and I identified myself with them to an extent it was possible for a human being to do. I saw trust in their eyes, which I now want to turn to good account in fighting this Empire upheld on untruth and violence.

However gigantic the preparations that the Empire has made, we must get out of its clutches. How can I remain silent at this supreme hour and hide my light under the bushel? Shall I ask the Japanese to tarry a while? If today I sit quiet and inactive, God will take me to task for not using up the treasure He had given me, in the midst of the conflagration that is enveloping the whole world. Had the condition been different, I should have asked you to wait yet awhile. But the situation now has become intolerable, and the Congress has no other course left for it.

Nevertheless, the actual struggle does not commence this moment. You have only placed all your powers in my hands. I will now wait upon the Viceroy and plead with him for the acceptance of the Congress demand. That process is likely to take two or three weeks. What would you do in the meanwhile? What is the programme, for the interval, in which all can participate? As you know, the spinning wheel is the first thing that occurs to me. I made the same answer to the Maulana. He would have none of it, though he understood its import later. The fourteenfold constructive programme is, of course, there for you to carry out. What more should you do? I will tell you. Everyone of you should, from this moment onwards, consider yourself a free man or woman, and act as if you are free and are no longer under the heel of this imperialism.

It is not a make-believe that I am suggesting to you. It is the very essence of freedom. The bond of the slave is snapped the moment he considers himself to be a free being. He will plainly tell the master: 'I was your bondslave till this moment, but I am a slave no longer. You may kill me if you like, but if you keep me alive, I wish to tell you that if you release me from the bondage of your own accord, I will ask for nothing more from you. You used to feed and clothe me, though I could have provided food and clothing for myself by my labour. I hitherto depended on you instead of on God, for food and raiment. God has now inspired me with an urge for freedom and I am today a free man and will no longer depend on you.'

You may take it from me that I am not going to strike a bargain with the Viceroy for ministries and the like. I am not going to be satisfied with anything short of complete freedom. May be, he will propose the abolition of salt tax, the drink evil, etc. But I will say:

'Nothing less than freedom.'

Here is a *mantra*, a short one, that I give you. You may imprint it on your hearts and let every breath of yours give expression to it.

The *mantra* is: 'Do or Die.' We shall either free India or die in the attempt; we shall not live to see the perpetuation of our slavery. Every true Congressman or [Congress] woman will join the struggle with an inflexible determination not to remain alive to see the country in bondage and slavery. Let that be your pledge. Keep jails out of your consideration. If the Government keep me free, I will spare you the trouble of filling the jails. I will not put on the Government the strain of maintaining a large number of prisoners at a time when it is in trouble. Let every man and woman live every moment of his or her life hereafter in the consciousness that he or she eats or lives for achieving freedom and will die, if need be, to attain that goal. Take a pledge with God and your own conscience as witness, that you will no longer rest till freedom is achieved and will be prepared to lay down your lives in the attempt to achieve it. He who loses his life will gain it; he who will seek to save it shall lose it. Freedom is not for the coward or the faint-hearted.

A word to the journalists I congratulate you on the support you have hitherto given to the national demand. I know the restrictions and handicaps under which you have to labour. But I would now ask you to snap the chains that bind you. It should be the proud privilege of the newspapers to lead and set an example in laying down one's life for freedom. You have the pen which the Government can't suppress. I know you have large properties in the form of printing presses, etc., and you would be afraid lest the Government should attach them. I do not ask you to invite an attachment of the printing press voluntarily. For myself, I would not suppress my pen, even if the press was to be attached. As you know my press was attached in the past and returned later on. But I do not ask from you that final sacrifice. I suggest a middle way. You should now wind up your Standing Committee, and you may declare that you will give up writing under the present restrictions and take up the pen only when India has won her freedom. You may tell Sir Frederick Puckle that he can't expect from you a command performance, that his Press notes are full of untruth, and that you will refuse to publish them. You will openly declare that you are whole heartedly with the Congress. If you do this, you will have changed the atmosphere before the fight actually begins.

From the Princes I ask with all respect due to them a very small thing. I am a well-wisher of the Princes. I was born in a State. My grandfather refused to salute with his right hand any Prince other than his own. But he did not say to the Prince, as I feel he ought to have said, that even his own master could not compel him, his minister, to act against his conscience. I have eaten the Princes' salt and I would not be false to it. As a faithful servant, it is my duty to warn the Princes that if they will act while I am still alive, the Princes may come to occupy an honourable place in free India. In Jawaharlal's scheme of free India, no privileges or the privileged classes have a place.

Jawaharlal considers all property to be State-owned. He wants planned economy. He wants to reconstruct India according to plan. He likes to fly; I do not. I have kept a place for the Princes and the zamindars in India that I envisage. I would ask the Princes in all humility to enjoy through renunciation. The Princes may renounce ownership over their properties and become their trustees in the true sense of the term. I visualize God in the assemblage of people. The Princes may say to their people: 'You are the owners and masters of the State and we are your servants.' I would ask the Princes to become servants of the people and render to them an account of their own services. The Empire too bestows power on the Princes, but they should prefer to derive power from their own people; and if they want to indulge in some innocent pleasures, they may seek to do so as servants of the people. I do not want the Princes to live as paupers. But I would ask them: 'Do you want to remain slaves for all time? Why should you, instead of paying homage to a foreign power, not accept the sovereignty of your own people?' You may write to the Political Department: 'The people are now awake. How are we to withstand an avalanche before which even the large Empires are crumbling? We, therefore, shall belong to the people from today onwards. We shall sink or swim with them.' Believe me, there is nothing unconstitutional in the course I am suggesting. There are, so far as I know, no treaties enabling the Empire to coerce the Princes. The people of the States will also declare that though they are the Princes' subjects, they are part of the Indian nation and that they will accept the leadership of the Princes, if the latter cast their lot with the People, but not otherwise. If this declaration enrages the Princes and they choose to kill the people, the latter will meet death bravely and unflinchingly, but will not go back on their word.

Nothing, however, should be done secretly. This is an open rebellion. In this struggle secrecy is a sin. A free man would not engage in a secret movement. It is likely that when you gain freedom you will have a C.I.D. of your own, in spite of my advice to the contrary. But in the present struggle, we have to work openly and to receive the bullets on our chest, without taking to heels.

I have a word to say to the Government servants also. They may not, if they like, resign their posts yet. The late Justice Ranade did not resign his post, but he openly declared that he belonged to the Congress. He said to the Government that though he was a judge, he was a Congressman and would openly attend the sessions of the Congress, but that at the same time he would not let his political views warp his impartiality on the bench. He held Social Reform Conference in the very *pandal* of the Congress. I would ask all the Government servants to follow in the footsteps of Ranade and to declare their allegiance to the Congress as an answer to the secret circular issued by Sir Frederick Puckle.

This is all that I ask of you just now. I will now write to the Viceroy. You will be able to read the correspondence not just now but when I publish it with the Viceroy's consent. But you are free to aver that you support the demand to be put forth in my letter. A judge came to me and said: "We get secret circulars from high quarters.

What are we to do?" I replied, "If I were in your place, I would ignore the circulars. You may openly say to the Government: 'I have received your secret circular. I am, however, with the Congress. Though I serve the Government for my livelihood, I am not going to obey these secret circulars or to employ underhand methods.' "

Soldiers too are covered by the present programme. I do not ask them just now to resign their posts and leave the army. Soldiers come to me, Jawaharlal and to the Maulana and say: "We are wholly with you. We are tired of the governmental tyranny." To these soldiers I would say: "You may say to the Government, 'Our hearts are with the Congress. We are not going to leave our posts. We will serve you so long as we receive your salaries. We will obey your just orders, but will refuse to fire on our own people.' "

To those who lack the courage to do this much I have nothing to say. They will go their own way. But if you can do this much, you may take it from me that the whole atmosphere will be electrified. Let the Government then shower bombs, if they like. But no power on earth will then be able to keep you in bondage any longer.

If the students want to join the struggle only to go back to their studies after a while, I would not invite them to it. For the present, however, till the time that I frame a programme for the the struggle, I would ask the students to say to their professors: 'We belong to the Congress. Do you belong to the Congress or to the Government? If you belong to the Congress, you need not vacate your posts. You will remain at your posts but teach us and lead us unto freedom.' In all fights for freedom, the world over, the students have made very large contributions.

If in the interval that is left to us before the actual fight begins, you do even the little I have suggested to you, you will have changed the atmosphere and will have prepared the ground for the next step.

There is much I should yet like to say. But my heart is heavy. I have already taken up much of your time. I have yet to say a few words in English also. I thank you for the patience and attention with which you have listened to me even at this late hour. It is just what true soldiers would do. For the last twenty-two years, I have controlled my speech and pen and have stored up my energy. He is a true *brahmachari* who does not fritter away his energy. He will, therefore, always control his speech. That has been my conscious effort all these years. But today the occasion has come when I had to unburden my heart before you. I have done so, even though it meant putting a strain on your patience; and I do not regret having done it. I have given you my message and through you I have delivered it to the whole of India.

[*Mahatma,* Vol. VI, pp. 154-64]

68. Do or Die

SPEECH AT A.I.C.C. MEETING

[Bombay,
August 8, 1942][1]

I have taken such an inordinately long time over pouring out what was agitating my soul to those whom I had just now the privilege of serving. I have been called their leader or, in military language, their commander. But I do not look at my position in that light. I have no weapon but love to wield my authority over anyone. I do sport a stick which you can break into bits without the slightest exertion. It is simply my staff with the help of which I walk. Such a cripple is not elated, when he is called upon to bear the greatest burden. You can share that burden only when I appear before you not as your commander but as a humble servant. And he who serves best is the chief among equals.

Therefore, I was bound to share with you, such thoughts as were welling up in my breast and tell you in as summary a manner as I can, what I expect you to do as the first step.

Let me tell you at the outset that the real struggle does not commence today. I have yet to go through much ceremonial as I always do. The burden is almost unbearable and I have got to continue to reason in those circles with whom I have lost my credit for the time being. I know that in the course of the last few weeks I have forfeited my credit with a large number of friends, so much so that some of them have now begun to doubt not only my wisdom but even my honesty. Now, I hold that my wisdom is not such a treasure which I cannot afford to lose; but my honesty is a precious treasure to me and I can ill afford to lose it.

Such occasions arise in the life of a man who is a pure seeker after truth and who would seek to serve humanity and his country to the best of his lights without fear or hypocrisy. For the last fifty years I have known no other way. I have been a humble servant of humanity and have rendered on more than one occasion such service as I could to the

1. From *The Indian Annual Register* 1942, Vol. II, p. 144.

Empire; and here let me say without fear of challenge that throughout my career never have I asked for any personal favour.

I have enjoyed the privilege of friendship, as I enjoy it today, with Lord Linlithgow. It is a friendship which has outgrown official relationship. Whether Lord Linlithgow will bear me out I do not know; but there has sprung up a personal bond between him and myself. He once introduced me to his daughter. His son-in-law, the A.D.C., was drawn towards me. He fell in love with Mahadev more than with me, and Lady Anne and he came to me. She is an obedient and favourite daughter. I take interest in their welfare. I take the liberty to give out these titbits only to give you an earnest view of the personal bond which exists between us. And yet let me declare here that no personal bond will ever interfere with the stubborn struggle which, if it falls to my lot, I may have to launch against Lord Linlithgow, as the representative of the Empire. It seems to me that I will have to resist the might of that Empire with the might of the dumb millions, with no limit but non-violence as policy confined to this struggle. It is a terrible job to have to offer resistance to a Viceroy with whom I enjoy such relations. He has more than once trusted my word, often about my people. I mention this with great pride and pleasure. I mention it as an earnest of my desire to be true to the British nation, to be true to the Empire. I mention it to testify that when that Empire forfeited my trust, the Englishman who was its Viceroy came to know it.

Then there is the sacred memory of Charlie Andrews which wells up within me at this moment. The spirit of Andrews hovers about me. For me he sums up the brightest tradition of English culture. I enjoyed closer relations with him than with most Indians. I enjoyed his confidence. There were no secrets between us. We exchanged our hearts every day. Whatever was in his heart he would blurt out without the slightest hesitation or reservation. It is true he was friend of Gurudev, but he looked upon Gurudev with awe, not that Gurudev wanted it. Andrews had that peculiar humility. But with me he became the closest friend. Years ago he came to South Africa[1] with a note of introduction from the late[2] Gokhale. He is unfortunately gone.[3] He was a fine Englishman.[4] I

1. The words "to South Africa" were added by Gandhiji.
2. The words "the late" were added by Gandhiji.
3. This is in Gandhiji's hand. The original had: "Pearson and he are both unfortunately gone."
4. This is in Gandhiji's hand. The original had: "They were the finest specimen of Englishmen."

know that the spirit of Andrews is listening to me. Then I have received a warm telegram from the Metropolitan (Dr. Westcote[1]) of Calcutta, conveying his blessings, though, I know, he is opposed to my move today. I hold him to be a man of God. I can understand the language of his heart, and I know that his heart is with me.

With this background, I want to declare to the world that, whatever may be said to the contrary, and although I might have forfeited the regard and even the trust of many friends in the West, and I bow my head low, but even for their friendship or their love, I must not suppress the voice within, call it 'conscience', call it the 'prompting of my inner basic nature'. There is something within me impelling me to cry out my agony. I have known humanity. I have studied something of psychology though I have not read many books on it. Such a man knows exactly what it is. That something in me which never deceives me tells me now: 'You have to stand against the whole world although you may have to stand alone. You have to stare the world in the face although the world may look at you with bloodshot eyes. Do not fear. Trust that little thing which resides in the heart.' It says, 'Forsake friends, wife, and all; but testify to that for which you have lived, and for which you have to die.'

Believe me, friends, I am not anxious to die. I want to live my full span of life. According to me, it is 120 years at least. By that time India will be free, the world will be free. Let me tell you, too, that I do not regard England, or for that matter America, as free countries.

They are free after their own fashion, free to hold in bondage the coloured races of the earth. Are England and America fighting for the liberty of these races today? You shall not limit my concept of freedom. The English and American teachers, their history and their magnificent poetry have not said you shall not broaden the interpretation of that freedom. And according to my interpretation of that freedom, I am constrained to say, they are strangers to that freedom which their poets and teachers have described. If they will know the real freedom, they should come to India. They have to come not with pride or arrogance but in the spirit of earnest seekers of Truth.

It is the[2] fundamental truth with[3] which India has been experimenting for 22 years. Unconsciously, from its very foundations, long ago, the Congress has departed though non-violently from what is

1. This name was added by Gandhiji.
2. This is in Gandhiji's hand. The original had 'a'.
3. The word "with" was added by Gandhiji.

known[1] as the constitutional method. Dadabhai and Pherozshah who held the Congress India in the palm of their hands had held on to the latter[2]. They were lovers of the Congress. They were its masters. But above all they were real servants. They never countenanced murder and secrecy and the like. I confess there are many black sheep amongst us Congressmen. But I trust the whole of India to launch upon a non-violent struggle on the widest scale[3]. I trust[4] the innate goodness of human nature which perceives the truth and prevails during a crisis as if by instinct. But even if I am deceived in this, I shall not swerve[5]. From its very inception the Congress based its policy on peaceful methods, and the subsequent generations added non-cooperation. When Dadabhai entered the British Parliament, Salisbury dubbed him as a black man, but the English people defeated Salisbury, and Dadabhai, went to Parliament by their vote. India was delirious with joy. These things, however, now India has outgrown.

It is with all these things as the background that I want Englishmen, Europeans and all the United Nations to examine in their heart of hearts what crime India has committed in demanding independence today. I ask: Is it right for you to distrust us? Is it right to distrust such an organization with all its background, tradition and record of over half a century and misrepresent its endeavours before all the world by every means at your command? Is it right, I ask, that by hook or by crook, aided by the Foreign Press, aided, I hope not, by the President of the U.S.A. or even by the Generalissimo of China, who has yet to win his laurels, you should present India's stand in shocking lights?

I have met the Generalissimo. I have known him through Madam Chiang who was my interpreter, and though he seemed inscrutable to me, not so Madam Chiang. And he allowed me to read his mind through her. He has not as yet said that we were wrong in demanding our independence. There is a chorus of disapproval and protest all over the world against us. They say we are erring, the move is inopportune. I had

---

1. This is in Gandhiji's hand. The original had "been building on non-violence known".
2. This is in Gandhiji's hand. The original had "become rebels".
3. The words "son the widest scale" were added by Gandhiji.
4. This is in Gandhiji's hand. The original had "because of my nature to rely upon".
5. This is in Gandhiji's hand. The original had "I shall not flinch".

great regard for the British, but now British diplomacy stinks in[1] my nostrils. Yet others are learning their lessons.

They may succeed in getting, through these methods, world opinion on their side for a time; but India will raise her voice against all the organized propaganda. I will speak against it. Even if the whole of the world forsakes me, I will say: 'You are wrong. India will wrench with non-violence her liberty from unwilling hands.'

Even if my eyes close and there is no freedom for India, non-violence will not end. They will be dealing a mortal blow to China and to Russia if they oppose the freedom of non-violent India which today is pleading with bended knees for the fulfilment of a debt long overdue. Does a creditor ever go to the debtor like that? And even when India is met with such angry opposition, she says: 'We won't hit below the belt. We have learnt sufficient gentlemanliness. We are pledged to non-violence.' I have been the author of the non-embarrassment policy of the Congress and yet today you find me talking this strong language. My non-embarrassment plea was always qualified by the proviso 'consistent with our honour and safety'. If a man holds me by the neck and wants to drown me, may I not struggle to free myself directly? There is no inconsistency in our position today.

There are representatives of the Foreign Press assembled here today. Through them I wish to say to the world that United Nations, who say that they have need for India, have the opportunity now to declare India free and prove their *bona fides*. If they miss it, they will be missing opportunity of their lifetime, and history will record that they did not discharge their obligations to India in time and lost the battle. I want the blessing of the whole world, so that I may succeed with them. I do not want the United Powers to go beyond their obvious limitations. I do not want them to accept non-violence and disarm today. There is a fundamental difference between Fascism and even this imperialism which I am fighting. Do the British get from India all they want? What they get today is from the India which they hold in bondage. Think what difference it would make if India was to participate as a free ally. That freedom, if it is to come, must come today. It will have no taste left in it if today you, who have power to help, do not exercise it. If you can exercise it, what seems impossible today will, under the glow of freedom, become possible tomorrow. If India feels that freedom, she will command that freedom for China.

1. This is in Gandhiji's hand. The original had "into".

The road for running to Russia's help will be opened. Englishmen did not die in Malaya or on the soil of Burma. What shall enable us to retrieve this situation? Where shall I go and where shall I take the forty crores of India? How is this vast mass of humanity to be aflame in the cause of world-deliverance, unless and until it has touched and felt freedom? Today they have no touch of life left. It has been crushed out of them. If lustre is to be put into their eyes, freedom has to come not tomorrow but today. I have, therefore, pledged the Congress and the Congress has pledged herself that she will do or die.

[*From a typed office copy.*
Courtesy: Nehru Memorial Museum and Library]

69. Independence

[New Delhi,
April 29, 1946]

Friends have repeatedly challenged me to define independence. At the risk of repetition, I must say that the independence of my dream means *Ramarajya*, i.e., the Kingdom of God on Earth. I do not know what it will be like in Heaven. I have no desire to know the distant scene. If the present is attractive enough, the future cannot be very unlike.

In concrete terms, then, the independence should be political, economic and moral.

'Political' necessarily means the removal of the control of the British army in every shape and form.

'Economic' means entire freedom from British capitalists and capital, as also their Indian counterparts. In other words, the humblest must feel equal to the tallest. This can take place only by capital or capitalists sharing their skill and capital with the lowliest and the least.

'Moral' means freedom from armed defence forces. My conception of *Ramarajya* excludes replacement of the British army by a national army of occupation. A country that is governed by even its national army can never be morally free and, therefore, its so-called weakest member can never rise to his full moral height.

Though Mr. Churchill is claimed to have won the war for the British, he has in his Aberdeen speech uttered words of wisdom from the standpoint of a radical non-violent reformer. He knows, if any panoplied warrior knows, what havoc the two wars of our generation have wrought. In another column I reproduce the summary of his speech as reported in the Public Press.[1] Only I must warn the public against the pessimistic note underlying the speech. Nothing will be found to have gone wrong if mankind recoils from the horrors of war.

The bloodletting that men have undergone to the point of whiteness will not have been in vain, if it has taught us that we must freely give our

1. *Vide* "Winston Churchill's Speech".

own blood in the place of taking other people's blood, be the cause ever so noble or ignoble.

If the Cabinet Mission 'delivers the goods', India will have to decide whether attempting to become a military power she would be content to become, at least for some years, a fifth-rate power in the world without a message in answer to the pessimism described above, or whether she will by further refining and continuing her non-violent policy prove herself worthy of being the first nation in the world using her hard won freedom for the delivery of the earth from the burden which is crushing her in spite of the so-called victory.,

[*Harijan*, 5-5-1946]

70. On Cabinet Mission's Proposal

SPEECH AT A.I.C.C.[1]

[Bombay,
July 7, 1946]

I have often said that man plans but the success of his plans depends not on him but on the will of Providence which is the supreme arbiter of our destinies. Unlike you, I am [here] not in my own right but on sufferance. I have been told that some of my previous remarks about the Cabinet Mission's proposals have caused a good deal of confusion in the public mind. As a *satyagrahi* it is always my endeavour to speak the whole truth and nothing but the truth. I never wish to hide anything from you. I hate mental reservations. But language is at best an imperfect medium of expression. No man can fully express in words what he feels or thinks. Even seers and prophets of old have suffered under that disability.

I have not seen what has appeared in the papers about what I am supposed to have said regarding the Cabinet Mission's proposals. I cannot read all the newspapers myself. I content myself with perusing only what my co-workers and assistants may place before me. I hold that I have lost nothing thereby. Because of what has appeared in the Press, an impression seems to have been created that I said one thing at Delhi and am saying something different now. I did say in one of my speeches at Delhi in regard to the Cabinet Mission's proposals that I saw darkness where I saw light before.[2] That darkness has not yet lifted. If possible it

---

1. On June 26 the Congress Working Committee had passed a resolution in New Delhi expressing willingness to "join the proposed Constituent Assembly with a view to framing the Constitution of a free, united and democratic India" and demanding the formation of "a representative and responsible Provisional National Government" at the earliest possible date.
   Gandhiji spoke on the motion moved by Abul Kalam Azad seeking ratification of the resolution of June 26 and the one on *satyagraha* in South Africa.
2. *Vide* "Speech at Prayer Meeting", 25-6-1946.

has deepened. I could have asked the Working Committee to turn down the proposals about the Constituent Assembly if I could see my way clearly. You know my relations with the members of the Working Committee. Babu Rajendra Prasad might have been a High Court Judge, but he chose instead to act as my interpreter and clerk in Champaran.[1] Then there is the Sardar. He has earned the nickname of being my yes-man. He does not mind it. He even flaunts it as a compliment. He is a stormy petrel. Once he used to dress and dine in the Western style. But ever since he decided to cast his lot with me my word has been law to him. But even he cannot see eye to eye with me in this matter. They both tell me that whereas on all previous occasions I was able to support my instinct with reason and satisfy their head as well as heart, this time I have failed to do so. I told them in reply that whilst my own heart was filled with misgivings, I could not adduce any reason for it or else I would have asked them to reject the proposals straightway. It was my duty to place my misgivings before them to put them on their guard. But they should examine what I had said in the cold light of reason and accept my view-point only if they were convinced of its correctness. Their decision, which they have arrived at after prolonged deliberations and which is almost unanimous, is before you. The members of the Working Committee are your faithful and tried servants. You should not lightly reject their resolution.

I am willing to admit that the proposed Constituent Assembly is not the Parliament of the people. It has many defects. But you are all seasoned and veteran fighters. A soldier is never afraid of danger. He revels in it. If there are shortcomings in the proposed Constituent Assembly, it is for you to get them removed. It should be a challenge to combat, not a ground for rejection. I am surprised that Shri Jayaprakash Narayan said yesterday[2] that it would be dangerous to participate in the proposed Constituent Assembly and, therefore, they should reject the Working Committee's resolution. I was not prepared to hear such defeatist language from the lips of a tried fighter like Jayaprakash. One line from a song composed by the late Choudhary Rambhaj Dutt has always made a very deep appeal to me. It means:

"We will never be defeated—nay, not even in death." That is the spirit in which I expect you to approach this resolution. A *satyagrahi* knows no defeat.

---

1. In 1917.
2. At the A.I.C.C. meeting.

Nor would I expect a *satyagrahi* to say that whatever Englishmen do must be bad. The English are not necessarily bad. There are good men and bad men among the English people as among any other people. We ourselves are not free from defects. The English could not have risen to their present strength if they had not some good in them. They have come and exploited India, because we quarrelled amongst ourselves and allowed ourselves to be exploited.

In God's world unmixed evil never prospers. God rules even where Satan seems to hold sway, because the latter exists only on His sufferance. Some people say that *satyagraha* is of no avail against a person who has no moral sense. I join issue with that. The stoniest heart must melt if we are true and have enough patience. A *satyagrahi* lays down his life, but never gives up. That is the meaning of the "Do or die" slogan. That slogan does not mean 'Kill or be killed'. That would be wilful distortion and travesty of its true meaning. The true meaning is that we must do our duty and die in the course of performing it if necessary. To die without killing is the badge of a *satyagrahi*. If we had lived up to that ideal we would have won *swaraj* by now. But our *ahimsa* was lame. It walked on crutches. Even so it has brought us to our present strength. I know what happened in 1942. You will perhaps say that it was sabotage and underground activity that had brought the country to its present strength. It cannot be denied that sabotage activity was carried on in the name of the Congress during the 1942 struggle but I deny *in toto* that the strength of the masses is due to that. Whatever strength the masses have is due entirely to *ahimsa* however imperfect or defective its practice might have been. Our *ahimsa* was imperfect because we were imperfect, because it was presented to you by an imperfect being like myself. If then, even in the hands of imperfect instruments it could produce such brilliant results, what could it not have achieved in the hands of a perfect *satyagrahi*?

In 1942 our people showed great valour. But greater valour will be required of us before our goal is reached. We have done much, but more remains to be done. For that we must have patience and humility and detachment. You should try to understand what happened in 1942, the inner meaning of that struggle and the reason why it stopped short where it did.

This is no time for dalliance or ease. I told Pandit Jawaharlal Nehru that he must wear the crown of thorns for the sake of the nation and he has agreed.[1] The Constituent Assembly is going to be no bed of roses for you but only a bed of thorns. You may not shirk it.

That does not mean that everybody should want to go into it. Only those should go there who are especially fitted for the task by virtue of their legal training or special talent. It is not a prize to be sought as a reward for sacrifices, but a duty to be faced even like mounting the gallows or sacrifice of one's all at the altar of service.

There is another reason why you should join the Constituent Assembly. If you asked me whether in the event of your rejecting the proposed Constituent Assembly or the Constituent Assembly failing to materialize, I would advise the people to launch civil disobedience, individual or mass, or undertake a fast myself, my reply is 'No'. I believe in walking alone. I came alone in this world, I have walked alone in the valley of the shadow of death and I shall quit alone when the time comes. I know I am quite capable of launching *satyagraha* even if I am all alone. I have done so before. But this is no occasion for a fast or civil disobedience. I regard the Constituent Assembly as the substitute of *satyagraha*. It is constructive *satyagraha*.

The alternative is constructive work which you have never done justice to. If you had, you would have today got the Constituent Assembly of Jayaprakash's dream instead of the present one. But a *satyagrahi* cannot wait or delay action till perfect conditions are forthcoming. He will act with whatever material is at hand, purge it of dross and convert it into pure gold. Whatever may be the defects in the State Document of May 16th, I have no doubt as to the honesty of those who have framed it. They know they have got to quit. They want to quit in an orderly manner. And to that end they have produced the Document they could under the circumstances. I refuse to believe that they came all the way from England to deceive us.

A polish lady[2] has sent me a note just today saying that all Europeans had received secret instructions to leave India as the British army would no longer be able to give them adequate protection. If it is so, it is a sad reflection on us. We would be unworthy of the name of *satyagrahi* if even an English child did not feel secure in our midst.

Even if we succeed in driving out the Europeans by these tactics, something worse will take their place. Our Quit India Resolution[3] has no malice about it. It only means that we will no longer be exploited.

---

1. Jawaharlal Nehru was elected President of the Indian National Congress.
2. Wanda Dynowska; *vide* "Letter to G. E. B. Abell", 9-7-1946.
3. *Vide* Appendix "C. Rajagopalachari's Formula", before 5-8-1942.

Let us not be cowardly, but approach out task with confidence and courage. Let not the fear of being deceived dismay us. No one can deceive a *satyagrahi*. Never mind the darkness that fills my mind.

He will turn it into light.[1] Continuing, Mahatma Gandhi referred to the draft resolution on the *satyagraha* movement now being carried on by Indians in South Africa. He said that the Indians in South Africa were being ill-treated not because they were not whites but because they were considered as coolies. The Indians in South Africa spoke English and many of them were doctors and lawyers. In spite of all this, the South African whites looked upon them as coolies and called them as such. The Indians, of course, were in a minority and yet they were putting up a brave fight. They had no swords or guns but they were determined to resist the anti-Indian laws by soul force, which was the only force available to *satyagrah* is. Durban owed its present prosperity to the Indians. The South African whites had agreed to give the Indians the vote though not as equals but as inferiors.

The white civilization in South Africa could not be kept alive by such means.

Mahatma Gandhi wondered how a brave man like General Smuts who had praised the Indians of their elementary rights.[2] Commenting on the doings of the white hooligans who were said to have beaten to death an Indian, whom they mistook for a *satyagrahi*, Gandhiji remarked: "It is a sad event. Nevertheless, I feel happy. A *satyagrahi* must always be ready to die with a smile on his face without retaliation and without rancour in his heart. Some people have come to have a wrong notion that *satyagraha* means only jail-going, perhaps facing lathi blows and nothing more. Such *satyagraha* cannot bring independence."

To win independence you have to learn the art of dying without killing.

I venture to submit that a civilization which needs such barbarous legislation for its protection is a contradiction in terms. The Indians are fighting for their honour. The land in South Africa does not belong to the whites. Land belongs to one who labours on it. I would not shed a single tear if all the *satyagrahis* in South Africa are wiped out. Thereby, they will not only bring deliverance to themselves but point the way to the

1. The report up to this point has been reproduced from *Harijan*. What follows is from *The Hindu*.
2. What follows is from Pyarelal's "Weekly Letter" in *Harijan*, 14-7-1946.

Negroes and vindicate the honour of India. I am proud of them and so should you be.

His object in speaking to them, he continued, was not to move them to tears or to incite them to anger and vituperation against the whites. Rather they should pray to God to guide the whites aright and grant strength and courage to their brethren to remain steadfast to the end.

The South African struggle may appear to be insignificant today but it is charged with momentous consequences. *Satyagraha* is today being tried in the land of its birth. The success of a handful of Indians, mostly descendants of indentured labourers, has excited the jealousy of the whites of South Africa. And they are now subjecting them to unspeakable indignities. They are sought to be segregated into *ghettos* and further humiliated by being offered an inferior franchise. That all this should happen under the imprimatur of Field Marshal Smuts fills me with shame and humiliation. Our sins have a strange way of coming home to roost. We turned a portion of ourselves into pariahs and today the whites of South Africa are doing the same to our compatriots there. Let us purge ourselves of this curse and bless the heroic struggle of our brethren in South Africa. They do not need our monetary help. But they need all our sympathy and moral support.[1]

[*The Hindu, 8-7-1946,* and
Harijan, 14-7-1946 and 21-7-1946]

1. After Gandhiji's address the debate was resumed. Prominent among those who opposed the resolution were Jayaprakash Narayan, Achyut Patwardhan and Aruna Asaf Ali, members of the Congress Socialist Party. The resolution was then put to vote and carried, 204 voting for and 51 against.

71. Move On

[SEVAGRAM,
August 16, 1946]

On reading about my persistent darkness, a correspondent sends me the following lines of comfort:

The path may be clouded;
Move on, for the orbit is fixed for your soul;
And though it may lead into darkness of night,
The torch of the Builder shall give it new light.

[*Harijan,* 1-9-1946]

72. No One Listen to Me

SPEECH AT PRAYER MEETING

[NEW DELHI,
April 1, 1947]

Today as soon as Manu Gandhi uttered the first word of the *Kalma* from the *Koran* a young man stood up, marched right up to the stage where Gandhiji sat and said, "You go away from here. This is a Hindu temple where we will not allow a Muslim prayer. You have been repeatedly telling this thing to us but our mothers and sisters continue to be slaughtered. We cannot tolerate it any longer." Gandhiji told him: You are free to go. If you do not want to pray let the others do it. This place does not belong to you. This is not the right way.[1] You did not do the right thing. You forcibly removed the young man from the meeting. You should not have done such a thing. It would give him a sense of triumph. He was very excited. He did not wish to listen to the prayer. But I know that you all wish to listen to it.

I do not wish to hold the prayer in spite of protests. Now I intend to give up the rest of the prayer. You are all familiar with the prayer I offer. You have heard it even before I went to Noakhali. In my sequence of prayers, the Muslim prayer is followed by the Parsi prayer. After that this girl would have sung to you a *bhajan* in her melodious voice and then there would have been *Ramdhun.* But now I am leaving out the Parsi prayer and also the *Ramdhun. Auz-o-Billahi* is the beginning of one of the verses of the *Koran*. You think that uttering this expression is an insult to Hinduism. But I am a true *Sanatani* Hindu. My Hinduism tells me that along with the Hindu prayer I should also offer the Muslim prayer and the Parsi and Christian prayers. True Hinduism lies in offering prayers of all religions because only he is a good Hindu who is also a good Muslim

1. But the young man could not be silenced. He came close to Gandhiji. People tried to pull him back but he stood firm and persisted in arguing. A lady put herself between Gandhiji and the young man. Gandhiji asked her to keep away, saying, "Let no one stand between me and him." But the people removed the young man from the meeting.

and a good Parsi. The young man said that this was a Hindu temple and such prayers could not be held here. But that is wild talk. This temple belongs to the *Bhangis*. Even a single *Bhangi* can throw me out of this place if he so desires. But these people love me. They know that I am a Hindu. Jugal Kishore Birla, on the other hand, is my brother. He is a big man in terms of money but he regards me an elder. He has put me up here because he considers me a pious Hindu.

He also takes me to the big temple built by him. If in spite of all this the young man insists that I should go away and I cannot pray here, it is merely his arrogance. But you should have won him over with love.

You threw him out by force. What is the point in offering prayers by resorting to force? The young man was in a rage and in his anger was talking wild things. It was out of such talk that all those things happened in the Punjab. This rage is what starts all the fanaticism.

The *shlokas* just recited by this girl say that when a man broods on objects of the senses—that is, all the five senses—he is caught up in craving. Then he is possessed by wrath which leads to stupefaction, i.e., insanity.[1]

Driven by such frenzy the simple folk of Bihar have indulged in such acts as make me hang my head down in shame. In the same mad fury the people of Noakhali indulged in excesses. But the law of the jungle was more in evidence in Bihar than in Noakhali and it was even more so in the Punjab.

If you are true Hindus, you should not act in such a manner. If in a meeting something is being said which we do not like to hear we must get up and leave the meeting. There is no need to shout and make a row. Moreover, this is a matter of religion. Leave alone religious discussion this man would not even allow people to pray.

Prayers should not be disturbed as was done by this young man. Such acts help no one. None of those who have died in the Punjab will ever come back.

Ultimately all of us have to go the same way. If is true that these people met their death by being slaughtered whereas others die of cholera or in some other way. He who is born is destined to die. In being born there is, to an extent, some human responsibility, but in the matter of dying, none but God has any hand. Death cannot be avoided on any account. Death is our companion, our friend. If people have died with courage, they have lost nothing. Rather, they have gained something. But

1. *Bhagavad Gita*, II.62 and 63.

the great problem is how to deal with those who committed these murders. True, to err is human. After all man is but a bundle of errors. But we ought to rectify the errors. God will not overlook our acts. When we go to Him He will look into our hearts. He knows our hearts. If there is a change of heart in us, he will pardon all our lapses.

I have many friends in the Punjab who call themselves my devoted followers. But who am I that they should describe themselves as such? All these friends insist that since I have already come as far as Delhi I should go over to the Punjab at least for one night, so as to comfort the people there. It would take only a few hours if I fly. But how can I go at somebody's bidding? I shall go there only at God's bidding or at the bidding of my own heart. I did not go to Noakhali at someone else's call. Before leaving this place I had said that I was going there because my heart urged me to do so. People had been for long asking me to go to Bihar but I had not gone there at anyone's call. I went when Dr. Mahmud Saheb wrote to me that my going there would alone clear the minds of the Biharis.

Bihar is a province where Hindus and Muslims can live together [in peace]. But there too women and children have been subjected to outrages no less violent. Blind with fury, people killed innocent children; they slaughtered the womenfolk and threw the bodies into the wells. I am not talking in the air. All these are facts that can be proved by evidence. After that the Muslims are bound to say that they would not live there. But once they are assured that they would not be treated like that again, they would come back. The Bihari Muslims had nearly come to appreciate this ; so much so that if we could have reassured them, I was confident that the Muslims who had fled to Asansol and Sind would have come back. They were on the point of returning. But now, should the atrocities in the Punjab be avenged in Bihar? Then, will it be repeated in Madras? And where will this end?

Will all of us become barbarous in this way? The Congress fought a non-violent battle against the British. Should we now start killing our own brethren? True, Muslims are perpetrating atrocities, but should we also do the same? Was there an act of atrocity that the British did not commit?

But now the British are going. The Viceroy told me that they had never retreated, but they were leaving India, as a result of her non-violent struggle. You might say that they are doing it for show, because in any case they had got to go. But, if anyone comes to us with honest intentions, why should we interpret his honesty as wickedness? I have learnt to accept honesty on the face of it till I have experience to the contrary. Just at the moment of the departure of the British should we present the spectacle of pleading for the retention of their army although they are leaving? In the Punjab today we are protected solely by them. But can we call it protection? I wish we could protect ourselves even if only a handful of us survived. Let us not be afraid of dying. If we are to be killed, would we not rather be killed by our Muslim brothers? Would a brother cease to be a brother because he has changed his religion? Moreover, do we not indulge in the same acts as they do? What have we not done to the women in Bihar? The Hindus have done it, which means I have done it. It is a matter of shame. Do you think I should hurl two abuses in return for one? But that is exactly what both the Hindus and the Muslims are secretly doing and they are possessed by a mad frenzy.

Here is Badshah Khan sitting right beside me. Who can remove him from here? How much prayer did I leave unfinished because of that young man? I did so because I wanted to demonstrate, I wanted to proclaim to one and all that I would be a good Hindu only if I am a good Parsi, a good Muslim. Would it be religious to abuse other religions? For me, there is nothing like different religions.

All these people who have come from all over Asia[1] talk very lovingly to Jawaharlal. They are all very pleased with him. By the grace of God, we have a gem of a man in our midst who wants to embrace the whole world. Should we not maintain peace if only to honour him?

Now let me say a few things about the Viceroy. I was with him yesterday for more than two hours and, therefore, could not come for the prayers. Fortunately, the girl started the prayers as I had instructed her. Today also I talked with the Viceroy for two hours.[2] He said that he was making an honest effort. He assured me that he was the last Viceroy. He said he never wanted to come to India. He wanted to be on the seas but he came here because he was prevailed upon.

He was sent here when the Labour Government of Great Britain decided to quit India, since he belongs to the royal family. The British want to depart from India with grace. He said he was eager to hand over this country even to a single Parsi if he came forward to take it, not to mention a Hindu or a Muslim. Why should I not listen to one who comes to me with such honest intentions? The British have done us enough

1. For the Inter-Asian Relations Conference.
2. *Vide* "Interview with Lord Mountbatten", 1-4-1947, and "Interview with Lord Mountbatten", 1-4-1947

harm in the past. But Lord Mountbatten has done us no harm. He says that he would like to be a servant right from today if it were possible. But it is not proper that he should run away while we are fighting with each other. He, after all, belongs to a brave race. Why should he run away? He is thinking of the manner in which he should leave the country. He is making good efforts. He is proceeding honourably. If we too proceed accordingly, what has never before happened will happen now. If anyone wants to accommodate a fellow who would not conduct himself honourably but would act barbarously, let him learn from me how to do it. I am a prisoner of the Viceroy till Friday. Jawahar also wants to detain me here. After three days I shall tell you everything. I do not want to hide anything.

But what can possibly happen? Whatever the Congress decides will be done; nothing will be according to what I say. Mr Writ runs no more.

If it did the tragedies in the Punjab, Bihar and Noakhali would not have happened. No one listens to me anymore. I am a small man. True, there was a time when mine was a big voice. Then everyone obeyed what I said; now neither the Congress nor the Hindus nor the Muslims listen to me. Where is the Congress today? It is disintegrating. I am crying in the wilderness. Today everyone can forsake me but God will not. He has His devotee tested. An English poem[1] describes God as the "Hound of Heaven". He is the retriever of *dharma*, i.e., He seeks out *dharma*. It would be enough if He hears me. When God rules your hearts you will do only as He bids. We should therefore behave like rational creatures. We ought not to let loose our tongues at the slightest provocation.

[From Hindi]

[*Prarthana-Pravachan*—Part I, pp. 5-11]

---

1. By Francies Thompson (1859-1907).

73. The Message of Asia

SPEECH AT INTER-ASIAN RELATIONS CONFERENCE[1]

[April 2, 1947]

I do not think that I should apologize to you for having to speak in a foreign tongue. I wonder if this loud speaker carries my voice to the farthest end of this vast audience. If some of those who are far away are unable to hear what I may say, it will be the fault of the loud speaker.

I was going to tell you that I do not wish to apologize. I dare not. You cannot understand the provincial language which is my mother tongue. I do not want to insult you by speaking in my own language (Gujarati). Our national speech in Hindustani. I know that it will be a long time before it can be made into an international speech.

For international commerce, undoubtedly, English occupies the first placĕ. I used to hear that French was the language of diplomacy. I was told when I was young that if I wanted to go from one end of Europe to the other, I must try to pick up French. I tried to learn French in order that I may be able to make myself understood. There is a rivalry between French and English. Having been taught English I have naturally to resort to that language.

I was wondering as to what I was to say to you. I wanted to collect my thoughts but, let me confess to you, I had no time. Yet I had promised yesterday that I would try to say a few words. While I was coming with Badshah Khan I asked for a little piece of paper and pencil. I got a pen instead of a pencil. I tried to scribble a few words.

You will be sorry to hear from me that that piece of paper is not by my side though I remember what I wanted to say.

You, friends, have not seen the real India and you are not meeting in conference in the midst of real India. Delhi, Bombay, Madras, Calcutta, Lahore—all these are big cities and are, therefore, influenced by the West.

---

1. The version in *Harijan* entitled "The Message of Asia", has been collated with *The Hindu* report. More than 25,000 persons attended the concluding session presided over by Sarojini Naidu. Gandhiji spoke in Hindi.

I then thought of a story. It was in French and was translated for me by an Anglo-French philosopher. He was an unselfish man. He befriended me without having known me because he always sided with the minorities. I was not then in my own country. I was not only in a hopeless minority but in a despised minority, if the Europeans in South Africa will forgive me for saying so. I was a coolie lawyer. At that time we had no coolie doctors, nor coolie lawyers. I was the first in the field. You know perhaps what is meant by the word coolie.

This friend—his mother was a French woman and his father an Englishman—said: "I want to translate for you a French story. There were three scientists who went out from France in search of truth.

They went to different parts of Asia. One of them found his way to India. He began to search. He went to the socalled cities of those times—naturally this was before British occupation, before even the Moghul period. He saw the so called high-caste people, men and women, and he felt at a loss. Finally, he went to a humble cottage in a humble village. That was the cottage of a Bhangi and there he found the truth that he was in search of."

If you really want to see India at its best [*sic*], you have to find it in the humble Bhangi homes of such villages. There are 7,00,000 of such villages and 38 crores of people inhabit them. If some of you see the villages, you will not be fascinated by the sight. You will have to scratch below the dung heap. I do not say that they ever were heavenly places. Today they are really dung-heaps.

They were not like that before. What I say is not from history but from what I have seen myself I have travelled from one end of India to the other and have seen the miserable specimen of humanity with lustreless eyes. They are India. In these humble cottages, in the midst of these dung-heaps, are to be found the humble Bhangis in whom you find the concentrated essence of wisdom.

Again, I have learnt from books—books written by English historians. We read books written in English by English historians but we do not write in our own mother tongue or in the national language—Hindustani. We study our history through English books rather than through the originals. That is the cultural conquest which India has undergone.

Stating that wisdom had come to the West from the East, Gandhiji said: "The first of these wise men was Zoroaster. He belonged to the East. He was followed by the Buddha who belonged to the East India. Who followed the Buddha? Jesus, who came from the East."

Before Jesus was Moses who belonged to Palestine though he was born in Egypt. After Jesus came Mohammed. I omit any reference to Krishna and Rama and other lights. I do not call them lesser lights but they are less known to the literary world. All the same I do not know of a single person in the world to match these men of Asia. And then what happened? Christianity became disfigured when it went to the West. I am sorry to have to say that. I would not talk any further.

I have told you the story in order to make you understand that what you see in the big cities is not the real India. Certainly, the carnage that is going on before our very eyes is a shameful thing. As I said yesterday, do not carry the memory of that carnage beyond the confines of India.

What I want you to understand is the message of Asia. It is not to be learnt through the Western spectacles or by imitating the atom bomb. If you want to give a message to the West, it must be the message of love and the message of truth. I want you to go away with the thought that Asia has to conquer the West through love the truth. I do not want merely to appeal to your heads. I want to capture your hearts.

Of course, I believe in "one world". How can I possibly do otherwise, when I became an inheritor of the message of love that these great unconquerable teachers left for us? In this age of democracy, in this age of awakening of the poorest of the poor, you can redeliver this message with the greatest emphasis. You will complete the conquest of the West not through vengeance because you have been exploited, but with real understanding. I am confident that if all of you put your hearts together—not merely heads—to understand the secret of the message these wise men of the East have left to us, and if we really become worthy of that great message, the conquest of the West will be complete. This conquest will be loved by the West itself.

The West is today pining for wisdom. It is despairing of the multiplication of the atom bomb, because atom bombs mean utter destruction not merely of the West but of the whole world, as if the prophesy of the *Bible* was going to be fulfilled and there was to be a perfect deluge. It is up to you to tell world of its wickedness and sin—that is the teaching your teachers and my teachers have taught Asia.

[*Harijan*, 20-4-1947, and *The Hindu*, 3-4-1947]

74. Religion admits No Coercion

SPEECH AT PRAYER MEETING

November 13, 1947

BROTHERS AND SISTERS,

Yesterday was Diwali and today is the New Year. I have heard and I heard it all the more yesterday that Delhi has great illuminations on Diwali day which perhaps beat even the illuminations in Bombay.

There are magnificent illuminations in Bombay every year. I was pleased to hear that people had realized that this is not the time to celebrate Diwali. But the superstition still persists that there should be at least some lights on Diwali day. Hence, oil lamps were seen at some places. There were some electric lights too, though very few. I do not go out but I get all the information.

The new year begins today. I had already mentioned it yesterday, but I may as well refer to it again. On New Year day we make some pious resolutions and by the grace of God try to follow them all through the year. If we do this, and if the atmosphere prevailing today changes and the Hindus and Muslims live together in amity, we shall have a right to celebrate the next Diwali with illuminations. We can accomplish nothing by regarding one another as enemies. That is why I stressed that this is no occasion for an outward celebration of Diwali. We should try to illumine our hearts. Rama resides in our hearts and there is a continuous battle between Rama and Ravana raging inside us. If, in our hearts and not outside, Ravana triumphs over Rama, it means that there is no light but darkness in our hearts. If, instead, it is Rama who triumphs over Ravana, then there is indeed light in our hearts and this entitles us to have illuminations outside as well. Hence, all is well if the light outside is the symbol of the light within. Instead, if there is darkness in our hearts and we have illuminations outside and try to convince ourselves that everything is fine, we are hypocrites and liars. I only hope that we are never untruthful.

I told you yesterday that I would say something about the meetings of Congress Working Committee. There was no time yesterday because I did not want to take more than fifteen minutes.

Today is the third day of the Congress Working Committee meeting. It is still in session. One important thing that I am entitled to tell you is that the members of the Working Committee and others[1] who have been specially invited by Acharya Kripalani[2] have been sitting together in the meetings for the last three days. It is a good thing that they are unanimously of the opinion that it has been the policy of the Congress since its inception, that is, for the last sixty years, that Congress is not an institution that propagates any particular religion.

There are people of all religions in the Congress or, say, because it belongs to people of different religions, it does not belong to any one particular religion. It is an organization of the masses and it has to function only for political goals. It does not remain a religious body if it functions that way. Supposing one of the policies of the Congress is to provide food to all the people, to be true to its name it must provide food for everybody. If the Congress provides food only to those who are with it or, say, only to the Hindus and the Sikhs because they are in a majority and allows others to starve and says that it is not bothered about them, it would be a religious body superficially but in fact it would become an irreligious organization. If it advocates service of only those who are its followers and wants others to be killed, it would not be *dharma*, but *adharma*[3] in the name of *dharma*.

If I am a worshipper of Rama and do not worship any god, the law cannot force me to do so. It is another matter if I act against my faith or become a coward and say that a particular man is carrying a sword and that if I do not obey him he would kill me. But, if I am not a coward, when I am forced to worship Allah instead of Rama, I should have, and I have, a right to insist that I would worship only Rama and not Allah. All that the other person can do is to cut my throat. Let him do so. Then it is a matter of faith, which we call personal or individual *dharma*. There is no power on earth which can destroy one's personal *dharma*. Of course, it can be destroyed when the individual himself wants to do it, or when,

---

1. The special invitees to the Congress Working Committee meeting were: B. G. Kher, Pattabhi Sitaramayya, S. K. Patil, Jayaprakash Narayan, Kamaraj Nadar, Dr. Saifuddin Kitchlew and Prof. N. G. Ranga.
2. J. B. Kripalani (1888-1982); Principal, Gujarat Vidyapith, 1920-27; General Secretary of the Indian National Congress, 1934-45; its President, 1946-47; Member, Constituent Assembly; started the Krishak Mazdoor Praja Party which later merged into the Praja Socialist Party; resigned from the Praja Socialist Party in 1954.
3. Contrary to *dharma*.

instead of light, there is only darkness in one's heart. In such circumstances, when he cannot make up his mind he takes help from someone or just follows the bidding of some other person because he is surrounded by darkness.

But the person who is steadfast in his faith would listen to the command only of God and none else. Likewise, when an organization functions for the welfare of the people, only the things which are consistent with *dharma* apply to everybody and nothing else. And in this way it embodies *dharma* and not *adharma*. That, in my view, is the true meaning of politics and the Congress has followed this from the time of its inception. You should be happy that it is so, whether you belong to the Congress or not. Even I do not belong to the Congress. But so what? After all, I have been a Congress worker and have served it. What does it matter if I do not pay four annas for membership? I must pay the membership fee of four annas if I want to be its President. But that is not the question. If all of you think like me, it is really remarkable. It is good if you have registered yourselves as Congress members. It is well, too, if you are serving the Congress from outside. I have been sitting with the Congress Working Committee for the past three days. There are many differences of opinion in the Working Committee. The members are human beings after all, they are not stones. One member says one thing and another member says something else. There may be differences of opinion, but there should be no contradiction in behaviour. That is why they spent three days in discussing these differences. But they are all united about one thing, that is, that the Congress should continue to be what it has been so far. If in the process it has to perish, let it perish. Of course it cannot be completely wiped out, though it can remain in minority. And I doubt if it is in majority at present. For there should have been no Pakistan if the Congress were in majority. I can quote many instances to show how much the Muslims have been oppressed in India. But what should I say? You know more than I do. Have the Hindus and the Sikhs in Pakistan been oppressed less? But let us not talk about it. It is not for us to think of those things. Should I stop following my religion because others in the world do not adhere to theirs? That is why the Congress, whether it is in majority or minority, must adhere to its original objective. It is framing its resolutions from that point of view. It wants to present its views in a straightforward, sincere manner. What can be more straightforward than that we do not wish to compel a single Muslim to go away from here? The point is not whether the Muslims are good or bad. Can we claim that only angels have a right to live in India, and, if not angels, only good people can remain here? And, if only the good people can live here, are there no bad or wicked people among the Hindus and the Sikhs?

And if there are wicked people among them, what would you say to them? Would you order them to leave and threaten to cut their throats with a sword if they refused to oblige? You have no right to consider anybody wicked or to kill him. We have committed excesses against the Muslims. There may be some exaggeration in the reports I receive every day. But ultimately I find that there is truth in those reports.

When anything is done in the name of the Congress, the A.I.C.C. has to be summoned. The plenary session of the Congress is held once a year. It is like a big show and because there is such a big crowd nobody can even think clearly. But they know that the A.I.C.C. carries on its work with due deliberation and so they put their seal on what it does. Thus the A.I.C.C. is always on the alert. It is going to meet the day after tomorrow. It is the Working Committee which has to place the agenda before the A I.C.C. It is subservient to the A.I.C.C. If the Working Committee does not place the agenda before it, then the A.I.C.C. can say that they have not functioned well and the members of the Working Committee have to resign. The A.I.C.C. can form the Working Committee or terminate it. If the A.I.C.C. does not accept its proposals or makes great amendments to those proposals, then also it should resign. That is why the Working Committee says that it wants to do everything in the name of the A.I.C.C. If it does anything in its own name, it does not have the same effect. For, what is the use of 15 individuals proclaiming that not a single Muslim should be killed? If the same thing is done in the name of the A.I.C.C., its effect is much greater. That is why I have been advising the Congress Working Committee for the past three days that it should categorically state that this is the only thing it wishes to carry out. Let us not worry if this pleases the people or displeases them. If we are true servants of the Congress, then this is the only thing we have to do. Let the A.I.C.C. brush it aside if it so wishes. After all we, and also Pakistan, have to stand before the world. We do many things because we are worried about what the world may say. I would say that you should do only what you think is correct. Then the world too would regard it as correct. It is said that the word of the *Panch*[1] is like the word of God. The world is like the *Panch*. That is why what the world says is divine justice in the true sense.

---

1. Elected members of a Village Panchayat; also, an arbitrator.

The Working Committee is in session today. It would be meeting again tomorrow. It is my prayer that it should place before the A.I.C.C. such a resolution which would bring victory to India and everybody would be able to live in peace here. It does not mean that we should let the traitors do as they please. But we should not take it for granted that a particular person is a traitor. If someone is proved to be a traitor, you may kill him, hang him, shoot him. But if you say that no Muslim can ever be loyal or that only the Hindus and the Sikhs have a monopoly of loyalty, then I would say that it would be a grave thing. I am confident that the Congress would never do such a thing. You must also pray that through the advice of the Congress we and the whole country as well as other parts of the world rise high.

The Congress is meant only to raise the country high. But the Congress does not wish to raise itself by depriving anybody of his wealth or other property. The Congress would die for the sake of the whole world, but would not kill anyone. This has been the objective of the Congress, not since I entered it, but for many years. The Congress has tried to prevent the Europeans who come here from looting the country, so that people of Asia and Africa could live in peace. India has to remain alive for this purpose. It is for this that India has attained her independence and for no other purpose.

[From Hindi]

[*Prarthana Pravachan*—II, pp. 71-7]

75. Pray With Me and For Me

SPEECH AT PRAYER MEETING[1]

[New Delhi,
January 12, 1948]

One fasts for health's sake under laws governing health or fasts as a penance for a wrong done and felt as such. In these fasts, the fasting one need not believe in *ahimsa*. There is, however, a fast which a votary of non-violence sometimes feels impelled to undertake by way of protest against some wrong done by society and this he does when he, as a votary of *ahimsa*, has no other remedy left.

Such an occasion has come my way. When on September 9, I returned to Delhi from Calcutta, I was to proceed to West Punjab.

But that was not to be. Gay Delhi looked a city of the dead. As I alighted from the train I observed gloom on every face. I saw even the Sardar, whom humour and the joy that humour gives never desert, was no exception this time.

The cause of it I did not know. He was on the platform to receive me. He lost no time in giving me the sad news of the disturbances that had taken place in the metropolis of the Union. At once I saw that I had to be in Delhi and do or die. There is apparent calm brought about by prompt military and police action. But there is storm within the breast. It may burst forth any day. This I count as no fulfilment of the vow to "do" which alone can keep me from death, the incomparable friend. I yearn for heart friendship between Hindus, Sikhs and Muslims. It subsisted between them the other day. Today it is non-existent. It is a state that no Indian patriot worthy of the name can contemplate with equanimity.

Though the voice within has been beckoning for a long time, I have been shutting my ears to it lest it might be the voice of Satan, otherwise called my weakness. I never like to feel resourceless; a *satyagrahi* never should. Fasting is his last resort in the place of the sword—his or others.

---

1. As Gandhiji was observing silence, his speech written in English was translated into Hindi and read out after the prayers.

I have no answer to return to the Muslim friends who see me from day to day as to what they should do. My impotence has been gnawing at me of late. It will go immediately the fast is undertaken. I have been brooding over it for the last three days. The final conclusion has flashed upon me and it makes me happy.[1] No man, if he is pure, has anything more precious to give than his life. I hope and pray that I have that purity in me to justify the step. I ask you all to bless the effort and to pray for me and with me.

The fast begins from the first meal tomorrow (Tuesday). The period is indefinite and I may drink water with or without salts and sour limes. It will end when and if I am satisfied that there is a reunion of hearts of all communities brought about without any outside pressure, but from an awakened sense of duty.

The reward will be the regaining of India's dwindling prestige and her fast-fading sovereignty over the heart of Asia and there through the world. I flatter myself with the belief that the loss of her soul by India will mean the loss of the hope of the aching, storm-tossed and hungry world. Let no friend or foe, if there be one, be angry with me.

There are friends who do not believe in the method of the fast for reclamation of the human mind. They will bear with me and extend to me the same liberty of action that they claim for themselves.

With God as my supreme and sole counsellor, I felt that I must take the decision without any other adviser. If I have made a mistake and discover it, I shall have no hesitation in proclaiming it from the house-top and retracing my faulty step. There is little chance of my making such a discovery. If there is a clear indication, as I claim there is, of the Inner Voice, it will not be gainsaid. I plead for all absence of argument and inevitable endorsement of the step. If the whole of India responds or at least Delhi does, the fast might be soon ended.

But whether it ends soon or late or never, let there be no softness in dealing with what may be termed as a crisis. Critics have regarded some of my previous fasts as coercive and held that on merits the verdict would have gone against my stand but for the pressure exercised by the fasts.

What value can an adverse verdict have when the purpose is demonstrably sound? A pure fast, like duty, is its own reward. I do not

1. Gandhiji had given no inkling of what was in his mind to his close associates—not even to Vallabhbhai Patel and Jawaharlal Nehru who had met him shortly before this announcement at the prayer meeting. This was the fifteenth fast to be undertaken by Gandhiji.

embark upon it for the sake of the result it may bring. I do so because I must. Hence, I urge everybody dispassionately to examine the purpose and let me die, if I must, in peace which I hope is ensured.

Death for me would be a glorious deliverance rather than that I should be a helpless witness of the destruction of India, Hinduism, Sikhism and Islam. That destruction is certain if Pakistan does not ensure equality of status and security of life and property for all professing the various faiths of the world and if India copies her. Only then Islam dies in the two Indias, not in the world. But Hinduism and Sikhism have no world outside India. Those who differ from me will be honoured by me for their resistance however implacable. Let my fast quicken conscience, not deaden it.

Just contemplate the rot that has set in in beloved India and you will rejoice to think that there is an humble son of hers who is strong enough and possibly pure enough to take the happy step. If he is neither, he is a burden on earth. The sooner he disappears and clears the Indian atmosphere of the burden, the better for him and all concerned.

I would beg of all friends not to rush to Birla House nor try to dissuade me or be anxious for me. I am in God's hands. Rather they should turn the searchlight inwards, for this is essentially a testing time for all of us. Those who remain at their post of duty and perform it diligently and well, now more so than hitherto, will help me and the cause in every way. The fast is a process of self-purification.

I told you yesterday of two letters from Andhra. One was from the aged friend, no other than Deshabhakta Konda Venkatappayyagaru. I give here extracts from it:

The one great problem, apart from many other political and economic issues of a very complicated nature, is the moral degradation into which the men in Congress circles have fallen. I cannot say much about other provinces but in my province the conditions are very deplorable. The taste of political power has turned their heads. Several of the M.L.A.s and M.L.C.s are following the policy of making hay while the sun shines, of making money by the use of influence, even to the extent of obstructing the administration of justice in the criminal courts presided over by magistrates. Even the District Collectors and other revenue officials do not feel free in the discharge of their duties on account of the frequent interference by the M.L.A.s and M.L.C.s on behalf of their partisans. A strict and honest officer cannot hold his position, for false reports are carried against him to the Ministers who easily lend their ears to these unprincipled self-seekers.

Swaraj was the only all-absorbing passion which goaded men and women to follow your leadership. But now that the goal had been reached, all moral restrictions have lost their power on most of the fighters in the great struggle, who are joining hands even with those who were sworn opponents of the national movement and who, now, for their personal ends enlist themselves as Congress members. The situation is growing intolerable every day with the result that the Congress as well as the Congress Government have come into disrepute.

The recent municipal elections in Andhra have proved how far and how fast the Congress is losing its hold upon the people. The municipal elections in the town of Guntur were suddenly ordered to be stopped by an urgent message from the Minister for Local Bodies (Madras) after every preparation was made for carrying on election. Only a nominated council was in power for, I believe, the last ten years or more and for nearly a year now the municipal administration has been in the hands of a commissioner. Now the talk prevails that the Government would soon nominate councillors to take charge of the municipal affairs of this town.

I, old, decrepit, with a broken leg, slowly limping on crutches within the walls of my house, have no axe to grind. I no doubt entertain certain strong views against some of the leading Congressmen in the two parties into which the members of the Provincial and District Congress Committees now stand divided. And I have made no secret of my views.

The factions in the Congress circles, the money-making activities of several of the M.L.A.s and M.L.Cs and the weakness of the Ministers have been creating a rebellious spirit among the people at large. The people have begun to say that the British Government was much better and they are even cursing the Congress.

Let the people of Andhra and the other provinces measure the words of this self-sacrificing servant of India. As he rightly says the corruption described by him is no monopoly of Andhra. He could only give first-hand evidence about Andhra. Let us beware.

My Bahawalpur friends, I have to ask you to be patient. Sardar Saheb saw me only at noon. Being silent and preoccupied I could say or write nothing. Shri Shanker[1] from his office was too busy to come so that I could not place your case before him and possibly save the Sardar's precious time.[2]

[*The Hindustan Times,* 13-1-1948, and *Harijan,* 18-1-1948]

1. V. Shankar, Private Secretary to Vallabhbhai Patel.
2. Gandhiji visited word Mountbatten after the prayers.

76. My Dream

SPEECH AT PRAYER MEETING

[New Delhi,
January 14, 1948]

BROTHERS AND SISTERS,

Yesterday I said I might not be able to come to the meeting today. But I have managed it. However, from tomorrow or the day after I may not be in a condition to move about. Doctors have advised me rest from today.[1] I have placed myself not in the hands of the doctors but in the hands of God. I have no such attachment for life that I must live under any circumstances. Whether I die or live is wholly in the hands of God. I can only pray that my faith may remain firm and no one may interfere in my acting on that faith. Today man has become weak. He asks: Where is God? I want everyone to become strong. Only then can we escape misery. The few things I wanted to say to you I had in fact dictated in English, because I was not sure what my physical condition would be. I thought if I could not speak to you, a translation of the message could be read out. It was intended not only for you but for the millions in the country who would hear it on the radio and those who want to hear in my own voice what I have to say. I am a prisoner of their love and I thought that they had better hear my own voice today. I feel that a thirty-six hours' fast is very useful physically. It cleanses the body and can cause no harm. True, I have to conserve my energy for the future but God will see to that. I have been receiving many telegrams from all quarters—a lot of them from Muslims. I have also had cablegrams from outside India. I have told Pyarelal to pick out the most relevant of them. Not all need be published; only the few that can teach something to the people should be published. There are others which say that I should give up the fast and

---

1. Gandhiji spent the second day of his fast as per his normal routine except for the morning and evening walks. He took hot water without salt or lime, participated in two meetings with the Cabinet Ministers and received a deputation of refugees from the N.W.F.P., besides a number of visitors and friends. Drs. Jivraj Mehta and Sushila Nayyar issued a health bulletin that each day's fast increased both immediate and future danger to Gandhiji's life.

all will be well. But how can I give up the fast? God inspired the fast and He alone may terminate it. I have a telephonic message from Mridulabehn. She is in Lahore. She has a large number of friends among Muslims. She is a Hindu girl. The fast has distressed her. I carried her in my arms when she was a little girl. Now she has grown up. She goes about everywhere all by herself. She says Muslims, even officers in the Pakistan Government are asking her what they can do for me, now that I am doing what I am doing for their sake. This pleased me. I do not know whether my message has reached them. By tomorrow it will certainly reach them. My answer is that there is no need for them to ask. Although this *yajna* is being performed in Delhi it is for the whole country.

The fast is for self-purification. You must have God enthroned where today Satan sits enthroned. There must be some indication of it. Everybody cannot undertake a fast. It has become my proud privilege to do so. If everyone had this privilege they would have lived in amity. Hindus say, 'Kill the Muslims.' Muslims say, 'Kill the Hindus.' Sikhs say, 'Kill the Muslims.' If Hindus, Muslims and Sikhs fight in this way it helps no one. If you want to participate in the *yajna*, you must become brothers and should have love instead of hate in your hearts. Let all Hindus, Muslims and Sikhs pledge that they will not touch liquor, they will not touch opium. They will have nothing to do with adulterous men and adulterous women. Everyone will look upon other women as mothers or sisters or daughters. Everyone must exercise self-restraint and become clean. If they do all these things and if even then I regard Pakistan as full of sin, I will have to repent and say that Pakistan is not a land of sin but a land of purity. But what is needed is action, not mere words. If the Muslims of Pakistan become thus transformed, it is bound to have an effect in India. I have never tried to hide my view that Pakistan has committed crimes against Hindus.

What has happened in Karachi? Innocent Sikhs were murdered and their properties looted. Now I understand the same thing has happened in Gujrat.[1] There was a caravan coming from Bannu or somewhere. They were all refugees running away to save their lives.

They were waylaid and cut down. I do not want to relate this grim tale. I ask the Muslims if in their name this kind of thing continues in

1. On January 13, a train carrying non-Muslim refugees from Bannu was attacked at the Gujrat (West Punjab) Station by the tribesmen who had assembled there on their way to Jammu. In spite of the heroic defence put up by the troops escorting the train, hundreds of refugees were killed or maimed and women and girls abducted by the tribesmen.

Pakistan, how long will the people in India tolerate it. Even if a hundred men like me fasted they would not be able to stop the tragedy that may follow. You should all become good. Whether you are Muslims or tribals, you must all say that you will have the Hindus and Sikhs back. The poet says, "If there is paradise it is here, it is here !" He had said it about a garden. I read it ages ago when I was a child. But paradise is not so easily secured. If Hindus, Muslims and Sikhs became decent, became brothers, then that verse could be inscribed on every door. But that will be only when Pakistan has become pure. But if you say one thing and do another, the place will become another hell. Cleanse your hearts and install God there. If that happens in Pakistan, we in India shall not be behind them. It does not matter that the country is geographically divided, so long as our hearts are one. There are so many different governments in the world. What does it matter if there are fifty or five hundred? There are seven hundred thousand villages in India. If each one of them had a government of their own it would be a good thing.

They tell me that I am mad and have a habit of going on fast on the slightest pretext. But I am made that way. When I was young I never even read the newspapers. I could read English with difficulty and my Gujarati was not satisfactory. I have had the dream ever since then that if the Hindus, Sikhs, Parsis, Christians and Muslims could live in amity not only in Rajkot but in the whole of India, they would all have a very happy life. If that dream could be realized even now when I am an old man on the verge of death, my heart would dance.

Children would then frolic in joy to see that there is no strife any more. I urge all of you to help me in this task. If we all persevere in our respective religions and become good there can be harmony between all religions. We must not fear whether a man is a Sikh or a Pathan. We must fear God. This is what I want to see.

You can all try and become such men. What after all is society?

Society is made up of individuals. It is we that make society. We are asleep and then say that we are helpless because society is such. The same goes for the Government. It is we who are the Government. If one man takes the initiative others will follow and one can become many; if there is not even one there is nothing. I am not sure that I shall be able to come here tomorrow. But the prayers will be held and the girls will sing the bhajans.

[From Hindi]

Courtesy: All India Radio. Also *Prarthana Pravachan*-II, pp. 300-4.

77. His Last Will*

DRAFT CONSTITUTION OF CONGRESS[1]

[NEW DELHI,
January 29, 1948]

Though split into two, India having attained political independence through means devised by the Indian National Congress, the Congress in its present shape and form, i.e., as a propaganda vehicle and parliamentary machine, has outlived its use. India has still to attain social, moral and economic independence in terms of its seven hundred thousand villages as distinguished from its cities and towns. The struggle for the ascendency of civil over military power is bound to take place in India's progress towards its democratic goal. It must be kept out of unhealthy competition with political parties and communal bodies. For these and other similar reasons, the A.I.C.C. resolves to disband the existing Congress organization and flower into a Lok Sevak Sangh under the following rules with power to alter them as occasion may demand.

---

1. Acharya Jugal Kishore, General Secretary of A. I. C. C., released this draft to the Press on February 7, with the note: "As something has already appeared in the Press . . . regarding the proposals which Mahatmaji had made concerning changes in the Congress Constitution I am releasing the full draft as was handed to me on the fateful forenoon of 30th January… ."

* This appeared in Harijan under the title "His Last Will and Testament".
This appeared in *Harijan* under the title "His Last Will and Testament".
In his article "The Fateful Friday", in Harijan, Pyarelal writes: "The whole of the 29th had been so cram-full with work that at the end of the day Gandhiji felt utterly fagged ou. "My head is reeling. And yet I Must finish this," he remarked to Abha, pointing to the Draft constitution for the Congress which he had undertaken to prepare, and then, "I am afraid I shall have to keep late hours."
The next morning Gandhiji revised the draft and gave it to Pyarelal to "go through it carefully". He added: "Fill in any gaps in thought that there might be. I wrote it under a heavy strain." When Pyarela took the revised draft to him be "went through the additions and alterations point by point with his characteristic thoroughness and removed an error in calculation that had crept in regard to the number of panchayats."

Every panchayat of five adult men or women being villagers or village-minded shall form a unit.

Two such contiguous panchayats shall form a working party under a leader elected from among themselves.

When there are one hundred such panchayats, the fifty-first grade leaders shall elect from among themselves a second-grade leader and so on, the first-grade leaders meanwhile working under the second-grade leader. Parallel groups of two[1] hundred panchayats shall continue to be formed till they cover the whole of India, each succeeding group of panchayats electing a second-grade leader after the manner of the first. All second-grade leaders shall serve jointly for the whole of India and severally for their respective areas. The second-grade leaders may elect, whenever they deem necessary, from among themselves a chief who will, during pleasure, regulate and command all the groups.

As the final formation of provinces or districts is still in a state of flux, no attempt has been made to divide this group of servants into provincial or district councils and jurisdiction over the whole of India has been vested in the group or groups that may have been formed at any given time. It should be noted that this body of servants derive their authority or power from service ungrudgingly and wisely done to their master, the whole of India.[2]

1. Every worker shall be a habitual wearer of *khadi* made from self-spun yarn or certified by the A. I. S. A. and must be a teetotaller. If a Hindu, he must have abjured untouchability in any shape or form in his own person or in his family and must be a believer in the ideal of inter-communal unity, equal respect and regard for all religions and equality of opportunity and status for all irrespective of race, creed or sex.
2. He shall come in personal contact with every villager within his jurisdiction.
3. He shall enrol and train workers from amongst the villagers and keep a register of all these.
4. He shall keep a record of his work from day to day.
5. He shall organize the villages so as to make them self contained and self-supporting through their agriculture and handicrafts.

---

1. The copy available in the A.I.C.C. files has a question-mark here.
2. A facsimile of the draft up to here is available in Mahatma Gandhi—The Last Phase.

6. He shall educate the village folk in sanitation and hygiene and take all measures for prevention of ill health and disease among them.
7. He shall organize the education of the village folk from birth to death along the lines of Nayee Talim, in accordance with the policy laid down by the Hindustani Talimi Sangh.
8. He shall see that those whose names are missing on the statutory voters, roll are duly entered therein.
9. He shall encourage those who have not yet acquired the legal qualification, to acquire it for getting the right of franchise.
10. For the above purposes and others to be added from time to time, he shall train and fit himself in accordance with the rules laid down by the Sangh for the due performance of duty.

The Sangh shall affiliate the following autonomous bodies:

1. A.I.S.A.
2. A.I.V.I.A.
3. Hindustani Talimi Sangh
4. *Harijan* Sevak Sangh
5. Goseva Sangh

FINANCE

The Sangh shall raise finances for the fulfilment of its mission from among the villagers and others, special stress being laid on collection of poor man's pice.

M.K.G

New Delhi, January 29, 1948

[*Harijan, 15-2-1948.* and A.I.C.C. File No. 1578.
Courtesy: Nehru Memorial Museum and Library]

Bibliography

Birla, G.D., *In the Shadow of the Mahatma*, Bombay: Orient Longmans Ltd., 1953.

Bose, N.K., *Gandhiji : The Man and his Mission*, Bharatiya Vidya Bhawan, Bombay, 1966.

Bose, N.K., *Selections from Gandhi,* Navajivan Publishing House, Ahmedabad, 1972.

Brown, Judith M., *Gandhi and Civil Disobedience,* London: Cambridge University Press, 1977.

Brown, Judith M., *Gandhi's Rise to Power : Indian Politics*, 1915-22, London: Cambridge University Press, 1972.

Brown, M. Judith, *Gandhi Prisoner of Hope*, Oxford University Press, Delhi, 1992.

Dhawan, Gopi Nath, *The Political Philosophy of Mahatma Gandhi*, Ahmedabad : Navajivan Publishing House, 1962.

Diwakar, R.R., *Saga of Satyagraha*, New Delhi, Gandhi Peace Foundation, 1969.

Doke, J.J., *M.K. Gandhi—An Indian Patriot*, Madras: Natesan, 1909. ,

Fischer, Louis, *The Essential Gandhi,* George Allen and Unwin Limited, London, 1962.

Gandhi, M.K., *An Autobiography or the Story of My Experiments With Truth,* Ahmedabad, Navajivan Publishing House, 1988.

Gandhi, M.K., *Hind Swaraj or Indian Home Rule*, Ahmedabad, Navajivan Publishing House, 1975.

Gandhi, M.K., *Satyagraha in South Africa*, Ahmedabad, Navajivan, Publishing House, 1975.

Gregg, Richard B., *The Power of Non-Violence*, Ahmedabad Navajivan Publishing House, 1960.

Iyer, Raghavan. *The Moral and Political Thought of Mahatma Gandhi,* Oxford University Press, Chicago, 1973.

Jack, A. Homer (Ed.). *The Gandhi Reader,* Samata Books, Madras, 1984.

Kalelkar, Kaka, *Stray Glimpses of Bapu*, Ahmedabad: Navajivan Publishing House, 1957.

Kripalani, J.B., *Gandhi: His Life and Thought*, New Delhi, Publications Division, Ministry of Information and Broadcasting, Government of India, 1968.

Mishra, Anil Dutta, *Understanding Mahatma Gandhi:Speeches and Writings that Reveal his Mind Methods and Mission*, New Delhi, Concept, 2011.

Mishra, Anil Dutta, *Reading Gandhi*, Delhi, Pearson, 2012.

Misra, K.P. and Gangal, S.C., *Gandhi and the Contemporary World : Studies in Peace and War*, Chanakya Publications, Delhi, 1981.

Mukerjee, Hiren, *Gandhi: A Study*, New Delhi: People's Publishing House, 1960.

Namboodiripad, E.M.S., *The Mahatma and the Islam*, New Delhi: People Publishing House, 1959.

Nanda, B.R., *Gandhi Pan-Islamism Imperialism and Nationalism*, Oxford University Press, Bombay, 1989.

Nanda, B.R., *Mahatma Gandhi: A Biography*, London: George Allen and Unwin Ltd., 1959.

Narayan, Shriman, *Selected Works of Mahatma Gandhi*, Navajivan Publishing House, Ahmedabad, 1956.

Nehru, Jawahar Lal, *Mahatma Gandhi,* Calcutta: Signet Press, 1949.

Prabhu, R.K., and Rao, U.R., *The Mind of Mahatma*, Ahmedabad: Navajivan Publishing House, 1967.

Pyare Lal, *Mahatma Gandhi* : *The Early Phase,* Volume 1, Ahmedabad: Navajivan Publishing House, 1965.

Pyare Lal, *Mahatma Gandhi* : *The Last Phase,* in 2 volumes, Ahmedabad: Navajivan Publishing House, 1956, 1958.

Pyarelal and Nayar Sushila, *In Gandhiji's Mirror,* Oxford University Press, Delhi, 1991.

Pyarelal, *Mahatma Gandhi* : *The Last Phase*, Ahmedabad, Navajivan Publishing House, 1958.

Radhakrishnan, S. (ed.), *Mahatma Gandhi* : *Essays and Reflections on His Life and Thought*, Allahabad: Kitabistan, 1944.

Radhakrishnan, S. (Ed.), *Mahatma Gandhi 100 Years,* Gandhi Peace Foundation, New Delhi, 1968.

Rajendra Prashad, *At the Feet of Mahatma Gandhi*, Bombay, Asia Publishing House, 1961.

Rao, U.S. Mohan (Ed.), *The Message of Mahatma Gandhi,* Publications Division, Ministry of Information and Broadcasting, Government of India, New Delhi, 1968.

Rolland, Romain, *Mahatma Gandhi* : *The Man Who Became One With The Universal Being,* (Translated by Catherine D. Groth), Agra: Shiva Lal Aggarwala & Co. Ltd.

Tendulkar, D.G., *Mahatma,* New Delhi, Publications Division, Ministry of Information and Broadcasting, Government of India, 1952.

The Collected Works of Mahatma Gandhi, New Delhi, Publications Division, Ministry of Information and Broadcasting, Government of India, 1965, (Vols. 1—100).

Index